Managing Dynamic IP Networks

Paul T. Ammann

Tata McGraw-Hill Publishing Company Limited
NEW DELHI

McGraw-Hill Offices

New Delhi New York St Louis San Francisco Auckland Bogotá
Caracas Lisbon London Madrid Mexico City Milan Montreal
San Juan Singapore Sydney Tokyo Toronto

To wife, Eve, who is my constant inspiration.

Tata McGraw-Hill
A Division of The McGraw·Hill Companies

Information contained in this work has been obtained by Tata McGraw-Hill, from sources believed to be reliable. However, neither Tata McGraw-Hill nor its authors guarantee the accuracy or completeness of any information published herein, and neither Tata McGraw-Hill nor its authors shall be responsible for any errors, omissions, or damages arising out of use of this information. This work is published with the understanding that Tata McGraw-Hill and its authors are supplying information but are not attempting to render engineering or other professional services. If such services are required, the assistance of an appropriate professional should be sought.

Copyright © 2000 by The McGraw-Hill Companies, Inc. All rights reserved.

No part of this publication may be reproduced or distributed in any form or by any means, or stored in a data base or retrieval system, without the prior written permission of the publisher.

Tata McGraw-Hill Edition 2000

Reprinted in India by arrangement with The McGraw-Hill Companies, Inc., New York

For Sale in India Only

ISBN 0-07-463675-8

Published by Tata McGraw-Hill Publishing Company Limited, 7 West Patel Nagar, New Delhi 110 008, and printed at Maharaj Printers, Shahdara, Delhi 110 032

CONTENTS

	Preface	xiii
Chapter 1	TCP/IP Basics	1
	Network Protocols	2
	IP Addresses	3
	IP Subnets	6
	IP Routing	10
	Assigning IP Addresses	11
	Name Servers	11
	Applications That Use TCP/IP	13
	Other TCP/IP Terms	13
	Related Publications	15
Chapter 2	DHCP Concepts and Overview	17
	BOOTP, the Predecessor of DHCP	18
	DHCP Overview	19
	How Does DHCP Work?	21
	How Is Configuration Information Acquired?	21
	How Are Leases Renewed?	26
	What Happens When a Client Moves Out of Its Subnet?	26
	How Are Changes Implemented in the Network?	27
	What Are BOOTP/DHCP Relay Agents?	28
	IP Address Pools	28
	Multiple Subnets per Pool	29
	Multiple Pools per Subnet	30
	Client Identification	30
	MAC Address as Qualifier	31
	Client ID as Qualifier	32
	User Class ID as Qualifier	33
	Qualification from Vendor Extensions	33
	Qualification from Relay Agents	34
	Multiple Qualifiers	36
	Server Administration	36
	Server Installation	37
	Database Initialization	37
	Runtime Database Manipulation	38

	Administrative Access Controls	39
	Remote Server Management	40
	Application Programming Interfaces (APIs)	41
	DHCP Server Availability	41
	DHCP Reliability	41
	Redundant DHCP Server Scenarios	42
	DHCP in IPv6	47
	Differences between DHCPv6 and DHCPv4	47
	Summary	48
Chapter 3	Serving Names	49
	Why Names?	50
	What Is a Domain Name System (DNS)?	50
	Domain vs. Zone of Authority	54
	Differentiating Name Servers	56
	Static Name Servers	56
	Dynamic Name Servers	56
	Primary Name Servers	56
	Secondary Name Servers	57
	Master Name Servers	58
	Caching-Only Name Servers	58
	Authoritative Name Servers	58
	Parent and Child Name Servers	58
	Root Name Servers	59
	Forwarders	60
	Firewall Name Servers	60
	Record Types	60
	Resolvers	62
	BIND's Treatment of DNS Database Entries	65
	What Is Dynamic IP?	68
	Dynamic Domain Name System (DDNS)	69
	What Does Dynamic IP Provide?	69
	How Does Dynamic IP Work?	71
	Configuring for Network Availability	74
	Enabling Host Mobility	76
	Securing Your Dynamic IP Network	77
	How Dynamic Addressing Is Made Usable with DDNS	78
Chapter 4	NetBIOS Name Servers	79
	Overview	80
	TCP/IP for the Enterprise	81

Contents

Name Server History	82
NetBIOS/NBNS Basic Functionality	83
Service Specification	83
Design	84
NetBIOS Naming	84
Names for Applications	85
Translating Names to IP Addresses	86
Name Database	86
Distributed Database	87
Probe Mechanisms	88
Roll Call Mechanisms	89
Centralized Database	90
Role of a NetBIOS Datagram	90
NetBIOS Datagram Distributor	91
Workstation Interoperability	92
NBNS Design Criteria	92
High Performance	93
Standard Hardware Platform	94
Dedicated Server	94
Fast Response Time	95
High Capacity	95
Reliability	95
Load Balancing	96
Scalability	96
Datagram Distribution	97
Distributed Algorithms	97
Extensibility	98
Transaction Capture	98
Static Names	98
Remote Management	99
Database Validation	99
NBNS Implementations	101
Microsoft WINS	101
Network TeleSystems Shadow IPserver	103
Summary	104

Chapter 5

Dynamic IP Routing Protocols	105
Basic IP Routing	106
Routing Processes	108
Autonomous Systems	109

	Routing Algorithms	109
	Static Routing	110
	Distance Vector Routing	111
	Link-State Routing	116
	Interior Gateway Protocols (IGPs)	118
	Routing Information Protocol (RIP)	118
	RIPng for IPv6	124
	Open Shortest Path First (OSPF)	126
	Exterior Routing Protocols	150
	Exterior Gateway Protocol (EGP)	152
	Border Gateway Protocol (BGP-4)	152
	References	166
Chapter 6	Mobile IP	169
	Mobile IP Overview	171
	Mobile IP Operation	173
	Mobile IP Registration Process	174
	Tunneling	178
	Broadcast Datagrams	178
	Move Detection	179
	Address Resolution Protocol (ARP) Considerations	180
	Mobile IP Security Considerations	180
	Mobile IP and Routers	181
	Background	181
	Emerging Examples Where Mobile IP Is Applicable	185
	Detailed Protocol Overview	186
	Other Important Issues	190
Chapter 7	Security of DHCP and Dynamic DNS	193
	Security Trade-Off	194
	RSA Public Key Authentication System	194
	Presecured Domain	198
	ProxyArec Considerations	198
	ProxyArec and Option 81	201
	Securing Lease Allocations	202
	Preventing Access to Unauthorized Devices	202
	"Rogue" DHCP Servers	203
	Connecting to Untrusted Networks—Firewalls	203
	Connecting through Untrusted Networks—VPN	205
	TFTP Security	206

Contents

Chapter 8	Reliability		
	Battlefield Questions		207
	Failure Events		208
	Severed Connections		208
	Facility Loss		209
	Router Outages		209
	DHCP Server Problems		210
	Name Server Difficulties		210
	Other Server Vulnerabilities		210
	Client Failures		
	AIX and UNIX Features		
	Shadow IPserver Features		
Chapter 9	Performance		
	Leases		
	What Is a Lease?		
	How Leases Work		
	Choosing a Lease Time		
	Multiple Leases		
	Monitoring and Troubleshooting		
	The ping Command		219
	The traceroute Command		219
	The iptrace Command		220
	The arp Command		221
	The netstat Command		221
	The host Command		222
	The nslookup Command		222
	Troubleshooting TCP/IP Networks		223
	Prerequisites for Troubleshooting		223
	A Bottom-Up Approach		224
	Tuning TCP/IP Networks		234
	An Approach to Tuning Your Network		234
	TCP/IP Tuning Parameters		235
	Bandwidth Efficiency		238
	Broadcast Traffic		238
	RSVP		239
	Communications Server		239
Chapter 10	Quality of Service		241
	Why QoS?		242

Contents

Integrated Services	243
Service Classes	246
The Reservation Protocol (RSVP)	250
The Future of Integrated Services	261
Differentiated Services	263
Differentiated Services Architecture	264
Using RSVP with Differentiated Services	273
Configuration and Administration of DS Components with LDAP	275
Using Differentiated Services with IPSec	276
Internet Drafts on Differentiated Services	277
References	278

Chapter 11

IP Version 6	279
IPv6 Overview	281
The IPv6 Header Format	281
Packet Sizes	285
Extension Headers	285
IPv6 Addressing	292
Priority	298
Flow Labels	298
Internet Control Message Protocol Version 6 (ICMPv6)	299
Neighbor Discovery	300
Stateless Address Autoconfiguration	310
Multicast Listener Discovery (MLD)	311
DNS in IPv6	314
Format of IPv6 Resource Records	315
DHCP in IPv6	318
Differences between DHCPv6 and DHCPv4	318
DHCPv6 Messages	319
Mobility Support in IPv6	320
Internet Transition: Migrating from IPv4 to IPv6	320
Dual IP Stack Implementation: The IPv6/IPv4 Node	321
Tunneling	322
Header Translation	329
Interoperability Summary	329
The Drive toward IPv6	330
References	331

Contents

Chapter 12	Dynamic DNS Review	333
	Cisco DNS/DHCP Manager	334
	Product Overview	334
	Key Features and Benefits	335
	Specifications	337
	Hardware	337
	Cisco DNS/DHCP Manager Overview	337
	Simplifying DNS Management with the Cisco Domain Name Manager Server	338
	Updating DNS Via the Cisco DHCP/BootP Server	341
	Supporting Multiple Logical Networks on the Same Physical Network	344
	Service Management	345
	Supporting Servers	345
	Service Configuration Manager	345
	Competitive Automation's JOIN BootP, DHCP, and DDNS	346
	BooTP	346
	Traditional BootP	347
	Dynamic BootP	347
	Finite BootP	348
	BootP Service: Details	349
	Server Logic	350
	How JOIN Resolves a Client Configuration	351
	Dynamic Naming	352
	Naming the Client	352
	VLSM	356
	Fixed Length vs. VLSM	356
	Addrmask	358
	JOIN DHCP/DDNS Features	359
	Platforms	360
	Lucent QIP Enterprise 5.0	360
	Automating IP Services Management	360
	Regulate User Access with Innovative Profiling Capabilities	361
	Eliminate Major Causes of Network Failure	361
	Exceed Industry Standards with High-Performance Servers	361
	Centralize Network Configuration and Planning	362

Contents

Lucent Advantage: QIP Enterprise 5.0	363
System Requirements	368
Bay Networks' NetID	372
Benefits	372
Features	374
NetID Architecture	377
System Requirements	379
MetaInfo's Meta IP	379
Features and Benefits of Meta IP	380
Extending Security	383
Meta DHCP	382
Meta DNS	385
User-to-Address Mapping	387
Multiplatform Support	389
Meta IP Solutions	390
System Requirements	392

Appendix

DHCP Options (RFC 2132)	393
A.1 Introduction	393
A.2 DHCP and BootP Options	394
A.2.1 Options 0 and 255: Pad and End	394
A.2.2 Option 1: Subnet Mask	394
A.2.3 Option 2: Time Offset	395
A.2.4 Option 3: Router	395
A.2.5 Option 4: Time Server	395
A.2.6 Option 5: IEN 116 (Old) Name Server	395
A.2.7 Option 6: Domain Name Server	396
A.2.8 Option 7: Log Server	396
A.2.9 Option 8: Cookie Server	396
A.2.10 Option 9: LPR Server	397
A.2.11 Option 10: Impress Server	397
A.2.12 Option 11: Resource Location Server	397
A.2.13 Option 12: Host Name	398
A.2.14 Option 13: Boot File Size	398
A.2.15 Option 14: Merit Dump File	398
A.2.16 Option 15: Domain Name	398
A.2.17 Option 16: Swap Server	399
A.2.18 Option 17: Root Path	399
A.2.19 Option 18: Extensions Path	399
A.2.20 Option 19: IP Forwarding Enable/Disable	400

Contents

A.2.21	Option 20: Non-Local Source Routing Enable/Disable	400
A.2.22	Option 21: Policy Filter	400
A.2.23	Option 22: Maximum Datagram Reassembly Size	401
A.2.24	Option 23: Default IP Time-to-Live	401
A.2.25	Option 24: Path MTU Aging Timeout	401
A.2.26	Option 25: Path MTU Plateau Table	402
A.2.27	Option 26: Interface MTU	402
A.2.28	Option 27: All Subnets Are Local	402
A.2.29	Option 28: Broadcast Address	403
A.2.30	Option 29: Perform Mask Discovery	403
A.2.31	Option 30: Mask Supplier	403
A.2.32	Option 31: Perform Router Discovery	403
A.2.33	Option 32: Router Solicitation Address	404
A.2.34	Option 33: Static Route	404
A.2.35	Option 34: Trailer Encapsulation	404
A.2.36	Option 35: ARP Cache Timeout	405
A.2.37	Option 36: Ethernet Encapsulation	405
A.2.38	Option 37: TCP Default Time-to-Live	405
A.2.39	Option 38: TCP Keep-Alive Interval	406
A.2.40	Option 39: TCP Keep-Alive Garbage	406
A.2.41	Option 40: Network Information Service Domain	406
A.2.42	Option 41: NIS Server	407
A.2.43	Option 42: Network Time Protocol Server	407
A.2.44	Option 43: Vendor-Specific Information	407
A.2.45	Option 44: NetBIOS over TCP/IP Name Server Option	408
A.2.46	Option 45: NetBIOS over TCP/IP Datagram Distribution Server	409
A.2.47	Option 46: NetBIOS over TCP/IP Node Type	409
A.2.48	Option 47: NetBIOS over TCP/IP Scope	409
A.2.49	Option 48: X Window System Font Server Option	410
A.2.50	Option 49: X Window System Display Manager	410

A.2.51	Option 64: NIS+ Domain	410
A.2.52	Option 65: S+ Server	411
A.2.53	Option 68: Mobile IP Home Agent	411
A.2.54	Option 69: Simple Mail Transport Protocol (SMTP) Server	411
A.2.55	Option 70: Post Office Protocol (POP3) Server	412
A.2.56	Option 71: Network News Transport Protocol (NNTP) Server	412
A.2.57	Option 72: Default World Wide Web (WWW) Server	412
A.2.58	Option 73: Default Finger Server	413
A.2.59	Option 74: Default Internet Relay Chat (IRC) Server	413
A.2.60	Option 75: StreetTalk Server	413
A.2.61	Option 76: StreetTalk Directory Assistance (STDA) Server	413
A.3	DHCP-Only Options	414
A.3.1	Option 50: Requested IP Address	414
A.3.2	Option 51: IP Address Lease Time	414
A.3.3	Option 52: Option Overload	415
A.3.4	Option 53: DHCP Message Type	415
A.3.5	Option 54: Server Identifier	415
A.3.6	Option 55: Parameter Request List	416
A.3.7	Option 56: Message	416
A.3.8	Option 57: Maximum DHCP Message Size	417
A.3.9	Option 58: Renewal (T1) Time Value	417
A.3.10	Option 59: Rebinding (T2) Time Value	417
A.3.11	Option 60: Vendor Class Identifier	418
A.3.12	Option 61: Client Identifier	418
A.3.13	Option 66: TFTP Server Name	419
A.3.14	Option 67: Boot File Name	419
A.4	Unofficial DHCP Options	419
A.5	Options Supported by Popular Operating Systems	421
A.5.1	Servers	421
A.5.2	Clients	422

Index   423

Preface

The ARPANET—the Department of Defense network that is the ancestor of today's Internet—was built in the late sixties using a proprietary protocol suite. This first protocol proved to have shortcomings for linking with other networks, which led to the development of Transfer Control Protocol/Internet Protocol (TCP/IP).

TCP/IP used 32-bit address numbers. These soon proved to be unwieldy for most users, even when expressed in the less daunting format of four 8-bit decimal numbers, delimited by periods. The obvious solution was a scheme for addressing computers by name. After all, people relate much better to names and find it much easier to remember the computer in the corner as "Frodo," rather than "192.168.1.2."

The First Generation: Host Tables

The desire to refer to machines by name instead of number led to the first IP address management scheme: the host table. The host table is a file that contains all the IP addresses in use on a network, along with their names. The host table provides a mapping from a host's name to its IP address, as well as reverse mapping: Given a host's IP address, the user can look up its name.

For a host table to be most useful, it must contain the names of all the hosts with which a given host might want to communicate. For the ARPANET, that meant that the host table had to contain the names and IP addresses of every host on the network. Such a file was maintained by the Network Information Center (NIC), the central organization responsible for managing the ARPANET. The file was called HOSTS.TXT and was similar in format to the /etc/hosts file on UNIX. Network administrators all over the network e-mailed host table changes to the NIC every time they added or deleted a host or changed a host's IP address. The NIC made the changes to its master host table, which it made available via File Transfer Protocol (FTP). Administrators periodically downloaded the latest version of the host table to stay current.

As the ARPANET exploded in size to eventually become the Internet, the rapid growth stressed the centralized host table scheme. The first problem was consistency: The file changed too quickly for everyone to have a current copy. Just as printed phone books are out-of-date as soon as they arrive, so too was the host table's information outdated after it was downloaded. A second problem was the lack of a hierarchical naming space for host names. The host table required short, single-label names for hosts. As the population of hosts grew, so did contention for popular names, and it became harder and harder to avoid duplicates. Worse, operator error at the NIC sometimes led to duplicates slipping into the file and wreaking havoc. Finally, the traffic and load just from downloading the file began to represent a significant portion of the ARPANET's total traffic. This model just didn't scale well.

From an IP address management perspective, the host table has both advantages and disadvantages:

Centralization. The centralized aspect of host tables is appealing from an IP address management standpoint: A host table provides a central location for an entire network's IP address information.

Simple format. The host table format (both the old HOSTS.TXT and the modern UNIX /etc/hosts) is simple and easy to edit. After all, the file contains only host names and IP addresses. It is easy for an administrator to make changes and make them correctly.

Limited contents. The simple format is also a drawback, since it limits the amount of additional information that can be stored easily, such as host location information and serial numbers.

The Second Generation: DNS "By Hand"

The problems with the centralized host table scheme led directly to the development of the Domain Name System (DNS) in the early 1980s. The two main design goals of DNS grew out of the biggest problems with the host table: distributed administration and a hierarchical naming scheme.

DNS defines a name space composed of hierarchical domains. Each organization is assigned a domain, such as *metainfo.com,* under which it can place hosts and create still more hierarchy by creating subdomains, such as *sales.infinity.com.* Domains are broken into units called *zones* for administrative purposes. Thus, administration is no longer centralized but divided along zone lines: Individual organizations administer the information corresponding to their zones. DNS is really just a distributed database with data maintained locally but available globally.

Programs called *name servers* are the workhorses of DNS. They store information about particular zones, loading this information from zone database files on disk. Name servers then answer questions from other

Preface

name servers about these zones. Name servers also know how to contact other name servers to find information about other zones.

DNS was good for the quickly growing Internet. It removed the central bottleneck at the NIC, and the now-familiar domain-based names paved the way for a truly vast number of hosts with unique names. But from a network administrator's IP address management standpoint, it made some things more difficult, including the following:

Zone database file complexity. The format of DNS zone database files is more complicated than the simple host table format, since DNS was designed to store more than just names and IP addresses. (For example, SMTP mail-routing information is also stored in DNS, something the host table is not capable of handling.) The more complicated format lends itself to the user making mistakes when editing the zone database files by hand.

Decentralization. With DNS, the information that was formerly centralized in the host table may now be spread among multiple name servers. Depending on how an organization creates zones, a network administrator looking for IP address information might have to consult multiple files on multiple name servers.

Limited contents. Like the host table, DNS lacks the ability to easily store additional host information, such as host location information and serial numbers. While this information can be stored as simple comments, it is difficult to search and any reporting would require add-on software.

The Third Generation: DNS with Homemade Tools

Editing DNS zone database files by hand tends to be a workable solution only for smaller organizations for the following reasons:

- Smaller organizations have fewer hosts and, therefore, a smaller and more comprehensible amount of DNS information.
- They often have fewer host moves, adds, and changes, resulting in less frequent changes to DNS information.
- They also usually have only a few people making these changes and, therefore, fewer people who need to understand the somewhat complicated zone database file syntax.

- Smaller organizations also tend to be more tolerant of the inevitable problems that arise from editing DNS information by hand.

Larger organizations usually decide that DNS by itself is not enough. Before the advent of commercially available IP address management software (discussed in the next section), organizations seeking to avoid DNS hand-editing were forced to use freely available software or write their own tools. However, freely available software to simplify IP address management tasks had several disadvantages:

Functionality. Software tended to focus on the automation of one particular function, rather than the larger feature set supported by later commercial IP address management software.

Support. No support is usually available for freely available software, which is unacceptable for most companies.

Quality. The quality of freely available software can be an issue, since anyone can write and distribute it. Commercial software is generally of higher quality.

An example of software in this category is h2n, a small Perl program distributed with the book *DNS and BIND*. The h2n program converts a host table into DNS zone database files. While designed to be used once during an organization's conversion from the use of host tables to DNS, it can also be used on a day-to-day basis: The host table becomes the canonical listing of IP addresses and host names, and h2n converts the information to DNS format. This offers the administrator the advantages of the host table—editing one file in a simple format—while using DNS, a necessity in today's Internet. But h2n is a simple tool focused on one task. It merely eliminates the need to hand-edit DNS zone database files.

Most large organizations made the decision to write some kind of customized application to avoid editing DNS files by hand and to implement some rudimentary IP address management features. This course of action also has disadvantages:

Development cost. Ambitious software packages with a large feature set are developed. Such development ended up taking a significant amount of time and money.

Support cost. Once developed, the software must be supported and maintained in-house, an ongoing burden.

Technical knowledge. This is difficult software to develop, potentially exceeding the capability of a company's internal development staff.

Of course, the tremendous advantage to developing one's own software is that it has exactly the features required.

We are aware of a Fortune 25 company that had no less than a dozen custom IP address management packages. Some were very simple and not much more complicated than h2n, while others performed some of the tasks later seen in commercial packages, such as tracking additional host information like serial and asset numbers. The cost to the company of maintaining all of these packages, however, was staggering.

The Advent of DHCP

The early 1990s saw the development and widespread implementation of the Dynamic Host Control Protocol (DHCP), which simplified the lives of network administrators but increased the complexity of IP address management. DHCP evolved from the Bootstrap Protocol (BootP), which allowed devices without permanent storage, such as printers, X terminals, and routers, to obtain an IP address and other configuration parameters at startup. The network administrator maintained a table of device hardware addresses and corresponding IP addresses. A device's hardware address had to be known and entered on the BootP server, along with the IP address that would always be assigned to that device.

A DHCP server also assigns IP addresses and configuration parameters to devices, but with a significant difference: A DHCP server does not need to know a device's hardware address ahead of time. DHCP servers own *lease pools,* or groups of IP addresses that may be dynamically assigned to DHCP clients on a first-come, first-served basis. The IP address assignment is called a *lease*. It may be permanent, but as the name suggests, it is more often valid for an interval called the *lease time*. Devices with nonvolatile storage—the norm today—attempt to renew their leases with the DHCP server upon startup.

DHCP represented a tremendous time savings for network administrators, who had previously been required to visit each device to configure its IP address and other parameters, such as default router and name servers. DHCP allows these devices to obtain this information out of the box, without any prior configuration; DHCP need only be enabled.

From an IP address management perspective, however, DHCP servers represented a whole new class of servers to configure and manage, along with name servers. Their configuration is similar. For example, DHCP lease pools are often entire subnets, which must also be configured on name servers as *in-addr.arpa* subdomains (the DNS construct that allows reverse mapping of IP address to host name).

Unfortunately, early DHCP servers didn't communicate with name servers, a situation still true today for almost all DHCP servers. Thus, the DHCP server generates new name-to-IP address mappings as it leases IP addresses, but this information is not reflected in DNS. Admittedly, the traditional DNS update mechanism is not conducive to this one-at-a-time-style update. The name server is designed for bulk updates and had to transfer an entire zone, even if only one piece of information had changed.

The DNS community recognized this deficiency, particularly in light of the growing popularity of DHCP and the desire for better integration between the two protocols. The result was a set of DNS protocol extensions developed in the mid-1990s and commonly referred to as *Dynamic DNS*. These extensions allow a DHCP server (or any authorized updater) to make changes to a running name server, which, in turn, notifies its peers immediately and propagates only the changed information.

By the mid-1990s, DHCP was in common use, which both increased and decreased the IP address management workload of network administrators. On the one hand, they no longer had to visit each host to configure its IP address and other parameters. On the other hand, they now had DCHP servers to maintain along with DNS servers. And while the protocols had been developed to allow DNS synchronization with DHCP lease activity, DHCP vendors did not implement them immediately. Finally, DNS and DHCP alone cannot track the additional physical information about a device associated with its IP address. The stage was set for software products to integrate these protocols and fill in the gaps.

The Fourth Generation: Commercial IP Address Management Software

By the mid-1990s, commercial IP address management software appeared from several vendors. It offered the following advantages and features:

Centralized management. The ability to centrally manage an entire organization's DNS and DHCP servers is probably the single largest advantage of commercial IP address management software. From one location, the software generates configuration and data files for all DNS and DHCP servers, transfers the files to the appropriate servers, and even restarts the servers so the changes take effect. A relatively recent feature is cross-platform support: Early packages focused on UNIX, but the growing popularity of Windows NT has generated support for it as well.

Graphical user interface. Many commercial packages support a graphical user interface (GUI), which is a great improvement over editing configuration files by hand on a terminal. A GUI simplifies the presentation of information, making it easier to interpret more information at once. It also simplifies data input and hides the underlying technical configuration, allowing more users than just the network administrator to make changes. Several commercial packages employ Java-based interfaces that can be accessed through a Web browser. These allow authorized users to perform management functions from anywhere on the network, without having to install separate software.

Consistency. All packages have a central data store from which configuration and data files for DNS and DHCP servers are created. In early packages, the data store is either a full-blown relational database from a third party or another, less complicated commercial database. This central data store, combined with the ability to do error and syntax checking in the GUI, increases the consistency and correctness of the data. For example, editing DNS files by hand requires two entries, one for the name-to-IP address mapping and another for the reverse. A common error is to forget one or the other, but this is easily avoided with IP address management software, along with all other syntax errors that stem from hand-editing.

Security. Most packages also implement access control lists, allowing the creation of different classes of users, from administrators with wide-ranging powers to operators who can only add and change host information.

Dynamic DNS. The commercial IP address management packages were the first to integrate DHCP and DNS information on a real-time basis. Early packages used proprietary protocols rather than the standards-based Dynamic DNS, but packages available today offer DHCP servers modified to provide true Dynamic DNS and the ability to update DNS servers in real time. This synchronization allows the DNS to provide an up-to-date view of the network at all times.

Extensible and customizable. Most packages allow the administrator to store considerable additional information along with each IP address, such as serial number, asset number, and physical location. Often these fields are customizable and additional fields may be added, allowing the administrator to track the desired information.

Reporting. Powerful reporting capabilities are a feature of most packages, allowing administrators to produce a report on just about any view of the IP address data: free subnets, allocated subnets, including percent used—the list goes on.

The Future

The future of IP address management products is, of course, still being written. Based on our experience in this field, I foresee the following features and trends:

Ubiquity. Eventually, IP address management products will be as common as the DNS and DHCP servers they currently manage. Software to manage these services effectively will be as necessary as the services themselves.

Directory-enabled applications. The entire industry is in the middle of a push to directory-enabled applications, and IP address management software is no exception. There are currently several packages available that use an LDAP-based directory server for their central data store, rather than a relational database. I expect this trend to continue. The directory-enabled model offers several advantages:

- *Simplicity.* A directory server is considerably less complicated than a relational database.
- *Content suitability.* Directory servers handle information in the format of attribute-value pairs. IP address management information is easily represented in this format and is thus an ideal choice for storage in a directory server.
- *Quantity.* The total amount of IP address information of most organizations does not require the nearly infinite scalability of relational databases but is well suited to the capacity of currently available directory servers.
- *Shared data store.* Multiple applications, including IP address management software, can share an organization's single directory server. In addition, the IP address management data in the directory server is easily accessible to all directory-enabled applications.

Integration with other protocols. It is inevitable that IP address management products will grow in scope to encompass other protocols.

User information. User-address mapping, which relates user information in the central data store to the currently assigned IP address, is a logical next step. This user information could be the basis for:

- *Authentication.* Servers could obtain users' information from IP address management software. This capability could also be used by any other device making authentication decisions, such as a firewall.
- *Authorization.* Software and devices making authorization decisions—whether or not a user is allowed access to a particular resource—could also use information in the central data store.
- *Usage tracking.* User activity could be correlated to other network information, such as DHCP lease activity, to obtain a picture of usage traits for different users.
- *Policy-based management.* The ability to relate IP addresses to user information enables policy-based management for controlling access to network resources on a per-user basis. While password schemes can allow or deny access to individual servers, this type of policy-based management would be built directly into the network's infrastructure, including bridges, routers, and firewalls. Uses include:

    Remote access. Remote users could be authenticated, then granted or denied access to all or part of the network according to their user profile.

    Virtual private networking. Firewalls could be configured to permit or deny access on a per-use basis, even though their IP addresses might be dynamically assigned.

    Bandwidth provisioning. In an actively managed network, packets destined for the CEO or for servers performing key business functions could be given priority over streaming video.

Management platform. Because network routers, bridges, firewalls, and other devices depend largely on IP addressing, address management software can provide a platform for actively managing the network. Just as current packages store configuration information centrally and download files to DNS and DHCP servers, future packages could do the same with network hardware. A dominant software developer could create a de facto standard mechanism for this integration.

IP address management is key to maintaining a reliable, robust network that works for its users. The new generations of management software will allow IT professionals to meet the demand for more TCP/IP services, extend services to remote sites, and efficiently manage the traffic on their growing networks.

Top Five Problems Solved by IP Address Management

Chances are, you are using DNS, DHCP (probably the free version available on NT 4.0), and some manual tracking system (spreadsheet or "homegrown" database) to manage your IP addresses and name space. This type of system may even work for you up to a point: up to the point where you are experiencing one or more of the costly problems inherent in these systems. Some of these problems include:

Duplicate IP addresses. With dynamically changing networks of thousands of IP addresses, one of the most common causes of network failures is duplicate IP addresses. It may seem like a small problem, but it can have huge consequences when mission-critical business functions fail. Not only is there lost productivity for people who cannot access the network during downtime, there is the potential for huge lost opportunity when online orders, for example, cannot function for a period of time.

Running out of IP addresses. As the Internet and intranets expand, a growing problem for many organizations is a shrinking pool of IP addresses. This problem is exacerbated by poor utilization of the existing IP address pool. Segmenting the lease pool in order to provide DHCP failover is one specific example of where many organizations are not maximizing the addresses they already have.

Troubleshooting difficulty. Many organizations do not realize they have an IP address management problem until disaster strikes. Once their network crashes, it becomes top priority. However, without the proper tools, solving IP address problems can be difficult and time-consuming. Tracking down a duplicate IP address or pinpointing a problem within pools of thousands of IP addresses can be difficult if there is no mechanism to know who had what address at what point in time.

Unauthorized IP address use. Many companies don't want their employees spending tons of time browsing the Internet while on the clock, or they may want to control how they utilize the Internet. Even

Preface

xxiii

so, with a little technical knowledge and a lot of patience, a person can sometimes grab an IP address they are not supposed to and browse freely. Most IP address management systems have no mechanism to know if this has happened or even how to track it if they know. Worse, this type of unknown activity could create a duplicate IP address situation that could bring the entire network down.

Inhibiting network growth. In today's network environments, change is ongoing. If the IP address management system cannot seamlessly allow for network changes (moving routers, redesigning subnet structures, and so on), then these changes are more time-consuming and costly. The last thing a network manager needs is a nonstandard, proprietary system that may solve this problem but requires a costly replacement of existing infrastructure and inhibits future network growth.

Solution

This book will introduce you to ideas and products that let you automatically and efficiently control your IP addresses and name-space services while ensuring a more reliable network.

You could continue to keep track of increasing numbers of static addresses in spreadsheets, or use the free DHCP services that come bundled with server packages. And those can work for you, up to a point.

They can work to the point where you're spending hours doing clerical work, to the point where an address conflict takes all or part of your network down, or to the point where users you can't identify are monopolizing your bandwidth.

Growing networks call for an automated solution. That solution is Dynamic IP management. Dynamic IP lets you centrally manage IP addresses and the IP name space across your entire network. A Dynamic IP solution integrates DHCP, DNS, and other IP services, and lets you administer them through a single interface. You get fully audited, easily administered, fail-safe addressing.

Fail-Safe Addressing and Naming

- Effectively eliminate the potential for conflicts.
- Ensure fault-tolerant services for every user and device on the network, through redundant fail-over capability.
- Extend IP services to remote users, via support for RADIUS protocol.

Complete Auditing and Reporting

- Accurately track and audit IP address assignments by MAC address and device name.
- Correlate lease assignments with login names, through the User-to-Address mapping service.
- View address assignments, names, and other status information in real-time displays.

Centralized, Automated Management

- Centrally administer the whole system, or delegate specified tasks to others on the network.
- Control IP services running on other servers including UNIX, Novell, and Windows NT.
- Administer all services via a password-protected Web interface.
- Set up the system quickly and make changes with re-entrant administration wizards.

The Objective of This Book

This book describes the requirements for a new type of Domain Name System (DNS) server implementation. These requirements are mandated by the rapid growth and dynamic nature of today's private intranets and the public Internet. In my opinion, DNS innovation has been thwarted by the domination of public domain DNS solutions and the heretofore static nature of TCP/IP network addressing. In today's networks, which increasingly rely on the Dynamic Host Configuration Protocol (DHCP) for Dynamic IP address assignments, a new and dynamic DNS server architecture is required. With the introduction of Windows 2000 (a.k.a. Windows NT 5.0) and Active Directory sometime in 1999 or 2000, this requirement will become a necessity.

Several companies have developed Dynamic DNS server implementations to address current requirements and to anticipate the future of dynamic, policy-based networking, while still maintaining full interoperability with traditional DNS implementations. This book describes the current DNS system, the requirements for change in this area, and Dynamic DNS servers solutions from Network TeleSystems, MetaInfo, Quadritek, and JOIN Systems.

Preface

The Domain Name System has evolved remarkably well to keep pace with the growth of the Internet and private TCP/IP networks that, by some estimates, now interconnect nearly 100 million computers. More remarkable still, most of the DNS servers in these networks are still based upon the BIND (Berkeley Internet Name Daemon) public domain software. For more than a decade, the DNS, supported by tens of thousands of BIND-derived servers, has met the needs of these networks based on a static IP address model.

However, today's networks are transitioning from static to dynamic address assignments in order to accommodate the rapid growth and change in such networks, and to a lesser extent, because we are running out of addresses in the current IP Version 4 protocol specification. In the future, networks will no longer assign static addresses to most of the computers that they interconnect. When addresses are assigned dynamically, the DNS directory service must accommodate the real-time, transactional nature of a system that is constantly being reconfigured.

The current DNS protocol and service standards have not fully addressed this change. Instead, these standards have evolved in a way that attempts to minimize the consequences of dynamic networks served by an offline, batch-oriented directory system. More radical change to the DNS is required, and even the vendors that offer BIND-derived DNS servers are beginning to enhance their products beyond the scope of the current standards. The deployment of an advanced DNS server is now a necessity for most commercial intranets.

The DNS of the future involves multiple types of clients, servers, and management stations interacting as a system. The boundaries that exist today between network clients and servers that support DHCP, DNS, security, directory, and related services will blur as these services become more sophisticated. The potential benefits of such an integrated system are considerable, but organizations that attempt to glue such a system together with multiple vendors' components may find themselves disappointed with the results. Organizations with a substantial investment in TCP/IP networking need to plan for the migration to such a system. At least in the short term, a system of services such as these should be engineered from the ground up to work together.

CHAPTER 1

TCP/IP Basics

Many excellent publications describe TCP/IP (Transmission Control Protocol/Internet Protocol) and the Internet in a comprehensive fashion. (References to several of these publications, including Requests for Comments, or RFCs, are included at the end of this chapter.) This chapter provides a short introduction to TCP/IP, so you can become acquainted (or reacquainted) with TCP/IP addressing. Familiarity with these concepts will help you master subsequent chapters.

After reading this chapter, you should understand what IP addresses, subnets, routers, and name servers are. You should also learn what the differences are between Class A, B, C, and D addresses. Static versus dynamic addressing will be discussed, along with basic information on so-called legacy protocols, such as NetBEUI.

Feel free to skip this chapter if you are already familiar with basic TCP/IP concepts.

Network Protocols

Computer networks simply deliver bits of information from one point to another. One requirement for transmitting such information is that the computer systems on each end both speak the same language, or *protocol*. You're already familiar with many protocols and how they're defined. For example, to address a regular letter or package in the United States, you need to write the destination address on the front of the envelope. That address might look like:

Dr. John Taylor
Sickville Eye and Foot Care Center
57 Pediatric Lane, Suite 300
Sickville, VT 05400

The protocol for U.S. mail requires a specific location where you write this destination address (the front of the envelope), the name of the recipient, the business name (if any), the street address (perhaps with a suite or apartment number), the city, the state, and a postal (zip) code. Additional requirements may apply, such as the amount of postage, a return address, proper packaging, and so on. All these requirements define the U.S. Postal Service protocol.

Computer network protocols require similar information in a precise format. A package of information sent over the network is called a *datagram*. Datagrams usually include at least a destination address, source address (where it came from), length (size of package), error detection information (such as a checksum), and package contents (the bits and bytes of information being carried).

Transmission Control Protocol/Internet Protocol (TCP/IP) is one of the most popular families of network protocols, and it happens to be the one used as the basis for the Internet. Many people think of TCP/IP in terms of layers or levels of functions. At the lowest layer, the network interface (such as a LAN) carries the network traffic over wires or other connections. The highest layer, the application layer (such as a Web browser), uses the various TCP/IP services to communicate. In between are two additional layers: the transport and internetwork layers.

The transport layer facilitates communication between applications, whether they are on the same or different systems. The main transport layer protocol is called *TCP*, and it can determine whether or not a message has been received at the other end of the connection. An alternative

TCP/IP Basics

is *User Datagram Protocol (UDP)*, which simply sends messages without checking to see whether the system at the other end has received each part. Applications that need maximum performance and that verify delivery themselves often use UDP.

Internet Protocol (IP) is one of the internetwork layer protocols, and it is responsible for properly routing datagrams to other computers across the network. (Other Internet layer protocols include ICMP, IGMP, ARP, and RARP, discussed in "Other TCP/IP Terms" later in this chapter.) IP depends on several important addresses in order to keep track of where messages should be delivered.

IP Addresses

IP uses addresses to specify both the source and destination systems on a TCP/IP network. Each address consists of 32 bits, usually broken into four decimal numbers separated by dots (.). Each decimal number represents an 8-bit byte (an *octet*) in the address. For example:

```
00001001 01000011 00100110 00000001  32-bit address
    9   .   67   .   38   .    1     decimal address
```

Each address can also be separated into two logical parts:

1. *Network address*—The network address is a lot like a postal code, because it identifies which region (or section) of the total network contains the system.

2. *System (or machine or host) address*—The system address is similar to an apartment or suite number, because it specifically identifies a particular system within that region.

As shown in Figure 1-1, IP addresses belong to one of four classes, depending on how the entire 32-bit address is split (a fifth class, Class E, is not commonly used).

Class A   Class A addresses use 7 bits for the network address portion and 24 bits for the host address. With Class A addresses, there are 126 (2^7-2) possible networks (regions), with 16,777,214 ($2^{24}-2$) possible hosts in each, for a total of over 2 billion addresses. (One bit is used to identify the address as Class A, to distinguish it from other classes.)

Figure 1-1
IP classes.

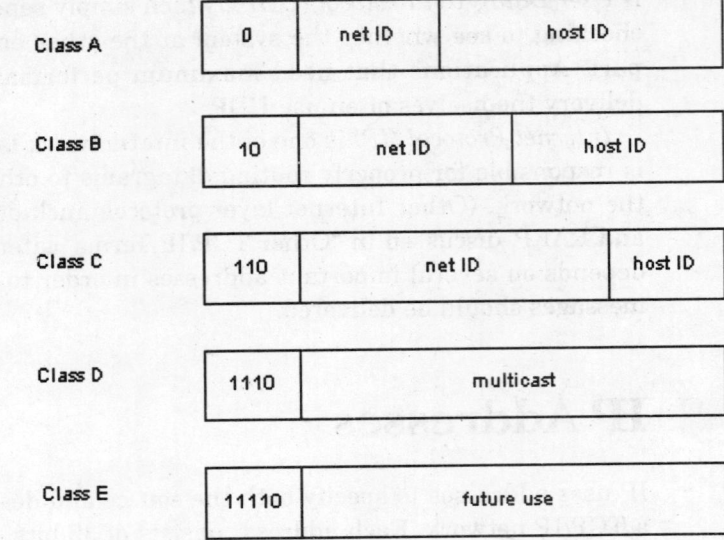

For example, the following Class A address can be broken apart into its network and host addresses:

```
00001001 01000011 00100110 00000001  32-bit address
   9    .   67   .   38   .    1     decimal address
^*******  ++++++++ ++++++++ ++++++++
```

The first bit (marked with ^), a 0, identifies this IP address as Class A. The next 7 bits (*) provide the network number (9). The remaining bits (+) identify the specific host within network 9, in this case $67*(2^{16})+38*(2^8)+1$, or 4,400,641. In other words, this IP address identifies the 4,400,641st system in the 9th network region.

Class B Class B addresses use 14 bits for the network portion and 16 bits for the host portion. These addresses provide an additional 16,382 ($2^{14}-2$) networks with 65,534 ($2^{16}-2$) hosts each, for a total of over 1 billion additional addresses. The first two bits of a Class B address are 1 and 0.

Class C Class C addresses use 21 bits for the network part and 8 bits for the machine part, providing 2,097,150 ($2^{21}-2$) networks with 254 (2^8-2) hosts each, for a total of over half a billion addresses. Class C addresses begin with 110.

TCP/IP Basics 5

As you can see, with Classes A through C and 32-bit addresses, TCP/IP can provide service for a theoretical maximum of approximately 3.5 billion different hosts.

Class D Class D addresses are reserved for multicasting, a limited form of broadcasting only to other hosts sharing the same Class D address. Class D addresses begin with bits 1110.

Class E Class E addresses (beginning with 11110) are not widely used at this point in time and are reserved for future use.

In addition, some special addresses are reserved and cannot be assigned to actual systems on the network. These special addresses include:

All bits 0 Means *this*. For example, if the network address part is set to 0, the host address refers to a system on *this* (its own) network. When making initial contact on the network, a system may use this method if it doesn't know the network address. Other systems will reply with the proper network address filled in, and this proper network address can be recorded for future use.

All bits 1 Means *all*. For example, if the host address is set to all 1s, the IP address identifies all systems within that particular network region. In other words, a Class B address of 128.2.255.255 refers to all systems on network 128.2. Such an address is also called a *directed broadcast* address, because it contains a valid network address and a broadcast (all 1s) host address.

Loopback The Class A network 127 (including addresses, such as 127.0.0.1) is defined as the *loopback* network. Systems will automatically route traffic destined for these addresses back into the same system without ever communicating across the real network. Loopback addresses are often used for testing new software, to separate network problems from simple programming errors.

Private addresses Several addresses have been reserved for private networks that are not directly connected to the Internet. These addresses include the Class A group of addresses in network 10, the 16 Class B groups of addresses in networks 172.16 through 172.31, and the 256 Class C groups of addresses in networks 192.168.0 through 192.168.255. Web servers, FTP sites, and other systems available to the public on the Internet will never have addresses beginning with 10, 172.16 through 172.31, or 192.168. These addresses are quite useful for testing purposes or for totally private use, and you can use them without having to contact someone to reserve real addresses.

You can determine whether an address is Class A, B, C, D, or E by simply examining the first octet, as shown in Table 1-1.

Table 1-2 builds on the information in Table 1-1, taking into consideration that 127.0.0.0 is defined as the loopback network. This table summarizes the properties of Class A, B, and C addresses.

IP Subnets

Suppose your company, MegaHuge Industries, is assigned a Class A address for all its systems around the world. Therefore, you have 16,777,214 possible IP addresses available to assign to all your systems. However, if you have many different buildings scattered across the globe,

TABLE 1-1

Class Determination.

For an address of **X.0.0.0**, if **X** is...

...from (lowest)...	...to (highest), then...	Class
00000000	01111111	A
0	127	
10000000	10111111	B
128	191	
11000000	11011111	C
192	223	
11100000	11101111	D
224	239	
11110000	11111111	E
240	255	

TABLE 1-2
Class Properties.

	Class A	Class B	Class C
Lowest network ID	1.0.0.0	128.0.0.0	192.0.0.0
Highest network ID	126.0.0.0	191.255.0.0	223.255.255.0
Number of networks	125	16,382	2,097,150
Number of hosts per network	16,777,214	65,534	254

it can be hard to manage such a large number of addresses. It might be much easier to have individuals in each location (or even within a particular department) manage their own smaller sets of addresses. In addition, it's often bad for network performance to have broadcast traffic throughout the Class A network. To cut down on network congestion, your company may wish to divide this huge range of addresses into more-manageable chunks.

Subnets, which are smaller groups of addresses, were introduced to help solve these problems. By sacrificing the total number of addresses (16,777,214 for a Class A), you can divide your network into separately managed subnets. Class A, B, and even C addresses can be divided into subnets. Then, address assignments within a subnet can be performed locally, without having to contact a central authority to obtain additional addresses. The whole network (with subnets) still appears to be one IP network to the outside world.

For example, consider the Class A address 9.67.38.1. The network address is 9, and the host address is 67.38.1. Subnets simply extend this basic address by treating part of the host address as a subnetwork address. IP addresses then consist of four parts: the class identifier (0 for Class A in this example), the network address (9), the subnetwork address (for example, bits 8 to 25), and the host address (for example, the remaining bits 26 to 31).

A bit mask, the *subnet mask,* identifies which bits are part of the subnet address and which are still part of the host address. This 32-bit subnet mask has the bits for the host address set to 0 and all the other bits set to 1. (By convention, the subnet mask never has a 1 following a 0. Both the network address and the subnet address are masked by 1s. Technically, however, only the subnet number needs to be masked.)

So, for 9.67.38.1, with only bits 26 to 31 representing the host address, the subnet mask would be as follows:

```
11111111 11111111 11111111 11000000
```

or 255.255.255.192 in decimal format. To extract the *subnet base address* (the network address and the subnet address together), a logical AND is performed. (If both bits in a particular bit position, for both the IP address and the subnet mask, are set to 1, then the result is also 1. Otherwise, the value is 0.) In this case:

```
00001001 01000011 00100110 00000001=9.67.38.1      (Class A address)
11111111 11111111 11111111 11----  = 255.255.255.192 (subnet mask)
                                                    (logical AND)
======== ======== ======== =========
00001001 01000011 00100110 00----  = 9.67.38        (subnet base address)
```

and the remainder is as follows:

```
-------- -------- -------- --000001 = 1            (host address)
```

Of course, the subnet number (by itself) is as follows:

```
-------- 01000011 00100110 00------ = 68760
```

Any subnet number can be chosen with the exception of all 0s (this subnet) or all 1s (all subnets).

One disadvantage of using subnets is that the total number of possible IP addresses available to you decreases. For example, if you have a Class C network address of 220.23.5, you have 8 remaining bits to control. Without subnets (or, more precisely, as one subnet), you have 254 possible host addresses. With two subnets, you sacrifice 2 bits (subnets 01 and 10; remember, all 1s and 0s are reserved), leaving 6 bits remaining. Therefore, you're left with two subnets with up to 62 host addresses in each for a total of 124 host addresses—less than half the previous number.

Bearing in mind both the advantages and disadvantages of using subnets, you can easily determine the number of available subnets and hosts in each subnet by using Table 1-3. By subnetting your network, you can more easily mix different network technologies (such as Ethernet and Token Ring), overcome limitations to the number of hosts per segment, and minimize network congestion by reducing broadcast traffic.

If you have...	...then your subnet mask is...
Class A	255.X.0.0
Class B	255.255.X.0
Class C	255.255.255.X

TCP/IP Basics

TABLE 1-3

Number of Subnets and Hosts per Subnet (Partial).

X	Number of Required Subnets	Number of Possible Hosts in Each Subnet		
		Class A	Class B	Class C
0	1	16,277,214	65,534	254
128	invalid	invalid	invalid	invalid
192	2	4,194,302	16,382	62
224	6	2,097,150	8,190	30
240	14	1,048,574	4,094	14
248	30	524,286	2,046	6
252	62	262,142	1,022	2
254	126	131,070	510	invalid
255	254	65,534	254	invalid
...	...	...	...	invalid

...where your choice of X yields the data in Table 1-3.

NOTE. *A Class C network cannot contain more than 62 subnets. Also, Table 1-3 only shows the possible number of subnets and hosts per subnet when only one octet is used for subnetting. For Class A and Class B networks, additional bits can be used for subnetting, as suggested by the last row in the table.*

Supernetting, the opposite of subnetting, treats multiple networks as if they belong to one larger network. For example, a company that may need up to 2,032 possible hosts could be assigned eight Class C network IDs (8*254 = 2,032) to form one supernet. For example, if those eight Class C networks are 220.78.168 through 220.78.175, then the subnet mask (to create the supernet) would be 255.255.248.0, which corresponds to the subnet mask used for a Class B network with 30 subnets of 2,046 possible hosts in each. Supernets are formed primarily to simplify routing on a TCP/IP network.

IP Routing

As mentioned in the preceding section, one reason for dividing a network into subnets is to cut down on the amount of broadcast traffic throughout the network. Generally, a system on one subnet can send IP datagrams to a system on another subnet only by working through an intermediary, called an *IP router* or *gateway*. Again, let's use the U.S. Postal Service as an example. A mail delivery system without subnets would mean that every delivery truck visits every home and business until all the packages and letters are delivered. Such a system might work, and pickup service would be quite frequent, but delivery would take a long time. Consequently, the Postal Service uses subnets, in essence, with one truck serving each particular neighborhood. Packages and letters picked up by that truck are routed to one or more central handling facilities, then further routed to other trucks on the delivery side. However, if your package or letter is destined for your neighbor's house (on the same subnet), there's very little routing involved, and the same truck will deliver that particular mail. The size of each truck route, the number of central facilities, the speed of transfers, and so on determine the overall level of service and performance.

Similarly, there are two types of IP routing. *Direct routing* (or *direct delivery*) means that an IP datagram can be sent directly to another system that is on the same subnet, without involving an intermediate gateway. *Indirect routing* occurs when the destination host is not on a network directly attached to the source machine. One or more gateways must handle the traffic, and the IP address of the first gateway must be provided to the machine trying to send the datagram. This address is called the *gateway address* or *router address*. Each system on the network maintains a routing table to help determine which type of routing to use—indirect or direct—to reach another system. Three types of routings can be found in the table:

1. Direct routes
2. Indirect routes
3. Default routes (in case the destination IP network is not found elsewhere in the table)

A routing table might look like this:

```
destination     router          interface
129.7.0.0       129.7.0.1       Ethernet
128.15.0.0      128.15.0.1      modem
```

TCP/IP Basics

```
128.10.0.0      128.10.0.5      Token Ring
default         128.10.0.5      Token Ring
127.0.0.1       127.0.0.1       loopback
```

Assigning IP Addresses

In short, there are generally three pieces of information a system needs in order to start communicating on a TCP/IP network: an IP address (to uniquely identify that system on the network), a subnet mask (to help divide that 32-bit address and determine the subnet and network parts), and at least one default router address. (If a machine does not need to communicate beyond its immediate subnet, the router address and the machine's own IP address are set the same.) These three values represent the bare minimum needed for a system to participate in the TCP/IP world, and they are vital. Yet, with networks changing so quickly, manually programming these values into each and every device attached to the network (and reprogramming them as they change) can quickly become tiresome.

IP addresses assigned to systems manually (by changing a setting at each individual system) are called *static addresses*. Bootstrap Protocol (BOOTP) and Dynamic Host Configuration Protocol (DHCP) can be used to assign *dynamic addresses*. *BOOTP* was one of the first attempts to automate delivery of these critical values. A client system (such as a PC) can boot up and obtain the address information needed to connect to the network from a BOOTP server, where all the information is kept and managed centrally.

Although BOOTP is still widely used, its successor, *DHCP,* provides much more flexibility. IP addresses can be used and reused according to rules set in the DHCP server, without having to make modifications for every change in the network. Also, many DHCP servers can still provide address information to older BOOTP clients. A well-designed DHCP server can save a lot of work and help get your TCP/IP network up and running more quickly. If you'd like to start exploring DHCP, read Chapter 2, "DHCP Concepts and Overview."

Name Servers

While 32-bit numbers are easy for computers to understand, human beings tend to prefer names. So, each system with an IP address can be assigned one or more alphanumeric names. For instance, 9.67.38.1 could be called *charlie,* and 9.67.38.2 might be *alice.* Subnets and network addresses can also be assigned names, such as *com, abc.net,* or *kingscollege.ac.uk.* Names assigned to subnets, networks, or any arbitrary collection of IP addresses are called *domain names.* Therefore, a system's *fully qualified name* might be *charlie.abcus2.abc.com* or *alice.kingscollege.ac.uk.* Domains are designed to save typing and to provide some structure to the naming of systems. Generally, you do not have to include the domain name if you're simply trying to reach another system within the same domain.

The system that has the job of keeping track of which names correspond to which IP addresses is called a *domain name system (DNS)* server. A DNS server simply contains a table of addresses with their corresponding names. Lookups can be performed in either direction, but usually a DNS server translates names into numeric addresses on behalf of clients. For any machine to take advantage of IP names, it must know the numeric address of at least one name server. This address is the fourth critical piece of information most machines need in order to get basic TCP/IP service, although it's optional, since it's still possible (albeit cumbersome) to reach other systems using nothing but numeric addresses.

Most systems can accept up to three name server addresses (a primary and up to two backups), contacting each in turn in order to look up the IP address that corresponds to a particular name. Yet there are thousands of DNS servers connected to the Internet, each handling a small portion of the vast list of names and addresses. To handle these lookups most efficiently, one DNS server can forward a lookup request it cannot satisfy to another DNS server. Often lookup responsibilities are divided according to the dots (.) in the fully qualified name. For example, *charlie* may be given one name server address, and that local name server (DNS 1) knows the names and addresses of all the systems in the *abcus2.abc.com* group. When *charlie* requests an IP address for *gadget.att.com* from DNS 1, DNS 1 may forward the request to DNS 2 (serving *abc.com*), which then forwards the request to DNS 3 (serving *com*), which then forwards the request to DNS 4 (serving *att.com*), which then answers with the proper IP address for *gadget.att.com.* In practice, name servers record many of the most recent lookups to help cut down on network traffic. For example, if *samuel.abcus2.abc.com* requests the IP address for *gadget.att.com* from DNS 1 just after *charlie* does, DNS 1 may be able to provide the answer without bothering DNS 2, DNS 3, or DNS 4.

Note that the capitalization of a TCP/IP name does not matter. For example, *charlie.abcus2.abc.com, CHARLIE.ABCUS2.ABC.COM,* and

ChArLiE.abcus2.ABC.cOm will all be treated by a DNS the same way, and the DNS will return an IP address of 9.67.38.1 for each of these variations. It's also quite common to have multiple listings, known as *alias names,* with several different names corresponding to the same numeric IP address. Many companies try to gain a marketing advantage by registering multiple names, hoping that someone will stumble into their Web site by typing one of several generic names, such as *www.casino.com* or *www.gambling.com.*

A *static DNS* requires someone to manually edit and update the lookup table whenever an IP address gets assigned or reassigned to a particular name, or when a name is no longer used because the system is out of service. Needless to say, this task can be tedious. Chapter 3, "Serving Names," explores how a *Dynamic DNS (DDNS)* server performs, with information on how to make communication between name servers and hosts more sophisticated.

Registration of IP addresses and domain names on the Internet is currently managed by a central administrative body called *InterNIC*, or the *Internet Network Information Center.* InterNIC's Internet Web page can be found at *http://rs.internic.net/rs-internic.html.*

Applications That Use TCP/IP

Programmers have written many applications that communicate using TCP/IP. Web browsers (HTTP), FTP (file transfer), Telnet (terminal emulation), LPR/LPD (printing over TCP/IP), REXEC and RSH (starting programs remotely over the network), POP/SMTP/IMAP (e-mail services), NFS (file sharing), X-Windows (graphics terminal emulation), NNTP (news), SNMP (network management), and Java, among other examples, can all use these common services. Although many variations exist for specific platforms (such as Winsock for Microsoft Windows), a *sockets interface* allows programmers to write applications that communicate with TCP/IP.

Other TCP/IP Terms

To work properly and manage traffic flow efficiently, IP needs some additional components, as described within the following list of terms. These terms are explained briefly; please consult the appropriate references for more detailed information:

- *Internet Control Message Protocol (ICMP),* a part of IP, helps report errors in datagram delivery. ICMP can also help discover routers and maximum transmission units (MTUs; see below) along the path the datagram travels. Ping, the popular TCP/IP application used to check the connection between two systems on the network, uses ICMP. RFC 792 describes ICMP in detail.

- *The maximum transmission unit (MTU)* is the size of the IP datagram, which can be adjusted depending on network conditions. All systems on a TCP/IP network are required to handle MTUs ranging from 576 to 65,535 octets. Each datagram typically packages 20 octets of identifying information, such as the destination address, as part of the structure.

- *Internet Group Management Protocol (IGMP)* allows systems to participate in IP multicasts and to cancel such participation. Additionally, IGMP provides routers with the ability to check hosts to see if they are interested in participating in multicasts. RFCs 966, 1112, and 1458 discuss IP multicasting.

- *Address Resolution Protocol (ARP)* maps IP addresses to hardware addresses on a network. (Hardware addresses are often Ethernet or token ring network adapter addresses consisting of 12 hexadecimal digits.) *Reverse ARP (RARP)* provides the reverse lookup. See RFC 826 for more information on ARP.

- *SLIP* (RFC 1055) and *PPP* (RFCs 1717 and 1661) provide TCP/IP services over serial lines, such as modems and ISDN (digital telephone) connections.

- *IPv6 (Internet Protocol version 6)* is proposed to help alleviate some of the address constraints and other shortcomings of TCP/IP as it becomes ever more popular, although an upgrade to these capabilities will take time. Fortunately, IPv6 simply extends today's TCP/IP; so the skills you develop in this book should help you prepare for these protocol enhancements as they become available. See RFCs 1883 through 1887 for more information on IPv6.

- *Firewalls* help protect an *intranet* (private TCP/IP network) from unwanted infiltration from the Internet, such as people trying to break into servers. At the same time, people on the intranet can still get access to Internet systems. Firewalls vary in capabilities, but the two basic types are *proxy* and *SOCKS* firewalls. Firewalls can also help link two separate intranets via the Internet (and still provide security) using a technology called *virtual private networks (VPN)*. Chapter 7, "Security of DHCP and Dynamic DNS," takes a look at firewalls in the context of overall TCP/IP network security.

- Traditional LAN (local area network) protocols can be carried by TCP/IP to provide file and print sharing services for PCs without contaminating a TCP/IP network with other protocols. (Many computer networks are perfectly capable of mixing protocols, but many network managers prefer to standardize on one protocol.) For example, RFC 1234 describes how Novell's IPX operates over TCP/IP; so traditional NetWare servers and clients can communicate via TCP/IP. NetBIOS over TCP/IP (used by Microsoft Windows 95, Windows 98, Windows NT, and Windows for Workgroups and explained by RFCs 1001 and 1002) supports applications written to the NetBIOS programming interface. NetBIOS isn't actually a protocol. Like the sockets interface, it's a widely accepted way of writing network-savvy applications. The NetBIOS interface can be supported by a number of underlying network protocols, including NetBEUI (NetBIOS over IEEE 802.2), TCP/IP (TCPBEUI), and even Systems Network Architecture (SNA). Like TCP/IP, NetBIOS also relies on names to communicate with other systems on the network, although these names behave much differently. A *NetBIOS Name Server (NBNS)* can help provide better NetBIOS service over a TCP/IP network.

Related Publications

This chapter has provided just enough information to understand most of the concepts explored in this book, but there's far more technical information on TCP/IP available. For more information on TCP/IP, please refer to the following publications:

- *Internetworking with TCP/IP,* Vol. I, *Principles, Protocols and Architecture,* 3rd ed., by Douglas E. Comer. Upper Saddle River, NJ: Prentice-Hall, Inc., 1995; ISBN 0-13-216987-8.
- *IPng and the TCP/IP Protocols,* by Steven A. Thomas. New York: John Wiley & Sons, Inc., 1996; ISBN 0-471-13088-5.
- *Communications for Cooperating Systems: OSI, SNA and TCP/IP,* by R. J. Cypser. Reading, MA: Addison-Wesley Publishing Company, Inc., 1992; ISBN 0-201-50775-7.

- **Requests for Comments (RFCs)**

    There are more than 2,200 RFCs today. For those readers who want to keep up-to-date with the latest advances in TCP/IP, the ever-increasing number of RFCs and Internet Drafts (IDs), published by the nonprofit Internet Engineering Task Force (IETF), are the best sources. RFCs can be viewed on the Internet at *http://www.isi.edu/rfc-editor*.

CHAPTER 2

DHCP Concepts and Overview

Dynamic Host Configuration Protocol, or DHCP, is a client/server protocol that enables you to centrally locate and dynamically distribute configuration information, including Internet Protocol (IP) addresses. This chapter provides an overview of DHCP concepts and components. The intention is to summarize concepts that you need to implement DHCP on network.

BOOTP, the Predecessor of DHCP

DHCP and its predecessor, Bootstrap Protocol (BOOTP), came about to fulfill the need of diskless workstations to acquire IP addresses and bootstrap information from a server in the network. BOOTP is an example of how you use the client/server paradigm to bootstrap a diskless workstation and to provide it with IP address configuration. The BOOTP server listens on well-known port 67, and diskless computers usually contain a startup program in nonvolatile storage, or ROM. Because all the workstations start from the same program, it is impossible to store IP addresses in that code. A diskless machine needs to know its IP address to participate in a TCP/IP network. It also needs to know the address of the file server machine where the bootstrap image is stored.

The BOOTP client uses the special broadcast IP address of all 1s (255.255.255.255) to obtain its IP address. It is responsible for retransmitting requests if the server does not respond. The mapping between the client hardware address and the IP address is kept in the BOOTP table, which is manually maintained by the administrator.

BOOTP is the first step of a two-step bootstrap procedure. It does not provide the clients with a memory image. Instead, it provides the client only with the information that it needs to obtain an image. The client obtains this memory image after initiating a Trivial FTP (TFTP) request to the server, whose IP address it received from the BOOTP server.

Figure 2-1 shows the BOOTP flow between a client and a server. When the server receives a BOOTP request from a client, the server looks up the defined IP address based upon the client's MAC address. It then replies with the client IP address and the name of the load file. The client initiates a TFTP request to the server for the load file.

BOOTP uses a limited broadcast address for the BOOTP request. It requires the server in the same subnet as the client that requests configuration information. BOOTP forwarding is a mechanism for routers to forward a BOOTP request between subnets. The agents that forward the BOOTP packets between clients and servers on different subnets are called *relay agents*. DHCP adds the capability of automatically allocating reusable network addresses and distributing additional host configuration options. DHCP clients and servers use existing BOOTP relay agents.

BOOTP clients can interact with DHCP servers, and DHCP servers and BOOTP servers can coexist if configured properly. DHCP clients cannot interoperate with BOOTP servers. BOOTP and DHCP servers cannot

DHCP Concepts and Overview

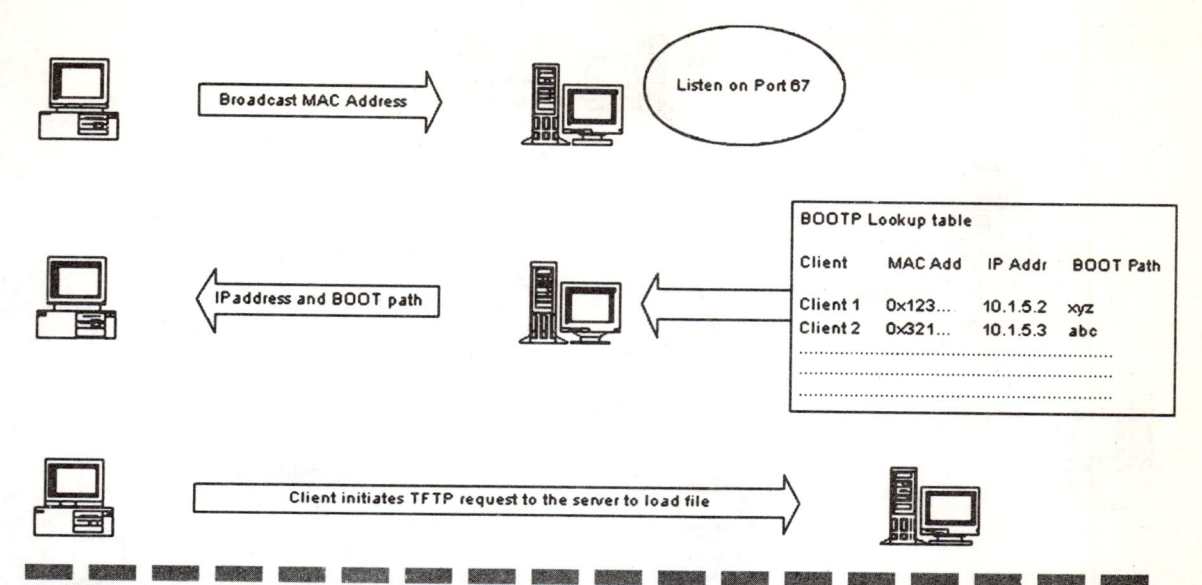

Figure 2-1 BOOTP flow between client and server.

run at the same time on the same system because both use the well-known ports 67 and 68.

IETF RFCs 2131 and 2132 describe DHCP protocols.

DHCP Overview

DHCP provides a framework for passing configuration parameters to hosts on a TCP/IP network (See Figure 2-2). The following three types of network components make up a DHCP network:

- *DHCP host clients.* These hosts run the DHCP client programs. The DHCP clients work together with their server counterparts to obtain and implement configuration information to automatically access IP networks.

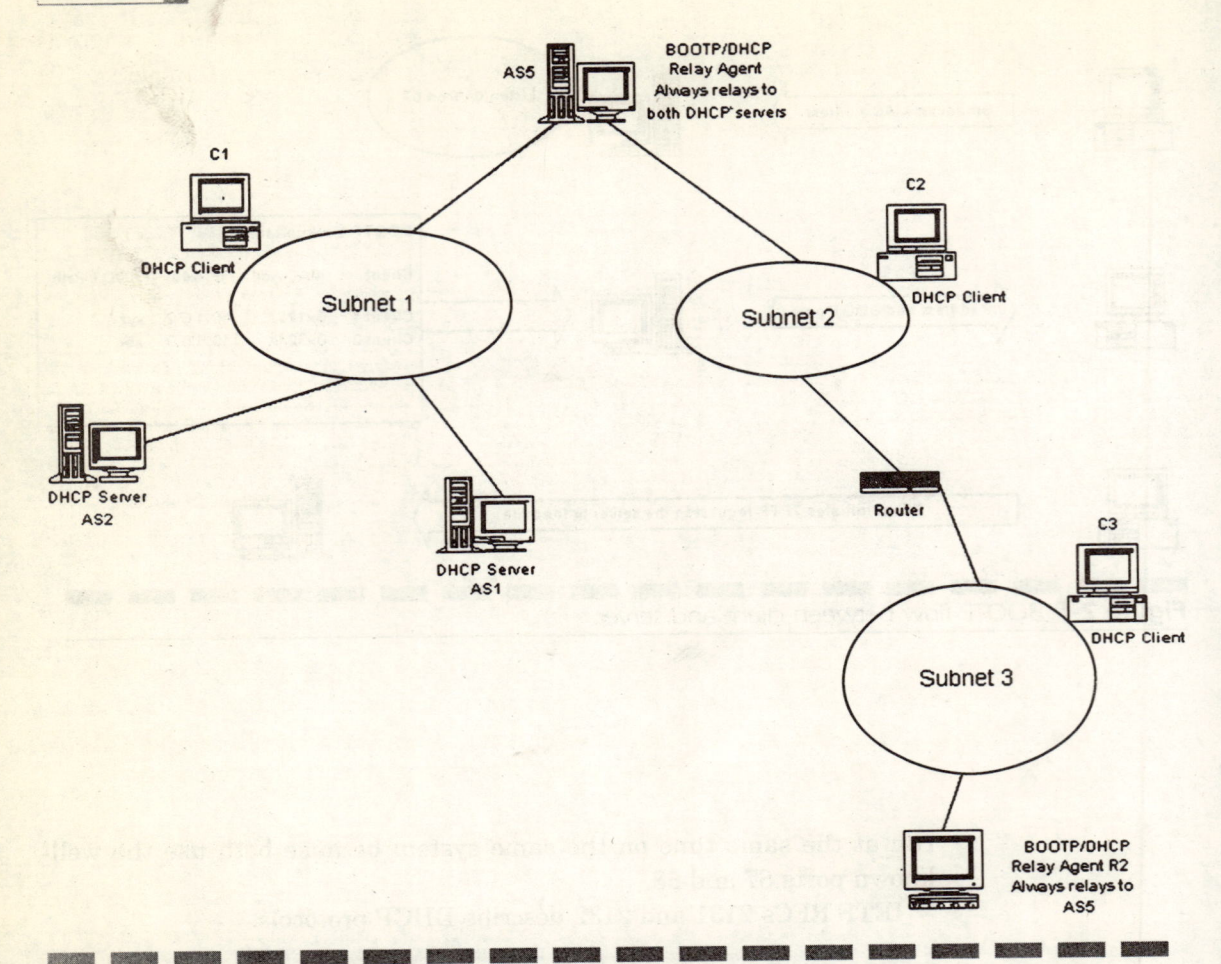

Figure 2-2 The various components in a DHCP network.

DHCP Concepts and Overview

- *DHCP servers.* DHCP servers provide the addresses and configuration information to DHCP and BOOTP clients on the network. DHCP servers contain information about the network configuration and host operational parameters, as specified by the network administrator.
- *BOOTP/DHCP relay agent.* Relay agents (also called *BOOTP helpers*) are used in IP router products to forward information between DHCP clients and servers on different subnets. BOOTP/DHCP relay agents eliminate the need for a DHCP server on each subnet to service the broadcast requests from DHCP clients.

How Does DHCP Work?

DHCP allows clients to obtain IP network configuration, including an IP address, from a central DHCP server. DHCP servers control whether the addresses they provide to clients are allocated permanently or leased for a specific period of time. When the server allocates a leased address, the client must periodically check with the server to revalidate the address and renew the lease.

The DHCP client and server programs handle address allocation, leasing, and lease renewal. All of these processes are transparent to end users.

To further explain how DHCP works, this section answers the following questions:

- How is configuration information acquired?
- How are leases renewed?
- What happens when a client moves out of the network?
- How are changes implemented in the network?
- What are BOOTP/DHCP relay agents?

How Is Configuration Information Acquired?

DHCP allows DHCP clients to obtain an IP address and other configuration information through a request process to a DHCP server. DHCP clients use RFC-architected messages to accept and use the options served them by the DHCP server. Figure 2-3 shows a high-level overview of the DHCP protocol cycle.

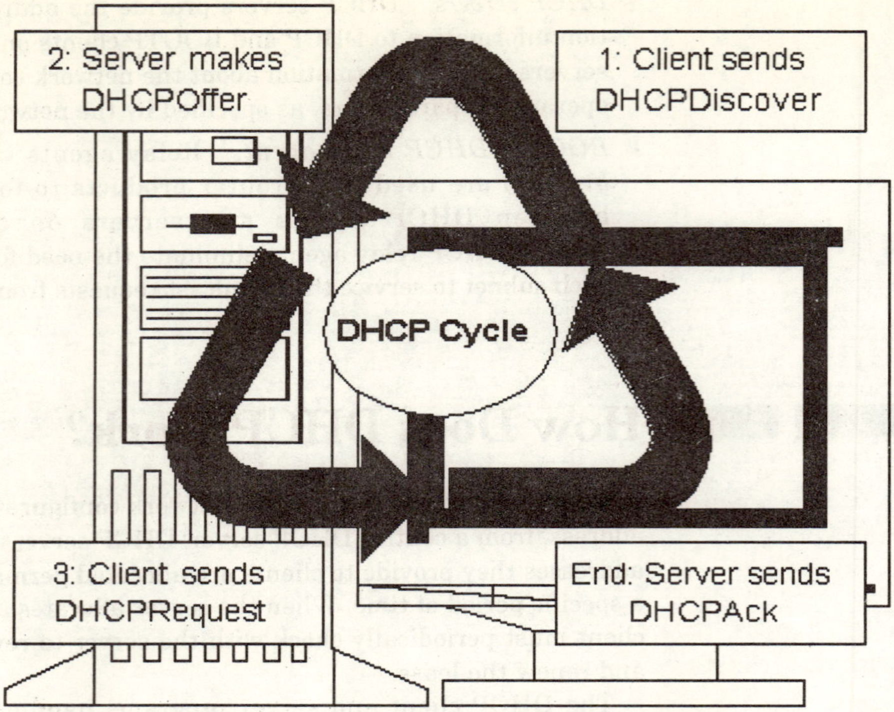
2: Server makes
DHCPOffer
1: Client sends
DHCPDiscover
DHCP Cycle
3: Client sends
DHCPRequest
End: Server sends
DHCPAck

Figure 2-3 DHCP cycle overview.

For example:

1. The client broadcasts a message that contains its client ID and announces its presence. The message also requests an IP address (DHCPDISCOVER message) and desired options, such as subnet mask, domain name server, domain name, and static route. See Figure 2-4.

NOTE. *If you configure routers on the network to forward DHCP and BOOTP messages (using BOOTP/DHCP relay agent capabilities), the broadcast message is forwarded to DHCP servers on the attached networks.*

2. Each DHCP server that receives the client's DHCPDISCOVER message can send a DHCPOFFER message to the client, offering an IP address. If the address has not been previously assigned, the DHCP server checks that the address is not already in use on the

DHCP Concepts and Overview

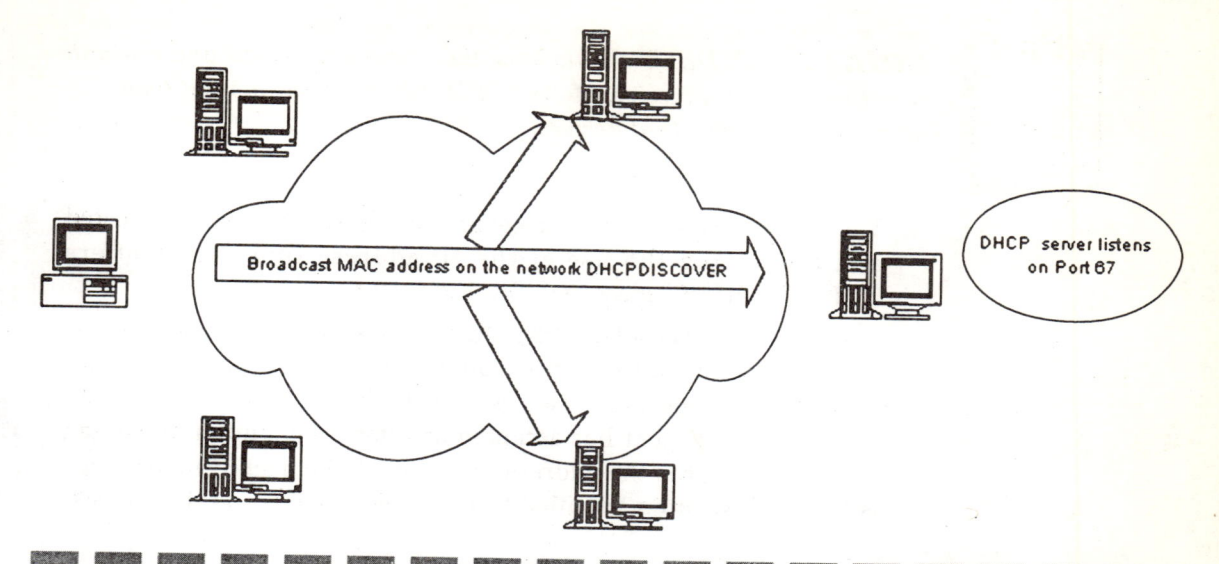

Figure 2-4 Step 1. DHCP client broadcasts DHCPDISCOVER on its subnet.

network before issuing an offer. The server checks the configuration file to see if it needs to assign a static or dynamic address to this client.

In the case of a dynamic address, the server selects an address from the address pool, choosing the least recently used address. An *address pool* is a range of IP addresses that are leased to clients. In the case of a static address, the server uses a client statement from the DHCP server configuration file to assign a static address to the client. Upon making the offer, the DHCP server reserves the offered address. See Figure 2-5.

3. The client receives the offer messages and selects the server it wants to use. Upon receiving an offer, some DHCP clients have the capability to make note of how many requested options are included in the offer. The DHCP client continues to receive offers from DHCP servers for a period of time after the first offer is received. The client takes note of how many requested options are included in each offer. At the end of that time, the DHCP client compares all offers and selects the one that meets its criteria.

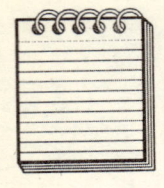

> **NOTE.** Not all DHCP clients have the capability to wait and evaluate the offers that they receive. Many DHCP clients on the market today accept the first offer that arrives.

4. The client broadcasts a message indicating which server it selected and requesting the use of the IP address that server offers (DHCPREQUEST message). See Figure 2-6.

5. If a server receives a DHCPREQUEST message indicating that the client has accepted the server's offer, the server marks the address as leased. If the server receives a DHCPREQUEST message indicating that the client has accepted an offer from a different server, the server returns the address to the available pool. If no message is received within a specified time, the server returns the address

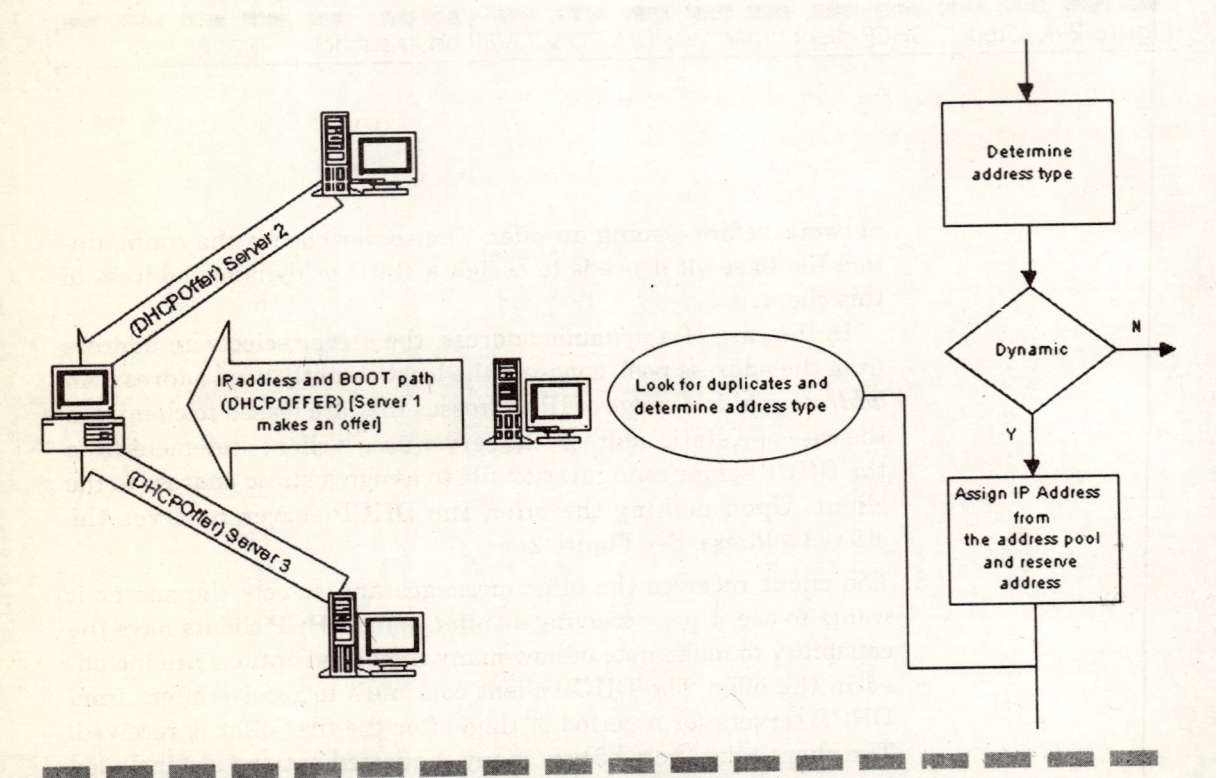

Figure 2-5 Step 2. DHCP in the subnet sends DHCPOFFER.

DHCP Concepts and Overview

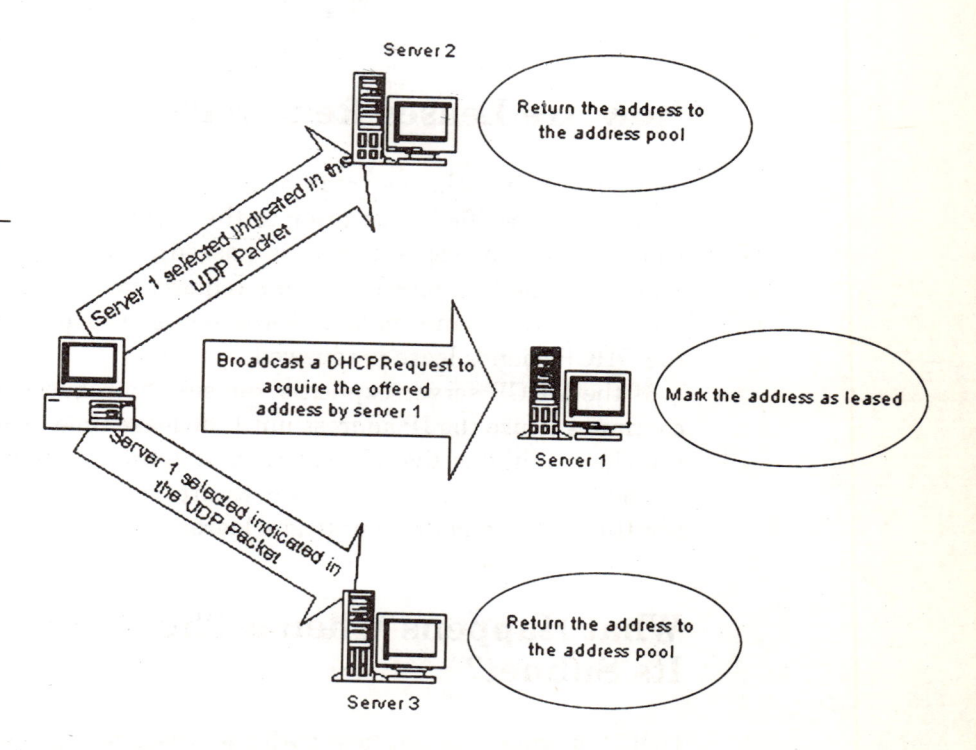

to the available pool. The selected server sends an acknowledgment that contains additional configuration information to the client (DHCPACK message). See Figure 2-7.

6. The client determines whether the configuration information is valid. Accepting a valid lease, the client specifies a *binding* state with the DHCP server and proceeds to use the IP address and options.

To DHCP clients that request options, the DHCP server typically provides options that include subnet mask, domain name server, domain name, static route, class identifier (which indicates a particular vendor), and user class. A DHCP client can request its own unique set of options. For example, Windows NT 4.0 DHCP clients are required to request options. The default set of client-requested DHCP options that IBM provides includes subnet mask, domain name server, domain name, and static route.

Figure 2-6
Step 4. DHCP client accepts DHCPOFFER from Server 1.

Figure 2-7
Step 5. Selected server sends acknowledgment with additional configuration to client.

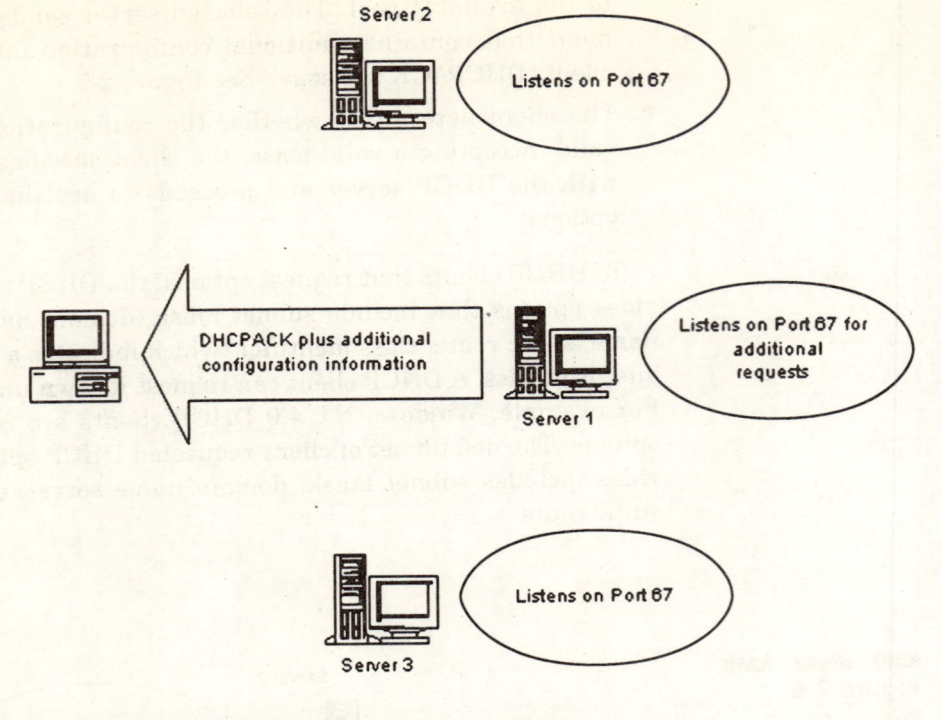

[Figure: Server 2 listens on Port 67; Server 1 sends DHCPACK plus additional configuration information to client and listens on Port 67 for additional requests; Server 3 listens on Port 67.]

How Are Leases Renewed?

The DHCP client keeps track of how much time is remaining on the lease. At a specified time prior to the expiration of the lease (usually when half of the lease time has passed), the client sends a renewal request to the leasing server. This request contains its current address and configuration information. If the server responds with a DHCPACK, the DHCP client's lease is renewed.

If the DHCP server explicitly refuses the request, the DHCP client continues to use the IP address until the lease time expires. At this time, the client initiates the address request process, including broadcasting the address request. If the server is unreachable, the client continues to use the assigned address until the lease expires (see Figure 2-8).

What Happens When a Client Moves Out of Its Subnet?

DHCP provides a client host with the freedom to move from one subnet to another without having to know what IP configuration information it

DHCP Concepts and Overview

Figure 2-8 How are leases renewed?

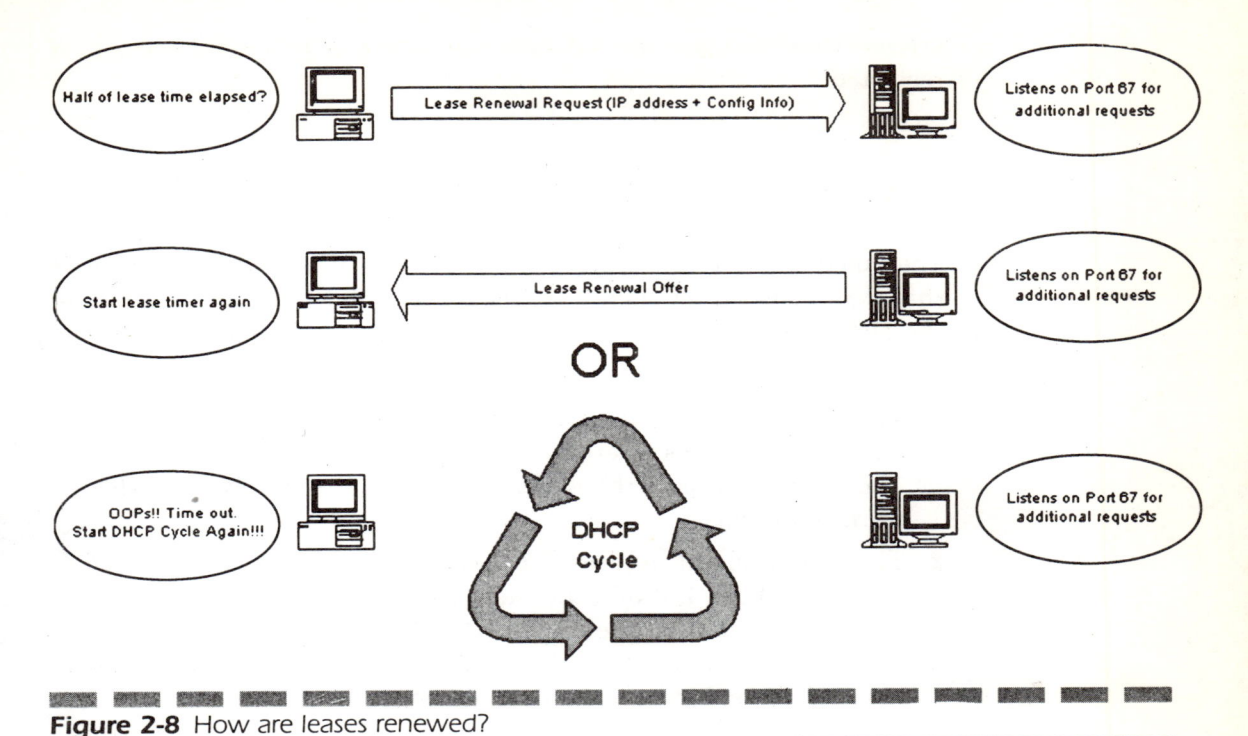

needs on the new subnet. As long as the subnets to which a host relocates have access to a DHCP server, a DHCP client automatically configures itself to access those subnets correctly. For DHCP clients to reconfigure and access a new subnet, the client host must be rebooted. When a host restarts on a new subnet, the DHCP client tries to renew its old lease with the DHCP server that originally allocated the address. The server refuses to renew the request because the address is not valid on the new subnet. The client then initiates the IP address request process to obtain a new IP address and access the network.

How Are Changes Implemented in the Network?

With DHCP, you make changes at the server, reinitialize the server, and distribute the changes to all the appropriate clients. A DHCP client retains DHCP option values that are assigned by the DHCP server for the duration of the lease. If you implement configuration changes at the server while a client is already up and running, the DHCP client does not process those changes until it either attempts to renew its lease or is restarted.

What Are BOOTP/DHCP Relay Agents?

The function of a relay agent is to forward any BOOTP/DHCP requests that it receives on its subnet or from other subnets in the direction of the DHCP server. The mechanism of operation of a relay agent is as follows:

1. The relay agent knows the address of the DHCP server beforehand, and it knows where to forward the requests for that server. The relay agent can, therefore, be a router that receives and forwards requests.
2. The DHCP client creates a packet with a special field called RELAY AGENT. Initially, the client places all zeros in it. The relay agent recognizes that the RELAY AGENT field is all zeros and puts its own IP address in this field. It then pushes the packet into the next subnet and increments the hop count.
3. The next relay agent, if any, sees that the RELAY AGENT field in the packet is not all zeros, forwards the packet to the next server, and increments the hop count by one. This process is repeated until the packet reaches the DHCP server.
4. The DHCP server sends the DHCPOFFER back to the first relay agent, and the relay agent forwards it to the originator client that broadcasted the DHCPDISCOVER. Once the client receives an IP address, the communication is direct between server and client.

IP Address Pools

As "potential" configurations, pools are the primordial soup from which actual configurations will spring to life. When a client has been awarded its IP address and DHCP options values from a pool, it can be registered in the DHCP server's database as a valid configuration. The IP address will be remembered by the server and associated with the client, even past lease expiration. The IP address of an expired, unnamed configuration is, in fact, available for reassignment if needed, but it should be reserved for the prior client if other never-used addresses are still lying fallow in the pool. In the absence of a change to the defining pool information, the server will attempt to award any subsequent DHCP petition from the same client with the configuration already recorded.

A valuable use of pools is their ability to name unique, common, or overlapping address space. Since different names can be defined for different purposes, servers are able to share address space for multiple uses. This completely removes the challenge of allocating space because network administrators can now define large blocks of IP space to be shared between individual stations or multiple groups of users.

Due to membership in different organizations (Marketing and Engineering, for example), an administrator may want to award two adjacent clients a different set of DHCP option values. And because of the differences in TCP stacks from different platforms (Microsoft and UNIX, for example), two adjacent DHCP clients may not be able to handle the same DHCP configuration options. DHCP pools define both an address range along with appropriate DHCP options and/or option sets. In this way, a pool defined for Engineering may allocate addresses from the same range as the pool defined for Marketing, but it may supply different IP configuration information.

The following subsections discuss two variations of IP address pools that are of particular interest to administrators.

Multiple Subnets per Pool

Physical network layouts often dictate that more than 256 clients reside on a single broadcast segment. If Class C addressing is used, not all clients can be covered by a single network value. If clients are assigned addresses from two Class C nets that cannot be amalgamated into one network number (using Classless Inter-Domain Routing, or CIDR), the clients on the broadcast segment will be segregated into two distinct subnets. To talk to one another, clients on the distinct subnets are programmed to send their packets through a router, even though they could do so directly. Since the router address used by a given client must be one on its own subnet, the clients of different subnets must have different IP addresses for the very same router. And since they derive the router address from their downloaded configuration, their configurations must be different. Hence, their configurations must be drawn from two different pools.

In support of multiple subnets on a common broadcast net, a DHCP server assigns addresses to clients on a broadcast segment using IP addresses drawn from two different pools (independent of user class and vendor class discriminators). It does this regardless of which of two relay agents forwards the DHCP packets and independent of the subnet to which the relay agent belongs. Of course, for the DHCP server to know how to assign IP addresses drawn from different pools, the administrator must declare within the pool the relay agent whose subnet does not match the one associated with the pool's set of addresses.

After the addresses from the first pool have all been assigned, the server automatically begins assigning subsequent addresses from the next pool that qualifies. With this strategy (others can be envisioned), the first clients configured by the server will all be on the same subnet and, thus, able to talk to one another directly without going through the router. The later clients will be able to talk among themselves directly but will need to use the router to reach the first group.

Multiple Pools per Subnet

A need for differences in configuration would seem to dictate a need for more than one pool on a given subnet. The pools can share a common set of IP addresses, if desired, since the addresses themselves may be neutral to these other distinctions. However, the pools must be defined with different DHCP options. With more than one pool per subnet, the DHCP server is faced with the problem: How are clients to be distinguished so they can be given their configuration from one pool or the other?

Once again, the RFCs supply a potential answer. They define two parameters, which can be sent by a client to serve as potential discriminators for the server to use in keying its database. DHCP user class ID can be used to identify the user by organization (such as Marketing or Engineering). DHCP vendor class ID can be used to identify the vendor of the TCP stack (such as Microsoft or IBM). It is then necessary both for the client to send these parameters and for the server to use them in qualifying the client for one or more pools. Details on client identification is discussed in the next section.

Client Identification

In non-DHCP systems, someone has to go to a host to tell it its network configuration. With DHCP, however, a DHCP server can send the configuration information that identifies a client. The principal role of the host

DHCP Concepts and Overview

(here, a DHCP client) is to ask for its own configuration and accept it when sent. The principal function of a DHCP server is to know the client's configuration and send it when asked.

The client's *configuration,* or the set of parameters belonging to a particular client, can be thought of as a database record on the DHCP server. DHCP servers can be differentiated by the mechanisms they offer for creating configurations. From a client's perspective, a DHCP server is the network resource that holds its configuration. It goes to the server to get it.

For administrators, who need to express specific configuration assignments on a per-client basis, DHCP servers provide the means for identifying clients and specifying their configuration parameters uniquely. In this way, administrators rely on DHCP servers to offer the following real-time information:

- A way to define specific configurations for specific clients and to name individual configurations for easy reference ("Color Lab Printer," for example)
- A way to automatically "learn" and save existing DHCP or BOOTP entries as defined configurations
- A way to view the status of a named configuration at any time during DHCP server operation
- The ability to view the status of the DHCP interactions at any time (for example, to see that a discover has been received from a client, a lease has been granted and will expire at time "Date/Time," a lease has expired, etc.)
- A means for an administrator to define pools that the server will award as appropriate to any of a number of qualifying clients, even though the clients may not be known in advance
- Once the server has assigned configuration parameters from a pool to a client, a means for the parameters to become a specific configuration that is an identifiable record in the DHCP server's database

The remainder of this section examines six ways in which clients may be identified: MAC address, client ID, user class ID, vendor extensions, relay agents, and multiple qualifiers.

MAC Address as Qualifier

The only mandated identification is the client's 48-bit MAC address. The MAC address is the address by which its network adapter card is uniquely branded at the factory. Prior to receipt of an operationally valid IP address, the MAC address is the only identifier that can be used to deliver packets to the client uniquely. Because of factory branding, this MAC address is typically "preconfigured" and does not require manual administration.

With a DHCP server, an administrator can associate a desired set of configuration parameters—including the very same IP address that would have been awarded under a manual regime—with the specific MAC address of the intended client. The DHCP server can then use the MAC address as a key into its database in order to locate and serve up the associated configuration. When this database key is used first in any access of the database, it ensures that specific assignments override any other, more general assignments for which the client might otherwise qualify. In other words, already-named configurations take precedence over "potential" configurations.

Client ID as Qualifier

The use of 48-bit addresses as keys to the server's database provides an excellent means for ensuring that parameter assignments can be made uniquely on a per-station basis. But 48-bit values were made for computers, not people. It is unlikely that administrators will know (or care to deal with) the 48-bit MAC addresses of any or all of their client systems. Fortunately, DHCP allows clients to send other parameters in their DHCP petitions that can also be tailored to identify the host uniquely. A system designed to spare administrators the need to deal with MAC addresses requires cooperation by both clients and servers: The client must send the optional parameter, and the server must allow it to key its DHCP database.

The DHCP "Client ID" option is defined by the DHCP RFCs as a parameter that can be used for client identification. But the RFCs do not mandate any particular treatment of the value or use of the client ID; they just allow it to be included by the client in packets it sends to the server. As a result of this laxness, DHCP product vendors are all over the map in their support for this potentially useful feature. For example, the standard Microsoft DHCP client uses the field to provide an ASCII encoding of the 48-bit MAC address.

With a third-party DHCP client, however, Microsoft and other network clients can use an enterprisewide scheme for assignment of these client IDs. Schemes that use employee name, employee ID, office phone

DHCP Concepts and Overview

extension, e-mail address, machine location (wall plug), or other easily mapped values not only makes these values more meaningful than MAC addresses to the administrator, it makes them meaningful to desktop users as well. Careful consideration of a candidate scheme ensures that users know how to specify their client ID string so that one-on-one interaction with the administrator is not usually required. Of crucial importance, of course, is that the DHCP server be able to use these string values as keys into the DHCP database. Administrators will probably want to avoid the complexity of tracking MAC addresses, and should check with DHCP server vendors to see what capabilities are provided for identifying clients by their client ID or other like parameter.

User Class ID as Qualifier

Similar to the Client ID option, the DHCP specification also defines an optional User Class ID parameter. The User Class ID field is typically used to name individual clients as part of a logical group, for example, a "Marketing" employee or "Temporary" clients. From the user class supplied by the client, the DHCP server is then able to make intelligent decisions on what set of configuration information to award. For example, assigning the appropriate lease time or selecting from a special IP address range.

Unlike the Client ID qualifier, broad groups can be defined with the user class, eliminating the need to define or track every specific client.

Qualification from Vendor Extensions

Support for the use of DHCP's Client ID may be important for systems that employ non-IEEE 802.2 techniques for MAC addressing. Dial-up lines, for example, typically have no agreed-on unique 48-bit value to offer DHCP servers. In such cases, discriminators at least as useful as Client ID will be required, and even more sophisticated extensions of DHCP—ones that include potential user authentication—may be of value if centralized administration (discussed later) is to be employed.

The use of DHCP for dial-up configuration assignment raises immediately the issue of security for DHCP. Following the common networking design practice of first getting something to work, and only then worrying about when to make it not work, security is not addressed at all by the current RFCs. Security in any form is possible at present only through the use of vendor extensions. DHCP clients that might provide for user authentication by, for example, sending extensions such as name and encrypted password can only favorably deal with DHCP servers that are equipped to check these extensions prior to sending the qualifying configurations to the client. Such a "systems" enhancement is likely to require both client and server elements to be from a common vendor.

Qualification from Relay Agents

The only IP addresses that should be offered to a client attached to a particular subnet are those that are valid for use on that subnet. A client that tries to operate using an IP address belonging to a subnet other than its own will find that nothing goes right. Unfortunately, the client is totally at the mercy of the server to provide it a usable IP address (and an accurate subnet mask), since it has no way of knowing where in the world it is located. The DHCP server is responsible for adhering to the rules that govern subnet addressing when awarding IP addresses to clients, but it has only the pool definitions to guide it. When a given client submits its DHCP petition (using a DISCOVER packet), the server must select the pool or set of pools that contain the configuration data appropriate for the subnet to which the client is attached.

This means the server must have a way of determining both the subnet from which the request is emanating and the subnet that a given pool is expected to serve. This is not as difficult as it might first seem. As discussed earlier, DHCP packets that are initiated from a broadcast segment to which the server is not directly attached will be handled by a relay agent, which inserts its own IP address in a special field in the packet and forwards it on to the server. The IP address used by the relay agent will be one associated with the MAC interface on which the agent received the client's broadcast. In most cases, this address will be on the same subnet as that to which the client will eventually be assigned. In such cases, the DHCP server must use the agent's IP address to key its pool database, and it can eliminate from consideration all pools that do not contain addresses belonging to the same subnet as the relay agent. Three possible scenarios are provided below.

Flat Switched Networks By definition, routers necessarily have a unique address on each subnet. However, during migration to flat switched networks, multiple subnets often coreside on a single broadcast segment. Therefore, it is possible that the address selected by the DHCP relay agent will be from a subnet other than the one from which the client will be assigned. Pools must then be specifically qualified to differentiate between these logical networks. This can be accomplished by the ability to override the implied source subnet qualifier. Networks with large switched segments supported by "one-arm routers" often need this capability.

Automated Subnet Mask DHCP servers can do a lot for the administrator to automate the match up of clients and pools. In fact, it is possible for the server to handle this task completely and transparently in most situations. For example, as soon as the administrator has declared even one IP address for inclusion in a pool, the server can automatically determine from the address's class (A, B, or C) a default subnet mask (of 255.0.0.0, 255.255.0.0, or 255.255.255.0, respectively). Given just the address and (inferred) subnet mask, the DHCP server will know the entire range of addresses that are valid on the associated subnet, and any relay agent will use one of these addresses. Thus, when all addresses in a pool belong to the same subnet—and, therefore, fall within the same address range—the matchup of client and pool becomes very straightforward. Of course, the server must provide a consistency check for the administrator as other addresses are assigned to the pool.

Overriding the Subnet Mask for CIDR At times, administrators will need to override the default subnet mask by explicitly declaring the SubnetMask option for use by the pool. For example, CIDR mechanics require subnet masks that can amalgamate multiple networks into one. So, if a subnet mask is given, the server then infers IP address ranges based on the given setting. Independent of whether the mask is given or computed, the server should always send the SubnetMask option to the client, since not all clients can be counted on to compute the mask for themselves.

Administrators may also need to override the server's computation of a range of qualifying relay agent addresses. This can be done by making the agent specification more precise. Precision is required whenever a particular pool is to be served by only a particular relay agent or when an agent outside the subnet defined by the pool is nonetheless able to forward requests on behalf of prospective subnet clients (as may be the case when multiple subnets share a single broadcast segment). Because two agents on a broadcast segment may both forward client packets to a DHCP server, an administrator needs the ability to distinguish the configurations offered on a per-agent basis.

Multiple Qualifiers

A DHCP server that supports multiple options for client identification should have a policy that allows an administrator to designate the use of one and/or multiple qualifiers for any or all clients. Examples are provided below.

If only the MAC address is designated, then only the client specifying a given MAC address will get its associated configuration data. This has been the practice for systems based on BOOTP, for example. In this way, an administrator can ensure that only a specific client receives a particular IP address.

If only the client ID is designated, then any station specifying the appropriate client ID will get its associated configuration data. For example, this allows stable IP configurations to track users when they move from one computer to another. If both MAC address and client ID are designated, then a given user can receive his or her configuration data only at a particular client. A DHCP packet from a client that is mismatched in a DHCP database entry designating "both" could mean one of two things: Either an interloper is masquerading by using the settable client ID, or a client machine has swapped its network adapter without prior arrangement with the administrator. In either case, the DHCP server will refuse to honor the request for operational parameters and let the client go begging until the situation is resolved by a change to either the client or the server's database.

NOTE. *It is tempting to think that a server supporting "both" qualifying parameters can be made to support "either" as well. A little analysis shows this is not the case, since there can be no protection against two different stations presenting the two different qualifiers. This would place the server in an untenable position: It must either deny service to the second requestor, or it must treat it as the first requestor performing a "second" DHCP request, albeit with possibly different qualifiers, in which case it will be tempted to allocate the same IP address it gave out "before."*

Server Administration

Administration of a DHCP server is required to initialize its operations, to modify its operations, and to examine and report on its operations.

Administrators require that servers offer a number of tools to support them in these activities. The following subsections discuss different server administration needs and the tools required to meet those needs: Server Installation, Database Initialization, Runtime Database Manipulation, Administrative Access Controls, Remote Server Management, and Application Programming Interfaces.

Server Installation

Servers may be run on conventional operating systems (OSs) including UNIX, Windows NT, NetWare, OS/2, and Mac OS, or on standalone servers in the manner of routers. Administrators who favor a DHCP server application that runs on a conventional platform they don't normally use may not necessarily find installation and configuration an easy task. However, if the server and the platform are both familiar, the task should be effortless.

Generally, the server must be easy to install and configure. Because a DHCP server will almost never reside on an employee's desktop machine, serious deployments will likely require the following:

- Use of a special system that is dedicated to the DHCP function or that includes DHCP along with other networking services such as DNS
- Procurement and bringup of the server's hardware platform, including network adapter card(s)
- Procurement and bringup of the server's software platform, including all relevant utility and communication software (for example, supporting TCP stacks)

Standalone servers should also be easy to install and configure initially, after which they never need to be touched again. Because standalone servers may often be installed in distributed or remote sites, these servers need to be managed remotely by tools with which the administrator is comfortable—for example, a Web browser, which can execute on any standard desktop OS.

Database Initialization

Tailoring a DHCP server for use in a particular enterprise setting requires a set of activities that gives the server its marching orders. The creation of configurations, pools, and option sets are possible by a variety of techniques, depending on the administrator's preference. Graphical user interfaces (GUIs) are expected, certainly. However, these must be carefully designed so that the repetitive nature of creating a database for networks with many entries does not become tedious. Not many GUIs can equal the power of even the simplest text editors for the cut-and-paste behaviors valued for database creation. Pointing and clicking one's way through 200 centralized configurations is likely to be an unacceptable chore. As a result, DHCP servers need to expose their configuration databases to text editing utilities for easy and quick replication, group editing, context searching, importing (via e-mail, for example), and so on.

If databases can be modified by editing tools, then consistency checking must be provided by the server at its initialization, since the checking or restrictions otherwise imposed by the GUI will not have been done. Error indications concerning the ASCII database can be described in the context of the editing tools to identify, for example, the line number, symbol name, and error condition. Errors encountered for initialization files created through GUI interactions need to be just as descriptive. If the GUI is used for database creation, then the initial assessment of configuration parameters by the server must be made in the context of the GUI paradigm.

Administrators whose IP address and configuration information reside in an existing database will be interested in tools that can convert or "import" their existing descriptions into the DHCP server's initialization file. The variations required for such conversions are beyond the scope of this book, but this will be an important consideration for large organizations and may require the active participation of the DHCP vendor.

Runtime Database Manipulation

If the server's operational databases are exposed to text editors, they are also exposed to other utility programs that can be crafted by the vendor or by the customer. The analysis, copying, and editing of configuration databases will be of use to most customers, but information taken from a running system will always be of greater interest. There are various schemes for retrieving formatted data from the running server in a form that can be manipulated by these same tools. Whatever the means a vendor supplies for instrumenting a DHCP server, however, facilities must

DHCP Concepts and Overview

be included for importing and exporting database information into other forms that are of interest to that administrator. A complete offering allows the following:

- Runtime display of the operational database in summary and detailed views
- ASCII representations of the initial database configuration
- ASCII representations of the operational database available at administrative command
- Server initialization from the (possibly modified) ASCII representations
- High-performance binary representations of the operational database
- Server initialization from the binary representations
- Error reporting for errors encountered on server initialization from binary representations
- Tools to convert from ASCII to binary and vice versa
- GUI utilities for offline initial database creation
- GUI support for starting the server with the initial database
- GUI error reporting for errors encountered on server initialization
- Extraction of the operational database for GUI display
- GUI modification of the extracted database
- Reloading of the (modified) database into any server
- Placement and reloading of the database information into commercial database repositories
- Tools to easily replicate configurations and policies between multiple servers
- Published application program interfaces (APIs) to enable tight integration with customer-written or third-party systems.

Administrative Access Controls

DHCP servers control information of interest to many different agencies within an enterprise. Server protection mechanisms must distinguish different classes of managers and constrain what they can view and change within the server.

Remote Server Management

A DHCP server created as a monolithic entity will have a user interface that is tightly coupled to its runtime behaviors, since the two are part and parcel of a single philosophy. Most servers are made this way (for example, FTP servers, NFS servers, mail servers, DNS servers, and most DHCP servers). It is possible, though, to create a server whose primary interface is decoupled from its runtime code so that the user interface can be located remotely. This is a necessary design condition for a server that is built to run in a standalone machine, and it is a familiar practice for routers, remote probes, smart switches, hubs, and other hardware systems managed by SNMP. DHCP servers built as applications for execution on common OS platforms are not often designed with a satisfactory decoupling of the user interface component. Thus, servers built as standalone components generally require remote management designed as an integral feature.

There are two types of remote console management: by Telnet and by a Web browser.

Telnet A Telnet connection with a command-line interface (CLI) is the most primitive—but most universally accepted—form of remote management. Telnet connections provide modest security through the use of passwords, and they provide a basic form of data presentation. Telnet commands can often be automated by scripts created on a management station, and Telnet responses can be captured as ASCII reports for subsequent analysis by offline tools. These connections can usually be supported through firewalls without special considerations, which enables the management of servers in multiple Internet sites from a single administrative location.

Web Browser The modern equivalent of Telnet is now based on Web technology. Web browsers can be fashioned to display information supplied by a remote server and can be made to submit management commands and parameters that change the operation of the server. Browsers provide the same modest security as Telnet, and they connect through firewalls with equal ease. Web management standards are emerging as this form of remote control becomes more popular. However, the automation of commands and the capture of responses for offline processing is only possible with the Java extensions now coming into vogue.

Application Programming Interfaces (APIs)

It should be possible for third-party and customer development personnel to write their own programs to interact with the DHCP server, independent of whether the server is an application on a standard OS or is a standalone utility. APIs should be supported for reading and writing all elements of the server, just as is done through the administrative GUIs supplied by the vendor. In fact, it would be particularly appropriate if the vendor's management tools were based on the same APIs as are made available to developers. In this way, customers can create arbitrary enhancements for their own management and report generation purposes. Of course, the server must protect itself from interaction with unauthorized users by demanding encrypted password authentication at each interaction.

DHCP Server Availability

When responsibility for IP address assignment is given over to a DHCP server, the server is elevated to "utility" status on a par with other networking equipment including routers, switches, and hubs. It becomes an indispensable element without whose services individual hosts cannot reliably join the network. For example, hosts wishing to commence network operations at a time when the server is unavailable will have to be manually configured. Any address assignment that takes place while the server is not active will have to be reflected in its database once it does resume operation so that the proper status of IP address allocations is taken into account. And because manually assigned addresses are not subject to lease expiration, resuming a host's use of DHCP is likely to require a second manual configuration. Generally speaking, nonavailability of the DHCP server is painful.

The subsections below—"DHCP Reliability" and "Redundant DHCP Server Scenarios"—discuss general server reliability, and then provide an analysis of several redundancy scenarios.

DHCP Reliability

DHCP service, though most frequently considered in the context of IP address assignment, is really useful for two purposes: the delivery and assignment of IP addresses, and the delivery and assignment of all of the other configurable parameters (DHCP options) of the client. Both of these valuable services are multiplexed onto a single mechanism: the four-way packet exchange between client and server that defines DHCP. It is not generally understood how best to implement both services from the single mechanism.

As mentioned, the only system design that can provide truly reliable DHCP service, whether IP addresses are abundant or scarce, is a system employing at least two DHCP servers acting as 100 percent replicates. In this design, each replicate provides DHCP services independent of one another to cover one another's possible absence, and each replicate maintains identical databases whenever both servers are present. Each replicate server must do the following:

- Detect the other's presence or absence
- Inform the other of all changes made to its mirrored database during operation
- Coordinate its allocation of IP addresses before consummating any client interaction
- Propagate remote management updates to the other
- Have a way of resolving database conflicts that arise during operation or remote management
- Be able to update its recovering peer completely with the database changes that occurred during its absence, whether planned or inadvertent

Redundant DHCP Server Scenarios

The four scenarios below examine the benefits of employing pairs of fully redundant DHCP backup servers.

Dependence on Single Server—Lots of IP Addresses If an organization has plenty of spare IP addresses, it can assign long lease times (L) and set t1 small enough to cause environment changes to be asked for in a timely fashion, with t2 set to be large enough that a renewal will be requested just before lease expiration. For example, set L = 30 days, t1 = 1 day, and t2 = 29 days.

Because every client will check with the DHCP server every day, changes to the environment can be reflected throughout the organization within a period of 24 hours. Every day, the client will also receive a new

30-day lease for its current IP address. This lease need not be changed because it need not be recovered. To handle the case where the daily renewal request is lost in transit, the client asks more than just once at t1. Several implementations of the DHCP client (but not all) are willing to retry the server with some regularity following t1 (and t2).

If the DHCP server crashes, the administrator has approximately 29 days to get it back up before leases expire. If the server recovers before 29 days, one of the client retries following t1 should be successful. Even after day 29, one of the client rebinding attempts (sent to "any" server, though there is only one here) after t2 should be successful. However, if clients only try once at t2, things are a little chancier.

Of course, while the server is down, administrators cannot change the configuration information of any client, serve addresses or configurations to any new client, or accommodate the move of any existing client to a new subnet. If the server is down, such clients must be configured manually. Then when the server comes back up, these clients must be reconfigured manually so they can use DHCP again. The server must be told of the manual assignment until the reconfiguration takes effect (so that it doesn't hand out the manually awarded addresses to any other client), and it must be told that the manual assignment has been canceled (unless it has so many addresses that losing these is not important).

Dependence on Single Server—Few IP Addresses If an organization has no spare IP addresses, it will want to assign fairly short lease times in order to allocate addresses only as they are needed and reclaim them quickly when they are no longer needed. This might be appropriate for a workforce that requires use of the network only during the day. Each morning, the previous day's leases will have expired and all addresses can be reassigned to the employees actually in need. In this type of system, polling for configuration changes is not important, so t1 and t2 can be relatively long, but leases must not be allowed to span even a full 24-hour day. For example, L can be set at 18 hours, and t1 and t2 can be set near enough to L that both renewal and rebinding will be requested just before lease expiration. For example, if L = 18 hours, then t1 = 16 hours, and t2 = 17 hours.

Machines left on overnight will retain their addresses, but all others will get new assignments each day. In this way, address conservation will occur naturally when employees don't come to work on a given day. In addition, every day the environment can be changed, since DHCP is performed at bootup. Even machines left on overnight will get new environmental information within a day.

If the server crashes in this type of system, administrators have only one night to get it back up before clients start failing. The problem of new clients arriving while the server is down is compounded because, in this system, every client is a new client every day. In this system, the DHCP server needs to be available or the network won't work.

It is apparent that a system built around a single DHCP server may have several undesirable failure modes no matter how many IP addresses are available.

Splitting Subnets between Two Servers It seems a shame to not service new clients while the DHCP server is down, so it is tempting to think that a second server can be used to cover a temporary outage. In certain situations this is actually the case, and it is possible that the servers need not even be aware of one another. Certainly, two servers can be configured with identical fixed address assignments, since regardless of which server provides the configuration, the information is identical. In this way, one could stand in for the other. Such a scheme is probably unacceptably restrictive, since no dynamic address assignment is possible, but it does increase reliability.

But in a network with many more addresses than clients, an even more dynamic scheme might be contemplated. Suppose the number of available addresses is twice the number of clients. Addresses can then be allocated half to each server, for example. As long as the managed addresses are disjoint, each server can offer clients addresses drawn from its own half without fear of conflict and without a requirement for coordination. If one server is down, the other has enough addresses to satisfy the entire client population.

Conflict will occur, of course, if one server crashes completely and stays out of service past one of its client's t2 intervals. Rebinding by the client to a server other than the one that originally served it may result in a mess, since the new server cannot award the same IP address that the old one did. The client must, therefore, change its address. Changing the address is an operation that may or may not be effected transparently within the client. A scheme where each client reboots every day would work better here because a new server could be used each day, though this doesn't help clients that remain powered on and in service past time t2.

To prevent conflicts, there must be double the available addresses on a per-subnet basis. Each server must be able to serve all clients on a given subnet in case the other server has crashed. In addition, the total must be double the number that could ever actually move to a given

DHCP Concepts and Overview

subnet, lest one server allocate all of its addresses to a given subnet and the other server crashes just before a client attempts to move to the subnet.

However, such a disjoint allocation scheme is likely to break down very quickly in any practical deployment, because in reality, IP addresses are a scarce commodity. Furthermore, IP addresses are structured in a way that confounds this type of assignment. Class C subnets have 256 addresses, for example, meaning that a Class C subnet can have 256 stations on it. Quite obviously, two servers cannot both have 256 addresses that are unique.

Several system designs for DHCP suggest a "nearby" server can be awarded almost all the needed addresses, and a far away (hence, slower to respond) server can have the remaining addresses (an 80-20 split is often envisioned), as though the distant server will only be needed when the nearby one fails. However, this design is problematic as well when the loss of the nearby server is taken into consideration. In such an instance, the distant server can only award the addresses it has. Other clients cannot be served.

Redundant Server Alternatives   If addresses are scarce, they cannot be allocated in disjoint sets to two servers. Furthermore, the servers cannot be statically configured, since the addresses must be allocated dynamically as needed by clients. Thus, there must be pools of addresses, and the servers must serve from the same pools. If system reliability is to be enhanced by the use of two servers, the servers must coordinate their activities somehow.

A discussion of two approaches to such coordination is provided below.

Hot-Standby Approach   A first-pass approach at providing coordination might be based on a "hot-standby" strategy in which a main server is made responsible for all dynamic assignments but keeps the standby informed of its database changes so that it can spring into action whenever the main server goes down. There are several problems with the hot-standby approach. One of them is how to determine that the main server has failed. What if it hasn't failed, but the standby thinks it has and begins serving clients? If both servers are simultaneously active but not coordinating their database changes, conflicts will surely arise. In particular, the danger exists that the two servers will allocate the same IP address to two different clients. It is not often factored into the hot-standby design that when the standby discovers its error, it must inform the main server of changes it made by mistake.

Further problems with the standby approach exist even when the failure assessment is properly made. With the main server down, the standby can surely take over operations. Since it is serving from the same information base, it can be expected to do well. However, while the standby is in control, it actually has assumed the role of the main. It will not be updating the original main (which has crashed), of course, so the standby itself has no hot-standby. What mechanism, then, will restore the system to its reliable status? When the main server is restored, shall the standby update the main with all its recent database changes? Should the original main take control once again, or should it merely assume the role of the standby? If the original main regains control, how do stations that were serviced by the standby renew their leases?

So if a hot-standby approach doesn't work, what else can there be? Standard shared database concepts are no good, of course, since a shared database becomes a single point of failure and frequent cross-net accesses to a central database will render a system too slow to be of practical use in any large-scale DHCP deployment.

Server-to-Server Protocol The IETF's DHCP working group has begun to design a server-to-server protocol that will specify guidelines for servers to coordinate the allocation of IP addresses in a consistent way. This activity is aimed at allowing DHCP servers from different vendors to achieve a form of reliability. However, it is not just address assignment that is provided by a DHCP server. The server is, after all, attempting to take over the role of the administrator and to do what, before DHCP, were manual configuration duties. In addition, the rules that one vendor's server follows in substituting for the administrator are going to be completely different from the rules another vendor's server follows. If a client can be served by one set of rules one day and a different set the next day, it is difficult to guess what its configuration will be at any given time.

As the discussion of the hot-standby approach has shown, the creation of a reliable system requires consideration of not only the operational modes but also of the failure and recovery modes. Merely coordinating the assignment of addresses is not enough. Reliable DHCP systems using the products of two different vendors is, at the moment, unthinkable.

Consider the problem of server coordination that arises from the notion of server database changes. Each interaction with a DHCP client produces a state change in one server that may not be known to the other. It is tempting to say the other will be informed when the changes are "complete," but it is often not possible to know what "complete" will ultimately mean. A client can halt its interactions with a server at any

DHCP Concepts and Overview

point in a DHCP exchange, so at any such point the server's database modifications may be "complete." For example, suppose a server removes an IP address from a pool intending to offer it to a client. It's intent is "complete" and should be communicated to its peer before the peer inadvertently allocates it to somebody else. Should the server really tell its peer now or wait until later? If later, then when? When the address is awarded? That's too late to resolve a conflict. And what if the address is declined by the client? Is the server-to-server protocol rich enough to tell the peer the address has somehow been returned?

To further expose the difficulty, consider the notion of server management and its relation to "completeness." A remote administrator can modify a DHCP server's database elements, creating anomalous temporary states along the way (a change to two options is typically done one at a time, for instance). The temporary nature of the changes may persist over a lunch break. This inconsistency may be of interest to the other server, though the modification may or may not be "complete."

DHCP in IPv6

Although IPv6 introduces stateless address autoconfiguration, DHCPv6 retains its importance as the stateful alternative for those sites that wish to have more control over their addressing scheme. Used together with stateless autoconfiguration, DHCP provides a means of passing additional configuration options to nodes once they have obtained their addresses.

There is currently no RFC covering DHCP in IPv6, although there is work in progress described in two Internet Drafts, "Dynamic Host Configuration Protocol for IPv6 (DHCPv6)" and "Extensions for the Dynamic Host Configuration Protocol for IPv6."

Differences between DHCPv6 and DHCPv4

DHCPv6 has some significant differences to DHCPv4, as it takes advantage of some of the inherent enhancements of the IPv6 protocol. Some of the principal differences are as follows:

- As soon as a client boots, it already has a link-local IP address, which it can use to communicate with a DHCP server or a relay agent.

- The client uses multicast addresses to contact the server, rather than broadcasts.
- IPv6 allows the use of multiple IP addresses per interface, and DHCPv6 can provide more than one address when requested.
- Some DHCP options are now unnecessary. Default routers, for example, are now obtained by a client using IPv6 neighbor discovery.
- DHCP messages (including address allocations) appear in IPv6 message extensions, rather than in the IP header as in IPv4.
- There is no requirement for BOOTP compatibility.
- There is a new reconfigure message, which is used by the server to send configuration changes to clients (for example, the reduction in an address lifetime). Clients must continue to listen for reconfigure messages once they have received their initial configuration.

Summary

This chapter has described the mechanisms required for reliable DHCP. The DHCP system you choose to implement should provide the following:

- Central administration of statically assigned and dynamically assigned IP addresses
- Identification and validation of statically configured clients using not only the client's MAC address but an administrator-configured client ID
- Identification and validation of a dynamically configured client using a user class ID, a vendor class ID, or both
- Support for vendor class extensions
- Simple configuration of IP address pools for multiple subnets and for clients separated from their servers by a router
- Most important, fault tolerance through pairs of fully redundant, fully active DHCP backup servers. (How could a reliable system be built with anything less?)

CHAPTER 3

Serving Names

This chapter describes how to assign unique names, statically and dynamically, to all devices on your TCP/IP network. We will see how a dynamic name server works and how it integrates with existing static name servers and firewalls. We will also discuss how to choose a naming scheme and whether your systems should have a host name.

Why Names?

Why would you want a Domain Name System (DNS) server, anyway (much less a dynamic one)? You do not really have to have one, but consider the following scenario. For this scenario, we will assume that you are not even using a DHCP server, that all IP addresses are hard-coded.

You have your network of, say, 20 (or even just 10) machines and a server. You have just configured all of the names in all of the host files of all of the machines. Now, you can reach Mary's machine without having to remember, for example, 192.168.20.32. A week later, Bob is hired, and you configure another machine for him. If you want all the other machines to be able to reach Bob without having to use the IP address, you will have to go to each and every machine and update the host files. Of course, you could be clever and download new files to each one and the associated verifications that would be involved.

Let's add a DNS server (also known as a name server) to the preceding scenario. Still, we will say there is no DHCP server; you are hard-coding addresses. All the machines are configured to resolve names to addresses by making requests to the name server (this is, of course, transparent to the user). You add Bob's machine to the network. You make some additions to the name server configuration files. Now all the machines know how to reach Bob, and Bob knows how to reach all the machines.

Now that we have a DHCP server in the network (setting up a DHCP server is covered in Chapter 2), when you plug Bob's machine into the network, you do not even have to assign an address to his machine. But we also have a Dynamic Domain Name System (DDNS) server. It's now as easy as plugging Bob's machine into the network. That's it. The address assignment is automatic, and the name server update is automatic (dynamic, right?). All machines can reach Bob, and Bob can reach all machines.

What Is a Domain Name System (DNS)?

The previous section explains what names can do for you, but just what is a Domain Name System? A Domain Name System (DNS) maps host IP addresses to hostnames. Just as you may have told your mom when you were young "I'm going over to Mary's to play," rather than "I'm going over to 1141 South Emerson Street to play," DNS servers allow you to reach another host from your host without having to provide the explicit address. DNS servers are constantly updated by system administrators and by other DNS servers.

Before DNS, the only way to get name/address mappings updated was from a single master list. In the earliest (1970s and early 1980s) days of the Internet, there was a single definitive source for the Internet hosts file. All other servers received the name/address mappings from a special file, the HOSTS.TXT file. When a host wanted to update its host file, it would connect to the definitive host and FTP the new file. There were fewer hosts on the Internet then. (This was back when the Internet was actually called ARPANET and was run primarily by the Department of Defense.) This system was not practical because the number of network hosts started growing. Hence, the development of the Domain Name System.

The DNS is a program consisting of a database of name and address information. The program responds to queries from other programs (called *resolvers* or *stub resolvers*). DNS servers can communicate amongst themselves to update one another with new information. This mechanism is what allows you to reach a Web page on a new server when a friend sends you a link. You do not have to know the IP address of the server that contains the Web page. Chances are that your own Internet service provider's name server may not contain the information you want, and so it queries another name server. The name servers cooperate in order to keep the information current. At least one of the DNS servers needs someone to manually update the information on it.

The structure of the DNS database is similar to the structure of a file system. The whole database or file system is pictured as an inverted tree with the root system at the top. Each node in the tree represents a partition of the database. Each domain or directory can be further divided into partitions, called *subdomains* (such as the file system's subdirectories).

The domain name space is tree structured. The top-level domains divided the Internet domain name space organizationally. Examples of top-level domains are as follows:

- *com.* Commercial organizations, such as Infinity (*infinity.com*), CNN (*cnn.com*), and mycompany (*mycompany.com*).
- *edu.* Educational organizations, such as the University of Minnesota (*umn.edu*) and New York University (*nyu.edu*).

- *gov.* Government organizations, such as the Federal Bureau of Investigation (*fbi.gov*) and the National Science Foundation (*nsf.gov*).

The tree is limited to 127 levels; this is a limit on subdomains, although there is no limit on the number of branches at each node.

Each node in the tree is labeled with a name (see Figure 3-1). The root has a null label (" "). The full domain name of any node in the tree is the sequence of names on the path, from the node up to the root, with a dot between node names. For example, in Figure 3-1, if you follow the arrows from the bottom label to the top, from the host, www, to the root label, you can form the full domain name for that host: *www.cars.infinity.com*.

In DNS, each domain can be administered by a different organization. Each organization can then break its domains into a number of subdomains and dole out the responsibility for those domains to other organizations. This is because DNS uses a distributed database, where you can manage your own domain (*company.com*), or parts of the name space (subdomains) can be delegated to other servers (*department.company.com*).

The DNS servers responsible for the top-level Internet domains, such as *com,* are also called *Internet root servers,* and they manage information about the top-level domains. For example, the Internet's Network Information Center runs the *edu* domain, but assigns U.C. Berkeley authority over the *berkeley.edu* subdomain.

Figure 3-1
DNS name space.

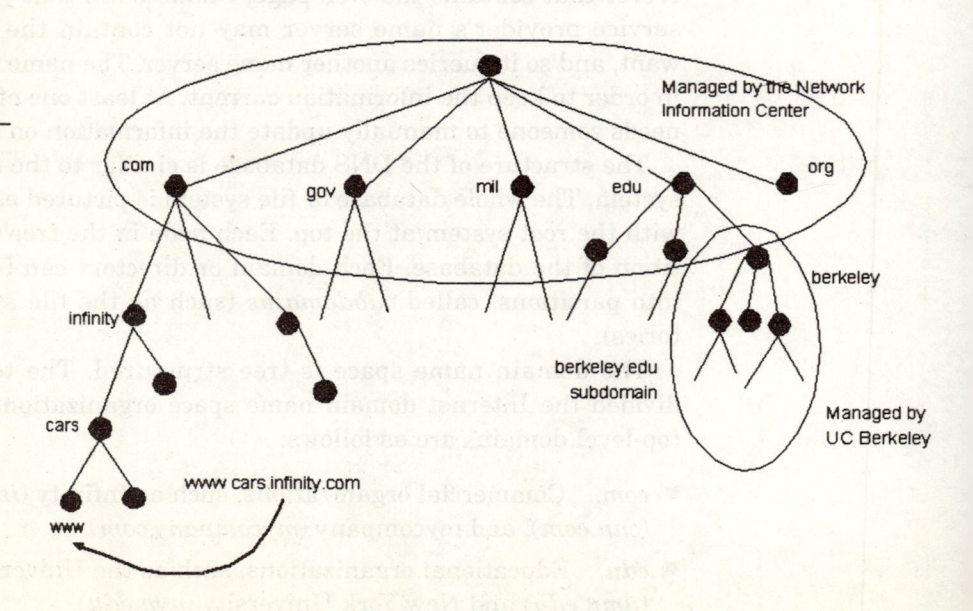

Serving Names

Domains can contain both hosts and other domains (their subdomains). For example, the *infinity.com* domain contains hosts, such as *www.infinity.com,* but it also contains subdomains, such as *cars.infinity.com.*

Domain names are used as indexes into the DNS database. In addition, each host on a network has a domain name with a DNS server that points to information about the host. This information may include an IP address, information about mail routing, and so on.

So why this complicated structure? It exists to solve the problems that a host table has. For example, making names hierarchical eliminates the problem of name collisions. Domains are given unique domain names; so organizations are free to choose names within their domains. Whatever name they choose, it does not conflict with other domain names, since it has its own unique domain name.

For example, we can have several hosts named *www,* such as *www.infinity.com* and *www.yahoo.com,* because they are in different domains managed by different organizations. See Figure 3-2. We can also have a host in the same domain that also has the same host name, such as *www.infinity.com* and *www.cars.infinitv.com,* because they belong to different subdomains.

Figure 3-2
Hosts with the same names in different domains.

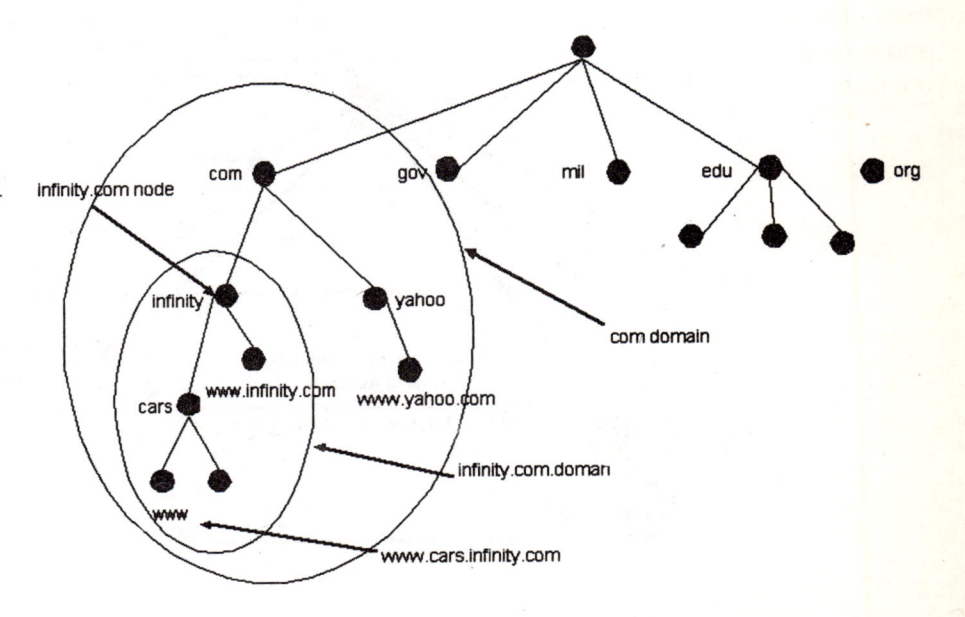

Domain vs. Zone of Authority

The concept of domains versus zones of authority can be a confusing one, which this section will try to explain.

One of the main goals of the design of the Domain Name System is decentralization. This is achieved through *delegation*. The central DNS administrator in a company administering the company's domain can divide it into subdomains. Each subdomain can be delegated to other administrators. This means that the administrator delegated to becomes responsible for maintaining the subdomain.

A *domain* is a subset or subtree of the name space tree. A *subdomain* is a subset of the domain. Figure 3-3 shows the domain *mycompany.com* as a subset of the *.com* name space. Under *mycompany.com*, there are other subdomains, such as *endicott.mycompany.com*, *rochester.mycompany.com*, and *otherdomain.mycompany.com*.

Name servers are programs running on a system with DNS support. In Figure 3-3, *as1.mycompany.com*, *rst.rochester.mycompany.com*, and *otherhost.otherdomain.mycompany.com* are hosts running name server pro-

Figure 3-3
Domain, subdomain, delegation, and zone of authority.

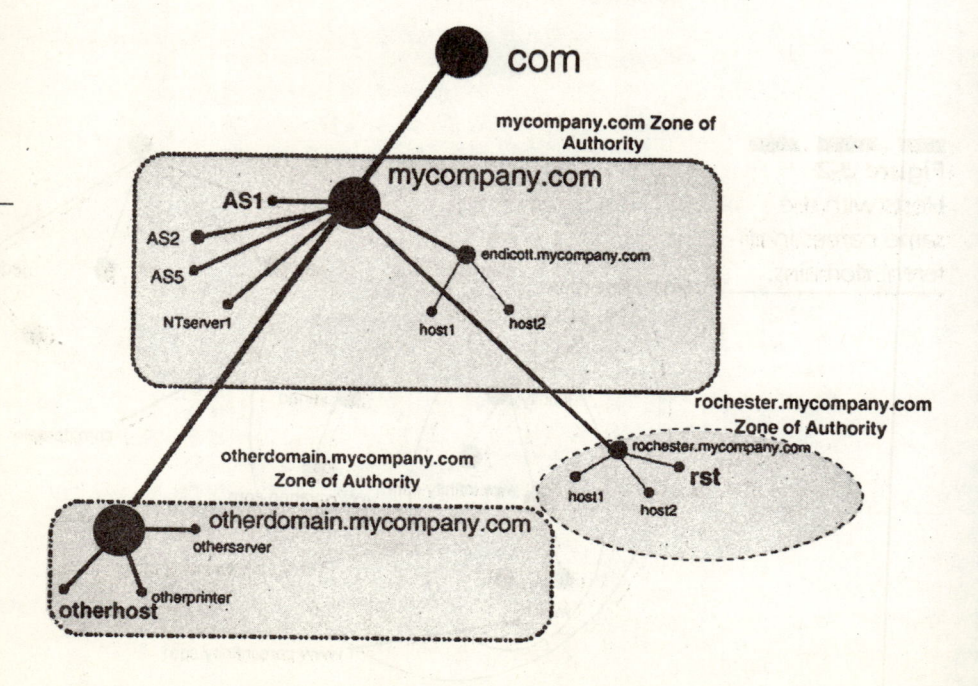

Serving Names

grams; they are called *Domain Name System (DNS) servers* or simply *name servers*.

Name servers have information about some part of the domain name space called a *zone* or *zone of authority*. Both domains and zones are subsets of the domain name space. A zone contains host information and data that the domain contains, excluding the information that is delegated somewhere else. If a subdomain of a domain is not delegated, the zone contains host information and data for the subdomain. Name servers have complete host information and data for a specific zone. Name servers are said to be "authoritative" for the zone for which they have this complete host information and data.

Refer to Figure 3-3. The *mycompany.com* domain is divided into the subdomains *endicott.mycompany.com, rochester.mycompany.com*, and *otherdomain.mycompany.com*. The zone *mycompany.com* contains the hosts: *AS1.mycompany.com, AS2.mycompany.com, AS5.mycompany.com*, and *NTserver1.mycompany.com*.

It also contains the host information and data in the subdomain *endicott.mycompany.com: host1.endicott.mycompany.com* and *host2.endicott.mycompany.com*. The subdomain *endicott.mycompany.com* has not been delegated, and its host information and data remain in the *mycompany.com* zone. The administration of the *endicott.mycompany.com* is the responsibility of the *mycompany.com* administrator. *AS1.mycompany.com* is the name server that has complete host information and data for the *mycompany.com* zone of authority. The zone *mycompany.com* does *not* contain information in the subdomains that have been delegated.

rochester.mycompany.com is a subdomain of *mycompany.com,* and its administration has been delegated. The zone *rochester.mycompany.com* includes host information and data in the subdomain *rochester.mycompany.com: rst.rochester.mycompany.com, host1.rochester.mycompany.com,* and *host2.rochester.mycompany.com*. *rst.rochester.mycompany.com* is the DNS server that has complete host information and data for the *rochester.mycompany.com* zone.

otherdomain.mycompany.com is a subdomain of *mycompany.com,* and its administration has been delegated. The zone *otherdomain.mycompany.com* includes host information and data in the subdomain *otherdomain.mycompany.com: otherhost.otherdomain.mycompany.com, otherprinter.otherdomain.mycompany.com,* and *otherserver.otherdomain.mycompany.com*. *otherhost.otherdomain.mycompany.com* is the

DNS server that has complete host information and data for the *otherdomain.mycompany.com* zone.

Differentiating Name Servers

Name servers are devices that store the information about the domain name space. Usually, they have complete information about some part of the name space or zone. There are several types of name servers, as illustrated in the following sections.

Static Name Servers

A static name server requires someone to manually edit and update the lookup table whenever an IP address gets assigned or reassigned to a particular name, or when a name is no longer required because the address or name are no longer required. When changes are made to the lookup table, the static DNS server needs to be restarted to make the changes active.

Dynamic Name Servers

A dynamic name server is capable of updating the lookup table itself whenever a DDNS client or DHCP server informs the DDNS server to update a client's hostname with a certain IP address that was assigned by a DHCP server. A dynamic name server never needs to be restarted. DDNS servers on UNIX and Windows can be used as static DNS servers also.

Primary Name Servers

The primary name server is the server on which the hosts in the zone of authority are configured. It is the server that the DNS administrator configures and maintains. When this server gives responses to queries from its primary domain files, the responses are called "authoritative." A name server for a primary domain reads the primary domain configuration information directly from files configured by DNS administrator and/or updated by dynamic clients.

Secondary Name Servers

This server has the same information as the primary name server. However, instead of getting its information directly from the DNS administrator configuring it, it gets its information from another name server through zone transfers over the network. Secondary name servers are authoritative servers, just like the primary name servers, and they act just like the primaries in terms of data storage and data queries.

NOTE. *A DNS server can be a primary name server for one or more domains, as well as a secondary name server for one or more domains. The terms* primary name server *and* secondary name server *are somewhat misnomers, because any given name server may be primary for some zones and secondary for other zones.*

A *zone transfer* is a TCP/IP transfer of domain files from another DNS server (called a *master name server*). This is done automatically when the secondary name server starts and also when the secondary name server detects that its domain files are downlevel from the master name server's domain files. The zone transfer is initiated from the secondary name server. The zone transfer cannot take place if the master name server is not active. A secondary name server is used for two reasons: spreading the DNS query workload over more than one server and as a backup in case the primary name server stops responding.

The name servers configured at the client very likely have no direct relationship to the zone being queried, and even if they do, the name servers might all be secondaries, or the first defined name server might be a secondary. Don't be confused with the terms *primary* and *secondary* name server at the client, which are applied when a client is configured with more than one DNS server for name resolving. If the first name server (also called the *primary name server*) does not respond, the client can query the second name server (also called the *secondary name server*). When the secondary name server gives out a response to a query, the response is also called authoritative. In other words, an answer from a secondary name server is considered to be just as good as if the answer came from a primary name server. The same applies if there is a third name server (also called the *tertiary name server*) defined at the client resolver configuration.

Master Name Servers

A master name server is the name server from which a secondary name server gets its zone transfer from. A master name server can either be a primary name server or another secondary name server.

Caching-Only Name Servers

A name server that does not have authority over any zone is called a *caching-only name server*. It gets all of its information by querying. A caching-only name server's responses are always nonauthoritative.

Authoritative Name Servers

A server that is considered to be authoritative for a domain is either the primary server or a secondary server for that domain. If another name server or a client queries either the primary or the secondary name server for information for which they are authoritative, the response is considered to be authoritative. Can a name server that is not authoritative over a domain give a response to a client about that domain and have that response considered an authoritative response? The answer is yes. If the nonauthoritative server does not know the answer and queries an authoritative name server on behalf of the client and then returns the answer to the client, this response is considered to be authoritative. The nonauthoritative name server caches this information. If a second client requests this same information from the nonauthoritative name server (and this information is still in its cache), the name server gives the response to the client, but now this same information is labeled nonauthoritative. Why? Because the information in the response this second time came out of the name server's cache. In other words, at some point, a nonauthoritative response came out of a name server's cache.

Parent and Child Name Servers

The concept of parent and child domains is equivalent to the concept of domain and subdomain: Once your domain grows to a certain size, you may need to distribute management by delegating authority of part of your domain to one or multiple subdomains. The upper-level domain is the parent, and its subdomains the children.

Serving Names

The name server authoritative for the parent domain is the parent name server, and the one authoritative for the subdomain is the child name server. For example, in Figure 3-3, *otherdomain* is a subdomain of *mycompany.com*. If a DNS server, AS1, is configured to be responsible for the *mycompany.com* zone of authority, and the authority for the zone *otherdomain.mycompany.com* is delegated to another DNS server, *otherhost*, then AS1 is considered to be the parent name server and *otherhost* is considered to be the child name server.

Root Name Servers

Internet root name servers know where name servers that are authoritative for the top-level domains are, and most of the Internet root name servers are authoritative for the top-level organizational domains (*.com, .edu, .net*, and so on). The top-level domain servers have information about the second-level domain that a given domain is in.

A company can implement internal root name servers. In this case, given a query for a company's subdomain, the internal root name server can provide information for the second-level subdomain the queried subdomain is in. In addition, a root name server is configured in a lower-level name server to help it navigate the name space tree from the top down, when it cannot answer a query with authoritative data or data in its cache.

If we use the example discussed in the previous section, the DNS server otherhost is authoritative for the zone *otherdomain.mycompany.com,* shown in Figure 3-3. The AS1 name server is authoritative for the *mycompany.com* zone of authority and is configured as the internal root for the whole company's name space. The internal roots can run on host systems all by themselves, or a given host can perform double duty as an internal root and as an authoritative name server for other zones. If otherhost cannot answer a query, it asks its root name server, which is AS1, the DNS server at the top of the *internal* name space tree. Please note the use of the term *internal* in this example, where these DNS servers are only part of an internal network. In this example, it is assumed that the network does not have Internet access; thus, the Internet com node is not part of this DNS name space tree. Therefore, the DNS server AS1 in the domain *mycompany.com* is at the top of tree. A root name server can be thought of as the name server at the *top* of the DNS name space tree. Remember, the DNS name space tree may be different, depending on whether the network is an internal network, or if the network includes the Internet DNS name space.

Forwarders

A DNS server can be configured to send queries to which it does not know the answer to a DNS server called a *forwarder name server*. Whereas going to a root name server for help in answering a query can be thought of as going to the top of the DNS name space tree, going to a forwarder can be thought of as going sideways in the DNS name space tree for help. The DNS administrator configures which DNS server is the forwarder. Usually, several DNS servers are configured to have the same forwarder. Then, the forwarder name server is configured with the root name servers (for example, the Internet root name servers). If the forwarders cannot answer the query, they query the root name servers, get the answer, and cache it. This way, a forwarder name server can build up a large cache of information. As the cache increases, chances are that the forwarder will receive a query for which it has a cached answer. This, in turn, reduces the number of times a root name server needs to be queried. Using a forwarder name server is an opportunity to build a large cache of information on one (or just a few) name servers.

Firewall Name Servers

A *firewall name server* is a special application of forwarding name servers. This could be useful when you want to connect a private network (intranet) to the Internet. You usually do not want all of your private DNS server information available to the Internet. You provide a more limited content DNS server to the public Internet (your firewall DNS server). When a host on your private network requests an address, it first queries the private DNS server. If that name server does not have the information desired, it sends the request to the firewall name server, which forwards the request out to the public Internet.

Please refer to the Chapter 8, "Security of DHCP and Dynamic DNS," to read how to connect your private network (intranet) to an untrusted network. This could be a customer's intranet or the global Internet. In either case, the information will help you protect your internal resources from the malicious attackers or just plain curious folks out there.

Record Types

Name server records are called *resource records* (RR) and are divided into classes for different kinds of networks. This subsection discusses

Serving Names

only the Internet class of records. The IN that you see as the second field in most records means "Internet." This list is not complete; see RFC 1035 for all RR types.

- *SOA* records are start-of-authority records, indicating that the name server is the main source of authoritative information for the domain. There is only one SOA record in the configuration files, and it is required to be in the zone and the address files.

- *NS* records are name server records. Each NS record should indicate a valid name server. Sometimes, this is not the case when you receive information from other name servers. As an aside, if you find a name server you know to provide bad information (or no information), you can use the bogusns directive in your boot file. For example, bogusns 192.168.6.11 would tell your name server not to query this name server (hopefully, there are other name servers that will be able to provide valid information for you).

- *RP* records are the responsible persons for the domain. If you found a name server that was delivering bad (or no) information, you would probably want to try to contact the RP for that name server and rectify the problem prior to adding a bogusns record to your name server.

- *TXT* records in the DDNS database may provide more information about how to contact the RP. A text record can contain arbitrary information in quotes (for example, a telephone number and name). It basically maps any kind of information to a host name. This is a feature that was created as a tool for the system administrator to map a host name and/or IP address lease to a real person. This is done by setting labels in the DHCP server in option 192

- *MX* records are mail exchanger records. An MX record indicates a host machine that will either deliver mail to the addressee or forward (using SMTP) the mail to another host that is closer to the addressee. The other host will either deliver or forward as necessary. MX records have a third parameter to prevent mail loops, the *preference value*. The preference value is a relative value for each mail host. The lowest value would indicate the highest preference for delivery (that is, a mailer should forward undeliverable mail to that host first). A preference value can be between 0 and 65535 (a 16-bit unsigned value).

- *A* records are address records. This is a record in the [D]DNS that maps a host name to an IP address so that you can resolve an IP address using by issuing a name. See also *PTR* records.

- *RR* entries are resource records in the name server database. A resource record maps information to a host name.

- *PTR* are pointer records. This is a record in the [D]DNS database that maps an IP address to a host name so that you can resolve a host name using its IP address. See also *A* records.
- *CNAME* records map a host alias name to the canonical name of the host (that is, the fully qualified domain name of the host that is defined by an address record).
- *HINFO* records contain host information and are generally not recommended, since you do not want to provide information that might be useful for any potential hackers. However, TCP/IP version 4.1 for OS/2 makes use of HINFO for ProxyArec clients. The ProxyArec client's MAC address is stored here in an encoded fashion to ensure that other clients cannot take over other clients' host names.
- *KEY* entries in the DDNS database contain all host name/domain name/primary name server settings that have been created and the associated keys to be able to update those host names.

Resolvers

The third component of the Domain Name System, *resolvers* are the clients making queries to the name servers on behalf of programs running on the host. These user programs make system or subroutine calls to the resolver, requesting information from the name server. The resolver, which runs on the same host as the user program, will transform the request into a search specification for resource records located (hopefully) somewhere in the domain name space. The request is then sent as a query to a name server, which will respond with the desired information to the resolver. This information is then returned to the user program in a format compatible with the local host's data formats.

What exactly does the resolver have to do for the client program? There are typically three functions that need to be performed:

1. *Host name-to-host address translation.* The client program (for example, FTP or Telnet) will provide a character string representing a host name. This will either be a fully qualified domain name (*host.net.com.*) or a simple unqualified host name. Let's use HO4. If the name is unqualified, the resolver code will append a domain origin name (in this case, *sample.net.*) to the name before passing it to the server. This domain origin name is one of four parameters that are configured on every IP host:

Serving Names

IP address of the host
Host name
Domain origin name—The domain to which this host belongs
IP address of the name server(s) being used

The resolver then translates this request into a query for address (type A) resource records and passes it to the specified name server. The server will return one or more 32-bit IP addresses.

2. *Host address-to-host name translation.* Presented with a 32-bit IP address from the client program (perhaps SNMP), the resolver will query the name server for a character string representing the name of the host in question. This type of query is for PTR-type resource records from the *in-addr.arpa* name space. The resolver will reverse the IP address and append the special characters `in-addr.arpa` before passing the query to the name server.

3. *General lookup function.* This function allows the resolver to make general queries to the name server requesting *all* matching resource records based on the name, class, and type specified in the query.

There are two types of resolvers, both making use of the routines `gethostbyname()` for name-to-address translation and `gethostbyaddr()` for address-to-name translation. The first, known as a *full resolver*, is a program distinct from the client user program. The full resolver has a set of default name servers it knows about. It may also have a cache to retain responses from the name server for later use.

Refer to Figure 3-4. The following steps correspond with the numbers on the figure:

1. The user program makes a call to the resolver.
2. The resolver translates the call into a resource record query and passes it to its default name server.
3. The name server attempts to resolve the query from its own database. Assume that this is the first query and there is nothing in the cache.
4. If unable to locate the requested records in its own database, the name server passes its own query to other name servers that it knows (if recursive mode is being used).
5. The remote name servers eventually reply with the required information.
6. The local name server passes the information back to the resolver.

Figure 3-4
A DNS full resolver.

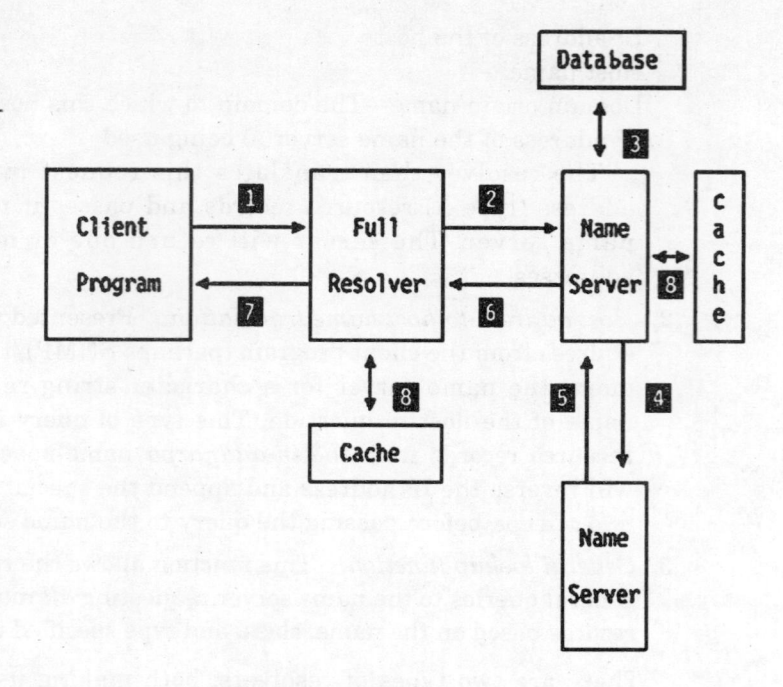

7. The resolver translates the resource records into local file format and returns the call to the user program.
8. Both the resolver and the name server update their caches with the information.

The second, and possibly more common, type of resolver is the *stub resolver*. This is merely a routine or routines that are linked to the user program. The stub resolver will perform the same function as the full resolver but generally does not keep a cache.

With reference to Figure 3-5, the stub resolver works as follows:

1. The user program invokes the stub resolver routines; the resolver creates an RR query and passes it to its default name server.
2. The name server attempts to resolve the query from its own database. Assume that this is the first query and there is nothing in the cache.
3. If unable to locate the requested records in its own database, the name server passes its own query to other name servers that it knows (if recursive mode is being used).
4. The remote name servers eventually reply with the required information.

Serving Names

Figure 3-5
A DNS stub resolver.

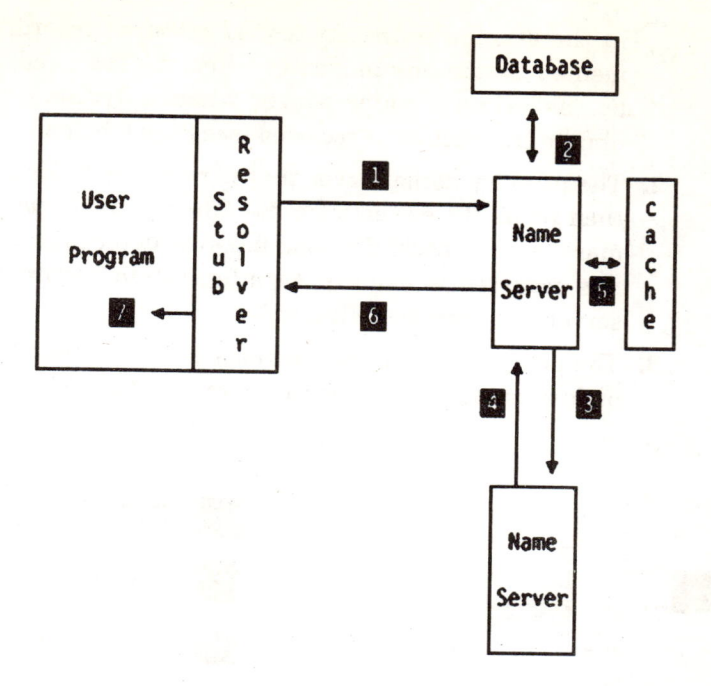

5. The name server updates its cache with the information.
6. The local name server passes the information back to the resolver.
7. The resolver translates the resource records into local file format and returns to the user program.

BIND's Treatment of DNS Database Entries

This section contains a brief example of how a new or changed resource record is propagated to all authoritative name servers using BIND (Berkeley Internet Name Domain) 8.1.1, which implements the latest RFCs pertaining to DNS updates, notifies, and incremental zone transfers:

1. To change a static DNS resource record, an administrator edits the zone file containing the resource record. Any time that zone data is changed, the serial number must also be incremented to indicate that the file has been changed. The serial number, which is a field

in the start of authority (SOA) resource record, must be incremented by the administrator when the file is edited or implicitly by the primary name server when a dynamic resource record update transaction is received (see Step 6 below).

2. The primary name server that is responsible for the changed zone then reads the edited zone file. The frequency with which the primary server checks its zone file(s) to determine whether a change has occurred is usually a configuration parameter of the name server software. See Figure 3-6.

3. The primary server then sends a notify message to all known secondary name servers for the changed zone. When multiple second-

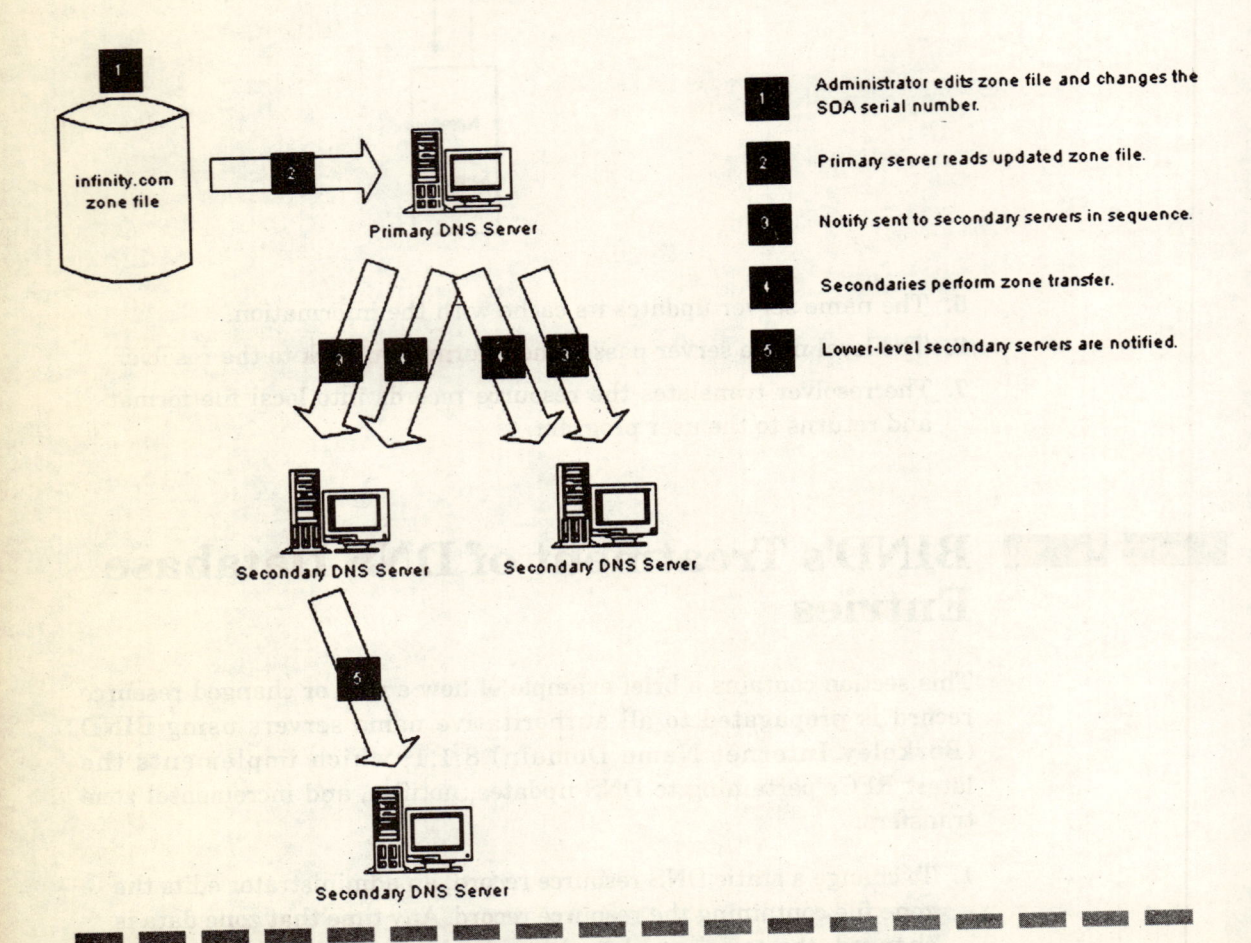

Figure 3-6 BIND's handling of zone file changes.

1. Administrator edits zone file and changes the SOA serial number.
2. Primary server reads updated zone file.
3. Notify sent to secondary servers in sequence.
4. Secondaries perform zone transfer.
5. Lower-level secondary servers are notified.

Serving Names

ary servers must be notified, which is usually the case, the primary server will wait about a minute between sending each notify to reduce the chance that all secondary servers request zone transfers at the same time.

4. If the secondary server(s) supports notify, it will initiate a zone transfer immediately upon receipt of the notify. Otherwise, the secondary server will discard the notify and wait until its next scheduled cycle to request a zone transfer from the primary server. An incremental zone transfer will occur if both primary and secondary servers support the capability; otherwise, a full zone transfer occurs. Present BIND documentation suggests that full zone transfers should be no more often than every 15 minutes and should be made at least every 24 hours if possible. Three hours is often recommended.

5. Once a secondary server has received the zone file change, it then notifies any other secondary servers that may be dependent upon it for zone transfers. This potentially multilevel zone transfer continues by repeating Steps 3 to 5 until all secondary servers for the changed zone have received the change.

6. If dynamic updates are supported by the primary server and a DNS client and/or a DHCP server, then a DNS client or DHCP server can send a resource record change (called an *update transaction*) to the primary server. If secondary name servers also support dynamic updates, then a DNS client or DHCP server may send an update transaction to a secondary server, which, in turn, will forward it to another secondary server until it reaches the primary server.

7. Once an update transaction is received by the primary server, it increments the zone SOA serial number and writes the changed zone data to a new zone file. The new zone file is the only permanent record of the update transaction. Once an update transaction is received and saved, it is propagated to secondary servers as described above.

In this standard-based scenario, the supposedly identical zone files in the primary and secondary name servers are out of synch for some period of time. In a system with static naming, resource record changes take place on a human timescale, so that delay is not problematic. In an emergency, network administrators can choose to restart their entire name system to synchronize the databases in a matter of minutes. However, in a network that uses dynamic naming, new address resource records are being created on computer timescales, which means that possibly hundreds of zone updates are required every second. Even with the new standards for notify and incremental zone transfers, zone changes propagate to the entire DNS very slowly.

What Is Dynamic IP?

Dynamic IP allows you to define network host configuration parameters at a central location and to automate configuration of IP hosts. Therefore, it simplifies both IP network access and IP network administration and is well suited for supporting mobile hosts. Essentially, Dynamic IP is the integration of the Dynamic Host Configuration Protocol (DHCP), which provides configuration information to IP hosts, and the Dynamic Domain Name System (DDNS), which provides dynamic host name-to-IP address (and IP address-to-host name) mapping for the Dynamic IP clients.

The design of Dynamic IP evolved from customer requirements for addressing the following challenges associated with network administration, particularly for large IP networks:

- Because each host on an IP network is typically configured and maintained individually, the task of implementing changes to the network infrastructure or services requires a massive coordinated effort to reconfigure all affected hosts.

- Similarly, when a host attaches to a new location in a network, the network administrator typically must assign a new IP address for the host, as well as manually change the host's host name-to-IP address mappings in the host's authoritative DNS server.

- For mobile hosts, an IP address must be *reserved* for each and every subnetwork location at which the mobile host may possibly attach. What's worse, the end user of the mobile host typically must manually reconfigure the IP software with the IP address and other IP network parameters appropriate to a given attachment location.

The goal of Dynamic IP is to simplify these tasks and to provide an easier way to access and administer IP networks. And because Dynamic IP uses only open-standard networking technologies, it is fully compatible and interoperable with existing IP network hosts.

In this section, we discuss what Dynamic IP provides and how it works. We also provide some recommendations for configuring for network availability, discuss how Dynamic IP can be used to enable mobile hosts, and discuss the security aspects of Dynamic IP.

Dynamic Domain Name System (DDNS)

DDNS is a protocol that defines extensions to the Domain Name System to enable DNS servers to accept requests to update the DNS database dynamically and securely. These extensions define mechanisms for adding and deleting a set of names and associated resource records.

Further, DDNS uses DNS security extensions to authenticate hosts that request to create or update entries in the DDNS server database. Without client authentication, another host could impersonate an unsuspecting host by remapping the address entry for the unsuspecting host to that of its own. Once the remapping occurs, important data, such as logon passwords and mail intended for the host, would unfortunately be sent to the impersonating host instead.

For more information about DDNS, refer to the Internet Drafts (IDs) "Dynamic Updates in the Domain Name System" and "Domain Name System Protocol Security Extensions".

What Does Dynamic IP Provide?

Dynamic IP uses open standards and existing IP network products to:

- Automate IP network access
- Simplify network administration
- Allow administration of site-specific host environments
- Enable customized, location-sensitive host serving

Automates IP Network Access A Dynamic IP client host can automatically obtain and use IP configuration information, including the network address and the routers and name servers to be used. This eliminates the need for each user to obtain and manually enter such information and, therefore, eliminates user frustration (and user error). In addition, this enables Dynamic IP hosts to freely move about the network and attach at arbitrary points without user or administrator intervention.

Dynamic IP also provides a mechanism to enable other hosts in the network to locate Dynamic IP hosts at their current points of attachment by maintaining up-to-date host name-to-IP address mappings. Automated IP network access also makes Dynamic IP well suited for laptops and other mobile computers that need to attach to IP networks at many different locations without losing their ability to access or be accessed by other hosts in a network.

Simplifies IP Network Administration Dynamic IP simplifies the job of configuring IP hosts by allowing a network administrator to provide configuration information for a network and its hosts from a central server. Therefore, changes to the network configuration, such as a change in the routing infrastructure or in network services, need only be made in a single server configuration file, from which the information is then automatically disseminated to affected network hosts. In addition, administrators can configure Dynamic IP hosts to maintain their own DNS mappings in a Dynamic DNS server, thus further reducing the workload of IP network administrators.

Allows Administration of Site-Specific Host Environments Many businesses supplement their off-the-shelf client/server applications with locally written network applications and frameworks. These locally written applications typically require some amount of configuration either by the user or by a system or network administrator.

Using Dynamic IP, you can distribute customer-defined configuration parameters, which simplifies the administration of these locally written application environments. For example, an administrator may instruct the Dynamic IP client host software to identify itself to a DHCP server as belonging to a user class called *accounting,* which requires a site-specific DHCP option #130 known by convention as *accounting database server IP address.* Further, the administrator can also instruct the client software to invoke a program called INVENDBS.EXE with the data passed in option #130 whenever that option is received. At the Dynamic IP server, the administrator can define option #130 as an IP address that is to be returned to all clients of class *accounting.* The administrator then specifies the value of option #130, which may vary depending on the client's location in the network. By defining both the data to be provided to clients as well as the way in which the clients process that data, an administrator can extend and customize your Dynamic IP setup to encompass applications and environments specific to the site.

Enables Customized, Location-Sensitive Host Serving Dynamic IP clients automatically receive the configuration parameters needed to access the network at a particular location. These configuration parameters can be considered *location-sensitive* because they are selected and served based on information about the host's location, specifically, the subnet to which it is attached. Thus, hosts can be served information and services that are relevant to their current location. This ability to provide location-sensitive information makes Dynamic IP ideal for supporting mobile hosts.

Taken a step further, administrators can use the site-customizing and host classing mechanisms previously mentioned to serve customized, location-sensitive information to mobile hosts as they move about a network.

Uses Only Open Standards Because all of the protocols employed by Dynamic IP conform to open networking standards, as specified in IETF RFC documents, implementation of Dynamic IP is compatible with and can interoperate with IP networking products from other manufacturers (OEM products) that implement these protocols. More specifically, Dynamic IP clients can be served by OEM DHCP and DNS servers, and by OEM Dynamic DNS servers, when they become available. Similarly, DHCP servers can support OEM BOOTP and DHCP clients. And because they are a functional superset of existing DNS servers, Dynamic DNS servers can serve traditional name resolvers and can be seamlessly inserted into existing customer DNS server hierarchies.

Leverages Existing IP Network Products and Infrastructure Dynamic IP clients and servers can interoperate with existing IP network products. Thus, you can integrate DHCP and DDNS servers and Dynamic IP clients into your network without change to your existing routers or routing tables and with little change to your existing DNS hierarchy. To use Dynamic IP in your network, you need only ensure that a BOOTP relay agent is present on subnets where a Dynamic IP DHCP server is not. These relay agents, also called BOOTP helpers, are widely available in today's IP router products.

How Does Dynamic IP Work?

This section provides an overview of the components of Dynamic IP and how they interact.

System Components Four types of network components can compose a Dynamic IP network:

1. *Dynamic IP hosts.* Dynamic IP hosts run the DHCP and Dynamic DNS client programs. The DHCP and DDNS clients work together and with their server counterparts to obtain and implement configuration information to automatically access IP networks.

2. *DHCP servers.* DHCP servers provide the addresses and configuration information to DHCP and BOOTP clients on the network. DHCP servers contain information about the network configuration and about host operational parameters as specified by the network administrator. Dynamic IP DHCP servers have the added capability of updating Dynamic DNS servers with IP address-to-host name mappings (PTR records), using host name information provided by the DHCP clients.

3. *Dynamic DNS servers.* Dynamic DNS servers are a superset of traditional BIND DNS servers. The *dynamic* enhancements enable client hosts to dynamically and securely register their name and address mappings in the DNS tables directly, rather than having an administrator manually perform the updates.

4. *BootP relay agents.* BOOTP Relay agents can be used in IP router products to forward information between DHCP clients and servers on different subnets. BOOTP relays eliminate the need for having a DHCP server on each subnet to service the broadcast requests from DHCP clients. BOOTP Relay agents are widely available as features of commercial internetworking router products.

System Operation To illustrate, here is an example of the Dynamic IP process. We have divided the process into two phases: acquiring configuration information and becoming known on the network. In this example:

- Client *CLIENT* is a workstation on subnet X that has been configured to use the DHCP client and Dynamic DNS client.
- Server *DHCPSERV* is a DHCP server on subnet Y.
- Server *DYNODNS* is a DDNS server on subnet Y.
- Router *ROUTER* is an IP router that connects subnets X and Y and that has been enabled for BOOTP relay and has been configured to forward IP broadcast messages to *DHCPSERV*.

Serving Names

Acquiring Configuration Information   In the first phase of the Dynamic IP process, the DHCP client must obtain the configuration information needed to access the network.

1. When CLIENT is started, the DHCP client program broadcasts a DHCP DISCOVER message onto the LAN, soliciting responses from any available DHCP servers.
2. When ROUTER receives the DHCP broadcast message, it inserts its IP address on subnet X and forwards the message to DHCPSERV.
3. When DHCPSERV receives the DHCP broadcast message, it reads the IP address inserted by ROUTER to determine where the DHCP DISCOVER request packet originated. DHCPSERV selects an IP address and a set of network parameters appropriate for the originating subnet, subnet X, and returns them in a DHCP OFFER packet to be forwarded to CLIENT by way of ROUTER.
4. CLIENT receives the OFFER, decides whether the OFFER meets its needs, and assuming so, sends a REQUEST message to DHCPSERV, requesting use of the configuration parameters for the specified lease time.
5. DHCPSERV receives the request and acknowledges the request by sending an ACK message to CLIENT.
6. Upon receipt of the ACK, CLIENT implements the configuration information to access the IP network.

Becoming Known on the Network   The client now has all the information it needs to access the network. One problem remains, however: No other hosts on the network know or can easily discover what address has been assigned to CLIENT. Therefore, CLIENT is essentially inaccessible to other hosts in the network.

The second phase of the process is needed to update the DNS server, DYNODNS, with the name and address information assigned to CLIENT so that others can discover the IP address assigned to CLIENT. In general, the following information is needed to update the Dynamic DNS server:

- The fully qualified domain name, consisting of a host name appended with a domain name
- The name or address of the primary DNS server, which is the DNS server that accepts dynamic updates for the domain

To become known on the network:

1. CLIENT creates a message to be sent to DYNODNS, which includes the necessary information.
2. At this point, CLIENT has not been configured with a DNS host name. So, the DDNS client configuration program prompts the user for the host name. In our example, we'll use WARPSPEED as the host name. The DHCP client appends the preconfigured domain name, for example, *dynamic.your-company.com* to the host name. The name of the primary Dynamic DNS server defaults to `ns-updates` in the specified domain. Therefore, for our example, WARPSPEED will be uniquely known as *warpspeed.dynamic.your-company.com,* and all associated DNS update requests for WARPSPEED will be sent to the DNS server known as *ns-updates.dynamic.your-company.com.*
3. WARPSPEED sends a name update message to DYNODNS indicating to its fully qualified host the lease time.
4. DYNODNS sends an acknowledgment to WARPSPEED that the information has been received and the database has been updated.

The initialization of host WARPSPEED is complete. Not only is WARPSPEED now able to access the network, it is also well known and accessible to other hosts in the network. All of this happens automatically without any intervention by a user or administrator.

NOTE. *For every name-to-address mapping in the DNS, there should also be a corresponding address-to-name mapping. Although not mentioned in the example above, the DHCPSERV is also notified of the host name assigned to WARPSPEED. DHCPSERV then sends a DDNS update request to DYNODNS specifying the reverse address mapping of the assigned IP address to the host name.*

Configuring for Network Availability

The DHCP protocols do not provide for server-to-server communication to enable sharing of information, such that one DHCP server could perform as a "hot backup" in the case the other one fails. Similarly, the Dynamic DNS protocols allow only one primary Dynamic DNS server to own a particular host DNS record. Therefore, with these limitations on component redundancy, Dynamic IP networks require careful planning in order to ensure network availability when using a single DHCP server or multiple DHCP servers and when using a Dynamic DNS server.

Using a Single DHCP Server If you choose to use a single DHCP server to service hosts on a subnet, consider the effects of the failure of that server. Generally, the failure of a sole server will affect only DHCP clients that are attempting to join the network. Typically, DHCP clients already on the network will continue operating unaffected until their lease expires. However, if the lease time is short, even those clients may lose their network access before the server can be restarted. To avoid this, if you have only one DHCP server for a subnet, you should choose a lease time that allows time to restart or respond to the failed DHCP server. This will minimize the impact of server downtime. Also, timers associated with client DHCP lease renewal algorithms can be set at the DHCP server to help ensure that server failures do not affect network operation.

Using Multiple DHCP Servers Two or more DHCP servers can be configured to serve the same subnet so that if one server fails, the other can continue to serve the subnet. The DHCP servers can be accessible either by direct attachment to the physical subnet or through a BOOTP relay function in an attached IP router.

Because two DHCP servers cannot serve the same addresses for a particular subnet, the address pools defined for a particular subnet must be unique among the DHCP servers. Therefore, when using two or more DHCP servers to service a particular subnet, the complete list of addresses for that subnet must be divided across those servers. If your routers support BOOTP Relay, you can configure each DHCP server to act as a primary server for the subnet to which it is directly attached and as a secondary DHCP server for another subnet. You could configure the primary server with an address pool consisting of 70 percent of the available addresses for the subnet and the secondary server with an address pool consisting of the remaining 30 percent of the available addresses.

Using multiple DHCP servers simply increases the probability of not having a DHCP-related network access failure; it does not guarantee against it. Even if only one of the DHCP servers for a particular subnet fails, the other DHCP server may not be able to serve all new hosts wishing to enter the network because the server may, for example, run out of its limited pool of available addresses.

DDNS Servers Because there is only one primary Dynamic DNS server owning the record information for any particular host, the failure of that DDNS server will prevent those hosts from registering new DNS record information. Further, primary DDNS server failure may also impair the ability of other hosts in the network to retrieve existing information about a particular host. Specifically, if the primary Dynamic DNS server is inoperative when a client host attaches to the network, the name registration step by the client host fails, and no information about the host is available in DNS in any case.

If, however, the primary DDNS server fails after a client host successfully registers its name, information about the host may still be available if there are other DNS servers in the network acting as secondaries for the zone of the client host. In this case, the information in the secondary DNS servers will be available for the period of time according to the DDNS record expiration time, which is based on the DHCP lease time in Dynamic IP hosts.

Accordingly, there is no strategy for having multiple DDNS servers service a pool of Dynamic IP hosts. There can be only one DDNS server primary for a particular DNS zone. You can, however, use one or more DNS servers as secondaries for a zone in order to enhance the availability of the information to other hosts in the network in the event of a primary DDNS server failure.

One important note is that you must configure the primary DNS servers to provide updates for the dynamic zones to its secondaries more frequently.

Enabling Host Mobility

Dynamic IP is well suited for use in networking mobile hosts, such as laptop computers. When accessing a Dynamic IP network, Dynamic IP clients can automatically obtain and implement configuration information and register their current location/address with the Dynamic DNS server. And, because the DHCP can provide location-specific configuration information, mobile clients can be assured of always having an accurate configuration.

If you move the Dynamic IP client computer out of its current subnet, you will simply need to restart it to obtain configuration information for the new location and to update the Dynamic DNS server with the new IP address. Because the Dynamic DNS server that you update remains constant, other hosts will be able to reach you using your fully qualified host name even if you move out of the domain.

Serving Names

To illustrate:

Fred works at the Phoenix location of Acme Corporation. His host name is *fredb* and his domain is *dynamic.acme.com*. Each time he starts his laptop, he is allocated an address by one of the DHCP servers in his network and updates are made to the local Dynamic DNS server, named *dynodns.dynamic.acme.com,* to map his new address to his host name (and vice versa). Fred's coworkers can reach him using the hostname of *fredb.dynamic.acme.com.*

One week, Fred is asked to help out in the Dallas office. He takes his laptop with him. When he starts his laptop, he is allocated an address by one of the DHCP servers in the Dallas network. He updates his home Dynamic DNS server, *dynodns.dynamic.acme.com*, with his new IP address. Therefore, assuming the Phoenix network and the Dallas network are connected, Fred can still be reached using *fredb.dynamic.acme.com.*

NOTE. *For efficient name resolution, the client will use the local DNS server to resolve host names.*

Securing Your Dynamic IP Network

The DHCP protocol specification does not include any mechanisms to limit access to DHCP services. Therefore, DHCP does not increase or decrease an IP network's exposure to unauthorized access. Dynamic DNS, however, does provide mechanisms to prevent unauthorized access to Dynamic DNS update services. DNS security extensions are used in DDNS to authenticate hosts that request to enter or change entries in the DDNS server database. Without client authentication, an unauthorized host, perhaps one with malicious intent, could impersonate an authorized host by remapping the address entry. Once the remapping occurred, data intended for the authorized host, such as logon passwords, could be intercepted by the impersonating host.

DDNS servers support two modes of controlling updates for a particular dynamic DNS zone: dynamic secured and dynamic presecured:

- With *dynamic secured mode,* the default mode, a DDNS server allows any host that complies with the DDNS protocol to make entries in a domain that is declared dynamic.

- With *dynamic presecured mode,* the Dynamic DNS administrator must preregister all hosts that are allowed to make updates to the DNS database.

In either mode, the Dynamic DNS client and server use RSA public-key digital-signature technology to authenticate DDNS update requests.

How Dynamic Addressing Is Made Usable with DDNS

Today, most DNS servers must be updated manually to change allocated names and addresses. Since most DNS entries are not updated very often, this isn't a big deal. But it becomes a different story when you're trying to keep up with the constant updates that are incurred by linking Dynamic DNS names to DHCP-leased addresses. If you also have slave DNS servers—servers that have cached their information for a set or lengthy period of time—they most likely won't get the information when it's needed.

Enter IP management systems. Most solutions run their own central DNS, DHCP, and database servers. Since DNS server updates are cached, dynamic addresses were resolved immediately. On the downside, since serial numbers have not been changed, secondary DNS servers do not know to reread the configuration files. However, if you combine these services with a periodic update of the zone file and serial number, your secondary DNS servers will be updated in a somewhat timely manner. This paradigm, however, is not true DDNS.

The IETF has a new RFC outlining how DDNS should work. RFCs 1996 and 2136 propose a solution that will be implemented in the standard DNS server, BIND 8.1. Once BIND 8.1 becomes widely used, vendors will likely support the methods of updating BIND servers.

DDNS strives to create an environment where DNS can function without causing a tremendous load on the DNS servers. As an IP address changes, the DHCP server sends a message to the DDNS server stating the change. The DDNS server then sends this update to its dependent slave servers. Additionally, a very short cache timeout will enable DNS servers on the Internet to receive changes while still providing for all the features DNS offers.

CHAPTER 4

NetBIOS Name Servers

A Network Basic Input-Output System (NetBIOS) over Transmission Control Protocol (TCP) has been defined by the governing TCP standards body, the Internet Engineering Task Force (IETF). The IETF standard describes how NetBIOS stations may interact with a NetBIOS name server (NBNS) in order to dynamically register their own applications' names and to learn the name-to-address mappings of other applications. Using the NBNS service, traditional client/server applications can be deployed over large, routed TCP/Internet Protocol (IP) networks.

It is the thesis of this chapter that the only design that can offer large networks truly dynamic NBNS servicing is one that has been designed to do the following:

- Enable system load balancing with secondary servers
- Collaborate with other servers to distribute algorithms
- Handle a high capacity of names
- Offer a caching strategy to provide for scalability
- Perform datagram distribution
- Enable the server's algorithms to be placed on top of standard workstation platforms
- Act as a dedicated system
- Provide failure resistance and overall reliability
- Allow for extensibility so it can be enhanced without jeopardizing its fundamental integrity
- Log records of every transaction
- Allow configuration of "static" name-to-address mapping entries
- Provide "wire speed" performance for name lookup requests
- Integrate with other standard TCP services like Dynamic Domain Name System servers (DDNSs)

Overview

The trend is clear—the Internet is real, and being accessible via the Internet is no longer an option for an enterprise network, but a necessity. The Internet's emergence has helped accelerate the shift in focus from shared resource computing in isolated workgroup nets to consolidated, enterprisewide "intranets," and ultimately to extended "affiliate" networks comprising a company's customers, prospects, and suppliers. The move away from proprietary workgroup protocols toward enterprise-oriented, routable protocols, coupled with the demonstrated success and extensibility of the global Internet, makes the Internet's protocol suite, TCP/IP, a natural choice for adoption within the enterprise. Enterprises with a TCP/IP network require an NBNS to ensure that the convenient and transparent view that workstations have of one another in a standalone workgroup environment can be maintained in the network.

The remainder of the Overview section discusses the following: TCP/IP for the Enterprise, Name Server History, and NetBIOS/NBNS Functionality.

TCP/IP for the Enterprise

The market share leaders of enterprise-oriented, PC-based network operating systems (NOSs) used for shared-resource computing are IBM, Microsoft, and Novell. Novell, once the dominant player, has based its NOS functionality on a tightly coupled implementation of system elements with a very efficient protocol. Until its endorsement of TCP/IP is complete, potential contributors can only offer added value from "outside" the Novell system elements.

Microsoft and IBM, on the other hand, have focused more on operating systems (OSs) than NOSs, and they have based their NOS functionality on designs more loosely coupled than Novell's. Since their file-sharing functionality is not inextricably bound up with a protocol of their own design, their NOSs are said to be "protocol-independent." A detailed specification (see the "Service Specification" subsection in this chapter) describes the services that the NOS needs from an underlying protocol stack in order to effect orderly network communications. It also dictates a way for the NOS services to be provided identically, exclusive of performance considerations, on any of a number of protocols. Given suitable interpretation of the service specifications, both Microsoft and IBM NOS services can be made to work over TCP/IP. And both companies, as well as a number of third-party vendors, have produced TCP/IP offerings that do provide such support.

Thanks in part to their early collaborative relationship, Microsoft and IBM agreed not only on the interface specification but also on the way in which their respective NOS systems would interact with one another for file and print sharing. This collaboration makes it possible for one company's "file redirector" to talk to the other company's "file server," enabling Microsoft clients to redirect their file accesses to IBM file servers and vice versa so that given a common underlying protocol, all manner of DOS, Windows, and OS/2 systems can interwork. When these redirectors and servers are placed on top of TCP/IP, it is possible for this cross-vendor interworking to be accomplished in workgroup, enterprise, or even Internet configurations of global proportions. As a result, the workgroup paradigms—except NetBIOS names, as will be discussed—can be preserved when swapping out IBM's NetBEUI, for example, and swapping in TCP.

Replacement of today's PC workgroup protocols by TCP/IP is hardly a straightforward undertaking, and many of the pieces needed to effect a properly functioning TCP/IP enterprise network are not well understood by all involved in the change. Even if a company's intent is only to swap out an old protocol and swap in a new one while maintaining the status quo in services, a number of problems and surprises will be encountered. But with the opportunities currently available to networking vendors, these deployment problems are probably already being worked on and will undoubtedly be solved.

Name Server History

NetBIOS, the service specification that defines the responsibility of the protocol stack in an IBM or Microsoft NOS, was designed in the mid-1980s to allow network-aware applications to communicate with one another across a local area net. When originally designing the NBNS, the TCP standards body did not attempt to elaborate on the workgroup solution. Rather, it based the design on the Internet's familiar Domain Name Service (DNS server), which translates Internet site names into IP addresses so browsers and other programs know where to connect. TCP/IP Request for Comments (RFCs) define the way in which this mapping is to be done, and DNS servers are the ones that must do it.

The NBNS RFCs (RFCs 1001 and 1002), written in 1987, define the standards by which PCs should interact with the server. Unfortunately, the conventions used for naming in the DNS are different from those used in the NBNS, rendering the two name spaces effectively disjoint. Thus, in addition to needing a DNS server to translate domain names to IP addresses, enterprise systems using NetBIOS "over" TCP/IP now need a separate NBNS to translate NetBIOS names to IP addresses.

It is worth noting that the TCP standards body is only now designing extensions to the DNS architecture that would allow dynamic registration and deregistration of name-to-address entries. Historically, domain names, which are usually associated with site (computer) names, have been generally thought of as "static." Once placed into the domain name database by an administrator, domain name-to-IP address mappings do not typically change. NetBIOS names, on the other hand, belong to individual applications with perhaps several names per application. These names must be inserted into and deleted from the NetBIOS name database as the applications are started and stopped on their respective PCs. As a result, NBNSs are much more "active" than traditional DNS servers. Today, an NBNS in a large network might be responsible for adding, deleting, and mapping hundreds or even thousands of names every second.

NetBIOS/NBNS Basic Functionality

The principal function of the NBNS is to maintain the name database for a community of NetBIOS stations. To do this, a simple NBNS need only provide for the registration, deregistration, and lookup of NetBIOS names. When an application instructs its underlying protocol stack to add a unique name into the net, the stack sends a name registration packet to the NBNS and waits for a definitive response. The NBNS scans its database to determine whether the name is already present. If it is not, the NBNS inserts the new name along with the requesting station's IP address and sends a response back to the originating station. If the name is already registered, the response will deny the originator's request. Looking up a name and deleting a name are just as straightforward.

Since duplicate registration and delete requests on a NetBIOS name do not significantly change its status, retransmissions may be used as often as necessary to provoke a definitive response from the NBNS. No broadcasts are required for NBNS service, so other stations on the net are not pestered by interactions not intended for them. The process of adding a name can be accomplished in most cases much more rapidly than in the broadcast case, where multiple broadcasts and multiple time-out periods are wasted (for each name) waiting to see if any other station objects. A TCP/IP station that knows how to interact with an NBNS for its name-to-address mapping services is called a point-to-point node, or P-node, station.

The remainder of this subsection discusses the NetBIOS service specification and the design of NetBIOS services and NBNSs.

Service Specification

The NetBIOS service specification defines an application programming interface (API) that details the calls that a program may make on a protocol stack and the services that the stack should provide to its callers. Client/server applications written to the NetBIOS API can be expected to work on a variety of networking systems. Many different vendors have built networking systems whose stacks supply NetBIOS services, and many more independent software vendors have built NetBIOS-based client/server applications that can run on any of the nets. This has been a boon to these vendors, since a single executable version of their product can be deployed in all NetBIOS-compliant settings. It has been a boon to IBM and Microsoft too, because their file redirectors and file servers are written to use the NetBIOS API.

The API defines its services at the session layer of the ISO reference model. True to the notion of protocol layering, it defines them in a way that is independent of the transport and lower layers on which they will ride. The utility of this approach is evidenced by the fact that similar attempts at fashioning a protocol-independent API—this time, at lower layers of the reference model—are being made (10 years later) by the authors of the Windows Sockets specification in Winsock, Version 2.0.

Design

NetBIOS's protocol-independent services were designed with small, workgroup-oriented networks in mind. The types of services offered through the NetBIOS API, while natural for use in small workgroups, are not entirely appropriate for use in large enterprise nets. In particular, the services offered for applications to refer to one another by "name"—a convenient, protocol-independent scheme for applications to locate one another in a simple workgroup environment—do not scale particularly well for large networks, where possibly thousands (or tens of thousands) of names might exist and where stations might be distributed over wide geographic regions, making them difficult to canvass.

For reasons such as this, NBNSs are particularly hard to implement in an enterprise network built upon the TCP/IP protocol suite, and they are apparently unthinkable in the context of the worldwide Internet with its millions of stations. This is, in part, because the writers of the NetBIOS service specification envisioned that the NetBIOS protocol could rely on broadcast packets, or single packets that propagate from a sending station to all other stations on its directly connected net. But in the Internet, broadcast packets are almost always prevented by routers from traveling from one IP segment to another. Worse, in an attempt to economize on bandwidth, broadcast packets are hardly ever passed over wide area links, suggesting that even users employing simple dial-in access to a corporate net cannot usually send or receive broadcast packets, regardless of the number of connected stations or IP segments.

NetBIOS Naming

Clients and servers need to know how to find one another in order to share information. The NetBIOS conventions built into DOS, Windows,

NetBIOS Name Servers

and OS/2 were defined to let PCs and, more specifically, individual client/server applications refer to one another by name. NetBIOS names, like "Steve's PC" or "the printer in the lab," can be created by humans and built into programs with relative ease. Also useful is the fact that NetBIOS names can be used as unambiguous identifiers even if a station is moved and is no longer "in the lab." However, in order to send packets of information, the TCP protocol drivers of the respective PCs must refer to one another by address. The problem exists, then, of having to translate NetBIOS names into IP addresses in order to effect PC-to-PC communication on an IP network.

To examine this difficulty, it is helpful to begin first with a discussion of the naming of applications, then follow with a comparison of the methods used to translate NetBIOS names into IP addresses.

Names for Applications

The NetBIOS specifications define the format of names but say very little about them otherwise. This leaves it to individual authors to invent the names used by their client and server correspondents. With a fixed limit of 16 bytes for each name, NetBIOS names usually aren't any more descriptive than DOS 8.3 filenames, especially since they are often used to encode the manufacturer's ID, the program's ID, and the station's ID. In some cases—for example, where the application implements more than one service—NetBIOS names even encode an internal selector to discriminate among multiple communications. In the example below, Microsoft's NT server NTMAILSERVER employs eight NetBIOS names just to establish its presence on the net.

These names are 16 bytes in length, and non-ASCII characters are shown in their hex equivalents enclosed in square brackets. The names shown here do not include an explicit manufacturer ID, in part because IBM and Microsoft adopted their naming conventions before anybody else had written NetBIOS applications. However, their special hex values in the sixteenth byte have mostly been avoided by all subsequent authors and, therefore, realistically perform the additional duty of acting as an implied manufacturer ID.

In addition to these "application" names, the TCP stack always registers a "permanent" unique name, "[zeros, then 12 hex digits]," which is the station's 48-bit hardware address. A Windows NT machine acting as a Primary Domain Controller registers 10 names exclusive of and in addition to the names used by any applications that may be started on the PC.

Translating Names to IP Addresses

To date, the translation of NetBIOS names into IP addresses has been handled in one of two ways: by use of static tables residing on each client and server, or by use of dynamic broadcast queries (packets sent to every client and server in the broadcast subnet) asking, in effect, "Where is Steve's PC?" The basic problem with static tables is that they must be continually updated and maintained, an activity far more troublesome than the maintenance of IP addresses alone. Every time any new station is added to the network, all of its applications' names must be added to the static table of each station that wants to send it data. Additionally, though names in static entries are always mappable, there is no way to tell whether the named application is actually active at the time interaction is desired by another station.

The basic problem with broadcast queries is that IP networks cannot propagate broadcasts beyond a single (logical) cable segment, so resources located on the "other" side of a router from the broadcasting station will not receive the query, while every station on the "same" side of the router will be pestered with queries for which it doesn't know the answer.

As has been mentioned, the NetBIOS over TCP protocol, as defined by the IETF, overcomes each of these translation problems. This will be discussed in greater detail in subsequent sections.

Name Database

When a NetBIOS application wants to talk to a particular remote correspondent, it supplies the correspondent's name to its own underlying protocol stack and asks it to effect the necessary communications setup. The stack does this by calling its counterpart stack on the remote correspondent's machine. To pick the right machine, given only an application level name, the stack must have a way of affiliating the name with its hosting station's address. In concept, the stack must refer to a "name database," a construct in which the mappings between names and addresses are kept.

The NetBIOS service specification presumes such a construct and defines several properties of NetBIOS naming that explain how the database is to be used. Of course, before an application is allowed to communicate on the network, its name must be "known" on the net. Therefore,

NetBIOS Name Servers

the properties of using the database to make its name known are as follows:

1. The application calls through the NetBIOS API and instructs its protocol stack to "add" the name into the net. In concept, this operation sets up an affiliation between the application's name and the protocol stack's own station address.
2. Both "group" and "unique" names are defined by NetBIOS.
   - When adding a unique name, the protocol stack is expected to ensure that the name is truly unique (i.e., that the name is not being used by any other station on the net).
   - When adding a group name, the protocol stack is expected to ensure that any other station using the name also thinks of it as identifying a group.
3. As an application ends its communication on the net, it instructs its stack to "delete" the application name, thereby ending its temporary affiliation with the station address and making the name "unknown" on the net. The NetBIOS service specification is not much more exhaustive in its naming discussion than this. But faithful implementation of even the simple services mentioned above can be remarkably hard. What is a protocol stack expected to do, for example, to ensure that a name that it "adds" is unique? The answer depends on the way in which the name database is implemented and the degree to which stack implementers believe strict adherence to the specification is important.

Distributed Database

In a (very) small workgroup, it is possible that the database can be statically defined. A file can be constructed that gives the name-to-address mappings for all applications expected to be deployed within the net, and this file is supplied to the protocol stacks of all participating stations. As a nondynamic entity, the file may not always be current, but in simple workgroup situations, the approximation will be "close enough." Administrators themselves are then charged with the responsibility of ensuring the uniqueness of names in the database.

For certain named applications that cannot be found by the dynamic techniques, static mappings can also be made to augment the more dynamic approaches discussed in the "Probe Mechanisms" and "Roll Call Mechanisms" subsections below.

> **NOTE.** Network administrators involved in making static mappings will recognize the use of LMHOST files—files that are on each user's PC—as an implementation of a static name database. Needless to say, this approach is impractical in a net of any meaningful size, since list maintenance becomes logistically untenable.

The remainder of this section discusses two mechanisms used to define the database: probe mechanisms and roll call mechanisms.

Probe Mechanisms

In a simple workgroup environment, the temptation is overwhelming to think of the name database as a "perfectly" distributed object, with each participating station responsible for just the segment of the database containing its own names. This is because name-to-address mappings seem almost trivial: Stations seeking the whereabouts of a particular name can effect a rapid retrieval by use of a single broadcast packet—a "probe"—which asks all stations at once to peruse their own database segment for the name. Any station finding the name is expected to respond. Apart from the annoyance of broadcasts, this scheme has several other drawbacks, most of which stem from the lack of any centralized authority. These drawbacks, however, are usually dismissed with the attitude that, in a simple workgroup, an approximate adherence to the NetBIOS service spec is probably "good enough."

An understanding of the drawbacks described above (and why they are generally dismissed) becomes clear in the analysis of what it means to add a unique name. A protocol stack instructed to add a unique name can, of course, look at its own database segment to ensure that the name isn't found. But to ensure that the name isn't found in the database as a whole, it must ask all the other stations as well. It can do this with just a single probe. A station receiving the probe that finds the name in its local database segment should send a protest to the requestor so that the name addition will not be allowed. Such an authoritative response will cause the requesting protocol stack to return an error to the application through the NetBIOS API. Stations that have no reason to protest will remain silent.

NetBIOS Name Servers

What should be assumed if the requestor gets no packet in protest? Is there really no protest, or did his or her probe get lost in transmission? Maybe a protest was generated but got lost before receipt. The results are not definitive. To resolve the uncertainty, the probe will be repeated a number of times, and a timeout period will be spent waiting for responses to each probe. Repetitions apparently reduce the possibility of lost packets to an "acceptable" level, though no quantitative measure of "acceptable" is ever attempted. "Three times ought to be enough" is about as scientific as it gets.

Many networking vendors have provided implementations of the NetBIOS service specification that employ broadcast packets, repetitions, timeout periods, and the other attendant operations associated with the perfectly distributed name database. The NetBIOS over TCP specification describes a subset mode of operation that uses precisely this scheme. A TCP/IP station relying on this type of broadcast servicing is called a broadcast node, or B-node, station. It is easy to see how these techniques lead to trouble in a network so large that broadcast traffic becomes a nuisance, or so dispersed that broadcasts cannot be made to reach all stations.

Roll Call Mechanisms

With a perfectly distributed implementation, each station maintains just that segment of the composite database that comprises its own applications' names. If a station adds a name to its own segment, that name then appears in the composite database. If it deletes the name, it will no longer be in the database. To determine whether a name is or is not in the database, it is necessary to canvass all stations. Broadcasts seem a convenient and efficient means for doing just this. But, in general, broadcasts aren't required—requestors could just probe other stations one at a time.

However, in nonbroadcast networks with a perfectly distributed database, such behavior is required. Routed IP networks are, in essence, nonbroadcast. Dial-in networks are also nonbroadcast, as are most networks based on any form of wide area communication links. And, quite importantly, tomorrow's ATM and other switched networks are decidedly nonbroadcast. But the prospect of canvassing all stations one at a time in a network of any meaningful size is almost unthinkable. Such a roll call mechanism would require that a list of stations be maintained, imposing a burden administrators would rather discard.

Centralized Database

Many economizing schemes might be designed to try to ameliorate the difficulties of database canvassing in nonbroadcast networks. Even "cluster-bomb" packets, which travel point-to-point to remote workgroup LANs and then explode into broadcasts, have been suggested. But if a PC has to send out any more than one packet to canvass all stations, other approaches are quickly seen to be superior.

The approach that has won favor with the TCP standards body is the authorization to use a "centralized" NBNS. Rather than leaving the database distributed and attempting to access it where it lies, the database is entrusted to the server. In practice, the name database is contained in both the central server and the individual stations, with the server calling the shots.

Role of a NetBIOS Datagram

Most NetBIOS applications talk to one another using the NetBIOS *connection-oriented* services. These services use TCP's reliable transmission capabilities to support communication between a calling and a called application. File redirectors talk to file servers using NetBIOS connections. When a calling application instructs its underlying protocol stack to "call" a remote named application, the protocol stack sends a name lookup packet to the NBNS to learn the IP address associated with the remote name, and then it executes the associated TCP connection.

NetBIOS also offers *transaction-oriented* services. These services allow NetBIOS datagrams to be sent from one named application to another using the User Datagram Protocol (UDP) services of the underlying stack. (For example, the browsing functions of the File Manager in Microsoft Windows are implemented with NetBIOS datagrams.) But whereas NetBIOS connections go between a caller and one other station, a datagram may be sent to a single remote station, a group of stations, or all stations on the net.

- To reach a group of stations or a single remote station, it specifies "Send Datagram" and supplies a destination name. The name can be either a unique or group name; at the outset, the underlying protocol stack does not know which.

NetBIOS Name Servers

- If unique, then it sends the datagram to a particular remote station, and its interactions with the NBNS require just a simple lookup to learn the IP address.
- If group, then the datagram must go to all the members of the group. The protocol stack must determine the group's membership and arrange for all members to receive a copy. In a simple workgroup environment, this may require just a single broadcast transmission. But if any group member lies outside the broadcast realm, directed packets must be used. The burden of sending multiple packets could be placed on the protocol stack itself, but the TCP standards writers favored placing the burden on the centralized server.
- To reach all stations, an application instructs the stack to "Send Broadcast Datagram."

The following subsections introduce the roles of a NetBIOS datagram in distribution and in a workstation.

NetBIOS Datagram Distributor

A protocol stack instructed to send a NetBIOS datagram asks the NBNS for a name-to-address translation. The response from the server reveals whether the destination name is unique or group, and it provides the IP address(es) of those members who should receive the datagram. If the NBNS supports the NetBIOS Datagram Distributor (NBDD) function as defined by the RFCs, the protocol stack sends the datagram to the server, which will forward it using directed packets to all the group members. Otherwise, the stack must do this distribution itself.

As may be imagined, there are many difficulties associated with having the stack perform its own distribution. Besides the inherent complexities (for example, what if the group's membership is so large that the list of IP addresses exceeds the space in the response packet?) and the wasted processor cycles spent sending the same datagram over and over again, one problem is intrinsic: A station at the end of a low-bandwidth link cannot perform this distribution without consuming unfavorable amounts of its networking bandwidth. Dial-in stations, wireless remotes, even small offices using leased lines to reach headquarters will find self-distribution of NetBIOS datagrams unnecessarily slow and wasteful.

Workstation Interoperability

There are many considerations for a protocol stack that implements the NetBIOS over TCP specification. Not all vendors have implemented the RFCs. Of those that have, many have implemented only B-node functionality and, therefore, must augment their limited workgroup reach by the use of LMHOSTS or other static administrative means. Of the vendors who do support P-node interactions with an NBNS, few also support interactions with an NBDD. Only these few vendors appear to have implemented the entire specification.

Stations that know how to interact with an NBNS (and NBDD) must have strategies for handling problem situations where the name server fails or becomes unavailable (e.g., a communications link is severed). In most cases, the stack can switch its attentions to a backup name server. If no backup exists, the RFCs suggest the stack revert to the more limited B-node operation so that communication—at least within the local workgroup—is still enabled. A TCP/IP station equipped to behave in this way is called a hybrid node, or H-node, station.

NBNS Design Criteria

The need for an NBNS and datagram distributor is much more apparent than the best way to build such a server. It would be a mistake to assume that making a name server is any easier than making a router. The intent of that observation is not that a router is hard to build—many programmers can code up a PC program that takes packets in from one LAN adapter and puts them out to another—but that an enterprise network router is hard to build. An enterprise network router is a fairly complex product, typically created by a vendor focused on the networking market, and it is a piece of networking equipment on which businesses depend. This perspective is central to the discussion of the NBNS design criteria that follows.

A truly dynamic NBNS needs to offer the following components and features, detailed further in the subsequent subsections:

- High performance
- Standard hardware platform
- Dedicated server

- Fast response time
- High capacity
- Reliability
- Load balancing
- Scalability
- Datagram distribution
- Distributed algorithms
- Extensibility
- Transaction capture
- Static names
- Remote management
- Database validation

High Performance

An NBNS should be able to handle every packet arriving on one or more network adapters. Even at 10 mbps, an Ethernet can carry over 10,000 NetBIOS-sized packets per second. It is unlikely that half of all packets on the network would be to the name server (and half from the name server), but should the server be designed to handle less? If one datagram can be distributed by the server to 100 members of a group, attempts by each member to reach every other would fill up the net. LAN technologies of 10 megabits cannot be the target design point. An NBNS deployed in a high-speed switched environment needs to be able to handle packets delivered on one or more links. And the only architecture that can sustain this type of packet flow is one built specifically for that purpose.

"Wire-speed" performance cannot be achieved by a complex, transaction-oriented application such as NBNS running over a commercial operating system, even if the system is dedicated to the application. A commercial operating system imposes latency in moving packets to and from the network by its general-purpose algorithms for allocating memory and other resources and by scheduling and dispatching application and system tasks. In many ways, an NBNS server is analogous to a high-performance router, and it should be implemented like a router. An NBNS server should be implemented by embedding finely tuned algorithms directly on a special hardware platform surrounded by a minimum amount of operating system code, usually just enough to tame the hardware's interrupt structure and handle lightweight task dispatching and timer management.

Standard Hardware Platform

Historically, enterprise routers have been deployed on proprietary hardware platforms. This is because the standard platforms used by enterprise networks for business purposes (PCs, UNIX workstations, etc.), have not been as fast, robust, scalable, or low priced as the proprietary systems offered by the pioneering router companies. While routers may still have requirements for proprietary hardware designs (for special bussing structures, perhaps, or large numbers of network connections), the same is not necessarily true for many new kinds of networking servers. It is now completely possible to place the special-purpose algorithms of servers like the NBNS on top of standard workstation platforms with which enterprise customers are already familiar. Doing so carries several advantages:

- PC platforms offer the scalability and pricing flexibility to allow wide latitude in NBNS deployments. An optimized NBNS can run on an inexpensive platform without requiring undue amounts of disk or memory resources.
- Standard Ethernet and Token Ring LAN adapters can be used.
- Upgrades from one hardware platform to another can be done in order to take advantage of enhancements in server functionality; such upgrades do not need to be done because of new OS requirements.
- As long as the NBNS software is able to provide the reliability and wire-speed performance required by its users, the hardware costs can be kept as low as possible.
- Hardware value-add can be focused on meeting the environmental and space demands as a communications infrastructure solution.

Dedicated Server

If a server system is to be serious, it must be thought of as a dedicated system. This is true whether the server rides directly on PC hardware or sits atop a commercial operating system. Even if the server only has to handle 10 packets a minute, attempting to use it for word processing, spreadsheet calculations, or Web surfing at the same time can still cause an accidental reboot.

Fast Response Time

How quickly can an NBNS respond to a name lookup request? The design point should relate to the expected offered load, but, in general, it is "as quickly as possible." Of principal concern, of course, is the size and nature of the server's name database. Even with a database of 64,000 names, lookup response times of about 1 millisecond are expected. Name insertion and retrieval algorithms are of paramount concern in the design of the server program. While it is tempting to imagine the database being built using commercial database technology, the overhead of such an approach would surely be prohibitive, and the flexibility is just not required. While administrators would benefit from reports to help them understand and manage its operation, the NBNS itself does not require multiple views of its data. Strategies for database dumping and restoration—both during operation and in cases of server shutdown—must be part of the server's offerings. Disk archiving, however, must be handled as a background task so that the server remains responsive to network requests. This may be a problem for application-based servers that depend on an underlying operating system's disk management services.

High Capacity

An NBNS must be designed to handle tens of thousands of names. Given that individual stations can easily supply 10 names just for file and print sharing reasons, a network with 1,000 PCs could generate 10,000 names. Corporate networks with 20,000 PCs need an NBNS with substantial capacity.

Reliability

Obviously, an individual NBNS must be resistant to failure. The software must be robust, the PC power must be clean, and the PC memory must not be hit by alpha particles. But reliability of the naming system as a whole also needs to be taken into account. Client PCs, which operate as P-node or H-node stations, are typically equipped to deal with both a "primary" and a "secondary" NBNS. If, for some reason, the PC loses contact with its primary, it must switch its attention to the secondary. (Various client-oriented algorithms govern the way in which switching between the two servers is managed.) For a secondary server to be of any use to a client PC when its primary fails, it needs to contain basically the same name database as the failed server. Since the database is a dynamic entity, the primary must keep the secondary up-to-date with all name additions and deletions. It can do this by forwarding database update information to the secondary at either predefined intervals or when the number of name additions or deletions meets or exceeds an administratively defined threshold.

Load Balancing

A secondary name server need not be thought of as just a "hot standby" for the primary, and database replication need not be just a one-way operation. If two name servers update one another with their respective database changes, each will contain the composite database so that the servers are backups of one another. System load balancing can then be achieved by giving all client PCs different primary/secondary assignments so that each server cuts its transaction count in half, for example. This architecture offers other benefits in addition to load balancing. For instance, an enterprise with two sites linked by a low-speed communications line may choose to deploy a server in each site. The servers use the remote link for communicating database synchronization information, but the client PCs at each site speak only to their local primary machine at normal transaction rates.

Scalability

Nobody imagines that the name database for the worldwide Internet can be held by just a single name server. For capacity reasons alone, thousands of DNS servers are required. A DNS server that is asked to supply a particular name-to-address mapping may find that it does not hold the entry in its own database segment, in which case it must begin a search through the segments held by other name servers. The DNSs are hierarchically arranged so that a search can be conducted through the compos-

NetBIOS Name Servers

ite name database by visiting a collection of servers in order (perhaps receiving some expediting search advice by servers it visits along the way). Name searches in the Internet can sometimes take up to a full minute, leaving requesting clients hanging all the while. Name mappings retrieved from other servers may be retained ("cached") by the receiving DNS, if space allows, so that subsequent requests for the same information can be answered more rapidly.

An NBNS should be designed to offer this kind of scalability. For load-balancing, capacity, geographic, or administrative reasons, an organization may choose to distribute its name database among multiple NBNSs. NetBIOS names do not lend themselves to a hierarchical arrangement because within a single organization, the name space is flat. If the name database is distributed among multiple servers, each NBNS must be able to interrogate all other servers to be able to canvass the composite database. When some sort of caching strategy is used by the initiating NBNS, subsequent lookups go faster.

Unlike the traditional BIND DNS, the NBNS is dynamic. Its name caching strategies must be fairly sophisticated because a name may be deleted from its "home" database segment while apparently still registered, according to some remote server's cache. As a result, NBNSs need a strategy allowing individual cached entries to decay at an appropriate rate—one governed by a suggested "time to live" recommendation received from the name's home server—so they can be removed from the cache.

Datagram Distribution

An NBNS is expected to perform the whole job called for by the RFCs. Datagram distribution has already been described as an extremely valuable and fundamental service of the centralized server approach. An NBNS must really be an NBNS/datagram distributor (DD).

Distributed Algorithms

Servers must work with one another to provide the services envisioned for the NetBIOS service specifications. It is important for the server's design to consider the nature of the distributed database in all operations. Suppose, for example, that two stations sharing a group name register themselves with separate name servers. Can a datagram sent to the group be sure to reach both?. The need for sophistication in the NBNS/DD algorithms seems nearly boundless.

Extensibility

The NBNS must be designed so that it can continue to be enhanced without jeopardizing its fundamental integrity. It is often the case that the breakthrough connectivity allowed by a new networking paradigm is soon followed by an equally important effort to bring the connectivity under control. An example of this is the Web's recent attempt to constrain viewing of offensive materials by minors. Such a pattern—achieve connectivity, then limit connectivity—can be expected for the distributed NBNS. An NBNS design should allow for such extensibility. If the mechanisms already at work in the NBNS are like the mechanisms being (re)invented for the new DDNS, an NBNS must be readily enhanced to take on DNS functionality as well.

Transaction Capture

An NBNS needs to be able to log to long-term storage a record of every transaction in which it is involved. Such transaction capture capabilities aid in understanding system behavior and help in possible troubleshooting.

Static Names

Not all vendors who support NetBIOS over TCP/IP have implemented the full P-node/H-node functionality. At this writing, in fact, only IBM, Microsoft, and Network Telesystems (NTS) are supportive of the full RFCs. However, the Microsoft TCP does not use a server for datagram distribution, and its Windows NT implementation does not offer H-node service.

Any station whose TCP does not dynamically register its names with the NBNS must have its names registered statically by a network administrator. In this way, since the name-to-address mapping is known to the NBNS, any station seeking out the name will be able to learn its address from the server. While this fallback grade of service is less desirable than the fully dynamic one (the mapping remains in place even when the application is not running), the server should allow the configuration of static name-to-address mapping entries.

Remote Management

Administrators need the ability to deploy name servers at any number of remote sites and to manage them from a central location as though they were at the site. Internet addressing offers the prospect for large enterprises to manage a global collection of servers from a headquarters facility. Different administrative privileges must be accorded different administrative personnel, and multiple accessors must be able to deal with a common server at the same time. Access restrictions are required in order to yield a hierarchy of permissions, such as the ability to read only—or read and write—the name database, to change the server's operational configuration, and to change the access control restrictions that govern these other operations.

Whereas a case has been made for the NBNS to be implemented on a PC platform directly with no hosting operating system, the same approach must not be used for the Manager application. This tool needs to be offered on standard Windows, UNIX, or OS/2 networked machines, thereby providing a familiar graphical interface for administrators to use. The Manager application must be able to upload and download database elements to and from the server(s), to move database components between the local file system and servers, and to move database components from server to server. Generation of reports about name server operations can be done on the management station using whatever commercial tools are appropriate for processing the management database. The Manager must also have the ability to retrieve a log of all server transactions for offline problem analysis or replay if needed.

Database Validation

Since the NBNS is attempting the management of a dynamic and important online database, it needs to ensure the consistency of the information it contains. The NetBIOS over TCP RFCs provide a number of mechanisms that can be used by a server to help do this job; among them are the mechanisms of name refresh and name challenge.

Name Refresh Well-behaved applications are expected not only to add their names to the NBNS's database but also to delete them from the database when no longer needed. Programs and PCs are not always well behaved, of course. Crashes occur and people use the ON/OFF switch with reckless abandon. Names that are not deleted at the time their application becomes unavailable need to be removed from the database on the NBNS's own initiative. The RFCs dictate that when an NBNS responds to a name registration request, it can tell the requesting station how long it will allow the entry to reside in the database. Unless the requestor's TCP stack "refreshes" the database entry before this time to live (TTL) period expires, the entry will be removed by the NBNS.

Used in combination, the TTL and name refresh mechanisms allow the NBNS to maintain its database in a reasonably consistent state with a tolerance—as set by the network administrator—of a few seconds to a few hours. (Note how the transaction load experienced by the NBNS will be increased if all applications have not just one name registration but a continual series of name refreshes as well.)

Name Challenge The RFCs also allow the NBNS to be proactive in policing the validity of its database entries. In order to determine whether a registered name is still in active use by the station whose IP address is recorded in the database entry, the NBNS is permitted to send a special "name challenge" packet to the TCP stack at that address. The TCP stack, in response, can either surrender or defend its right to the use of the name. While an NBNS could do its database pruning in this proactive fashion, the preferred approach is to have the individual stations do name refreshes as described above. Nonetheless, an NBNS can make good use of the name challenge mechanism to maintain database validity in a number of other situations.

Consider what might be done, for example, when a name registration request cannot be honored because of an apparent conflicting database entry. The entry could represent a true conflict, in which case the requesting application should be denied use of the name; or it could represent an out-of-date mapping, in which case the mapping should be expunged so that the new mapping can take its place. An NBNS must use the name challenge mechanism to resolve the issue unambiguously.

The problem of out-of-date entries has been exacerbated by the introduction of Dynamic Host Configuration Protocol (DHCP) into the enterprise networking world. DHCP allows a station (host) to receive all the operational parameters that govern its TCP behaviors from a server on the net, instead of receiving the parameters from a file on the station itself. For example, DHCP might be used to tell a station where its primary and secondary NBNSs are located.

DHCP requires the server to assign the station an IP address, and it allows the address to be different at each assignment. A station normally uses DHCP at startup time and presents the assigned address when it interacts with the NBNS to register all its names. Consider, for example, that a precipitous shutdown of the station keeps it from deregistering its names with the NBNS, and a subsequent reboot has it reregister its names under a possibly different IP address. In this case, the station is in conflict with itself. An NBNS must resolve this difficulty through the use of name challenges.

NBNS Implementations

NBNSs are relatively scarce commodities. The first commercially available NBNS, a fairly full-featured product developed to run as an application in OS/2, was developed at Ungermann-Bass (UB) in 1989. This NBNS was also a datagram distributor that employed a primary/secondary orientation for reliability and could be managed remotely from another OS/2-based station. Network Telesystems (NTS) licensed this technology from UB and enhanced it to the limits possible in such an application-based architecture.

Microsoft has recently implemented an NBNS as well. Their product, called Windows Internet Naming Service (WINS), is an application program that runs on top of Windows NT, and it provides some of the same services of UB's OS/2-based product. WINS does not provide datagram distribution, however, and it includes a number of nonstandard mechanisms that are needed to enforce certain Microsoft product strategies.

NetBIOS name servers dynamically register NetBIOS-to-IP mappings for P-, H-, and M-node workstations as they are initialized, and the servers respond to requests for those mappings. The NBNS is the simplest NetBIOS over IP solution to manage, as it removes the requirement for manual configuration of files, either on the client workstations or on the DNS.

Microsoft WINS

WINS is Microsoft's implementation of an NBNS. WINS only supports Microsoft's proprietary clients with its implementation of native NetBIOS and NetBIOS over TCP/IP.

How WINS Works Each Microsoft client needs to be configured with the IP address of a primary WINS server and, optionally, with the IP address of a secondary WINS server. Whenever a client (configured to use TCPBEUI and WINS) starts, it will attempt to register its NetBIOS name and IP address with the primary WINS server. The registration occurs when services or applications are started (for example, Workstation or Messenger) and is sent directly to the primary WINS server. If the name is not already registered to another client, the server responds with a message detailing the NetBIOS name that has been registered, and the name time to live (TTL).

If after attempting three times to register its name with the primary server and failing, the client will attempt to register its name using the secondary server. If the secondary server also fails to respond, the client will revert to broadcasting in order to register its name. The name registrations are made on a temporary basis, and the client is responsible for maintaining the lease of the registered name.

At one-eighths of the TTL, the client will attempt to refresh its name registration with the primary WINS server. If the client does not receive a response from the server, it will continue to attempt to refresh the registration every 2 minutes until half the TTL has expired. At this point it will repeat the procedure, but this time using the secondary WINS server.

With WINS enabled, the client acts as an H-node client for name registration. For resolution, it is H-node with a few modifications. The sequence used by a WINS client for name resolution is as follows:

- Check to see if it is the local machine name.
- Check the cache. (Any resolved name is placed in a cache for 10 minutes.)
- Try to use the primary WINS server. (Use the secondary server if the primary does not answer after three attempts.)
- Try a name query broadcast.
- Check the LMHOSTS file. (If the computer is configured to use LMHOSTS.)
- Try the HOSTS file.
- Try the DNS.

WINS Limitation According to RFC 1001/1002, a NetBIOS name server should support all group names. WINS, however, only keeps a list of IP addresses for group names ending in 0x1C. Warp Server domains however, are registered with a 0x00 suffix and, as such, are not stored by a WINS server. Therefore, when an IBM client requests an IP address from a WINS server, a broadcast address (an IP address of all 1s) is returned. This makes it difficult for IBM clients to communicate across a routed network when using WINS as the NBNS.

In addition, as mentioned, WINS does not provide datagram distribution, and a number of nonstandard mechanisms are included to enforce certain Microsoft product strategies. For example, only certain names are thought of as "Internet" names that can span workgroups. Such an approach often limits workgroup membership to stations that are physically adjacent (i.e., reachable by broadcast). DOS, Windows, and OS/2 clients that are equipped with TCP software that supports the full NetBIOS over TCP specification (P-node and H-node) can all use IBM or Microsoft redirector components in order to talk with either IBM Warp Server or Microsoft NT file servers through WINS. Because it is a Windows application component, WINS also suffers from the same architectural limitations as UB's OS/2 NBNS.

Network TeleSystems Shadow IPserver

Shadow IPserver is a software system for managing name and address assignments and desktop configuration information within a TCP/IP network. IPserver includes a robust set of network services offered through standards-based protocol interactions, such as:

- DHCP (Dynamic Host Configuration Protocol) service
- DNS (Domain Name Service)
- NBNS (NetBIOS Name Server) and NBDD (NetBIOS Datagram Distributor) services

The Shadow IPserver NBNS service is an integrated NetBIOS name server and datagram distributor. The IPserver NBNS service fully implements RFCs 1001 and 1002. The NBNS service provides name resolution services similar to those provided by Microsoft WINS.

NOTE. To use the datagram distributor, both the NBNS server and TCP/IP client stack must support datagram distribution.

If you plan to use the Shadow IPserver Datagram Distributor functionality, you can use the Network TeleSystems TCP Pro protocol stack on the DLS client. The TCP Pro protocol stack fully supports datagram distribution. The Microsoft Windows 95 and Windows NT protocol stacks do not support datagram distribution.

The Shadow IPserver NBNS server supports both IBM and Microsoft NetBIOS networks; the same NBNS server can be used with OS/2 Warp, DOS/Windows workstations with DOS LAN services installed, Windows 95, and Windows NT workstations. The idea of the NBNS is that instead of broadcasting the NetBIOS names to the whole IP subnet, the names to be registered are sent to a NBNS server. The NBNS server then checks if the name is already in use, and if not, the name is registered. All the future queries to that name will be resolved with one single query to the NBNS.

Summary

An NBNS can be used in networks built on the Internet's TCP/IP protocol suite to support NetBIOS-based client/server application connectivity, without the need for broadcast packet exchanges or maintenance of local (LMHOSTS) configuration files. In particular, an NBNS can support the use of Microsoft or IBM NOSs for enterprisewide file- and print-sharing services. An NBNS supports the dynamic maintenance of a NetBIOS name database and the dynamic distribution of NetBIOS datagrams among member stations so that administrators can define workgroup connectivity in terms of logical—not physical—topologies. NBNSs are just as critical a part of the network infrastructure as are routers, and they should be designed with performance, reliability, scalability, extensibility, and remote manageability in mind.

CHAPTER 5

Dynamic IP Routing Protocols

One of the basic functions of IP is its ability to form connections between different physical networks. This is due to the flexibility of IP to use almost any physical network below it, and to the IP routing algorithm. A system that does this is termed a *router*, although the older term *IP gateway* is also used.

> **NOTE:** The position of each protocol is often shown in the layered model of the TCP/IP protocol stack. The routing function is part of the internetwork layer, but the primary function of a routing protocol is to exchange *routing information with other routers*, and in this respect the protocols behave more like application protocols. Therefore, an attempt is not made to represent the position of these protocols in the protocol stack with a diagram as we do with the other protocols.

Basic IP Routing

The fundamental function for routers is present in *all* IP implementations:

An *incoming* IP datagram that specifies a destination IP address other than one of the local host's IP address(es), is treated as a normal *outgoing* IP datagram.

This outgoing IP datagram is subject to the IP routing algorithm of the local host, which selects the next hop for the datagram (the next host to send it to). (See Figure 5-1.) This new destination can be located on any of the physical networks to which the intermediate host is attached. If it is a physical network other than the one on which the host originally received the datagram, then the net result is that the intermediate host has *forwarded* the IP datagram from one physical network to another.

The normal IP routing table contains information about the locally attached networks and the IP addresses of other routers located on these networks, plus the networks they attach to. It can be extended with information on IP networks that are farther away, and can also contain a default route, but it still remains a table with limited information; that is, it represents only a part of the whole IP networks. That is why this kind of router is called a *router with partial routing information*.

Some considerations apply to these routers with partial information:

- They do not know about all IP networks.
- They allow local sites autonomy in establishing and modifying routes.
- A routing entry error in one of the routers can introduce inconsistencies, thereby making part of the network unreachable.

Some error reporting should be implemented by routers with partial information via the Internet Control Message Protocol (ICMP). They should be able to report the following errors back to the source host:

Dynamic IP Routing Protocols

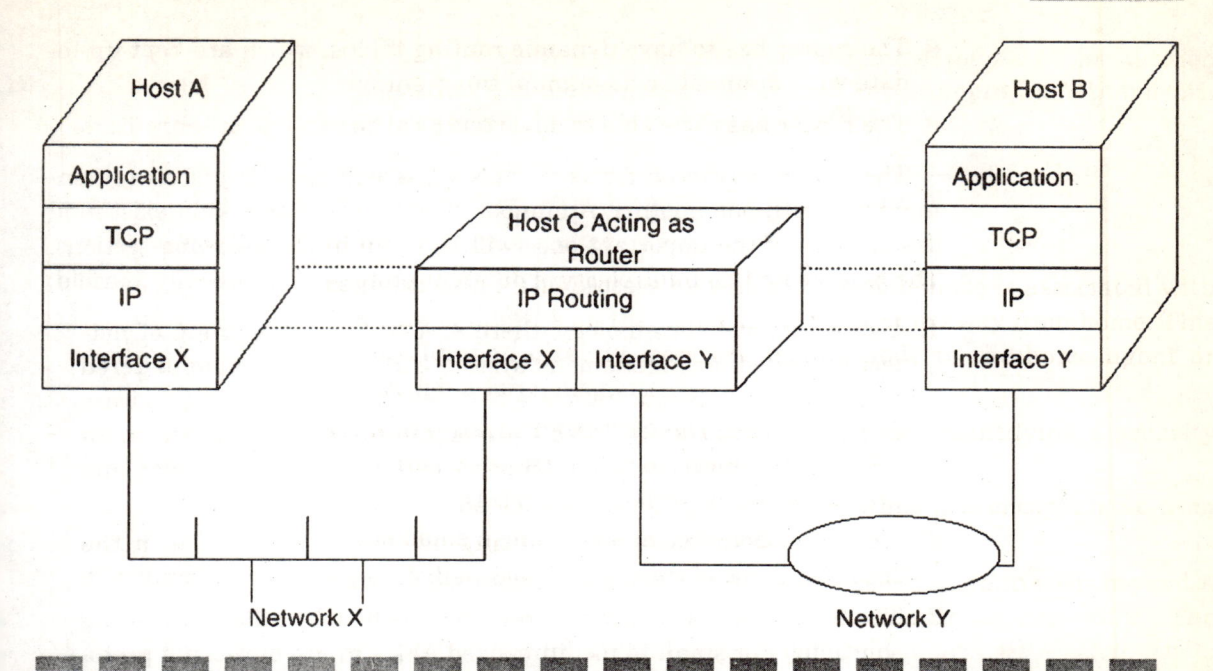

Figure 5-1 Router Operation of IP.

- Unknown IP destination network by an ICMP *Destination Unreachable* message.
- Redirection of traffic to more suitable routers by sending ICMP *Redirect* messages.
- Congestion problems (too many incoming datagrams for the available buffer space) by an ICMP *Source Quench* message.
- The Time-to-Live field of an IP datagram has reached zero. This is reported with an ICMP *Time Exceeded* message.
- Also, the following base ICMP operations and messages should be supported:
    Parameter problem
    Address mask
    Time stamp
    Information request/reply
    Echo request/reply
  A more intelligent router is required if:
- The router has to know routes to *all* possible IP networks, as was the case for the Internet backbone routers.

- The router has to have dynamic routing tables, which are kept up-to-date with minimal or no manual intervention.
- The router has to be able to advertise local changes to other routers.

These more advanced forms of routers use additional protocols to communicate with one another. A number of protocols of this kind exist, and descriptions of the important ones will be given in the following sections. The reasons for this multiplicity of different protocols are basically fourfold:

1. Using Internet terminology, there is a concept of a group of networks, called an autonomous system (AS), which is administered as a unit. The AS concept arose because the TCP/IP protocols were developed with the ARPANET already in place. Routing within an AS and routing outside an AS are treated as different issues and are addressed by different protocols.
2. Over two decades several routing protocols were tested in the Internet. Some of them performed well; others had to be abandoned.
3. The emergence of ASs of different sizes called for different routing solutions. For small to medium-sized ASs a group of routing protocols based upon Distance Vector, such as RIP, became very popular. However, such protocols do not perform well for large interconnected networks. Link-State protocols, such as OSPF, are much better suited for such networks.
4. To exchange routing information between ASs, border gateway protocols were developed.

Routing Processes

In TCP/IP software operating systems, routing protocols are often implemented using one of two daemons*:

1. *routed.* Pronounced "route D." This is a basic routing daemon for interior routing supplied with the majority of TCP/IP implementations. It uses the RIP protocol.

---

*Daemon, pronounced "demon," is a UNIX term for a background server process. Usually, daemons have names ending with a *d*. An analogous concept for MVS is a server running in a separate address space from TCP/IP; for VM it is a separate service virtual machine, for Windows NT it is a separate NT process, and so on. Although TCP/IP servers are often implemented differently on different platforms, the routed daemon is implemented like this on each of these platforms.

2. *gated.* Pronounced "gate D." This is a more sophisticated daemon on UNIX-based systems for interior and exterior routing. It can employ a number of additional protocols such as OSPF and BGP.

In TCP/IP hardware implementations, mainly in dedicated router operating systems such as the Common Code for IBM routers or Cisco's Internetworking Operating System (IOS), the routing protocols are implemented in the operating system.

Autonomous Systems

The dynamic routing protocols can be divided into two groups:

1. *Interior Gateway Protocols (IGPs).* Examples of these protocols are Open Short Path First (OSPF) and Routing Information Protocol (RIP).
2. Exterior Gateway Protocols (EGPs). An example of these routing protocols is Border Gateway Protocol Version 4 (BGP-4).

In this chapter, the term *gateway* is frequently used to imply an IP router.

Gateway protocols are referred to as interior or exterior, depending on whether they are used within or between ASs.

Interior gateway protocols allow routers to exchange routing information within an AS. Exterior gateway protocols allow the exchange of summary reachability information among separately administered ASs.

An autonomous system is defined as a logical portion of larger IP networks that are administered by a single authority. The AS would normally comprise the internetwork within an organization, and would be designated as such to allow communication over public IP networks with ASs belonging to other organizations. It is mandatory to register an organization's internetwork as an AS in order to use these public IP services.

Figure 5-2 illustrates three interconnected ASs. It shows that IGPs are used within each AS, and an EGP is used between the three ASs.

Routing Algorithms

Dynamic routing algorithms allow routers to exchange route or link information, from which the best paths to reach destinations in an inter-

Figure 5-2
Distance Vector—
Routing Table
Calculation.

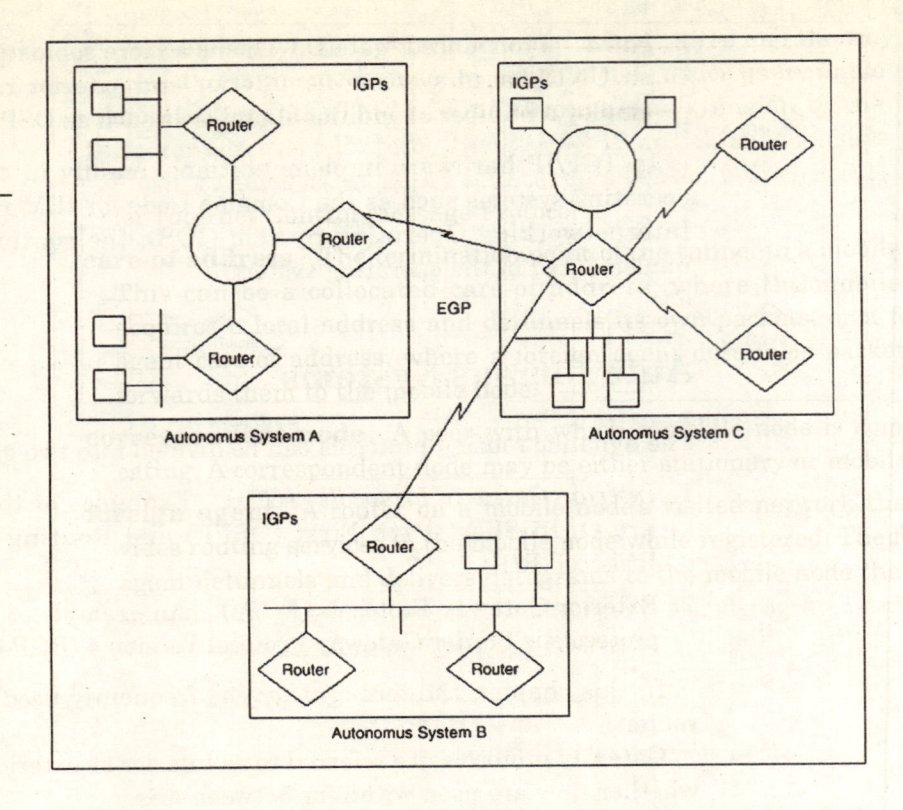

network are calculated. Static routing can also be used to supplement dynamic routing.

Static Routing

Static routing requires that routes be configured manually for each router, which constitutes one major reason why system administrators shy away from this technique, if they have a choice.

Static routing has the disadvantage that network reachability is not dependent on the existence and state of the network itself. If a destination is down, the static routes would remain in the routing table, and traffic would still be sent toward that destination in vain without awareness of an alternate path to the destination, if any.

To simplify the task of network administrators, normally the manual configuration of routes is avoided, especially in large networks. However, in certain circumstances static routing can be attractive. For example, static routes can be used in the following cases:

Dynamic IP Routing Protocols

- To define a default route, or a route that is not being advertised within a network
- To supplement or replace exterior gateway protocols when:
  Line tariffs between ASs make it desirable to avoid the cost of routing protocol traffic.
  Complex routing policies are to be implemented.
  It is desirable to avoid disruption caused by faulty exterior gateways in other ASs.

Distance Vector Routing

The principle behind *distance vector* routing is very simple. Each router in an internetwork maintains the distance from itself to every known destination in a *distance vector table.* Distance vector tables consist of a series of destinations (vectors) and costs (distances) to reach them and define the lowest costs to destinations at the time of transmission.

The distances in the tables are computed from information provided by neighbor routers. Each router transmits its own distance vector table across the shared network. The sequence of operations for doing this is as follows:

1. Each router is configured with an identifier and a cost for each of its network links. The cost is normally fixed at 1, reflecting a single hop, but can reflect some other measurement taken for the link such as the traffic or speed.
2. Each router initializes with a distance vector table containing 0 for itself, 1 for directly attached networks, and infinity for every other destination.
3. Each router periodically (typically every 30 seconds) transmits its distance vector table to each of its neighbors. It can also transmit the table when a link first comes up or when the table changes.
4. Each router saves the most recent table it receives from each neighbor and uses the information to calculate its own distance vector table.
5. The total cost to each destination is calculated by adding the cost reported to it in a neighbor's distance vector table to the cost of the link to that neighbor.
6. The distance vector table (the routing table) for the router is then created by taking the lowest cost calculated for each destination.

Figure 5-3 shows the distance vector tables for three routers within a simple internetwork.

The distance vector algorithm produces a stable routing table after a period directly related to the number of routers across the network. This period is referred to as the *convergence time* and represents the time it takes for distance vector information to traverse the network. In a large internetwork, this time may become too long to be useful.

Routing tables are recalculated if a changed distance vector table is received from a neighbor or if the state of a link to a neighbor changes. If a network link goes down, the distance vector tables that have been received over it are discarded and the routing table is recalculated.

The chief advantage of distance vector is that it is very easy to implement. There are also the following significant disadvantages:

- The instability caused by old routes persisting in an internetwork
- The long convergence time on large internetworks
- The limit to the size of an internetwork imposed by maximum hop counts

Figure 5-3
Distance Vector—
Routing Table Calculation.

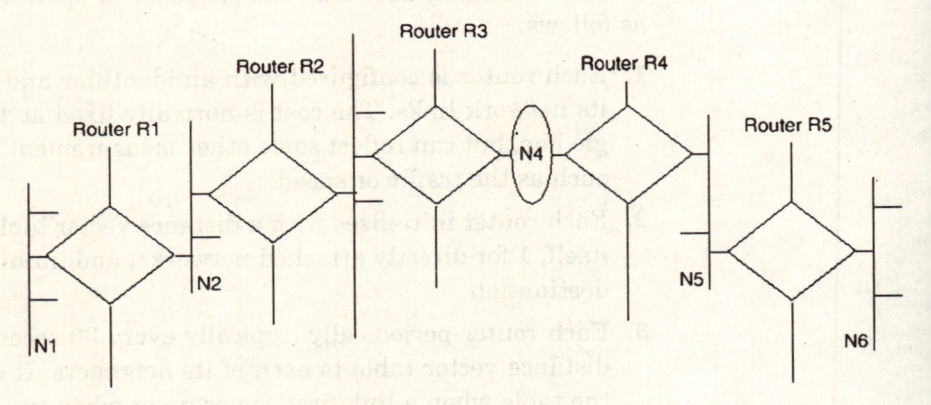

Router R2 Distance Vector Table

Net	Next Hop	Metric
N1	R1	2
N2	=	1
N3	=	1
N4	R3	2
N5	R3	3
N6	R3	4

Router R3 Distance Vector Table

Net	Next Hop	Metric
N1	R2	3
N2	R2	2
N3	=	1
N4	=	1
N5	R4	2
N6	R4	3

Router R4 Distance Vector Table

Net	Next Hop	Metric
N1	R3	4
N2	R3	3
N3	R3	2
N4	=	1
N5	=	1
N6	R5	2

Dynamic IP Routing Protocols

- The fact that distance vector tables are always transmitted even if their contents have not changed

Enhancements to the basic algorithm have evolved to overcome the first two of these problems. They are described in the following subsections.

The Count-to-Infinity Problem The basic distance vector algorithm will always allow a router to correctly calculate its distance vector table.

Figure 5-4 illustrates one of the problems of distance vector protocols known as *counting to infinity*. Counting to infinity occurs when a network becomes unreachable, but erroneous routes to that network persist because of the time for the distance vector tables to converge.

Figure 5-4
Counting to Infinity—Example Network.

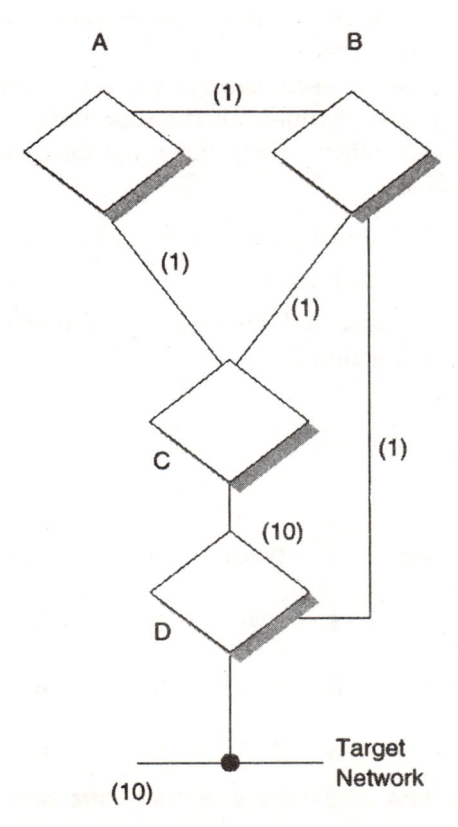

```
          A              B
           \   (1)      /
            \          /
             \        /
          (1) \      / (1)
               \    /
                \  /
                 C
                 |
                 | (10)
                 |
                 D ―――――― (1)
                 |
                 |       ● Target
                 |         Network
                (10)
```

(n) = Network Cost

The network shown in Figure 5-4 shows four routers interconnected by five network links. The networks all have a cost of 1, except for that from C to D, which has a cost of 10.

Each of the routers, A, B, C and D, has routes to all networks. The routes to the target network are as follows:

For D : Directly connected network. Metric 1.

For B : Route via D. Metric 2.

For C : Route via B. Metric 3.

For A : Route via B. Metric 3.

If the link from B to D fails, then all routes will be adjusted in time to use the link from C to D. However, the convergence time for this can be considerable.

Distance vector tables begin to change when B notices that the route to D has become unavailable. Figure 5-5 shows how the routes to the target network will change, assuming all routers send distance vector table updates at the same time.

The problem can be seen clearly. B is able to remove the failed route immediately because it times out the link. Other routers, however, have tables that contain references to this route for many update periods after the link has failed.

1. Initially A and C have a route to D via B.

2. The link from D to B fails.

3. A and C then send updates based on the route to D via B, even after the link has failed.

Time →							
D:	Direct 1	Direct 1	Direct 1	Direct 1	....	Direct 1	Direct 1
B:	Unreachable	C 4	C 5	C 6		C 11	C 12
C:	B 3	A 4	A 5	A 6		A 11	D 11
A:	B 3	C 4	C 5	C 6	....	C 11	C 12

Figure 5-5 Counting to Infinity.

Dynamic IP Routing Protocols

4. B then believes it has a route to D via either A or C. But, in reality, it does not have such a route, as the routes are vestiges of the previous route via B, which has failed.

5. A and C then see that the route via B has failed but believe a route exists via each other.

Slowly the distance vector tables converge, but not until the metrics have counted up, in theory, to infinity. To avoid this happening, practical implementations of distance vector have a low value for infinity; for example, RIP uses a maximum metric of 16.

The manner in which the metrics increment to infinity gives rise to the term *counting to infinity*. It occurs because A and C are engaged in an extended period of mutual deception, each claiming to be able to get to the target network D via each other.

Split Horizon Counting to infinity can easily be prevented if a route to a destination is never reported back in the distance vector table that is sent to the neighbor from which the route was learned. *Split horizon* is the term used for this technique.

The incorporation of split horizon would modify the sequence of distance vector table changes to that shown in Figure 5-6. The tables can be seen to converge considerably faster than before (see Figure 5-6).

Split Horizon with Poison Reverse *Poison reverse* is an enhancement to split horizon, whereby routes learned from a neighbor router are reported back to it, but with a metric of infinity (that is, network unreachable).

Figure 5-6
Split Horizon.

Time								
D:	Direct	1	Direct	1	Direct	1	Direct	1
B:	Unreachable		Unreachable		Unreachable		C	12
C:	B	3	A	4	D	11	D	11
A:	B	3	C	4	Unreachable		C	12

Note: Faster Routing Table Convergence

The use of poison reverse is safer than split horizon alone because it breaks erroneous looping routes immediately. If two routers receive routes pointing at each other, and they are advertised with a metric of infinity, the routes will be eliminated immediately as unreachable. If the routes are not advertised in this way, they must be eliminated by the timeout that results from a route not being reported by a neighbor router for several periods (for example, six periods for RIP).

Poison reverse does have one disadvantage. It significantly increases the size of distance vector tables that must be exchanged between neighbor routers, because all routes are included in the distance vector tables. While this is generally not a problem on LANs, it can cause real problems on point-to-point connections in large internetworks.

Triggered Updates   Split horizon with poison reverse will break routing loops involving two routers. It is still possible, however, for there to be routing loops involving three or more routers. For example, A may believe it has a route through B, B through C, and C through A. This loop can only be eliminated by the timeout that results from counting to infinity.

Triggered updates are designed to reduce the convergence time for routing tables—and hence reduce the period during which such erroneous loops are present in an internetwork.

When a router changes the cost for a route in its distance vector table, it must send the modified table immediately to neighbor routers. This simple mechanism ensures that topology changes in a network are propagated quickly rather than at a rate dependent on normal periodic updates.

Link-State Routing

The growth in the size of internetworks in recent years has necessitated the replacement of distance vector routing algorithms with alternatives that address the shortcomings identified in the previous section entitled "Distance Vector Routing."

These new protocols have been based on link-state or shortest-path-first algorithms (see "Shortest-Path-First (SPF)," below). The best example is the OSPF Interior Gateway Protocol.

The principle behind link-state routing is straightforward, although its implementation can be complex:

Dynamic IP Routing Protocols

- Routers are responsible for contacting neighbors and learning their identities.
- Routers construct link-state packets that contain lists of network links and their associated costs.
- Link-state packets are transmitted to all routers in a network.
- All routers therefore have an identical list of links in a network and can construct identical topology maps.
- The maps are used to compute the best routes to all destinations.

Routers contact neighbors by sending hello packets on their network interfaces. Hello packets are sent directly to neighbors on point-to-point links and nonbroadcast networks. On LANs, hello packets are sent to a predefined group or multicast IP address that can be received by all routers. Neighbors who receive hellos from a router should reply with hello packets that include the identity of that originating router. Once neighbors have been contacted in this way, link-state information can be exchanged.

Link-state information is sent in the form of *link-state packets* (LSPs), also known as link-state advertisements. LSPs provide the database from which network topology maps can be calculated at each router. LSPs are normally sent only under the following specific circumstances:

- When a router discovers a new neighbor
- When a link to a neighbor goes down
- When the cost of a link changes
- When basic refresh packets are sent every 30 minutes

Once a router has generated an LSP, it *must* be received successfully by all other routers in a network. If this does not happen, routers on the network will calculate network topology based on incorrect link-state information.

Distribution of LSPs would normally be on the basis of each router's routing tables. However, this leads to a *chicken and egg* situation. Routing tables would rely on LSPs for their creation, and LSPs would rely on routing tables for their distribution. A simple scheme called *flooding* overcomes this and ensures that LSPs are successfully distributed to all routers in a network.

Flooding requires that a router that receives an LSP transmits it to all neighbors except the one from which it was received. All LSPs must be explicitly acknowledged to ensure successful delivery, and they are sequenced and time-stamped to ensure duplicates are not received and retransmitted.

When a router receives an LSP, it looks in its database to check the sequence number of the last LSP from the originator. If the sequence number is the same as, or earlier than, the sequence number of the LSP in its database, then the LSP is discarded. Otherwise the LSP is added to the database.

The flooding process ensures that all routers in a network have the same link-state information. All routers are then able to compute the same shortest-path tree topology map for the network (see the discussion below under "Shortest-Path-First (SPF)"), and hence they select best routes to all destinations.

Shortest-Path-First (SPF) SPF is an algorithm that each router in the same AS has an identical link-state database, leading to an identical graphical representation by calculating a tree of shortest paths with the router itself as root. The tree is called the shortest-path tree, giving an entire path to any destination network or host. Figure 5-7 shows the shortest-path-tree example from router A. Each router, A, B, C, D, and E, has an identical link-state database, as shown. Router A generates its own shortest-path tree by calculating a tree of shortest paths, with router A itself as root.

Interior Gateway Protocols (IGPs)

There are many standard and proprietary interior gateway protocols. Products by IBM and Cisco, such as operating systems and routers, support only standard IGPs. This section describes the following IGPs:

- Routing Information Protocol (RIP)
- Routing Information Protocol, Version 2 (RIP-2)
- Open Shortest Path First (OSPF)

Routing Information Protocol (RIP)

RIP is an Internet Architecture Board (IAB) standard protocol; its status is elective. This means that it is one of several interior gateway protocols available, and it may or may not be implemented on a system. If a

Dynamic IP Routing Protocols

Figure 5-7
Shortest-Path-First (SPF) Example.

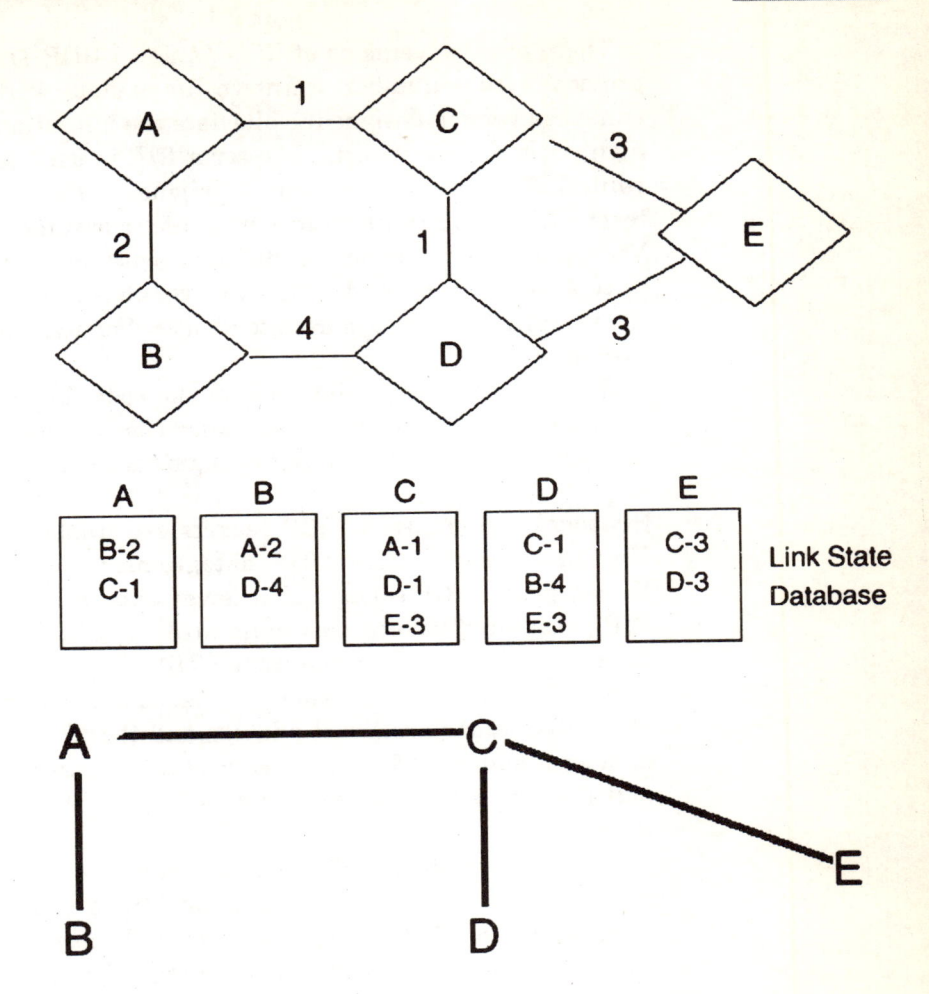

A	B	C	D	E	
B-2 C-1	A-2 D-4	A-1 D-1 E-3	C-1 B-4 E-3	C-3 D-3	Link State Database

system does implement it, however, the implementation should be in line with the RFC 1058.

RIP is based on the Xerox PUP and XNS routing protocols. The RFC was issued after many RIP implementations had been completed. For this reason, some do not include all the enhancements to the basic distance vector routing protocol (such as poison reverse and triggered updates).

RIP is a distance vector routing protocol more suitable for small networks than OSPF (see the discussion under "Open Shortest Path First (OSPF)" below). This is because of the shortcomings of distance vector routing identified in the section "Distance Vector Routing," above.

There are two versions of RIP. Version 1 (RIP-1) is a widely deployed protocol with a number of known limitations. Version 2 (RIP-2) is an enhanced version designed to alleviate the limitations of RIP while being highly compatible with it. The term RIP is used to refer to Version 1, while RIP-2 refers to Version 2. Whenever the reader encounters the term RIP in TCP/IP literature, it is safe to assume that it is referring to Version 1 unless explicitly stated otherwise. Such nomenclature is used in this section except when the two versions are being compared, when the term RIP-1 is always used to identify Version 1 to avoid possible confusion.

RIP is very widely used because the code (known as ROUTED) was incorporated in the Berkeley Software Distribution (BSD) UNIX operating system and in other UNIX systems based on it.

Protocol Description RIP packets are transmitted on a network in *User Datagram Protocol* (UDP) datagrams, which in turn are carried in IP datagrams. RIP sends and receives datagrams using UDP port 520. RIP datagrams have a maximum size of 512 octets, and tables larger than this must be sent in multiple UDP datagrams.

RIP datagrams are normally broadcast onto LANs using the LAN MAC all-stations broadcast address and the IP network or subnetwork broadcast address. They are specifically addressed on point-to-point and multi-access non-broadcast networks, using the destination router IP address.

Routers normally run RIP in *active mode*; that is, they advertise their own distance vector tables and update them based on advertisements from neighbors. End nodes, if they run RIP, normally operate in *passive* (or *silent*) mode; that is, they update their distance vector tables on the basis of advertisements from neighbors, but they do not in turn advertise them.

RIP specifies two packet types: request and response.

A request packet is sent by routers to ask neighbors to send part of their distance vector table (if the packet contains destinations), or all their table (if no destinations have been specified).

A response packet is sent by routers to advertise their distance vector table in the following circumstances:

- Every 30 seconds
- In response to a request packet
- When distance vector tables change (if triggered updates are supported)

Dynamic IP Routing Protocols

Active and passive systems listen for all response packets and update their distance vector tables accordingly. A route to a destination, computed from a neighbor's distance vector table, is kept until an alternate is found with lower cost or until it is not readvertised in six consecutive RIP responses. In this case, the route is timed out and deleted.

When RIP is used with IP, the address family identifier is 2 and the address fields are 4 octets. To reduce problems of counting to infinity, the maximum metric is 16 (unreachable) and directly connected networks are defined as having a metric of 1.

The RIP packet format for IP is shown in Figure 5-8.

RIP makes no provision for passing subnet masks with its distance vector tables. A router receiving a RIP response must already have subnet mask information to allow it to interpret the network identifier and host identifier portions of the IP address correctly.

In the absence of subnet mask information, a router will interpret routes as best as it can. If it knows an IP network has a specific subnet mask, it will interpret all other route information for that network on the basis of that single mask. If it receives a packet with bits set in the field

Figure 5-8
RIP Message.

Number of Octets	Field	Notes
1	Command	Request = 1, Response = 2
1	Version	Version = 1
2	Reserved	
2	2	Address Family Identifier for IP
2	Reserved	
4	IP Address	May be Repeated
8	Reserved	
4	Metric	

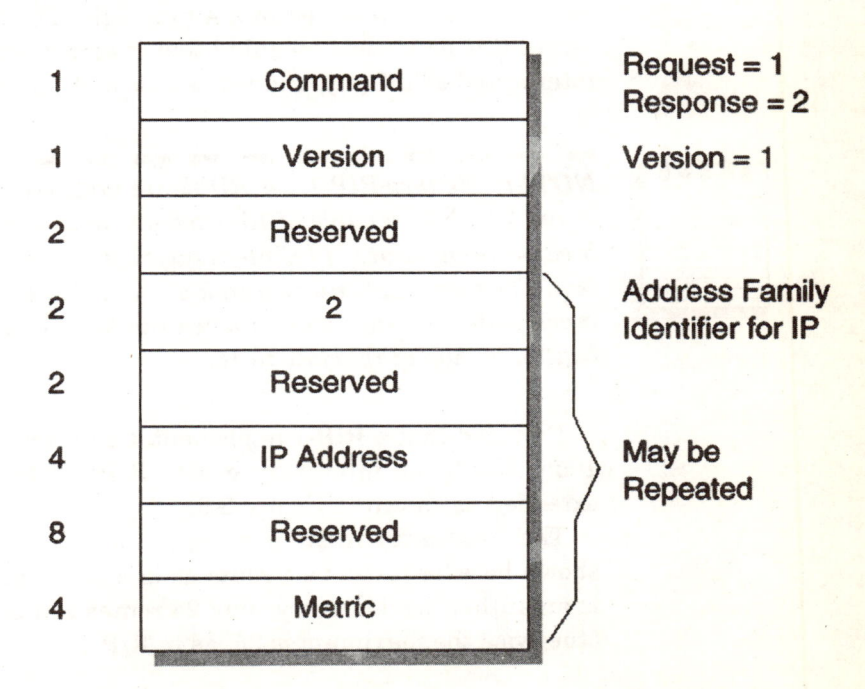

that it regards as the host field, it will interpret it as a route to a host with a mask of 255.255.255.255.

The above makes it impossible for RIP to be used in an internetwork with variable-length subnet masks.

Routing Information Protocol Version 2 (RIP-2)   RIP-2 is a draft standard protocol. Its status is elective.

RIP-2 extends RIP-1. It is less powerful than other recent IGPs such as OSPF (see "Open Shortest Path First (OSPF)," below), but it has the advantages of easy implementation and lower overheads. The intention of RIP-2 is to provide a straightforward replacement for RIP that can be used on small to medium-sized networks, can be employed in the presence of variable subnetting or supernetting, and importantly, can interoperate with RIP-1. In fact, the major reason for developing and deploying RIP-2 was the use of Classless Inter-Domain Routing (CIDR), which cannot be used in conjunction with RIP-1.

RIP-2 takes advantage of the fact that half of the bytes in a RIP-1 message are reserved (must be 0) and that the original RIP-1 specification was well designed with enhancements in mind, particularly in the use of the version field. One notable area where this is not the case is the interpretation of the metric field. RIP-1 specifies it as being a value between 0 and 16 stored in a 4-byte field. For compatibility, RIP-2 preserves this definition, meaning that it agrees with RIP-1 that 16 is to be interpreted as infinity, and wastes most of this field.

> ***NOTE:*** *Neither RIP-1 nor RIP-2 are properly suited for use as an IGP in an AS where a value of 16 is too low to be regarded as infinity, because high values of infinity exacerbate the counting to infinity problem. The more sophisticated link-state protocol used in OSPF provides a much better routing solution when the AS is large enough to have a legitimate hop count close to 16.*

Provided that a RIP-1 implementation obeys the specification in RFC 1058, RIP-2 can interoperate with RIP-1. The RIP message format is extended as shown in Figure 5-9.

The first entry in the message can be an authentication entry, as shown here, or it can be a route as in a RIP-1 message. If the first entry is an authentication entry, only 24 routes can be included in a message; otherwise the maximum is 25, as in RIP-1.

Dynamic IP Routing Protocols

Figure 5-9
RIP-2 Message.

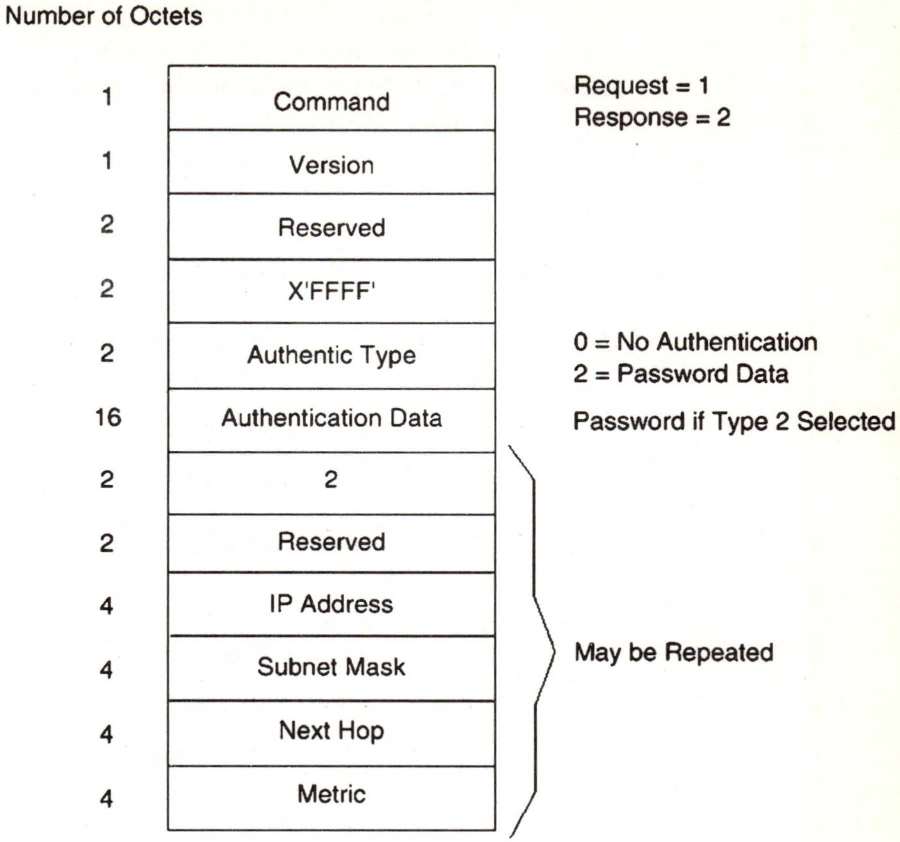

Number of Octets	Field	Notes
1	Command	Request = 1, Response = 2
1	Version	
2	Reserved	
2	X'FFFF'	
2	Authentic Type	0 = No Authentication, 2 = Password Data
16	Authentication Data	Password if Type 2 Selected
2	2	
2	Reserved	
4	IP Address	
4	Subnet Mask	May be Repeated
4	Next Hop	
4	Metric	

The fields in a RIP-2 message are the same as for a RIP-1 message except as follows:

Version   Is 2. This tells RIP-1 routers to ignore the fields designated as "must be zero." (If the value is 1, RIP-1 routers are required to discard messages with non-zero values in these fields since the messages originate with a router claiming to be RIP-1-compliant but sending non-RIP-1 messages.)

Address Family   May be X'FFFF' in the first entry only, indicating that this entry is an authentication entry.

Authentication Type   Defines how the remaining 16 bytes are to be used. The only defined types are 0, indicating no authentication, and 2, indicating that the field contains password data.

Authentication Data   The password is 16 bytes, plain-text ASCII, left-adjusted and padded with ASCII NULLs (X'00').

Route Tag   Is a field intended for communicating information about the origin of the route information. It is intended for interoperation between RIP and other routing protocols. RIP-2 implementations must preserve this tag, but RIP-2 does not further specify how it is to be used.

Subnet Mask   The subnet mask associated with the subnet referred to by this entry.

Next Hop   A recommendation about the next hop that the router should use to send datagrams to the subnet or host given in this entry.

To ensure safe interoperation with RIP, RFC 1723 specifies the following restrictions for RIP-2 routers sending over a network interface where a RIP-1 router may hear and operate on the RIP messages.

1. Information internal to one network must never be advertised into another network.
2. Information about a more specific subnet cannot be advertised where RIP-1 routers would consider it a host route.
3. *Supernet* routes (routes with a subnet mask shorter than the natural or unsubnetted network mask) must not be advertised where they could be misinterpreted by RIP-1 routers.

RIP-2 also supports the use of multicasting rather than simple broadcasting. This can reduce the load on hosts that are not listening for RIP-2 messages. This option is configurable for each interface to ensure optimum use of RIP-2 facilities when a router connects mixed RIP-1/RIP-2 subnets to RIP-2-only subnets. Similarly, the use of authentication in mixed environments can be configured to suit local requirements.

RIP-2 is implemented in recent versions of the *gated* daemon, often termed *gated Version 3*.

RIPng for IPv6

RIPng is intended to allow routers to exchange information for computing routes through an IPv6-based network. It is documented in RFC2080.

Protocol Description   RIPng is a distance vector protocol and similar to RIP-2 in IPv4 (see "Distance Vector Routing," above). RIPng is a UDP-based protocol and sends and receives datagrams on UDP port number

Dynamic IP Routing Protocols

521. RIPng should be implemented only in routers; IPv6 provides other mechanisms for router discovery. Any router that uses RIPng is assumed to have interfaces to one or more networks; otherwise, it isn't really a router. RIPng has the following limitations, just as those of RIP-2 in IPv4, which are specific to a distance vector protocol:

- There is a limited number of networks, where the longest path is 15.
- RIPng depends on counting to infinity. The resolution of a loop would require much more time (refer to "The Count-to-Infinity Problem," above).
- There is a fixed metric. It is not appropriate for situations where routers need to be chosen based on real-time applications.

The RIPng message format is extended, as shown in Figure 5-10. The basic blocks of a RIPng message are the following:

Command   It is the same idea as in RIP-1 and RIP-2 in IPv4 (see also Figures 5-8 and 5-9).

Route Table Entry (RTE)   It is a different concept than RIP-1 and RIP-2. RIPng provides the ability to specify the immediate next hop IPv6 address to which packets to a destination specified by an RTE should be forwarded in much the same way as RIP-1 and RIP-2 (see RTE in Figure 5-11).

In RIP-2, each route table entry has a next-hop field. Including a next-hop field for each RTE in RIPng would nearly double the size of the RTE. Therefore, in RIPng, the next hop is specified by a special RTE and applies to all of the address RTEs following the next-hop RTE until the end of the message or until another next-hop RTE is encountered (see Figure 5-12).

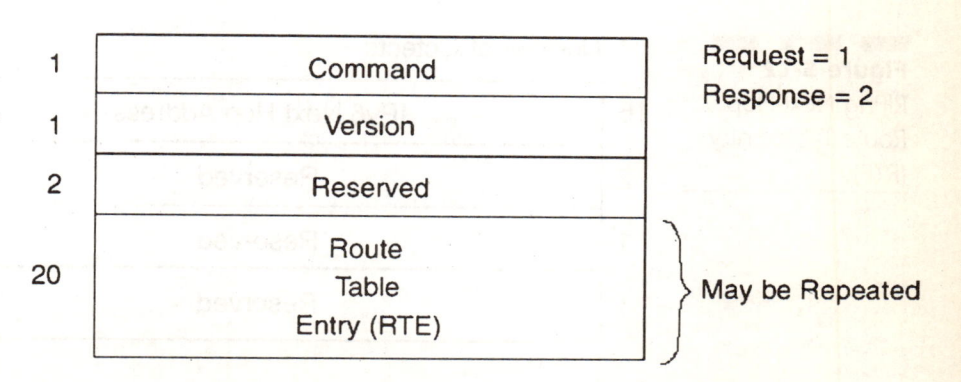

Figure 5-10
RIPng Message.

Bytes	Field	
1	Command	Request = 1, Response = 2
1	Version	
2	Reserved	
20	Route Table Entry (RTE)	May be Repeated

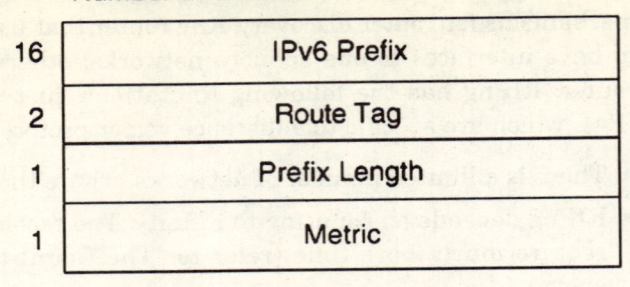

Figure 5-11
RIPng Route Table Entry (RTE).

Number of Octects

Octets	Field	Range
16	IPv6 Prefix	
2	Route Tag	
1	Prefix Length	Between 0 and 128
1	Metric	Between 1 and 15 Infinity = 16

Next-Hop Route Table Entry (RTE)   The next-hop RTE is identified by a value of 0xFF in the metric field of an RTE. The prefix field specifies the IPv6 address of the next hop.

Open Shortest Path First (OSPF)

The Open Shortest Path First (OSPF) V2 Protocol is an interior gateway protocol defined in RFC 2328. A report on the use of OSPF V2 is contained in RFC 1246, "Experience with the OSPF Protocol."

OSPF is an IAB standard protocol; its status is elective. However, RFC 1812, "Requirements for IPv4 Routers," lists OSPF as the only required dynamic routing protocol.

OSPF is important because it has a number of features not found in other interior gateway protocols. Support for these additional features makes OSPF the preferred choice for new IP internetwork implementations, especially in large networks. The following features are covered within OSPF; it:

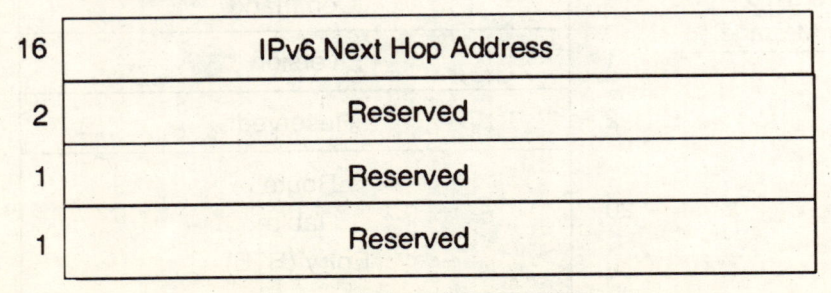

Figure 5-12
RIPng Next-Hop Route Table Entry (RTE).

Number of Octects

Octets	Field	
16	IPv6 Next Hop Address	
2	Reserved	
1	Reserved	
1	Reserved	0xFF

Dynamic IP Routing Protocols

- Supports *type-of-service* (*TOS*) routing*
- Provides *load balancing*
- Allows site partitioning into subsets by using *areas*
- Has information exchange between routers which requires *authentication* (also covered in RIP-2; see "Routing Information Protocol Version 2 (RIP-2)," above)
- Supports *host-specific* routes as well as network-specific routes
- Reduces table maintenance overhead to a minimum by implementing a *designated router*
- Allows definition of *virtual links* to provide support to a noncontiguous area
- Allows the usage of *variable-length subnet masks* (also covered in RIP-2; see "Routing Information Protocol Version 2 (RIP-2)," above)
- Will *import* RIP and EGP routes into its database

OSPF Terminology OSPF uses specific terminology which must be understood before the protocol can be described.

AREAS OSPF internetworks are organized into *areas*. An OSPF area consists of a number of networks and routers that are logically grouped together. Areas can be defined on a per-location or a per-region basis, or they can be based on administrative boundaries. All OSPF networks consist of at least one area, the backbone, plus as many additional areas as are demanded by network topology and other design criteria. Within an OSPF area, all routers maintain the same topology database, exchanging link-state information to maintain their synchronization. This ensures that all routers calculate the same network map for the area.

Information about networks outside an area is summarized by an *area border* or *AS boundary routers* (see "Intra-Area, Area Border and AS Boundary Routers," below) and flooded into the area. Routers within an area have no knowledge of the topology of networks outside the area, only of routes to destinations provided by area borders and AS boundary routers.

The importance of the area concept is that it limits the size of the topology database that must be held by routers. This has direct impact on the processing to be carried out by each router, and on the amount of link-state information that must be flooded into individual networks.

---

*The use of TOS has been dropped in recent OSPF implementations.

THE OSPF BACKBONE All OSPF networks must contain at least one area, the *backbone,* which is assigned an area identifier of 0.0.0.0. (This is a different definition from IP address 0.0.0.0.) The backbone has all the properties of an area, and has the additional responsibility of distributing routing information between areas attached to it. Normally an OSPF backbone should be contiguous, that is with all backbone routers attached to one another. This may not be possible because of network topology, in which case backbone continuity must be maintained by the use of *virtual links* (see below). Virtual links are backbone router-to-backbone router connections that traverse a nonbackbone area.

Routers within the backbone operate identically to other intra-area routers and maintain full topology databases for the backbone area.

INTRA-AREA, AREA BORDER, AND AS BOUNDARY ROUTERS There are three possible types of routers in an OSPF network. Figure 5-13 shows the location of intra-area, area border, and AS boundary routers within an OSPF internetwork.

1. *Intra-Area Routers* Routers that are situated entirely within an OSPF area are called *intra-area routers.* All intra-area routers flood router-link advertisements into the area to define the links they are attached to. If they are elected designated or backup-designated routers (see "Designated and Backup Designated Router," below), they also flood network links advertisements to define the identity of all routers attached to the network. Intra-area routers maintain a topology database for the area in which they are situated.

2. *Area Border Routers* Routers that connect two or more areas are referred to as *area border routers.* Area border routers maintain topology databases for each area to which they are attached, and exchange link-state information with other routers in those areas. Area border routers also flood summary link-state advertisements into each area to inform them of inter-area routes.

3. *AS Boundary Routers* Routers that are situated at the periphery of an OSPF internetwork and exchange reachability information with routers in other ASs using exterior gateway protocols are called *AS boundary routers.* Routers that import static routes or routes from other IGPs, such as RIP, into an OSPF network are also AS boundary routers. AS boundary routers are responsible for flooding AS external link-state advertisements into all areas within the AS to inform them of external routes.

Dynamic IP Routing Protocols

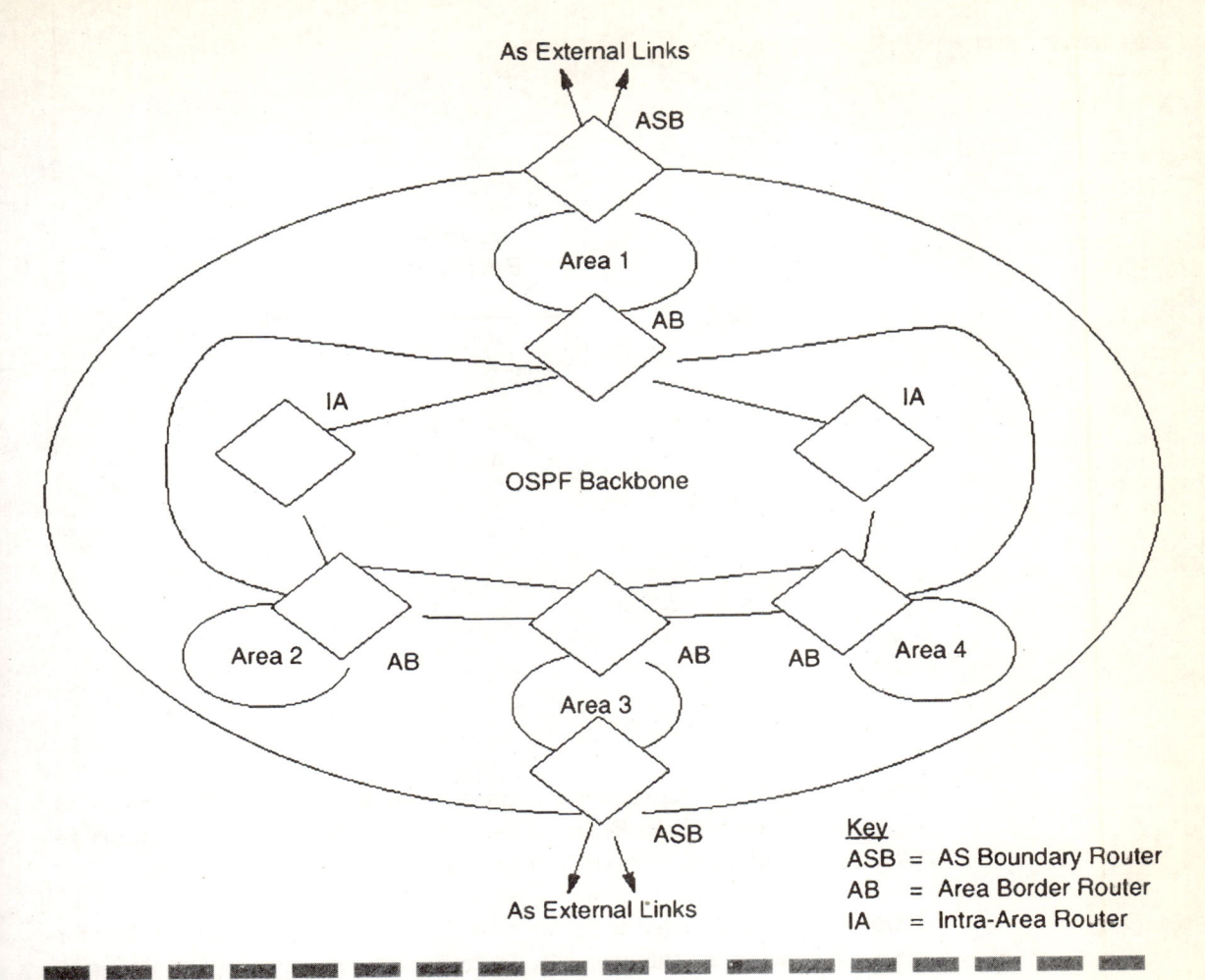

Figure 5-13 OSPF Network.

VIRTUAL LINK A virtual link is part of the backbone. Its endpoints are two area border routers that share a common nonbackbone area. The link is treated as a point-to-point link with metrics cost equal to the intra-area metrics between the endpoints of the links. The routing through the virtual link is done using normal intra-area routing (see Figure 5-14). Virtual endpoints are area border routers (ABRs) that share Area 2 as a transit area.

Figure 5-14
OSPF Virtual Link, Transit Area.

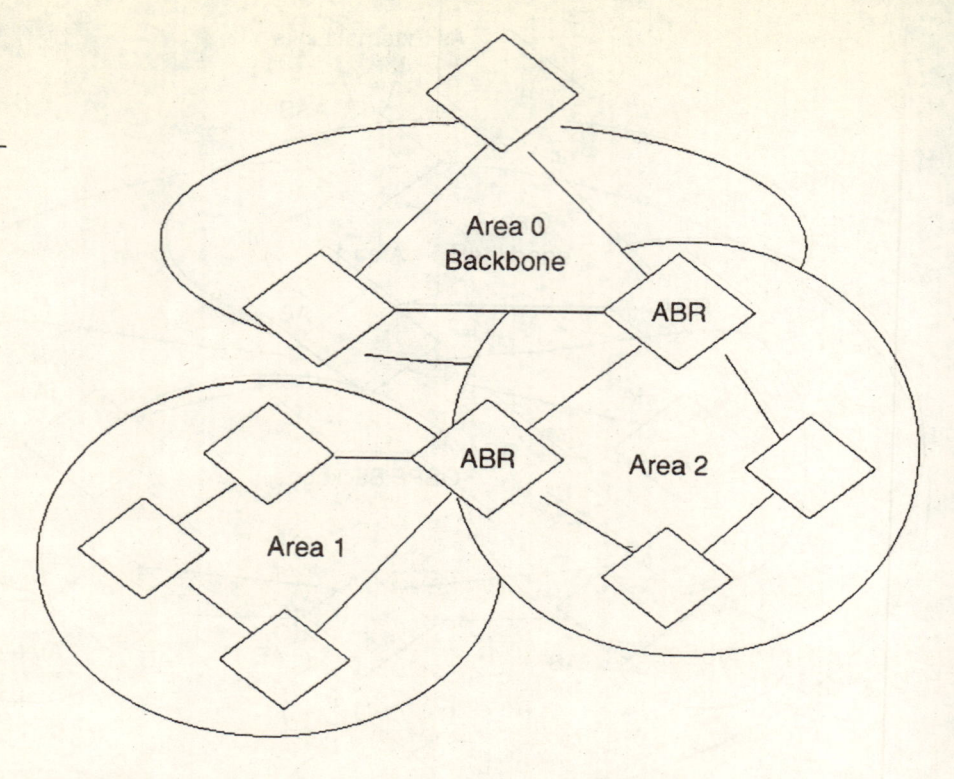

TRANSIT AREA A transit area is one through which a virtual route is physically connected. In Figure 5-14, Area 2 is transit area. In Figure 5-14, virtual endpoints are ABRs that share area 2 as a transit area.

STUB AREA A stub area is an area configured to use default routing for inter-AS routing. A stub area can be configured where there is only a single exit from the area, or where any exit can be used without preference for routing to destinations outside the autonomous system. By default, inter-AS routes are copied to all areas, so the use of stub areas can reduce the storage requirements of routers within those areas for autonomous systems where a lot of inter-AS routes are defined.

NEIGHBOR ROUTERS Neighbor routers are two routers that have interfaces to a common network. On multi-access networks, neighbors are dynamically discovered by the Hello protocol.

Each neighbor is described by a state machine, which describes the conversation between this router and its neighbor. A brief outline of the meaning of the states follows. See the section immediately following for a definition of the terms *adjacency* and *designated router*.

Down Initial state of a neighbor conversation. It indicates that there has been no recent information received from the neighbor.

Attempt A neighbor on a nonbroadcast network appears down and an attempt should be made to contact it by sending regular hello packets.

Init A hello packet has recently been received from the neighbor. However, bidirectional communication has not yet been established with the neighbor (that is, the router itself did not appear in the neighbor's hello packet).

2-way In this state, communication between the two routers is bidirectional. Adjacencies can be established, and neighbors in this state or higher are eligible to be elected as (backup) designated routers.

ExStart The two neighbors are about to create an adjacency.

Exchange The two neighbors are telling each other what they have in their topological databases.

Loading The two neighbors are synchronizing their topological databases.

Full The two neighbors are now fully adjacent; their databases are synchronized.

Various events cause a change of state. For example, if a router receives a hello packet from a neighbor that is `down`, the neighbor's state changes to `init`, and an inactivity timer is started. If the timer fires (that is, if no further OSPF packets are received before it expires), the neighbor will return to the `down` state. A complete description of the states and information on the events that cause state changes can be found in RFC 2173.

ADJACENT ROUTER Neighbor routers can become *adjacent*. They are said to be adjacent when they have synchronized their topology databases through the exchange of link-state information. Link-state information is exchanged only between adjacent routers, not between neighbor routers.

And not all neighbor routers become adjacent. Neighbors on point-to-point links do so, but on multi-access networks adjacencies are only formed between individual routers and the designated and backup designated routers.

The exchange of link-state information between neighbors can create significant amounts of network traffic. Limiting the number of adjacencies on multi-access networks in this way achieves considerable reductions in network traffic.

DESIGNATED AND BACKUP DESIGNATED ROUTER All multi-access networks have a *designated* and a *backup designated router.* These routers are elected automatically for each network once neighbor routers have been discovered by the Hello protocol.

The designated router performs two key roles for a network:

1. It generates network-link advertisements that list the routers attached to a multi-access network.
2. It forms adjacencies with all routers on a multi-access network and therefore becomes the focal point for forwarding of all link-state advertisements.

The backup designated router forms the same adjacencies as the designated router. It therefore has the same topology database and is able to assume designated router functions should it detect that the designated router has failed.

PHYSICAL NETWORK TYPES All OSPF areas consist of aggregates of networks linked by routers. OSPF categorizes networks into the following different types.

Point-to-Point Network Point-to-point networks directly link two routers.

Multi-Access Network Multi-access networks are those that support the attachment of more than two routers. They are further subdivided into two types:
- Broadcast
- Nonbroadcast

Point-to-Multipoint Network Point-to-multipoint networks describe a special case of multiaccess nonbroadcast where not every router has a direct connection to any other router (also referred to as *partial mesh*).

Broadcast networks have the capability of directing OSPF packets to all attached routers, using an address that is recognized by all of them. An Ethernet LAN and token-ring LAN are examples of a broadcast multi-access network.

Nonbroadcast networks do not have this capability and all packets must be specifically addressed to routers on the network. This requires that routers on a nonbroadcast network be configured with the addresses of neighbors. Examples of a nonbroadcast multi-access network are the X.25 public data network or a frame relay network

INTERFACE The connection between a router and one of its attached networks. Each interface has state information associated with it that is obtained from the underlying lower-level protocols and the OSPF protocol itself. A brief description of each state is given here. For more details, and for information on the events that cause an interface to change its state, refer to RFC 2173.

Down The interface is unavailable. This is the initial state of an interface.

Loopback The interface is looped back to the router. It cannot be used for regular data traffic.

Waiting The router is trying to determine the identity of the designated router or its backup.

Point-to-Point The interface is to a point-to-point network or is a virtual link. The router forms an adjacency with the router at the other end.

NOTE: The interfaces do not need IP addresses. Since the remainder of the internetwork has no practical need to see the routers' interfaces to the point-to-point link, just the interfaces to other networks, any IP addresses for the link would be needed only for communication between the two routers. To conserve the IP address space, the routers can dispense with IP addresses on the link. This has the effect of making the two routers appear to be one to IP, but this has no ill effects. Such a link is called an unnumbered link.

DR Other The interface is on a multi-access network but this router is neither the designated router nor its backup. The router forms adjacencies with the designated router and its backup.

Backup The router is the backup designated router. It will be promoted to designated router if the present designated router fails. The router forms adjacencies with every other router on the network.

DR The router itself is the designated router. The router forms adjacencies with every other router on the network. The router must also originate a network-link advertisement for the network node.

TYPE-OF-SERVICE (TOS) METRICS In each type of link-state advertisement, different metrics can be advertised for each IP type of service. A metric for TOS 0 (used for OSPF routing protocol packets) must always be specified. Metrics for other TOS values can be specified; if they are not, these metrics are assumed to be equal to the metric specified for TOS 0.*

LINK-STATE DATABASE Also called the *directed graph* or the *topological database,* the link-state database is created from the link-state advertisements generated by the routers in the area.

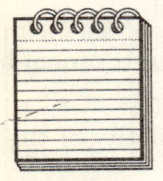

> *NOTE:* RFC 2328 uses the term link-state database *in preference to* topological database. *The former term has the advantage in that it describes the contents of the database; the latter is more descriptive of the purpose of the database: to describe the topology of the area. The term* topological database *was used previously in this chapter for this reason, but for the remainder of this section, where the operation of OSPF is discussed in more detail, the database will be referred to as the* link-state database.

SHORTEST-PATH TREE Each router runs the SPF algorithm (see "Shortest-Path First (SPF)," above) on the link-state database to obtain its shortest-path tree. The tree gives the route to any destination network or host as far as the area boundary. It is used to build the routing table.

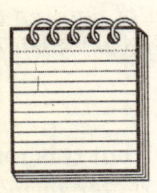

> *NOTE:* Because each router occupies a different place in the area's topology, application of the SPF algorithm gives a different tree for each router, even though the database is identical.

Area border routers run multiple copies of the algorithm but build a single routing table.

ROUTING TABLE The routing table contains entries for each destination: network, subnet, or host. For each destination, there is information for one or more types of service (TOS). For each combination of destination and type of service, there are entries for one or more optimum paths to be used.

AREA ID A 32-bit number identifying a particular area. The backbone has an area ID of 0.

---

*The use of TOS has been dropped in recent OSPF implementations.

Dynamic IP Routing Protocols

ROUTER ID A 32-bit number identifying a particular router. Each router within the AS has a single router ID. One possible implementation is to use the lowest numbered IP address belonging to a router as its router ID.

ROUTER PRIORITY An 8-bit unsigned integer, configurable on a per-interface basis, indicating this router's priority in the selection of the (backup) designated router. A router priority of 0 indicates that this router is ineligible to be the designated router.

LINK-STATE ADVERTISEMENTS Link-state information is exchanged by adjacent OSPF routers to allow area topology databases to be maintained and inter-area and inter-AS routes to be advertised.

Link-state information consists of five types of link-state advertisements (see Figure 5-15). Together these provide all the information needed to describe an OSPF network and its external environment:

Figure 5-15
OSPF Link-State Advertisements.

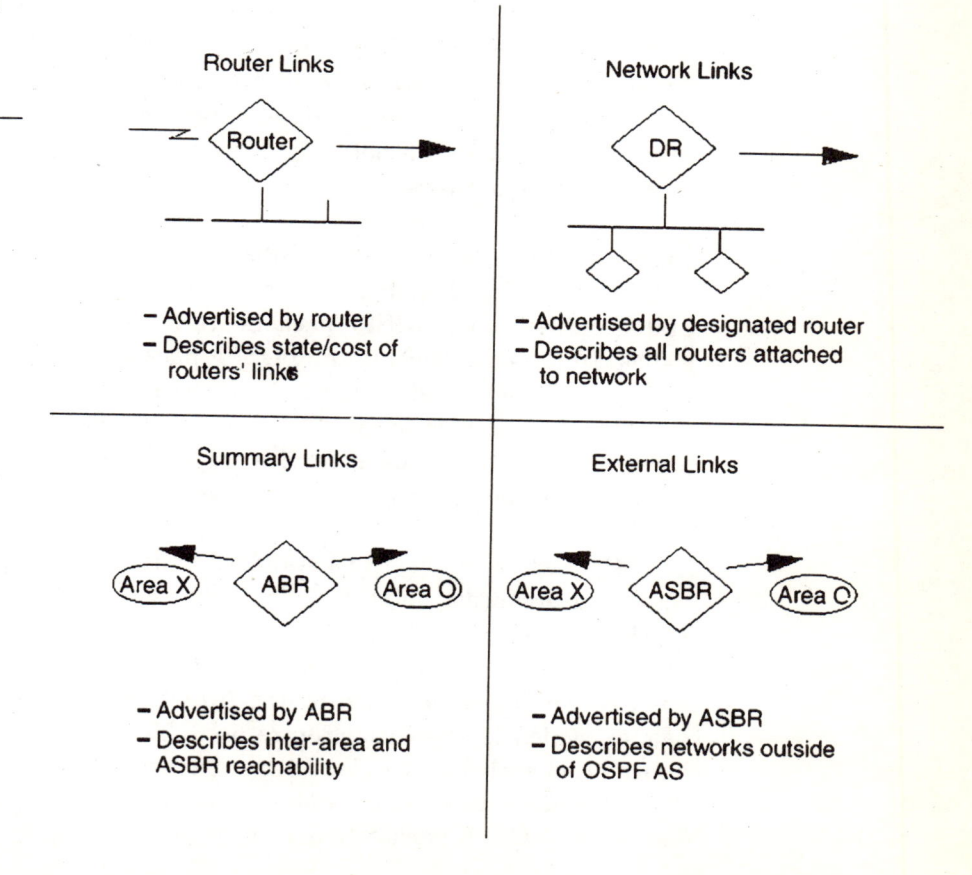

Router Links
- Advertised by router
- Describes state/cost of routers' links

Network Links
- Advertised by designated router
- Describes all routers attached to network

Summary Links
- Advertised by ABR
- Describes inter-area and ASBR reachability

External Links
- Advertised by ASBR
- Describes networks outside of OSPF AS

1. Router links
2. Network links
3. Summary link (type 3)
4. Summary link (type 4)
5. AS External links

Router link advertisements   Router link advertisements are generated by all OSPF routers and describe the state of the router's interfaces (links) within the area. They are flooded throughout a single area only.

Network link advertisements   Network link advertisements are generated by the designated router on a multi-access network and list the routers connected to the network. They are flooded throughout a single area only.

Summary link advertisements   Summary link advertisements are generated by area border routers. There are two types: one describes routes to destinations in other areas; the other describes routes to AS boundary routers. They are flooded throughout a single area only.

AS external link advertisements   AS external link advertisements are generated by AS boundary routers and describe routes to destinations external to the OSPF network. They are flooded throughout all areas in the OSPF network.

Protocol Description   The OSPF protocol is an implementation of a link-state routing protocol, as described in the section entitled "Link-State Routing," above. OSPF packets are transmitted directly in IP datagrams. IP datagrams containing OSPF packets can be distinguished by their use of protocol identifier 5-21 in the IP header. OSPF packets are not, therefore, contained in TCP or UDP headers. OSPF packets are always sent with IP type of service set to 0 and the IP precedence field set to internetwork control. This is to aid them in getting preference over normal IP traffic.

OSPF packets are sent to a standard multicast IP address on point-to-point and broadcast networks. This address is 224.0.0.5, referred to as AllSPFRouters in the RFC. They are sent to specific IP addresses on non-broadcast networks using neighbor network address information that must be configured for each router. All OSPF packets share a common header, which is shown in Figure 5-16. This header provides general information such as area identifier and originating router identifier, and it also includes a checksum and authentication information. A type field defines each OSPF packet as one of five possible types:

Dynamic IP Routing Protocols

Figure 5-16
OSPF Common Header.

Number of Octets	Field	Notes
1	Version	Version = 2
1	Packet Type	1 = Hello 2 = Database Description 3 = Link State Request 4 = Link State Update 5 = Link State Acknowledgment
2	Packet Length	
4	Router ID	
4	Area ID	
2	Checksum	
2	Authentication Type	0 = No Authentication 1 = Simple Password
8	Authentication Data	Password if Type 1 Selected

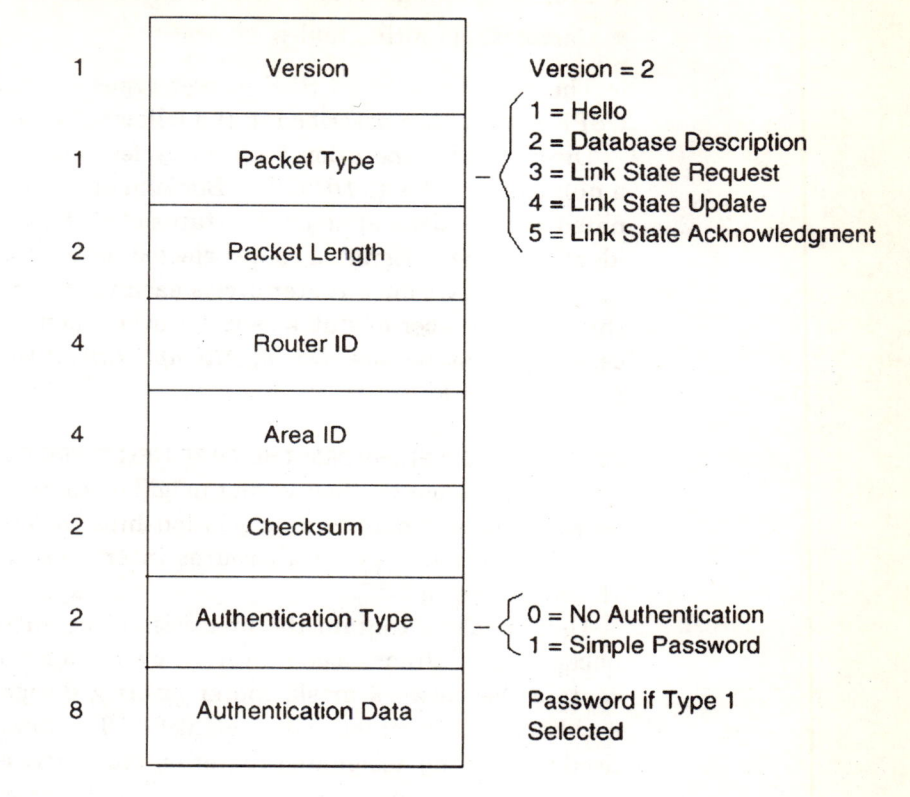

1. Hello
2. Database description
3. Link-state request
4. Link-state update
5. Link-state acknowledgement

The router identifier, area identifier, and authentication information are configurable for each OSPF router.

The OSPF protocol defines a number of stages which must be executed by individual routers. They are as follows:

- Discovering neighbors
- Electing the designated router
- Initializing neighbors

- Propagating link-state information
- Calculating routing tables

The use of the five OSPF packet types to implement stages of the OSPF protocol are described in the following subsection.

During OSPF operation a router cycles each of its interfaces through a number of states to *DR Other*, *BackupDR*, or *DR* (DR stands for designated router), depending on the status of each attached network and the identity of the designated router elected for each of them.

At the same time a router cycles each neighbor interface (interaction) through a number of states as it discovers them and then becomes adjacent. These states are: *Down, Attempt, Init, 2-Way, ExStart, Exchange, Loading,* and *Full*.

DISCOVERING NEIGHBORS: THE OSPF HELLO PROTOCOL The Hello protocol is responsible for discovering neighbor routers on a network and for establishing and maintaining relationships with them. Hello packets are sent out periodically on all router interfaces. The format of these is shown in Figure 5-17.

Hello packets contain the identities of neighbor routers whose hello packets have already been received over a specific interface. They also contain the network mask, router priority, designated router identifier, and backup designated router identifier. The final three parameters are used to elect the designated router on multi-access networks.

The network mask, router priority, hello interval, and router dead interval are configurable for each interface on an OSPF router.

A router interface changes state from *Down* to *Point-to-Point* (if the network is point-to-point), to *DR Other* (if the router is ineligible to become designated router), or otherwise to *Waiting* as soon as hello packets are sent over it.

A router receives hello packets from neighbor routers via its network interfaces. When this happens, the neighbor interface state changes from *Down* to *Init*. Bidirectional communication is established between neighbors when a router sees itself listed in a hello packet received from another router. Only at this point are the two routers defined as true neighbors, and the neighbor interface changes state from *Init* to *2-Way*.

ELECTING THE DESIGNATED ROUTER All multi-access networks have a designated router. There is also a backup designated router that takes over in the event that the designated router fails. The use of a backup, which maintains an identical set of adjacencies and an identical topology

Dynamic IP Routing Protocols

Figure 5-17
OSPF Hello Packet.

Number of Octets	Field	
24	Common Header	Packet Type = 1
4	Network Mask	
2	Hello Interval	
1	Reserved | E | T	E = Subarea; T = Multiple TOS Metrics Supported
1	Router Priority	
4	Router Dead Interval	
4	Designated Router	
4	Backup Designated Router	
4	Neighbor	Repeated for Each Current Valid Neighbor

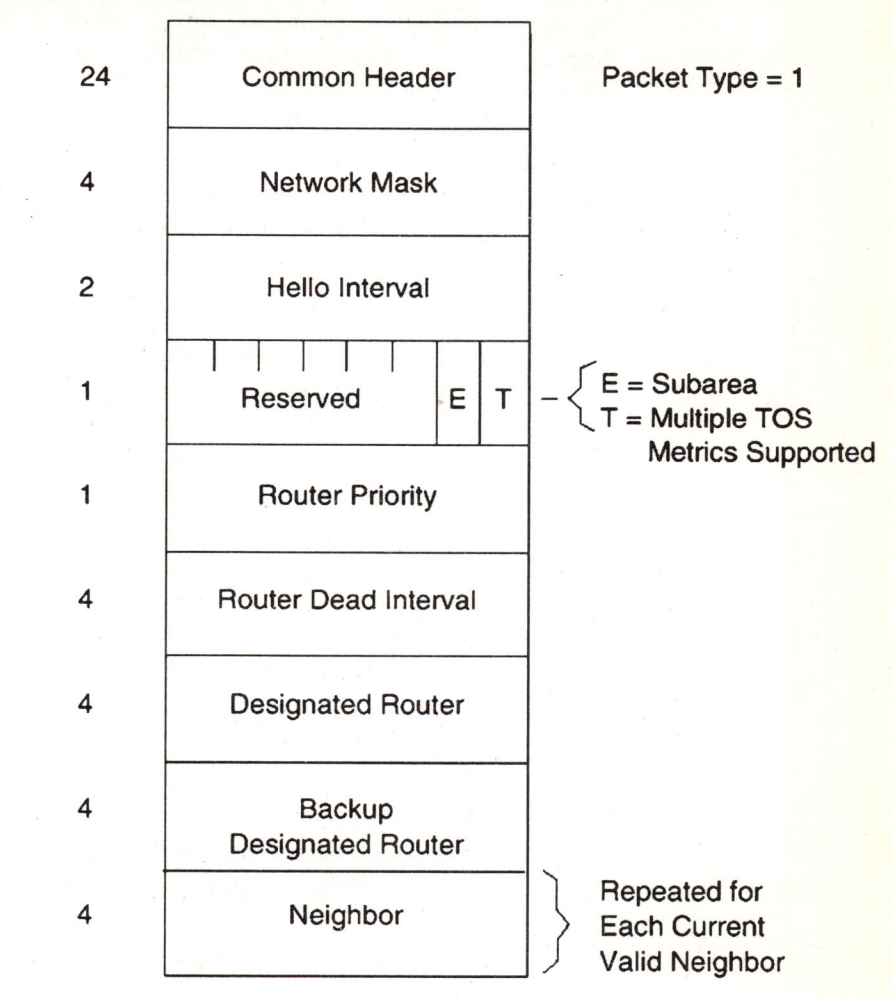

database to the designated router, ensures that there is no extended loss of routing capability if the designated router fails. The designated router performs two major functions on a network:

1. It originates network link advertisements on behalf of the network.
2. It establishes adjacencies with all other routers on the network. Only routers with adjacencies exchange link-state information and synchronize their databases.

The designated router and backup designated router are elected on the basis of the router identifier, router priority, designated router, and backup designated router fields in hello packets. Router priority is a single octet field that defines the priority of a router on a network. The lower the value of the priority field, the more likely the router is to become the designated router; hence the higher its priority. A zero value means the router is ineligible to become a designated or backup designated router.

The process of designated router election is as follows:

1. The current values for designated router and backup designated router on the network are initialized to 0.0.0.0.
2. The current values for router identifier, router priority, designated router, and backup designated router in hello packets from neighbor routers are noted. Local router values are included.
3. Backup designated router election:
   - Routers that have been declared as designated router are ineligible to become a backup designated router.
   - The backup designated router will be declared to be:
   The highest-priority router that has been declared as a backup designated router.
   The highest-priority router, if no backup designated router has been declared.
   - If equal priority routers are eligible, the one with the highest router identifier is chosen.
4. Designated router election:
   - The designated router will be declared to be:
   The highest-priority router that has been declared the designated router.
   The highest-priority router, if no designated router has been declared.
5. If the router carrying out the above determination is declared the designated or backup designated router, then the above steps are re-executed. This ensures that no router can declare itself both designated and backup designated router.

Once designated and backup designated routers have been elected for a network, they proceed to establish adjacencies with all routers on the network.

Completion of the election process for a network causes the router interface to change state from *Waiting* to *DR, BackupDR,* or *DR Other,*

Dynamic IP Routing Protocols

depending on whether the router is elected the designated router, the backup designated router, or none of these.

ESTABLISHING ADJACENCIES: DATABASE EXCHANGE A router establishes adjacencies with a subset of neighbor routers on a network.

Routers connected by point-to-point networks and virtual links always become *adjacent*. Routers on multi-access networks form adjacencies with the designated and backup designated routers only.

Link-state information flows only between adjacent routers. Before this can happen, it is necessary for them to have the same topological database and to be synchronized. This is achieved in OSPF by a process called *database exchange*.

Database exchange between two neighbor routers occurs as soon as they attempt to bring up an adjacency. It consists of the exchange of a number of database description packets that define the set of link-state information present in the database of each router. The link-state information in the database is defined by the list of link-state headers for all link-state advertisement in the database. (See Figure 5-22 for information on the link-state header.)

The format of database description packets is shown in Figure 5-18.

During the database exchange process the routers form a *master-slave* relationship, the master being the first to transmit. The master sends database description packets to the slave to describe its database of link-state information. Each packet is identified by a sequence number and contains a list of the link-state headers in the master's database. The slave acknowledges each packet by sequence number and includes its own database of headers in the acknowledgements.

Flags in database description packets indicate whether they are from a master or slave (the M/S bit), the first such packet (the I bit), and if there are more packets to come (the M bit). Database exchange is complete when a router receives a database description packet from its neighbor with the M bit off.

During database exchange each router makes a list of the link-state advertisements for which the adjacent neighbor has a more up-to-date instance (all advertisements are sequenced and time-stamped). Once the process is complete, each router requests these more up-to-date instances of advertisements using link-state requests.

The format of link-state request packets is shown in Figure 5-19.

The database exchange process sequences the neighbor interface state from *2-Way* through:

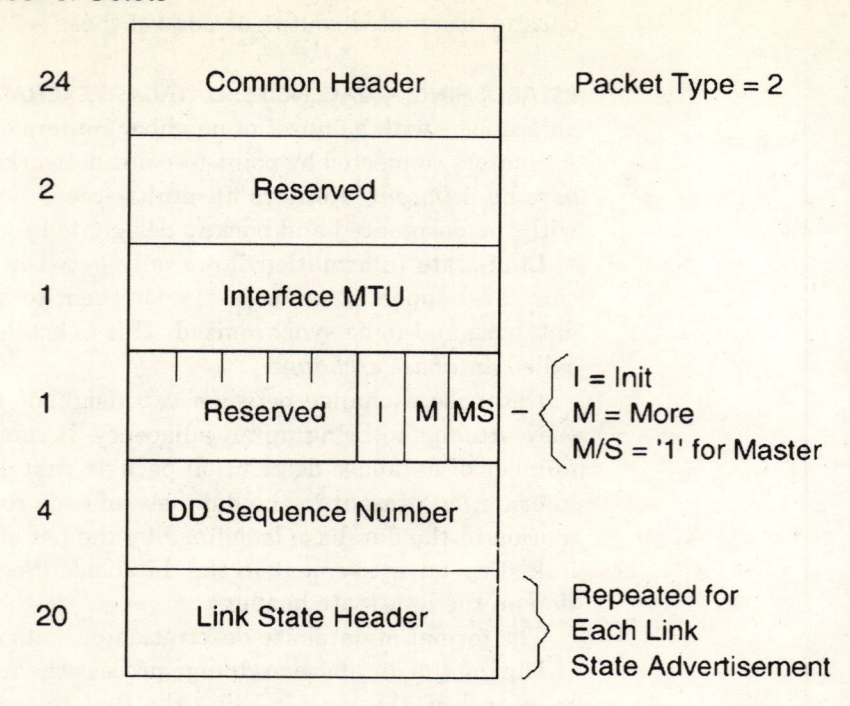

Figure 5-18
OSPF Database Description Packet.

Number of Octets	Field	
24	Common Header	Packet Type = 2
2	Reserved	
1	Interface MTU	
1	Reserved | I | M | MS	I = Init, M = More, M/S = '1' for Master
4	DD Sequence Number	
20	Link State Header	Repeated for Each Link State Advertisement

- *ExStart* as the adjacency is created and the master agreed upon
- *Exchange* as the topology databases are being described
- *Loading* as the link-state requests are being sent and responded to
- And finally to *Full* when the neighbors are fully adjacent

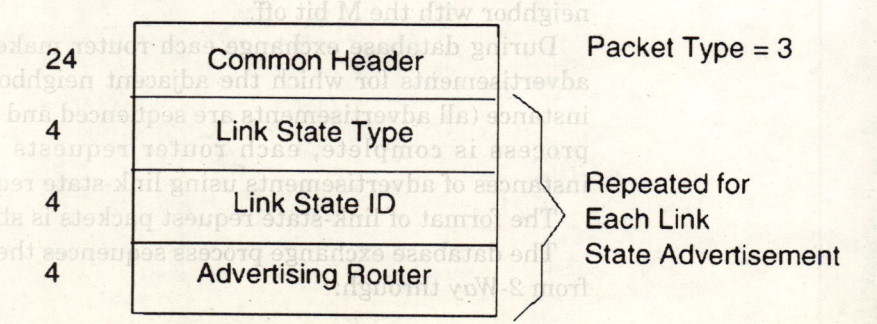

Figure 5-19
OSPF Link-State Request Packet.

Number of Octets	Field	
24	Common Header	Packet Type = 3
4	Link State Type	Repeated for Each Link State Advertisement
4	Link State ID	
4	Advertising Router	

Dynamic IP Routing Protocols

In this way, the two routers synchronize their topology databases and are able to calculate identical network maps for their OSPF area.

LINK-STATE PROPAGATION Information about the topology of an OSPF network is passed from router to router in link-state advertisements. Link-state advertisements pass between adjacent routers in the form of *link-state update packets,* the format of which is shown in Figure 5-20.

Link-state advertisements are of five types—router links, network links, summary link (type 3), summary link (type 4), and AS external links—as noted earlier in this section.

Link-state updates pass as a result of link-state requests during database exchange and also in the normal course of events when routers wish to indicate a change of network topology. Individual link-state update packets can contain multiple link-state advertisements. It is essential that each OSPF router in an area have the same network topology database; hence the integrity of link-state information must be maintained.

For that reason, link-state update packets must be passed without loss or corruption throughout an area. The process by which this is done is called *flooding*. A link-state update packet floods one or more link-state advertisements one hop farther away from their originator. To make the flooding procedure reliable, each link-state advertisement must be acknowledged separately. Multiple acknowledgements can be grouped together into a single *link-state acknowledgement packet*. The format of the link-state acknowledgement packet is shown in Figure 5-21.

In order to maintain database integrity all link-state advertisements *must be* rigorously checked to ensure validity.

The following checks are applied, and the advertisement discarded if:

The link-state checksum is incorrect

The link-state type is invalid

Figure 5-20
OSPF Link-State Update Packet.

Number of Octets

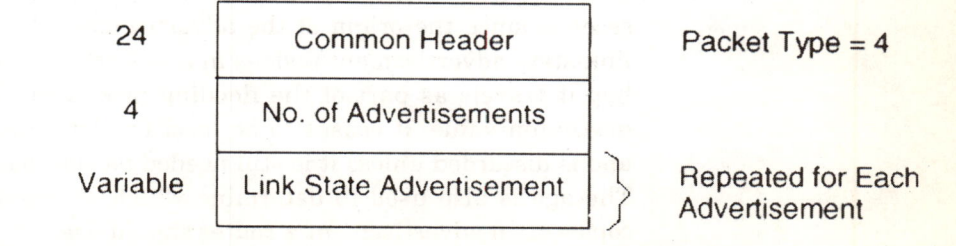

Octets	Field	Notes
24	Common Header	Packet Type = 4
4	No. of Advertisements	
Variable	Link State Advertisement	Repeated for Each Advertisement

Figure 5-21
OSPF Link-State Acknowledgement Packet.

Number of Octets

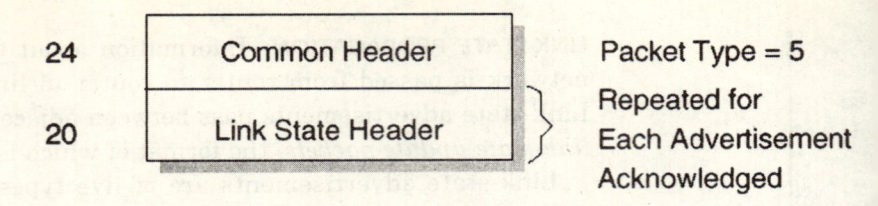

| 24 | Common Header |
| 20 | Link State Header |

Packet Type = 5

Repeated for Each Advertisement Acknowledged

- The advertisement's age has reached its maximum
- The advertisement is older than or the same as one already in the database

If an advertisement passes the above checks, then an acknowledgement is sent back to the originator. If no acknowledgement is received by the originator, then the original link-state update packet is retransmitted after a timer has expired. Once accepted, an advertisement is flooded onward over the router's other interfaces until it has been received by all routers within an area.

Advertisements are identified by their link-state type, link-state ID, and the advertising router. They are further qualified by their link-state sequence number, link-state age, and link-state checksum number. The age of a link-state advertisement must be calculated to determine if it should be installed into a router's database. Only a more recent advertisement should be accepted and installed. Valid link-state advertisements are installed into the topology database of the router. This causes the topology map or graph to be recalculated and the routing table to be updated.

Link-state advertisements all have a common 20-byte header. This is shown in Figure 5-22. The four link-state advertisement types are shown in Figures 5-23 through 5-26.

The fields in the link-state advertisement header are:

Link-Stage Age This consists of a 16-bit number indicating the time in seconds since the origin of the advertisement. It is increased as the link-state advertisement resides in a router's database, and with each hop it travels as part of the flooding procedure. When it reaches a maximum value, it ceases to be used for determining routing tables and is discarded unless it is still needed for database synchronization. The age is also used to determine which of two otherwise identical copies of an advertisement a router should use.

Dynamic IP Routing Protocols

Figure 5-22
OSPF Link-State Header.

Number of Octets	Field
2	Link State Age
1	(options, E bit)
1	Link State Type
4	Link State ID
4	Advertising Router
4	Link State Sequence Number
2	Link State Checksum
2	Length

Options
- 1 = Router Links
- 2 = Network Links
- 3,4 = Summary Links
- 5 = AS External

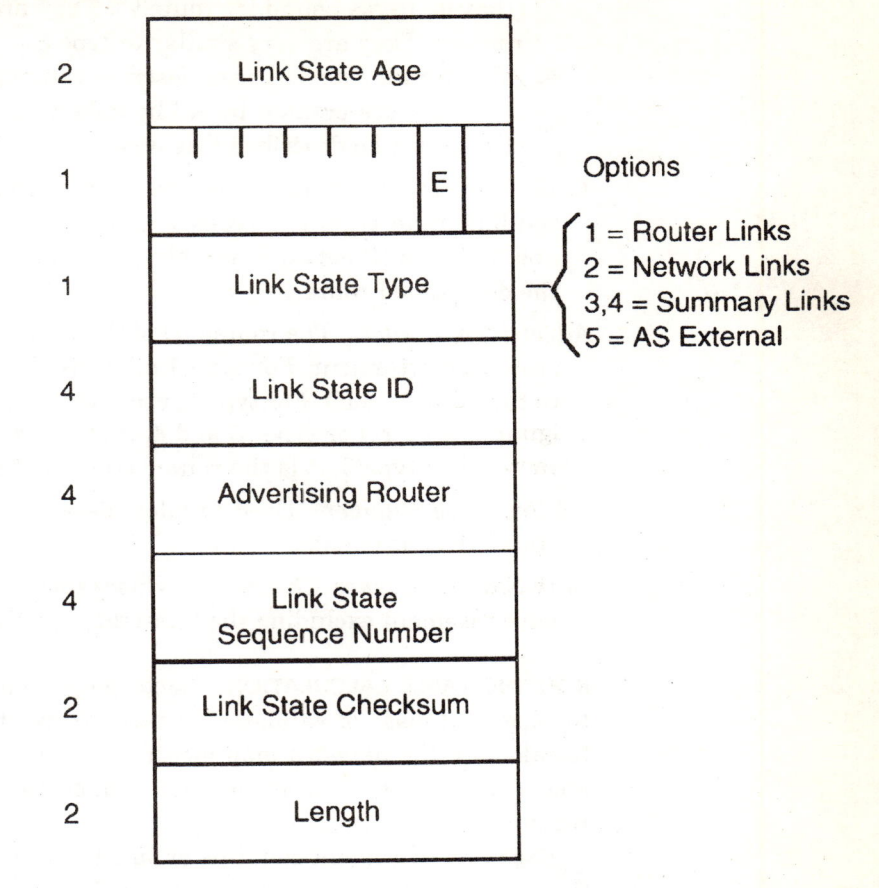

Option(s) This consists of 1 bit that describes optional OSPF capability. The E-bit indicates an external routing capability. It is set unless the advertisement is for a router, network link, or summary link in a stub area. The E-bit is used for information only and does not affect the routing table.

Link-State Type The types of the link-state advertisement are (see "Link-State Advertisements," above):

1. *Router links* These describe the states of a router's interfaces.
2. *Network links* These describe the routers attached to a network.
3. *Summary links* These describe inter-area, intra-AS routes. They are created by area border routers and allow routes to networks within the AS but outside the area to be described concisely.

4. *Summary links* These describe routes to the boundary of the AS (that is, to AS boundary routers). They are created by area border routers. They are very similar to type 3.
5. *AS external links* These describe routes to networks outside the AS. They are created by AS boundary routers. A default route for the AS can be described this way.

Link-State ID A unique ID for the advertisement that is dependent on the link-state type. For types 1 and 4 it is the router ID; for types 3 and 5 it is an IP network number; and for type 2 it is the IP address of the designated router.

Advertising Router The router ID of the router that originated the link-state advertisement. For type 1 advertisements, this field is identical to the link-state ID. For type 2, it is the router ID of the network's designated router. For types 3 and 4, it is the router ID of an area border router. For type 5, it is the router ID of an AS boundary router.

LS Sequence Number Used to allow detection of old or duplicate link-state advertisements.

Link-State Sequence Checksum Checksum of the complete link-state advertisement excluding the link-state age field.

ROUTING TABLE CALCULATION Each router in an OSPF area builds up a topology database of validated link-state advertisements and uses them to calculate the network map for the area. From this map, the router is able to determine the best route for each destination and insert it into its routing table.

Each advertisement contains an age field, which is incremented while the advertisement is held in the database. An advertisement's age is never incremented past *MaxAge*. When age reaches *MaxAge*, it is excluded from routing table calculation and reflooded through the area as a newly originated advertisement.

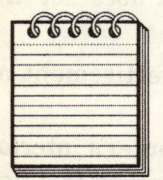

NOTE: MaxAge *is an architecture constant and the maximum age an LSA can attain. The value of* MaxAge *is set to 1 hour.*

Routers build up their routing table from the database of link-state advertisements in the following sequence:

1. The shortest-path tree is calculated from router and network links advertisements allowing best routes within the area to be determined.

Dynamic IP Routing Protocols

2. Inter-area routes are added by examination of summary link advertisements.
3. AS external routes are added by examination of AS external link advertisements.

The topology graph or map constructed from the above process is used to update the routing table. The routing table is recalculated each time a new advertisement is received.

The fields in the router link advertisement header (see Figure 5-23) are:

Figure 5-23
OSPF Router Links Advertisement.

Number of Octets

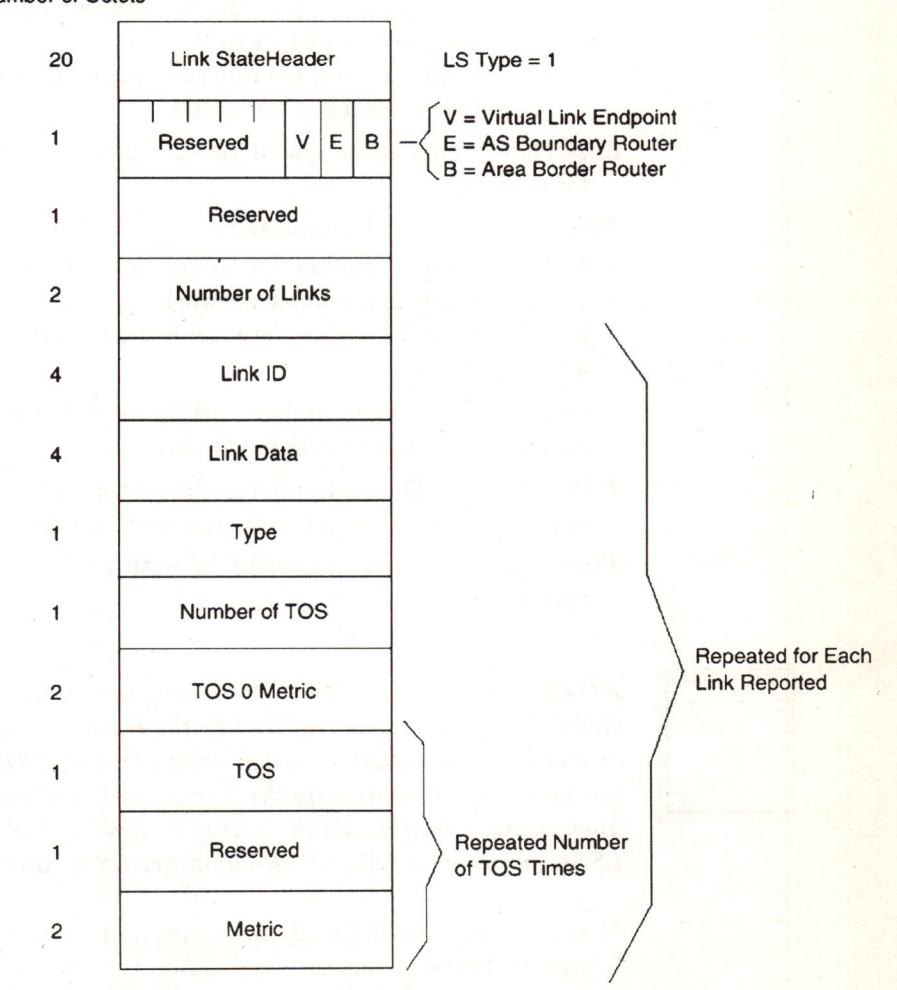

Octets	Field	Notes
20	Link StateHeader	LS Type = 1
1	Reserved V E B	V = Virtual Link Endpoint / E = AS Boundary Router / B = Area Border Router
1	Reserved	
2	Number of Links	
4	Link ID	
4	Link Data	
1	Type	
1	Number of TOS	
2	TOS 0 Metric	
1	TOS	
1	Reserved	
2	Metric	

Repeated for Each Link Reported

Repeated Number of TOS Times

V Bit   When set, this router is the endpoint of a virtual link that is using this area as a transit area.

E Bit   When set, the router is an AS boundary router.

B Bit   When set, the router is an area border router.

Number of Links   The number of links described by this advertisement.

Link ID   Identifies the object that this link connects to. The value depends upon the type field (see below).
   1. Neighboring router's router ID
   2. IP address of the designated router
   3. IP network/subnet number—this value depends on what the inter area route is to:
      For a stub network, it is the IP network/subnet number.
      For a host, it is X'FFFFFFFF'.
      For the AS-external default route, it is X'00000000'.
   4. Neighboring router's router ID

Link Data   This value also depends upon the type field (see RFC 2328 for details).

Type   What this link connects to.
   1. Point-to-point connection to another router
   2. Connection to a transit network
   3. Connection to a stub network or to a host
   4. Virtual link

Number of TOS   The number of different TOS metrics given for this link in addition to the metric for TOS 0.

TOS 0 Metric   The cost of using this outbound link for TOS 0. All OSPF routing protocol packets are sent with the IP TOS field set to 0.

TOS   For backward compatibility with previous versions of the OSPF specification.

NOTE: *In RFC 2328 the TOS routing option has been deleted from OSPF. This action was required by the Internet standards process, due to lack of implementation experience with OSPF's TOS routing. However, for backward compatibility the formats of OSPF's various LSAs remain unchanged, maintaining the ability to specify TOS metrics in router-LSAs, summary-LSAs, ASBR-summary-LSAs, and AS-external-LSAs.*

Metric   The cost of using this outbound router link for traffic of the specified type of service.

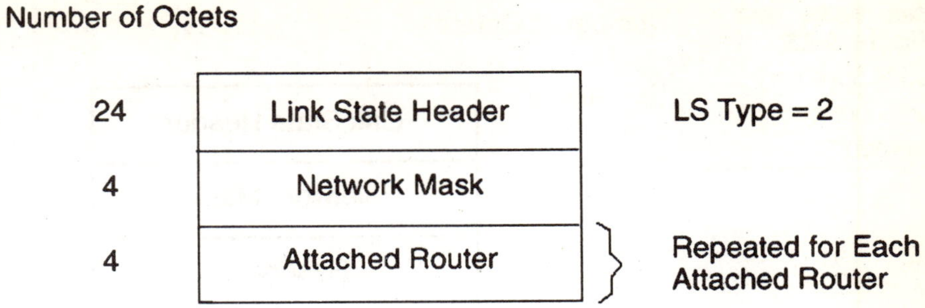

Dynamic IP Routing Protocols

Figure 5-24
OSPF Network Links Advertisement.

Number of Octets

Octets	Field	
24	Link State Header	LS Type = 2
4	Network Mask	
4	Attached Router	Repeated for Each Attached Router

The format of a network links advertisement (type 2) is shown in Figure 5-24.

The fields in the network link advertisement header are:

Network Mask   The IP address mask for the network. For example a CIDR prefix length /20 network would have the mask 255.255.240.0 (dotted-decimal) and the mask 1111 1111 1111 1111 1110 0000 0000 0000 (binary).

Attached Router   The router IDs of each of the routers attached to the network that are adjacent to the designated router (including the sending router). The number of routers in the list is deduced from the length field in the header.

The fields in the summary link advertisement header (see Figure 5-25) are:

Network Mask   For a type 3 link-state advertisement, this is the IP address mask for the network. For a type 4 link-state advertisement, this is not meaningful and must be 0.

Reserved   All zero.

Metric   The cost of this route for this type of service in the same units used for TOS metrics in type 1 advertisements.

TOS   Zero or more entries for additional types of service. The number of entries can be determined from the length field in the header.

The fields in the external links advertisement header (see Figure 5-26) are:

Network Mask   The IP address mask for the network.

Bit E   The type of external metric. If set, the type is 2, otherwise it is 1.
  1. The metric is directly comparable to OSPF link-state metrics
  2. The metric is considered larger than all OSPF link-state metrics

Figure 5-25
OSPF Summary Links Advertisement.

Number of Octets		
20	Link State Header	LS Type = 3 or 4
4	Network Mask	0 for LS Type 4
1	Reserved	
3	Metric	
1	TOS	Repeated for Each TOS
3	Metric	

Reserved All zero.

Metric The cost of this route. Interpretation depends on the E-bit.

Forwarding Address The IP address that data traffic for this type of service intended for the advertised destination is to be forwarded to. The value 0.0.0.0 indicates that traffic should be forwarded to the AS boundary router that originated the advertisement.

External Route Tag A 32-bit value attached to the external route by an AS boundary router. This is not used by the OSPF itself. It can be used to communicate information between AS boundary routers.

TOS Zero or more entries for additional types of service. The number of entries can be determined from the length field in the header.

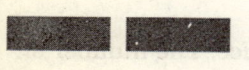

Exterior Routing Protocols

Exterior routing protocols or exterior gateway protocols (EGPs) are used to exchange routing information among routers in different autonomous systems.

NOTE: The term exterior routing protocol *has no abbreviation commonly used, so this book uses the abbreviation EGP as does most TCP/IP literature.*

Dynamic IP Routing Protocols

Figure 5-26
OSPF External Links Advertisement.

Number of Octets	Field	
20	Link State Header	LS Type = 5
4	Network Mask	
1	E / Reserved	⎫
3	Metric	⎬ Repeated for Each TOS
4	Forwarding Address	
4	External Route Tag	⎭
1	E / TOS	
3	TOS Metric	
4	Forwarding Address	
4	External Route Tag	

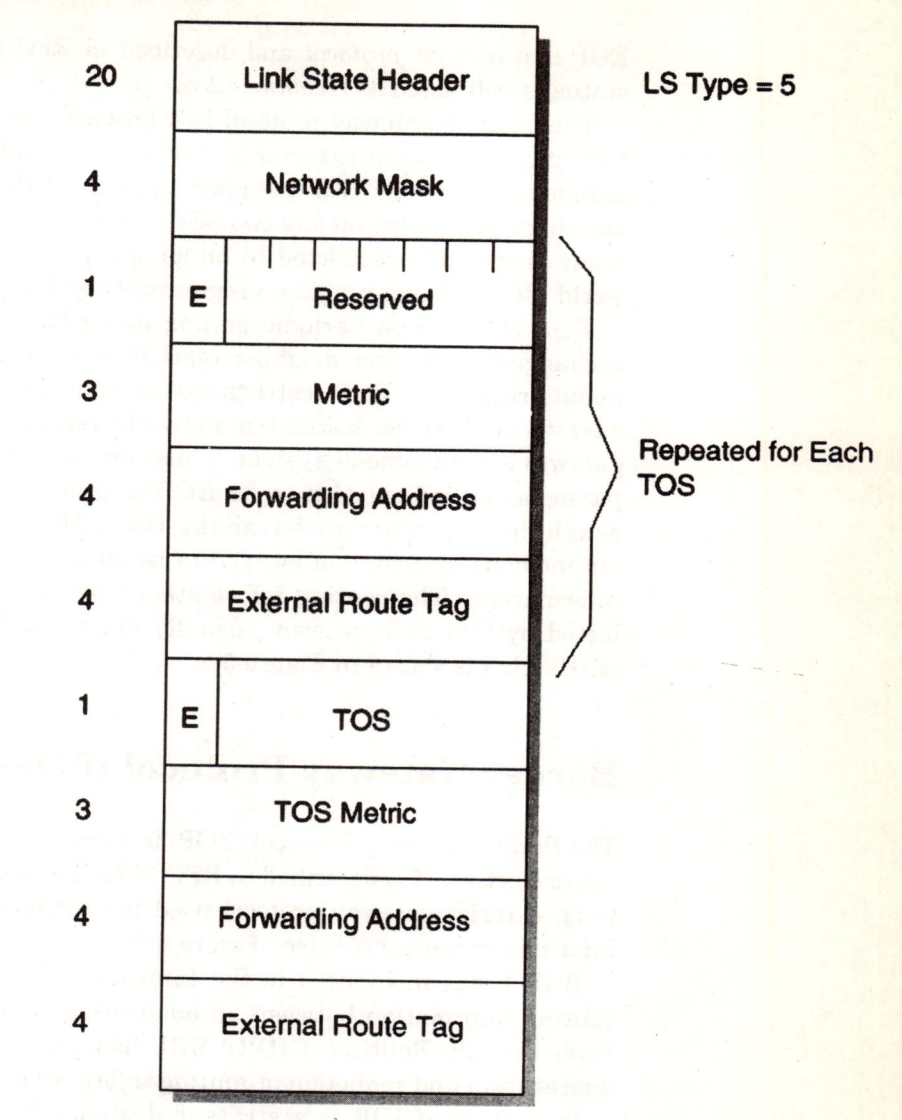

Two EGPs are commonly used:

- Exterior Gateway Protocol (see "Exterior Gateway Protocol (EGP)," below)
- Border Gateway Protocol (see "Border Gateway Protocol (BGP-4)," below)

Exterior Gateway Protocol (EGP)

EGP is a *historic protocol* and described in RFC 904. Interestingly, its status is still listed as *recommended*.

The exterior gateway protocol is a protocol used to exchange routing information among *exterior* gateways (not belonging to the same autonomous system). EGP assumes a single backbone and therefore only one single path between any two ASs. Therefore, the practical use of EGP today is virtually restricted to building a private Internet. In the real world, EGP is being replaced progressively by BGP.

EGP is based on periodic polling using Hello/I Hear You message exchanges, to monitor neighbor reachability and poll requests to solicit update responses. EGP restricts exterior gateways by allowing them to advertise only those destination networks reachable entirely within that gateway's autonomous system. Thus, an exterior gateway using EGP passes along information to its EGP neighbors but does not advertise reachability information about its EGP neighbors outside the autonomous system. (Gateways are neighbors if they exchange routing information.) The routing information from inside an AS must be collected by this EGP gateway, usually via an interior gateway protocol (IGP). This is shown in Figure 5-2.

Border Gateway Protocol (BGP-4)

The Border Gateway Protocol (BGP) is a draft standard protocol. Its status is elective. It is described in RFC 1771. The Border Gateway Protocol is an exterior gateway protocol used to exchange network reachability information among ASs (see Figure 5-2).

BGP-4 was introduced in the Internet for the loop-free exchange of routing information between autonomous systems. Based on Classless Inter-Domain Routing (CIDR), BGP has since evolved to support the aggregation and reduction of routing information.

In essence, CIDR is a strategy designed to address the following problems:

- Exhaustion of Class B address space
- Routing table growth

CIDR eliminates the concept of address classes and provides a method for summarizing *n* different routes into single routes. This significantly

Dynamic IP Routing Protocols

reduces the amount of routing information that BGP routers must store and exchange.

Before giving an overview of the BGP protocol, some terms used in BGP should be defined:

BGP speaker   This is a system running BGP (see Figure 5-27).

BGP neighbors   A pair of BGP speakers exchanging inter-AS routing information are known as BGP neighbors. BGP neighbors may be of two types:

Internal.   Internal BGP neighbors consist of a pair of BGP speakers in the same autonomous system. Internal BGP neighbors must present a

Figure 5-27
BGP Speaker and AS Relationship.

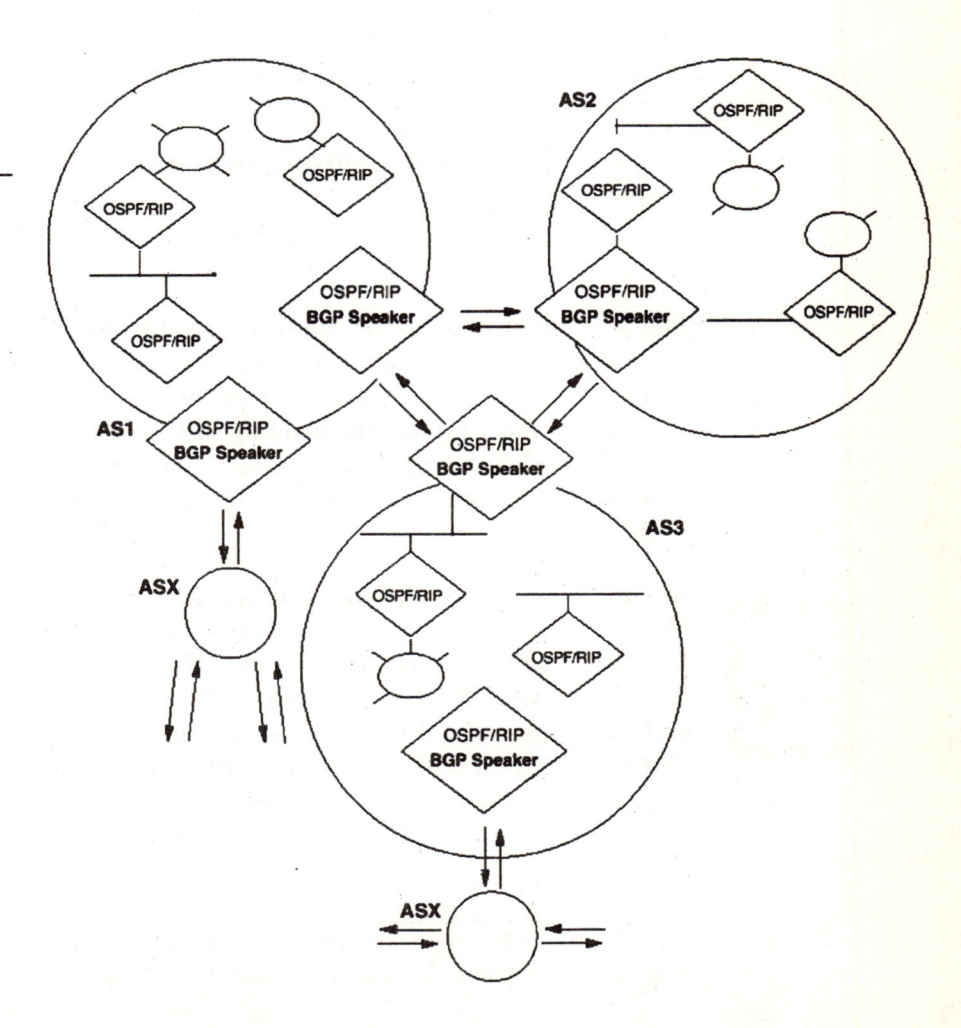

consistent image of the AS to their external BGP neighbors. This is explained in more detail below.

External. External BGP neighbors consist of a pair of BGP neighbors in different autonomous systems. External BGP neighbors must be connected by a BGP connection as defined below. This restriction means that in most cases where an AS has multiple BGP inter-AS connections, multiple BGP speakers are also required.

BGP session This type of TCP session is between BGP neighbors that are exchanging routing information using BGP. The neighbors monitor the state of the session by sending a *KEEPALIVE* message regularly. (The recommended interval is 30 seconds.)*

AS border router (ASBR) An AS border router is a router that has a connection to multiple autonomous systems. ASBRs may be of two types:

Internal This type is a next-hop router in the same AS as the BGP speaker.

External This type is a next-hop router in a different AS from the BGP speaker.

The IP address of a border router is specified as a next-hop destination when BGP advertises an AS path (see below) to one of its external neighbors. Next-hop border routers must share a physical connection (see below) with both the sending and receiving BGP speakers. If a BGP speaker advertises an external border router as a next hop, information about that router must have been learned from one of the BGP speaker's peers.

NOTE: The nomenclature for this type of router is somewhat varied. RFC 2328, which describes OSPF, uses the term AS boundary router. *RFC 1771 and 1772, which describe BGP, use the terms* border router *and* border gateway. *Here, the first term is used consistently when both OSPF and BGP are being described. BGP defines two types of AS border routers, depending on its topological relationship to the BGP speaker that refers to it.*

---

*This KEEPALIVE message is implemented in the application layer, and it is independent of the KEEPALIVE message available in many TCP implementations.

Dynamic IP Routing Protocols

AS connection   BGP defines two types of inter-AS connections:

Physical connection   An AS shares a physical network with another AS, and this network is connected to at least one border router from each AS. Since these two routers share a network, they can forward packets to each other without requiring any inter-AS or intra-AS routing protocols. (That is, they require neither an IGP nor an EGP to communicate.)

BGP connection   A BGP connection means that there is a BGP session between a pair of BGP speakers, one in each AS. This session is used to communicate the routes through the physically connected border routers that can be used for specific networks. BGP requires that the BGP speakers must be on the same network as the physically connected border routers so that the BGP session is also independent of all inter-AS or intra-AS routing protocols. The BGP speakers do not need to be border routers, and vice versa.

> **NOTE:**   *The term* BGP connection *can be used to refer to a session between two BGP speakers in the same AS.*

Traffic type   BGP categorizes traffic in an AS as one of two types:

local   Local traffic is traffic that either originates in or terminates in that AS. That is, either the source or the destination IP address is in the AS.

transit   Transit traffic is all nonlocal traffic.

One of the goals of BGP is to minimize the amount of transit traffic.

AS type   An AS is categorized as one of three types:

stub   A stub AS has a single inter-AS connection to one other AS. A stub AS only carries local traffic.

multihomed   A multihomed AS has connections to more than one other AS but refuses to carry transit traffic.

transit   A transit AS has connections to more than one other AS and carries both local and transit traffic. The AS may impose policy restrictions on what transit traffic will be carried.

AS number   An AS number is a 16-bit number uniquely identifying an AS. This is the same AS number used by EGP.

AS path An AS path is a list of all of the AS numbers traversed by a route when exchanging routing information. Rather than exchanging simple metric counts, BGP communicates entire paths to its neighbors.

Routing policy A routing policy is a set of rules constraining routing to conform to the wishes of the authority that administers the AS. Routing policies are not defined in the BGP protocol but are selected by the AS authority and presented to BGP in the form of implementation-specific configuration data. Routing policies can be selected by the AS authority in whatever way that authority sees fit. For example:

- A multihomed AS can refuse to act as a transit AS. It does this by not advertising routes to networks other than those directly connected to it.
- A multihomed AS can limit itself to being a transit AS for a restricted set of adjacent ASs. It does this by advertising its routing information to this set only.
- An AS can select which outbound AS should be used for carrying transit traffic.

An AS can also apply performance-related criteria when selecting outbound paths:

- An AS can optimize traffic to use short AS paths rather than long ones.
- An AS can select transit routes according to the service quality of the intermediate hops. This service quality information could be obtained using mechanisms external to BGP.

It can be seen from the definitions above that a stub AS or a multihomed AS has the same topological properties as an AS in the ARPANET architecture. That is, it never acts as an intermediate AS in an inter-AS route. In the ARPANET architecture, EGP was sufficient for such an AS to exchange reachability information with its neighbors, and this remains true with BGP. Therefore, a stub AS or a multihomed AS can continue to use EGP (or any other suitable protocol) to operate with a transit AS. However, RFC 1772 recommends that BGP be used instead of EGP for these types of AS because it provides an advantage in bandwidth and performance. Additionally, in a multihomed AS, BGP is more likely to provide an optimum inter-AS route than EGP, since EGP only addresses reachability and not distance.

Path Selection Each BGP speaker must evaluate different paths to a destination from the border router(s) for an AS connection, select the best one that complies with the routing policies in force, and then advertise that route to all of its BGP neighbors at that AS connection.

BGP is a vector-distance protocol, but it is unlike such traditional vector-distance protocols as RIP that use a single metric. BGP determines an order of preference by applying a function that maps each path to a preference value. The protocol accordingly selects the path with the highest value. This function is generated by the BGP implementation according to configuration information. However, BGP does not associate a cost metric to any path, which is sometimes thought of as a shortcoming. BPG has no mechanism to collect a uniform cost for paths across the multitude of today's service provider networks.

When there are multiple viable paths to a destination, BGP maintains all of them but only advertises the one with the highest preference value. This approach allows a quick change to an alternate path should the primary path fail.

Routing Policies   RFC 1772 includes a recommended set of policies for all implementations:

- A BGP implementation should be able to control which routes it announces. The granularity of this control should be at least at the network level for the announced routes and at the AS level for the recipients. For example, BGP should allow a policy of announcing a route to a specific network to a specific adjacent AS. Care must be taken when a BGP speaker selects a new route that cannot be announced to a particular external peer, when the previously selected route was announced to that peer. Specifically, the local system must explicitly indicate to the peer that the previous route is now infeasible.
- BGP should allow a weighting policy for paths. Each AS can be assigned a weight and the preferred path to a destination is then the one with the lowest aggregate weight.
- BGP should allow a policy of excluding an AS from all possible paths. This can be done with a variant of the previous policy; each AS to be excluded is given an *infinite* weight and the route selection process refuses to consider paths of infinite weight.

See Figure 5-28 regarding the following BGP process and routing policies:

1. Routing updates are received from other BGP routers.
2. The input policy engine filters routes and performs attribute manipulation.

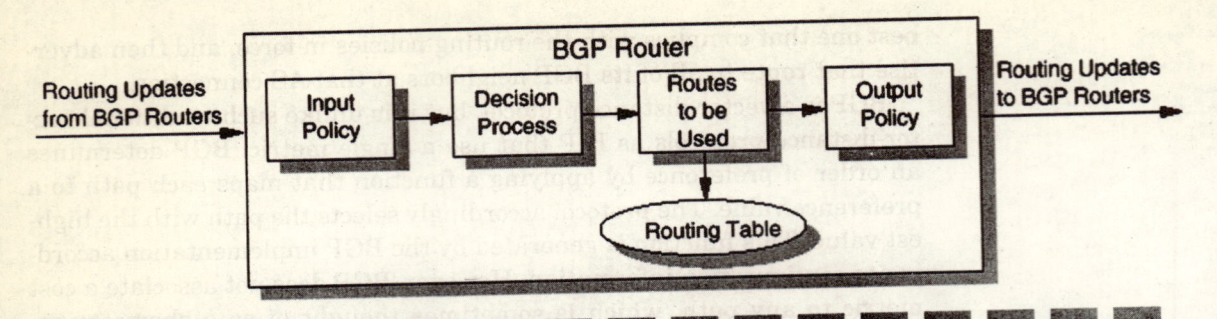

Figure 5-28 BGP Process and Routing Policies.

3. The decision process decides what routes the BGP router will use.
4. The output policy engine filters routes and performs attribute manipulation for routes to be advertised.
5. Routing updates are advertised to other BGP routers.

AS Consistency BGP requires that a transit AS present the same view to every AS using its services. If the AS has multiple BGP speakers, they must agree on two aspects of topology: intra-AS and inter-AS. Since BGP does not deal with intra-AS routing at all, a consistent view of intra-AS topology must be provided by the interior routing protocol(s) employed in the AS. Naturally, a protocol such as OSPF (see "Open Shortest Path First (OSPF)," above) that implements synchronization of router databases lends itself well to this role. Consistency of the external topology *may* be provided by all BGP speakers in the AS having BGP sessions with one another, but BGP does not require that this method be used, only that consistency be maintained.

Routing Information Exchange BGP only advertises routes that it uses itself to its neighbors. That is, BGP conforms to the normal Internet hop-by-hop paradigm, even though it has additional information in the form of AS paths and theoretically could be capable of informing a neighbor of a route it would not use itself.

When two BGP speakers form a BGP session, they begin by exchanging their entire routing tables. Routing information is exchanged via UPDATE messages (see below for the format of these messages). Normally the routing information contains the complete AS path to each listed destination in the form of a list of AS numbers in addition to the usual reachability and next-hop information used in traditional vector

Dynamic IP Routing Protocols

distance protocols. But it can be used to suppress routing loops and to eliminate the *counting-to-infinity* problem found in RIP. After BGP neighbors have performed their initial exchange of their complete routing databases, they only exchange updates to that information.

Protocol Description BGP runs over a reliable transport layer connection among neighbor routers. BGP relies on the transport connection for fragmentation, retransmission, acknowledgement, and sequencing. It assumes that the transport connection will close in an orderly fashion, delivering all data, in the event of an error notification.

Practical implementations of BGP use TCP as the transport mechanism. Therefore, BGP protocol data units are contained within TCP packets. Connections to the BGP service on a router use TCP port 179.

The BGP protocol comprises four main stages (see Figure 5-29):

1. Opening and confirming a BGP connection with a neighbor router
2. Maintaining the BGP connection
3. Sending reachability information
4. Notification of error conditions

OPENING AND CONFIRMING A BGP CONNECTION BGP communication between two routers commences with the TCP transport protocol connection being established.

Once the connection has been established, each router sends an *OPEN* message to its neighbor.

The BGP OPEN message, like all BGP messages, consists of a standard header plus packet-type specific contents. The standard header consists of a 16-octet marker field, which is set to all 1s when the authen-

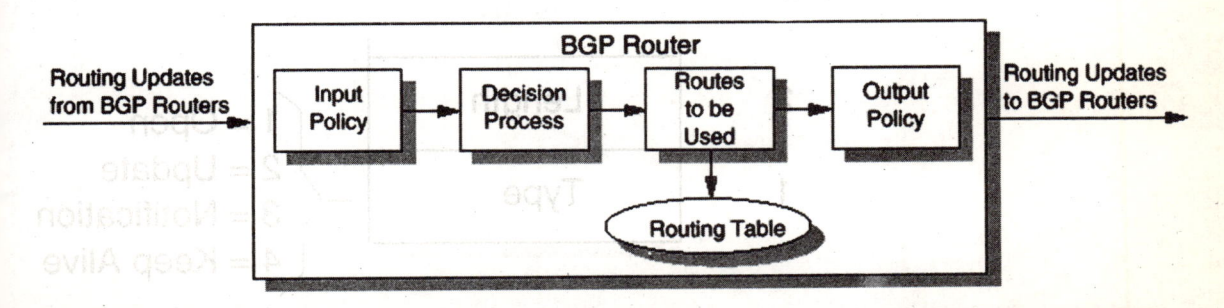

Figure 5-29 BGP Messages Flow between BGP Speakers.

tication code is 0, the length of the total BGP packet, and a type field that specifies the packet to be one of four possible types:

1. OPEN*
2. UPDATE
3. NOTIFICATION
4. KEEPALIVE

The format of the BGP header is shown in Figure 5-30.

The OPEN message defines the originating router's AS number, its BGP router identifier, and the hold time for the connection. If no KEEPALIVE, UPDATE, or NOTIFICATION messages are received for a period of hold time, the originating router assumes an error, sends a notification message, and closes the connection.

The OPEN message also provides an optional parameter length and optional parameters. These fields may be used to authenticate a BGP peer.

The format of the OPEN message is shown in Figure 5-31.

An acceptable OPEN message is acknowledged by a *KEEPALIVE* message. Once neighbor routers have sent KEEPALIVE messages in response to OPENs, they can proceed to exchange further KEEPALIVEs, NOTIFICATIONs, and UPDATEs.

MAINTAINING THE BGP CONNECTION BGP messages must be exchanged periodically between neighbors. If no messages have been received for

Figure 5-30
BGP Message Header.

Number of Octets

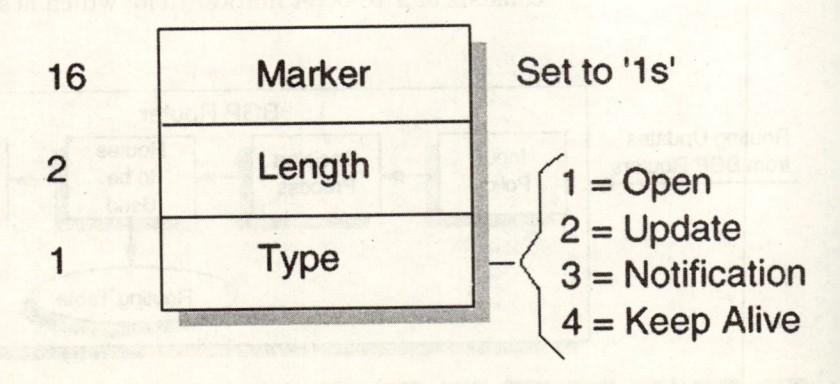

Octets	Field	
16	Marker	Set to '1s'
2	Length	1 = Open
1	Type	2 = Update
		3 = Notification
		4 = Keep Alive

*RFC 1771 uses uppercase to name BGP messages, so this section will do the same.

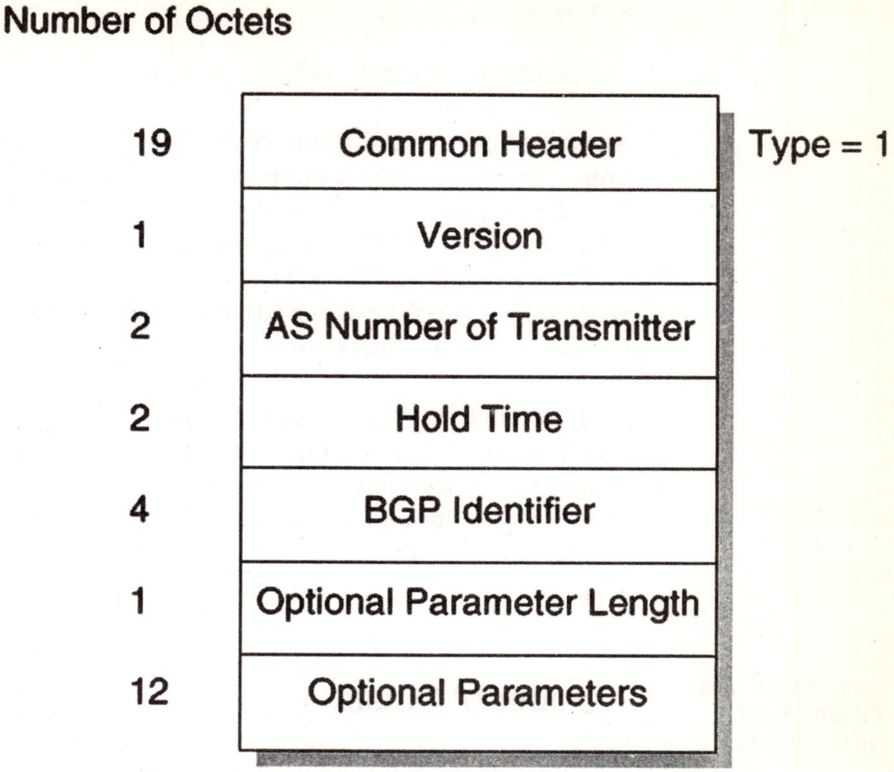

Dynamic IP Routing Protocols

Figure 5-31
BGP OPEN Message.

Number of Octets

Octets	Field	
19	Common Header	Type = 1
1	Version	
2	AS Number of Transmitter	
2	Hold Time	
4	BGP Identifier	
1	Optional Parameter Length	
12	Optional Parameters	

the period of the hold timer, which is calculated by using the smaller of its configured hold time and the hold time received in the OPEN message, then an error on the connection is assumed.

BGP uses KEEPALIVE messages to maintain the connection between neighbors. KEEPALIVE messages consist of the BGP packet header only, with no data. The RFC recommends that the hold time timer is 5 to 22 seconds and KEEPALIVE timer is 30 seconds.

SENDING REACHABILITY INFORMATION Reachability information is exchanged between BGP neighbors in UPDATE messages.

An UPDATE message is used to advertise a single feasible route to a peer or to withdraw infeasible routes from service. An UPDATE may simultaneously advertise a feasible route and withdraw multiple infeasible routes from service. The following are the basic blocks of an UPDATE message:

Network Layer Reachability Information (NLRI)

Path attributes

- Withdrawn routes

The format of these is shown in Figure 5-32.

NETWORK LAYER REACHABILITY INFORMATION (NLRI) NLRI is the mechanism by which BGP-4 supports classless routing. NLRI is a variable field indication, in the form of an IP prefix route, of the networks being advertised. The NLRI is also represented by the tuple `<length,prefix>`. A tuple of the form `<14,220.24.106.0>` indicates a route to be reachable of the form 220.24.106.0 255.252.0.0 or 220.24.106.0/14 in the CIDR format (see Figure 5-33).

PATH ATTRIBUTES Each path attribute consists of a triple set of values: attribute flag, attribute type, and attribute value. Three of the attribute flags provide information about the status of the attribute types, and they may be optional or well-known, transitive or non-transitive, and partial or complete.

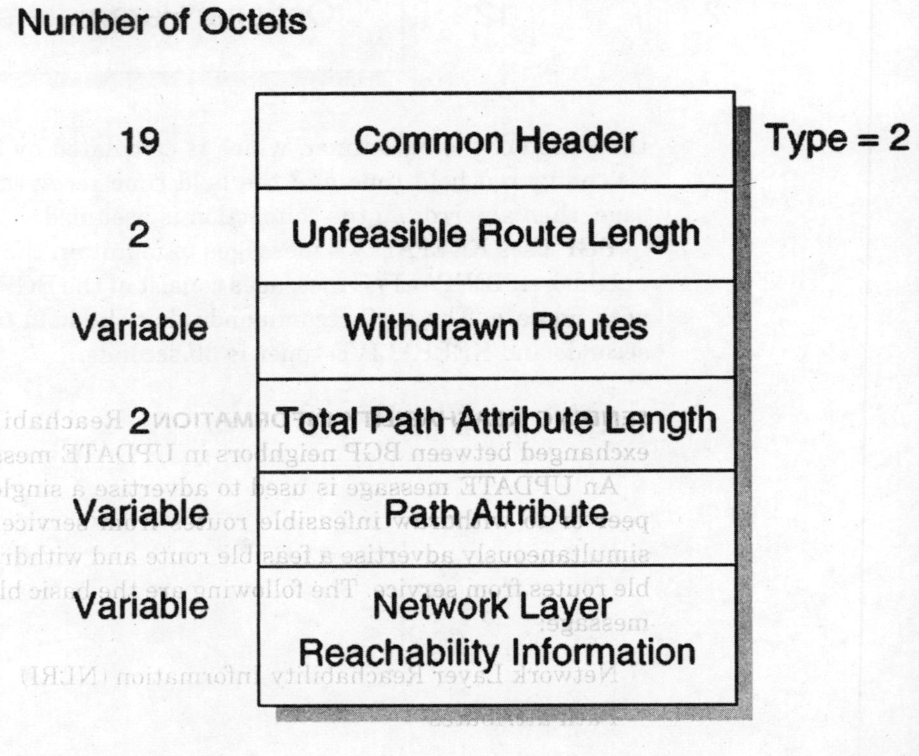

Figure 5-32
BGP UPDATE Message.

Number of Octets

Octets	Field	
19	Common Header	Type = 2
2	Unfeasible Route Length	
Variable	Withdrawn Routes	
2	Total Path Attribute Length	
Variable	Path Attribute	
Variable	Network Layer Reachability Information	

Dynamic IP Routing Protocols

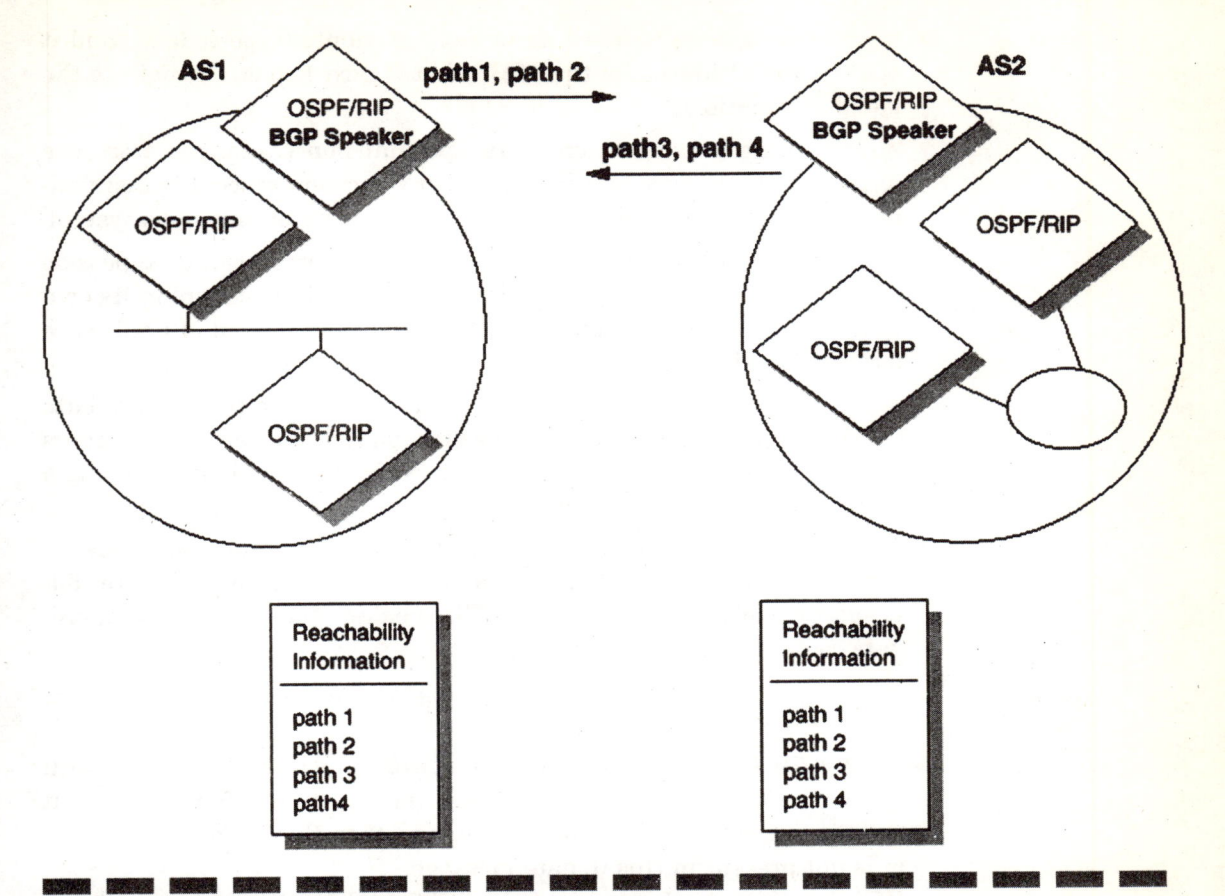

Figure 5-33 BGP Exchanging NLRI.

Attribute flags must be read in conjunction with their associated attribute types. There are seven attribute types that together define an advertised route:

- Origin, which is a well-known mandatory attribute (type code 1), and defines the origin of the route as an IGP, an EGP, or INCOMPLETE (for example a static route).
- AS path is a well-known mandatory attribute (type code 2), and it defines the AS that must be crossed to reach the network being advertised. It is a sequence of AS numbers a route has traversed to reach a destination. The AS that originates the route adds its own AS number when sending the route to its external BGP peer. Each AS that receives the route and passes it on to another BGP peer will prepend its own AS number as the last element of the sequence.

- `Next hop` is a well-known mandatory attribute (type code 3), and it defines the IP address of the ASBR that is next hop on the path to the listed destination(s).
- `Multi_exit_disc`, which is an optional non-transitive attribute (type code 4), is used by a BGP speaker's decision process to discriminate among multiple exit points to a neighboring autonomous system.
- `Local_pref`, which is a well-known discretionary attribute (type code 5), is used by a BGP speaker to inform other BGP speakers in its own autonomous system of the originating speaker's degree of preference for an advertised route.
- `Atomic_aggregate`, which is a well-known discretionary attribute (type code 6), is used by a BGP speaker to inform other BGP speakers that the local system selected a less specific route without selecting a more specific route that is included in it.
- `Aggregator`, which is an optional transitive attribute (type code 7), indicates the last AS number that formed the aggregate route, followed by the IP address of the BGP speaker that formed the aggregate route.

The format of BGP path attributes is shown in Figure 5-34.

WITHDRAWN ROUTES An infeasible route length indicates the total length of the withdrawn routes field in octets. A value of 0 indicates that no routes are withdrawn from service, and that the *Withdrawn Routes* field is not present in this update message.

Withdrawn routes is a variable length field. Updates that are not feasible or that are no longer in service need to be withdrawn from a BGP

Figure 5-34
BGP Path Attributes.

Number of Octets		
1	O T P EL Reserved	O = Optional, T = Transitive, P = Partial, EL = Extended Length
1	Attribute Type	
1 or 2	Attribute Length	
Variable	Attribute Value	

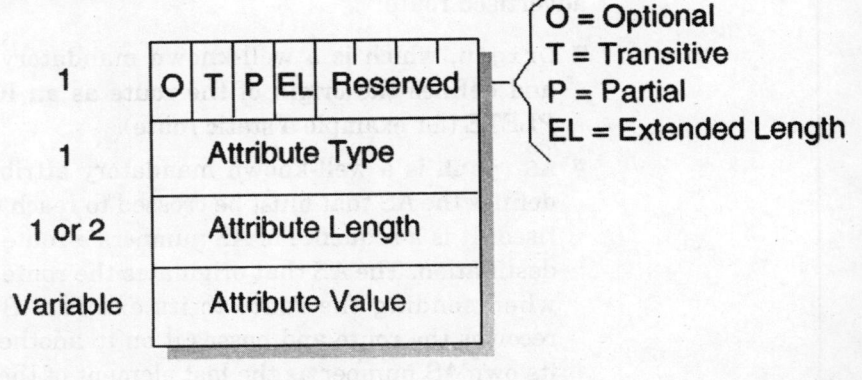

Dynamic IP Routing Protocols

routing table. The withdrawn routes have the same formats as the NLRI. Withdrawn routes are also represented by the tuple `<length,prefix>`. A tuple of the form `<15,220.24.106.0>` indicates a route to be withdrawn of the form 220.24.106.0 255.254.0.0 or 220.24.106.0/15 in the CIDR format (see Figure 5-35).

NOTIFYING ERRORS Notification messages are sent to a neighbor router when error conditions are detected. The BGP transport connection is closed immediately after a notification message has been sent.

Notification messages consist of an error code and an error subcode, which further qualifies the main error. The format of notification messages is shown in Figure 5-36.

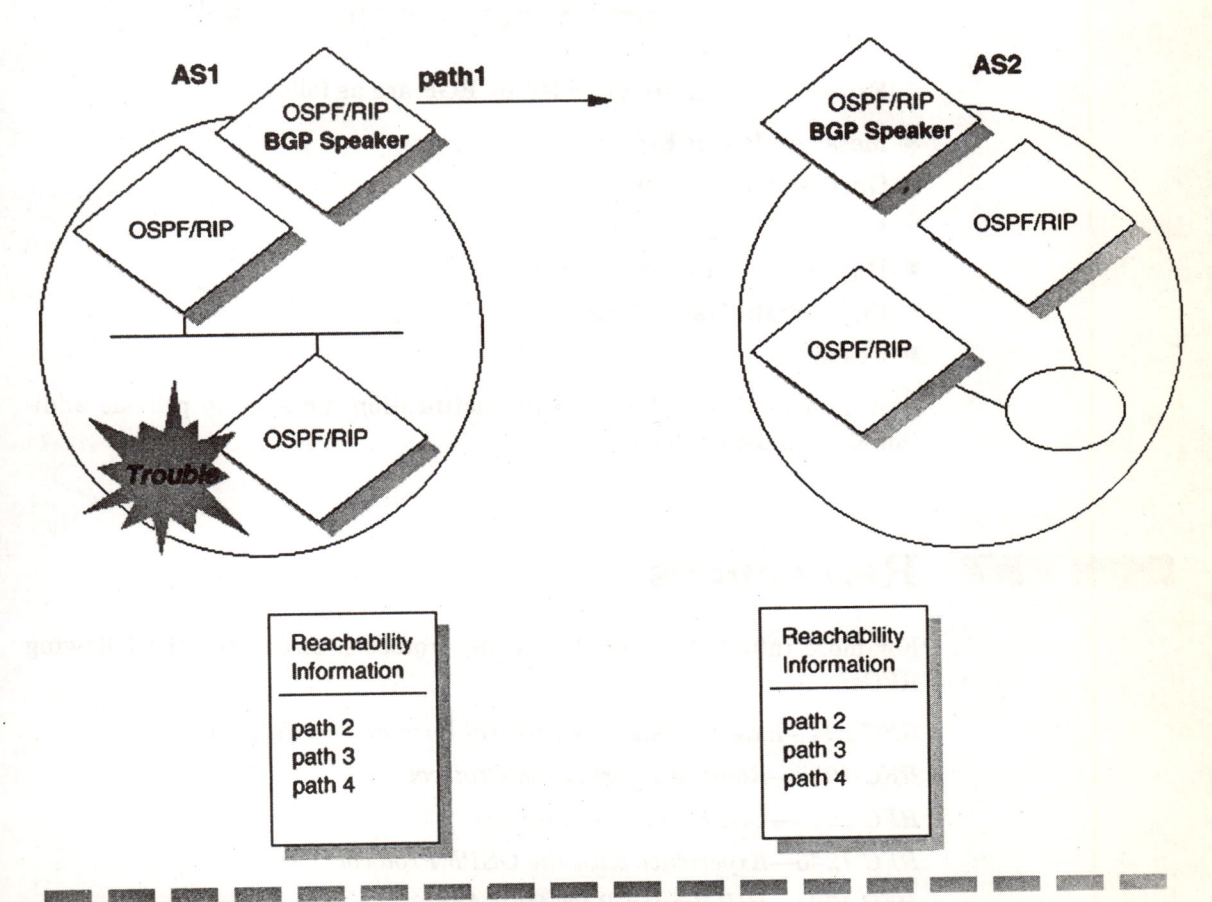

Figure 5-35 BGP Exchanging Withdraw Routes.

Figure 5-36
BGP Notification Message.

Number of Octets

Octets	Field	
19	Common Header	Type = 3
1	Error Code	
1	Error Subcode	
Variable	Data	

Error codes that are provided by BGP are as follows:

- Message Header Error
- Open Message Error
- Update Message Error
- Hold Timer Expired
- Finite State Machine Error
- Cease

A data field is included in the notification message to provide additional diagnostic information.

References

For more information on IP routing protocols, please see the following RFCs:

RFC 904—*Exterior Gateway Protocol Formal Specification*

RFC 1058—*Routing Information Protocol*

RFC 1245—*OSPF Protocol Analysis*

RFC 1246—*Experience with the OSPF Protocol*

RFC 1721—*RIP Version 2 Protocol Analysis*

Dynamic IP Routing Protocols

RFC 1722—RIP Version 2 Protocol Applicability Statement

RFC 1723—RIP Version 2—Carrying Additional Information

RFC 1724—RIP Version 2 MIB Extension

RFC 1771—A Border Gateway Protocol 4 (BGP-4)

RFC 1772—Application of the Border Gateway Protocol in the Internet

RFC 1812—Requirements for IP Version 4 Routers

RFC 1850—OSPF Version 2: Management Information Base

RFC 2080—RIPng for IPv6

RFC 2328—OSPF Version 2

CHAPTER 6

Mobile IP

As Personal Digital Assistants (PDAs) and the next generation of data-ready cellular phones become more widely deployed, a greater degree of connectivity is almost becoming a necessity for the business user on the go. Data connectivity solutions for this group of users is a very different requirement than it is for the fixed dial-up user or the stationary wired LAN user. Solutions here need to deal with the challenge of movement during a data session or conversation. Cellular service providers and network administrators wanting to deploy wireless LAN technologies need to have a solution that will grant this greater freedom.

In the Dynamic Host Configuration Protocol (DHCP) and Dynamic Domain Name Service (DDNS) environment, DHCP provides a device with a valid Internet Protocol (IP) address for the point at which it is attached to the network. DDNS provides a method of locating that device by its host name, no matter where that device happens to be attached to a network and what IP address it has been allocated. An alternative approach to the problem of dealing with mobile devices is provided in RFC 2002 "IP Mobility Support." IP Mobility Support, commonly referred to as Mobile IP, is a *proposed standard*, with a status of *elective*.

Routers, such as Cisco IOS, have integrated new technology into their routing platforms to meet these new networking challenges. Mobile IP is a tunneling-based solution that takes advantage of the Cisco-created generic routing encapsulation (GRE) tunneling technology, as well as simpler IP-in-IP tunneling protocol. This tunneling enables a router on a user's home subnet to intercept and transparently forward IP packets to users while they roam beyond traditional network boundaries. This solution is a key enabler of wireless mobility, both in the wireless LAN arena, such as the 802.11 standard, and in the cellular environment for packet-based data offerings that offer connectivity to a user's home network and the Internet.

Mobile IP provides users the freedom to roam beyond their home subnet while consistently maintaining their home IP address. This enables transparent routing of IP datagrams to mobile users during their movement, so that data sessions can be initiated to them while they roam; it also enables sessions to be maintained in spite of physical movement between points of attachment to the Internet or other networks. Cisco's implementation of Mobile IP is fully compliant with the Internet Engineering Task Force's (IETF's) proposed standard defined in Request for Comments (RFC) 2002.

Mobile IP is most useful in environments where mobility is desired and the traditional land line dial-in model or DHCP does not provide adequate solutions for the needs of the users. If it is necessary or desirable for users to maintain a single address while they transition between networks and network media, Mobile IP can provide them with this ability. Generally, Mobile IP is most useful in environments where a wireless technology is being utilized. This includes cellular environments as well as wireless LAN situations that may require roaming. Mobile IP can go hand in hand with many different cellular technologies like Code Division Multiple Access (CDMA), Time Division Multiple Access (TDMA), Global System for Mobile Communications (GSM), Advanced Mobile Phone Service (AMPS), and Narrowband Advanced Mobile Phone Service (NAMPS), as well as with other proprietary solutions, to provide a mobile system that will scale for many users.

Each mobile node is always identified by its home address, no matter what its current point of attachment to the Internet, allowing for transparent mobility with respect to the network and all other devices. The only devices that need to be aware of the movement of this node are the mobile device and a router serving the user's topologically correct subnet.

Mobile IP Overview

Mobile IP allows a device to maintain the same IP address (its *home address*) wherever it attaches to the network. (Obviously, a device with an IP address plugged into the wrong subnet will normally be unreachable.) However, the mobile device also has a *care-of address*, which relates to the subnet where it is currently located. The care-of address is managed by a home agent, which is a device on the home subnet of the mobile device. Any packet addressed to the IP address of the mobile device is intercepted by the *home agent* and then forwarded on to the care-of address through a tunnel. Once it arrives at the end of the tunnel, the datagram is delivered to the mobile device. The mobile node generally uses its home address as the source address of all datagrams that it sends.

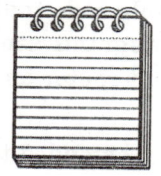

> ***NOTE:*** *To configure home agent functionality on your router, you need to determine IP addresses or subnets for which you would like to allow roaming service. If you intend to support roaming without having a physical home location for the roaming devices, you need to identify the subnets for which you will allow this service and place these virtual networks appropriately within your network on the home agent. It is possible to enable home agent functionality for a homed or non-homed subnet. In the case of non-homed addresses, it is necessary to define virtual networks on the router. Mobile IP Home Agent and Foreign Agent services can be configured on the same router or on separate routers to enable Mobile IP service to users.*
>
> *Since Mobile IP requires support on the host device, it is necessary that each mobile node is appropriately configured for the desired Mobile IP service. Please refer to the manual entries in your mobile-aware IP stack vendor's documentation for details on this.*

Mobile IP can help resolve address shortage problems and reduce administrative workload, because each device that needs to attach to the network at multiple locations requires a single IP address only.

The following terminology is used in a mobile IP network configuration:

agent discovery   The method by which a mobile node determines whether it is currently connected to its home network or a foreign network and by which it detects whether it has moved and the way it has moved. It is the mechanism by which mobile nodes query and discover mobility agents. This is done through an extension of the ICMP Router Discovery Protocol, IRDP (RFC 1256), which includes a mechanism to advertise mobility services to potential users. (ICMP stands for Internet Control Message Protocol.)

care-of address The termination point of the tunnel to a mobile node. This can be a collocated care-of address, where the mobile node acquires a local address and detunnels its own packets, or a foreign agent care-of address, where a foreign agent detunnels packets and forwards them to the mobile node.

correspondent node A peer with which a mobile node is communicating. A correspondent node may be either stationary or mobile.

foreign agent A router on a mobile node's visited network that provides routing services to the mobile node while registered. The foreign agent detunnels and delivers datagrams to the mobile node that were tunneled by the mobile node's home agent. For datagrams sent by a mobile node, the foreign agent may serve as a default router for registered mobile nodes.

home address An IP address that is assigned for an extended time to a mobile node. It remains unchanged regardless of where the node is attached to the Internet.

home agent A router on a mobile node's home network that tunnels packets to the mobile node while it is away from home. It keeps current location information for registered mobile nodes called a *mobility binding*.

home network The network or virtual network that matches the subnet address of the mobile node.

mobile node A host or router that changes its point of attachment from one network or subnet to another. A mobile node may change its location without changing its IP address; it may continue to communicate with other Internet nodes at any location using its home IP address, assuming link-layer connectivity to a point of attachment is available.

mobility agent A home agent or a foreign agent.

mobility binding The association of a home address with a care-of address and the remaining lifetime.

mobility security association A collection of security contexts between a pair of nodes, which may be applied to Mobile IP messages

Mobile IP

exchanged between them. Each context indicates an authentication algorithm and mode, a secret (a shared key or appropriate public/private key pair), and a style of replay protection in use.

Maximum transmission unit (MTU) Maximum packet size, in bytes, that a particular interface can handle.

node A host or router.

registration The process by which the mobile node is associated with a care-of address on the home agent while it is away from home. This may happen directly from the mobile node to the home agent or through a foreign agent.

security parameter index (SPI) The index identifying a security context between a pair of nodes.

tunnel The path followed by a datagram while it is encapsulated from the home agent to the mobile node.

virtual network A network with no physical instantiation beyond a router (with a physical network interface on another network). The router (a home agent, for example) generally advertises reachability to the virtual network using conventional routing protocols.

visited network A network other than a mobile node's home network to which the mobile node is currently connected.

visitor list The list of mobile nodes visiting a foreign agent.

Mobile IP Operation

Mobility agents (home agents and foreign agents) advertise their presence on the network by means of *agent advertisement messages,* which are ICMP router advertisement messages with extensions. A mobile node may also explicitly request one of these messages with an agent solicitation message. When a mobile node connects to the network and receives one of these messages, it is able to determine whether it is on its home network or a foreign network. If the mobile node detects that it is on its home network, it will operate normally, without the use of mobility services. In addition, if it has just returned to the home network, having previously been working elsewhere, it will deregister itself with the home agent. This is done through the exchange of a registration request and registration reply.

If, however, the mobile node detects from an agent advertisement that it has moved to a foreign network, then it obtains a care-of address for the foreign network. This address may be obtained from the foreign agent (a foreign agent care-of address, which is the address of the foreign agent itself), or it may be obtained by some other mechanism such as DHCP (in which case it is known as a *co-located* care-of address). The use of co-located care-of addresses has the advantage that the mobile node does not need a foreign agent to be present at every network that it visits, but it does require that a pool of IP addresses is made available for visiting mobile nodes by the DHCP server.

NOTE: Foreign Agent services need to be enabled on a router attached to any subnet into which a mobile node may be roaming. Therefore, you need to configure Foreign Agent functionality on routers connected to conference room or lab subnets, for example. For administrators wanting to utilize roaming between wireless LANs, Foreign Agent functionality would be configured on routers connected to each base station. In this case, it is conceivable that both Home Agent and Foreign Agent functionality will be enabled on some of the routers connected to these wireless LANs.

Note that communication between a mobile node and a foreign agent takes place at the link-layer level. It cannot use the normal IP routing mechanism, because the mobile node's IP address does not belong to the subnet in which it is currently located.

Once the mobile node has received its care-of address, it needs to register itself with its home agent. This may be done through the foreign agent, which forwards the request to the home agent, or directly with the home agent (see the next section, "Mobile IP Registration Process").

Once the home agent has registered the care-of address for the mobile node in its new position, any datagram intended for the home address of the mobile node is intercepted by the home agent and tunneled to the care-of address. The tunnel endpoint may be at a foreign agent (if the mobile node has a foreign agent care-of address), or at the mobile node itself (if it has a co-located care-of address). Here the original datagram is removed from the tunnel and delivered to the mobile node.

The mobile node will generally respond to the received datagram using standard IP routing mechanisms. Mobile IP operation is shown in Figure 6-1.

Mobile IP Registration Process

RFC 2002 defines two different procedures for mobile IP registration. The mobile node may register via a foreign agent, which relays the reg-

Mobile IP

Figure 6-1
Mobile IP operation.

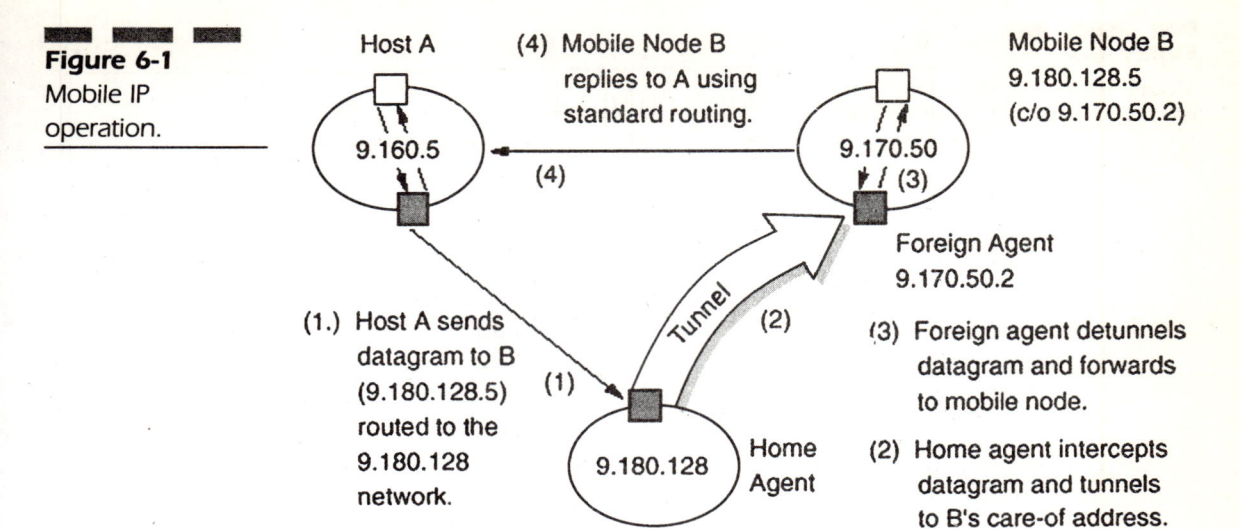

Host A — 9.160.5
(1.) Host A sends datagram to B (9.180.128.5) routed to the 9.180.128 network.
(2) Tunnel
9.180.128 Home Agent
(2) Home agent intercepts datagram and tunnels to B's care-of address.
(3) Foreign agent detunnels datagram and forwards to mobile node.
Foreign Agent 9.170.50.2
9.170.50
(4) Mobile Node B replies to A using standard routing.
Mobile Node B 9.180.128.5 (c/o 9.170.50.2)

istration to the mobile node's home agent, or it may register directly with its home agent. The following rules are used to determine which of these registration processes is used:

- If the mobile node has obtained its care-of address from a foreign agent, it must register via that foreign agent.

- If the mobile node is using a co-located care-of address but has received an agent advertisement from a foreign agent on this subnet, which has the R bit (registration required) set in that advertisement, then it should register via the agent. This mechanism allows for accounting to take place on foreign subnets, even if DHCP and co-located care-of address is the preferred method of address allocation.

- If the mobile node is using a co-located care-of address but has not received such an advertisement, it must register directly with its home agent.

- If the mobile node returns to its home network, it must register (or deregister) directly with its home agent.

The registration process involves the exchange of registration request and registration reply messages, which are User Datagram Protocol (UDP) datagrams. The registration request is sent to port 434. The request consists of a UDP header, followed by the fields shown in Figure 6-2.

Figure 6-2
Mobile IP—Registration request.

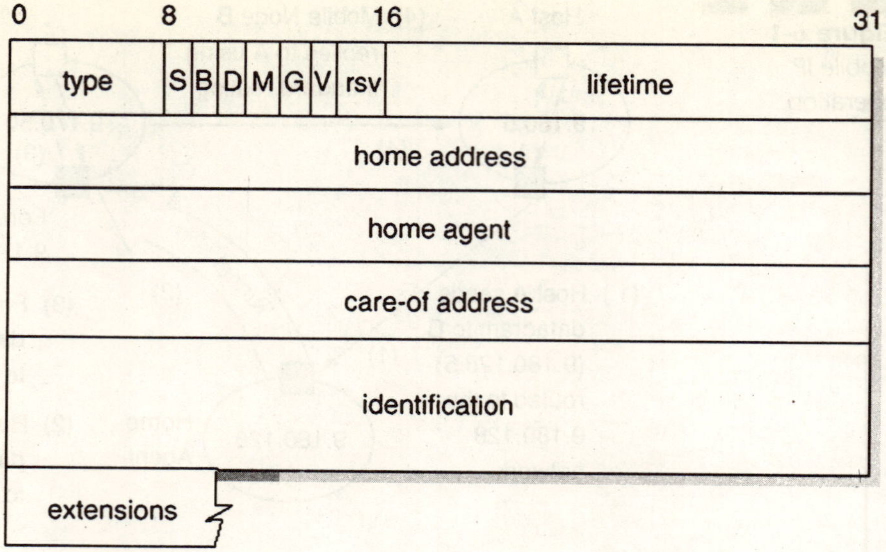

```
0                8              16                              31
+----------------+--+--+--+--+--+--+------+----------------------+
|     type       |S |B |D |M |G |V | rsv  |       lifetime       |
+----------------+--+--+--+--+--+--+------+----------------------+
|                         home address                           |
+----------------------------------------------------------------+
|                          home agent                            |
+----------------------------------------------------------------+
|                        care-of address                         |
+----------------------------------------------------------------+
|                         identification                         |
+----------------------------------------------------------------+
|   extensions
```

Type. 1

S—Simultaneous bindings. If this bit is set, the home agent should keep any previous bindings for this node, as well as add the new binding. The home agent will then forward any datagrams for the node to multiple care-of addresses. This capability is intended particularly for wireless mobile nodes.

B—Broadcast datagrams. If this bit is set, the home agent should tunnel any broadcast datagrams on the home network to the mobile node.

D—Decapsulation by mobile node. The mobile node is using a co-located care-of address and will itself decapsulate the datagrams sent to it.

M—Minimal encapsulation. This should be used for datagrams tunneled to the mobile node.

G—GRE encapsulation. This should be used for datagrams tunneled to the mobile node.

V—Van Jacobson compression. This should be used over the link between agent and mobile node.

rsv—Reserved bits. Sent as zero.

Lifetime. The number of seconds remaining before the registration will be considered expired. A value of zero indicates a request for deregistration. 0xffff indicates infinity.

Home address. The home IP address of the mobile node.

Home agent. The IP address of the mobile node's home agent.

Care-of address. The IP address for the end of the tunnel.

Identification. 64-bit identification number constructed by the mobile node and used for matching registration requests with replies.

Extensions. A number of extensions are defined, all relating to authentication of the registration process. Please see RFC 2002 for full details.

The mobility agent responds to a registration request with a registration reply, with a destination port copied from the source port of the registration request. The registration reply is of the format shown in Figure 6-3.

Type. 3

Code. Indicates the result of the registration request.
   0—Registration accepted
   1—Registration accepted, but simultaneous bindings unsupported
   64-88—Registration denied by foreign agent
   128-136—Registration denied by home agent

Lifetime. The number of seconds remaining before the registration is considered expired. (Code field must be 0 or 1.)

Home address. Home IP address of the mobile node.

Home agent. IP address of the mobile node's home agent.

Figure 6-3
Mobile IP—Registration reply.

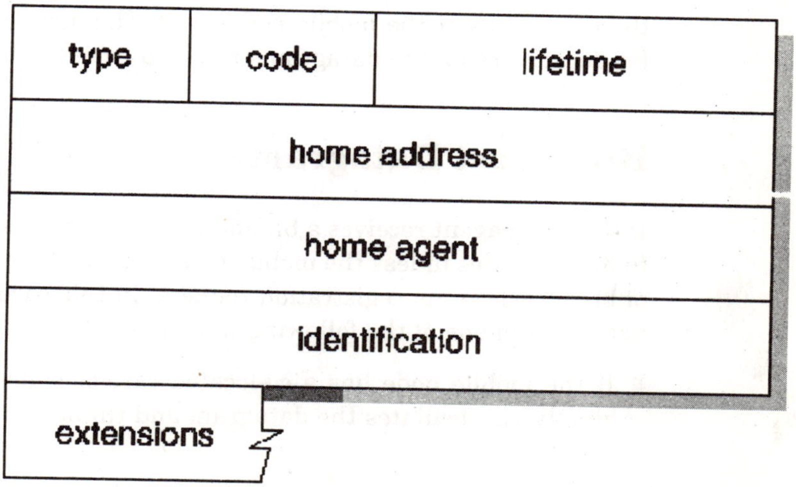

Identification. 64-bit identification number used for matching registration requests with replies.

Extensions. A number of extensions are defined, all relating to authentication of the registration process.

For full details of these messages, please refer to RFC 2002.

Tunneling

The home agent examines the destination IP address of all datagrams arriving on the home network. If the address matches any of the mobile nodes currently registered as being away from home, then the home agent tunnels (using IP-in-IP encapsulation) the datagram to the care-of address for that mobile node. It is likely that the home agent will also be a router on the home network. In this case, it is likely that it will receive datagrams addressed for a mobile node that is not currently registered as being away from home. In this case, the home agent assumes that the mobile node is at home and forwards the datagram to the home network.

When a foreign agent receives a datagram sent to its advertised care-of address, it compares the inner destination address with its list of registered visitors. If it finds a match, the foreign agent forwards the decapsulated datagram to the appropriate mobile node. If there is no match, the datagram is discarded. (The foreign agent must not forward such a datagram to the original IP header; otherwise, a routing loop will occur.)

If the mobile node is using a co-located care-of address, then the end of the tunnel lies at the mobile node itself. The mobile node is responsible for decapsulating the datagrams received from the home agent.

Broadcast Datagrams

If the home agent receives a broadcast datagram, it should not forward it to mobile nodes unless the mobile node specifically requested forwarding of broadcasts in its registration request. In this case, it will forward the datagram in one of the following manners:

- If the mobile node has a co-located care-of address, the home agent simply encapsulates the datagram and tunnels it directly to the care-of address.

- If the mobile node has a foreign agent care-of address, the home agent first encapsulates the broadcast in a unicast datagram addressed to the home address of the node. It then encapsulates and tunnels this datagram to the care-of address. In this way the foreign agent, when it decapsulates the datagram, knows to which of its registered mobile nodes it should forward the broadcast.

Move Detection

Mobile IP is designed not just for mobile users who regularly move from one site to another and attach their laptops to different subnets each time, but also for truly dynamic mobile users (for example, users of a wireless connection from an aircraft). Two mechanisms are defined that allow the mobile node to detect when it has moved from one subnet to another. When the mobile node detects that it has moved, it must reregister with a care-of address on the new foreign network. The two methods of move detection are as follows:

1. Foreign agents are consistently advertising their presence on the network by means of agent advertisements. When the mobile node receives an agent advertisement from its foreign agent, it starts a timer based on the Lifetime field in the advertisement. If the mobile node has not received another advertisement from the same foreign agent by the time the lifetime has expired, then the mobile node assumes that it has lost contact with that agent. If, in the meantime, it has received an advertisement from *another* foreign agent, it may immediately attempt registration with the new agent. If it has not received any further agent advertisements, it should use agent solicitation to try and locate a new foreign agent with which to register.

2. The mobile node checks whether any newly received agent advertisement is on the same subnet as its current care-of address. If the network prefix is different, the mobile node assumes that it has moved. On expiry of its current care-of address, the mobile node registers with the foreign agent that sent the new agent advertisement.

Returning Home When the mobile node receives an agent advertisement from its own home agent, it knows that it has returned to its home network. Before deregistering with the home agent, the mobile node must configure its routing table for operation on the home subnet.

Address Resolution Protocol (ARP) Considerations

Mobile IP requires two extensions to Address Resolution Protocol (ARP) to cope with the movement of mobile nodes. These are as follows:

Proxy ARP. An ARP reply sent by one node on behalf of another that is either unable or unwilling to answer ARP request on its own behalf

Gratuitous ARP. An ARP packet sent as a local broadcast packet by one node that causes all receiving nodes to update an entry in their ARP cache

When a mobile node is registered as being on a foreign network, its home agent will use proxy ARP in response to any ARP request seeking the mobile node's MAC (Message Authentication Code) address. The home agent responds to the request giving its own MAC address.

When a mobile node moves from its home network and registers itself with a foreign network, the home agent does a gratuitous ARP broadcast to update the ARP caches of all local nodes on the network. The MAC address used is again the MAC address of the home agent.

When a mobile node returns to its home network, having been previously registered at a foreign network, gratuitous ARP is again used to update ARP caches of all local nodes, this time with the real MAC address of the mobile node.

Mobile IP Security Considerations

The mobile computing environment has many potential vulnerabilities with regard to security, particularly if wireless links are in use, which are particularly exposed to eavesdropping. The tunnel between a home agent and the care-of address of a mobile node could also be susceptible to interception, unless a strong authentication mechanism is implemented as part of the registration process. RFC 2002 specifies implementation of keyed Message Digest 5 (MD5) for the authentication protocol and advocates the use of additional mechanisms (such as encryption) for environments where total privacy is required.

Mobile IP and Routers

The ability to provide ubiquitous mobility limited only by the scope of the Internet can be enabled with the availability of Mobile IP in a router. This protocol provides users the ability to roam through and beyond their enterprise while maintaining their home IP address. This IETF-proposed standard protocol enables transparent routing of IP datagrams to mobile users despite their physical movement. Mobile IP itself is very straightforward and based on IP tunneling. Valuable data can be constantly forwarded to mobile users wherever they roam. Packets originated by a mobile user can either be sent normally, without a tunneling requirement, or they can be forwarded back to a user's enterprise for increased security. The benefits of Mobile IP include transparent mobility and the low per-packet overhead, which make this solution very attractive for wireless applications. Cisco Systems will be integrating Mobile IP support in the IOS software Release 12.0(1)T.

In this section, Cisco's solutions are used as examples. However, other manufacturers—IBM, 3Com, Bay Networks, and Xylan—offer equal solutions to Cisco.

Background

Movement toward Boundless Networking With the advent of new technologies, the communications and networking paradigm is changing. The most important pieces of information reside on users' networks, with e-mail and Web servers containing all of the information needed for daily business operations. "Road warriors" are in need of connectivity to their home networks and the Internet from just about anywhere, and wireless services are sprouting up to meet this demand. Devices to enable these communications, such as PDAs, are getting smaller, smarter, and more efficient. They are also more reliable in performing useful business functions with their extended battery lifetimes. The need for nonstop networking from areas where there is no wired connectivity is becoming a requirement for many users who find themselves away from their own networks. Cisco IOS software provides the networking technology that will enable this cutting-edge connectivity.

Wireless Services The applicability of Mobile IP is not restricted to wireless applications. However, it is likely to be deployed in this arena first. It is an ideal way to enable data services unencumbered by the wired infrastructure. There are many wireless technologies that offer customers alternative data solutions, from the low-earth orbit (LEO) satellite constellations currently being launched, offering traveling users voice and data services anywhere on the planet, to the household wireless LAN. Some service providers are using microwave technology to offer Local Microwave Distribution Service (LMDS), Multipoint Microwave Distribution Service (MMDS), and similar services to users that include voice, data, and video functionality. Cellular technologies also offer voice and growing amounts of data service to customers to connect them to the Internet. Cellular phone networks are well established to support the voice needs of customers, and now these providers are anxious to start offering the data services that their users have long sought.

Although cellular service has been around for quite some time, only recently have technological advances allowed cellular service providers to offer compelling data services. The first generation of cellular data service is circuit-switched and utilizes resources in much the same way as traditional voice services. This type of service is inefficient at utilizing the carrier network and, more importantly, wasteful of scarce air-link resources. Further, the accompanying billing model is somewhat cost-prohibitive for the majority of subscribers. As second- and third-generation cellular offerings emerge, such as those being referred to as *personal communication systems (PCSs)*, the model is evolving into a packet-based data service, enabling better use of resources in the network and especially the air-link. Packet data enables more efficient use of the air-link, which means per-packet, rather than per-circuit, consumer charging.

Special Needs Are Emerging With the advent of these offerings and the availability of new devices, users are beginning to see real uses for these wireless services. These services can enable users to connect to their enterprise networks. While business professionals wait in airports, sit in conferences, commute on trains, or visit customers and vendors, they don't need to be out of touch with their home office. The extension of the enterprise network, in the form of mobile virtual private networks (VPNs), is a truly compelling use of these new wireless services. Corporations are willing to pay for services that make employees more productive. Just as 42 percent of business professionals now carry a cellular phone to stay in touch with their offices while they are on the road, it is likely that a similarly large number of professionals would be eager to carry a device that would tie them into their corporate network.

Mobile IP

A special set of requirements emerges from this new set of connectivity services. When devices and users don't have wires, there is the likelihood that they will move from one location to another. This is apparent when users are on trains or in cars, but it can also be an issue when users are stationary. As increased data rates are offered, there is a corresponding shrinkage in coverage area. Users are even more likely to move from one cell to another, sometimes without physically moving, because as conditions change in the area, such as having a large truck roll by, a cell hand-off can take place. The rerouting of data packets will need to be dealt with for both directions of data flow. Loss of sessions due to street traffic conditions cannot occur, and emerging push applications will require constant knowledge of a device's location. There must be a way to adequately deal with these relocation and rerouting issues.

Mobile IP: Solutions for Emerging Networking Needs Mobile IP, as outlined in RFC 2002, enables a host to be identified by a single IP address even while the device physically moves its point of attachment from one network to another, allowing for the transparent forwarding of data packets to a single address. This IETF-proposed standard functionality provides the unique ability to maintain sessions, regardless of movement between locations on different networks, because there are no address changes to be dealt with. Mobility becomes an issue that the Mobile IP protocol can transparently negotiate to allow users new free-

Figure 6-4
Wireless technology applicability by bandwidth and situation.

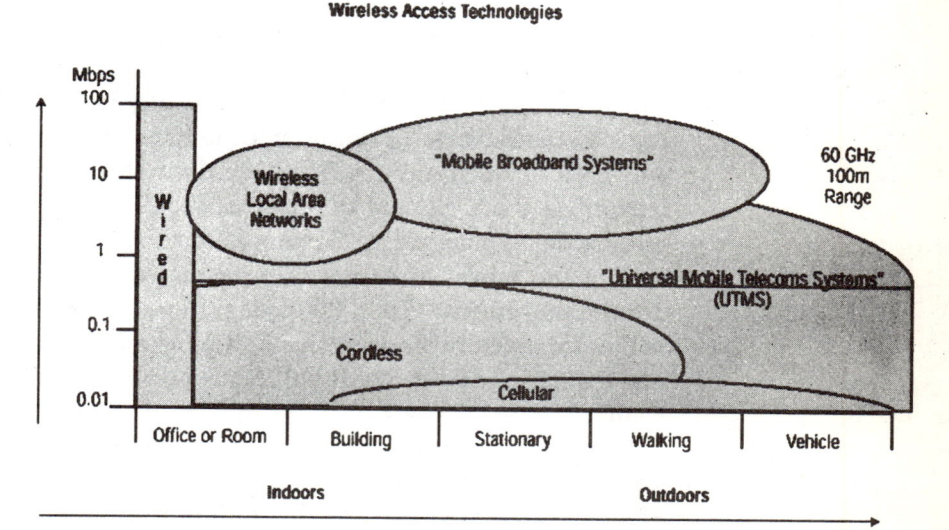

Figure 6-5
The challenges of mobility vary depending on the user's circumstances.

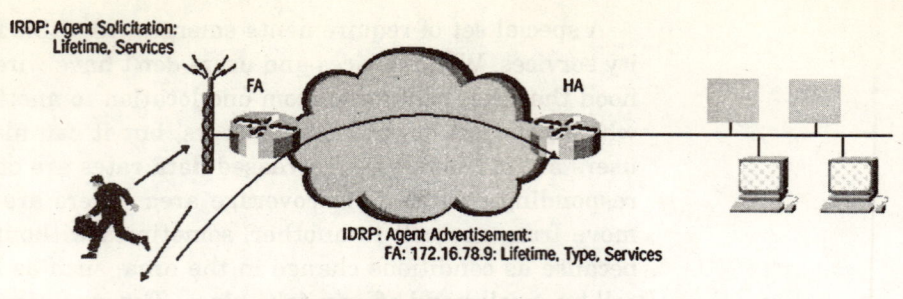

IRDP: Agent Solicitation: Lifetime, Services

FA   HA

IDRP: Agent Advertisement:
FA: 172.16.78.9: Lifetime, Type, Services

Registration through the FA back to the HA

doms. Movement from one point of attachment to another is seamlessly achieved without the intervention or the knowledge of the user. Mobile IP is the first protocol to offer such mobility transparently to applications. Roaming from a wired network to a wireless or wide area network can also be achieved with ease. Therefore, Mobile IP provides ubiquitous connectivity for users whether they are within their enterprise networks or away from home. Access to the resources within the network remains the same from the perspective of the user. This allows for truly transparent mobility with respect to all devices that communicate with the mobile node and all intermediate devices within networks.

An added benefit of Mobile IP is that it allows users to gain access to their enterprise networks and the Internet in the same way no matter where they are physically. They can access resources in the same way while they are within the bounds of their enterprise network and also when they dial in from hotel rooms or customer sites. Mobile IP provides a solution that can work in all connectivity situations. It enables users to connect to media of any kind, automatically locate a mobility agent, and register their current location with a home gateway. The home gateway will then forward any traffic received for this mobile user to his or her current location. Should the user move, since the Mobile IP software is automatically monitoring for this condition, it will notify the home gateway of the move. In this way, sessions can be seamlessly maintained despite movement. When the user returns home, the Mobile IP protocol will automatically discover this and inform its home gateway that it has arrived home, and the host will behave as any other IP device normally would.

Cisco IOS software increases the overall offering of this mobility solution, since many value-added features can be used in conjunction with Mobile IP. All IOS features for differentiation of services, accounting, traffic engineering, and queuing can be used in conjunction with Mobile

IP. By always being able to identify a user by an IP address, it is also possible to simplify certain configurations within the network. Access lists and queuing or traffic shaping configurations could remain static, for example. Netflow statistics and accounting data would be obtained in a straightforward manner. And it could be possible to manage the Mobile IP functionality in the network in the same way the rest of the IOS platform elements are monitored. Cisco has implemented full MIB support for Mobile IP as specified in RFC 2006.

Emerging Examples Where Mobile IP Is Applicable

Delivery Vehicles The need for wireless data communication is not new. Today there are several industries that rely on it to save time and money. One of the places where it is absolutely necessary is in the delivery industry. These people need to be in touch with schedule changes or road conditions. Drivers need to be updated immediately when pickup schedule changes occur or when there are hazards to be aware of. Drivers require directions in order to arrive at the new destination on time. A tremendous amount of time can be wasted printing schedules, updating them with changes, and trying to ensure that the drivers have correct information. If this data is constantly kept current on a device in the vehicle, the drivers can plan accordingly and immediately contact home base when they have questions. This saves a tremendous amount of time, allows more deliveries to be made efficiently, and ensures that the schedule is kept at all times. Most of the systems that are performing these functions today were developed specifically for each organization's applications in a proprietary manner. The pressing need to make a generalized solution for the expanding service industry is rapidly emerging. This will enable even greater savings, by using standard protocols and off-the-shelf platforms that can be managed in conjunction with the rest of the network elements.

The Business Traveler As the pace and frequency of business communication increases, time spent out of touch hurts businesses. "Road warriors" often find themselves wasting valuable workday hours without any communication with the home office. Business travelers could make better use of time spent while in cabs, in hotel lobbies, and in airport terminals, or even on airplanes. Availability of services to tie users back into their corporate networks could prove invaluable. Even more compelling would be a service that would allow users to be automatically notified of new developments as they occurred. Carrying a device that would allow users to constantly receive relevant information would be very liberating. This information could include stock and news updates, as well as sports scores and entertainment schedules. If users then had the ability to access any Web pages referenced in e-mail and immediately reply directly from this same device, users could be as effective on the road as they are at their desks. This would go a long way toward ensuring that communication would not break down when users have to visit customers or attend conferences. Services that will allow this sort of communication can be offered in the very near future.

Wired/Wireless VPN One benefit of this new era of communication is the extension of the wired VPN into the emerging wireless world. Paging services that require users to call back into the office are less compelling. More compelling will be the new class of services that enable users to carry a small device that is always on and always connected and gives users the capability to be tied directly into what is going on in their home environment. New products are coming to market that will have the ability to recognize whether a user is at home or away and adapt the forwarding of information to fit a profile the user sets up to match different situations. These will provide users with the ability to get what they need when they need it, with mobile IP providing the underlying network service.

Detailed Protocol Overview

Location Discovery Mobile IP works because the mobile node (MN) is able to discover whether it is at home or away from home. A host determines whether it is on its home network by using extensions to ICMP Router Discovery Protocol (IRDP) as specified in (RFC 1256). These IRDP extensions indicate mobility agent information that facilitates agent discovery. Routers acting as home agents (HAs) or foreign agents (FAs) will advertise their existence. HAs are routers located on the mobile node's home network that are capable of tunneling the mobile node's datagrams to it while it is away. FAs are devices on a network that are capable of acting as a detunneling point for datagrams to the mobile node. Agent discovery, like router discovery, works through advertisements, solicitations, and responses. A mobile-aware host, which is a host that is capable of utilizing mobile IP, will listen for agent advertisements

Mobile IP

or solicit them. An agent advertisement will indicate a mobility agent's IP address, as well as whether it is able to serve as an HA or FA. Agents will also advertise the registration options they are capable of supporting, as well as their availability, by using the appropriate fields. If the mobile node notices its own HA's advertisement, it knows it is at home and does not need to register or do anything special in order to receive its datagrams.

If, on the other hand, a mobile node receives an IRDP advertisement from another mobility agent, it will be able to determine it is not on its home network. When this is the case, a mobile node will need to register with its own home agent in order to receive datagrams, since they would not otherwise be directed to the host at its current location. The mobile node will try to locate a suitable foreign agent. It can find one if the IRDP advertisement contains mobility information, and then it can register its location via this foreign agent if it desires. If this IRDP advertisement does not contain mobility information, or if the FA does not support the options the mobile node desires, the mobile node can register directly with its home agent. In either case, the MN will send a registration request to its HA.

Care-Of Addresses and Registration. While away from home, the mobile node will be associated with a care-of address. This address will identify the mobile node's current, topological point of attachment to the Internet and will be used to route packets to the mobile node while the user visits other locations. Either a foreign agent's address or an address obtained by the MN for use while it is present on a particular network will be used as the care-of address. The former is called a *foreign agent care-of address* and the latter a *co-located care-of address*. After the MN

Figure 6-6
Location discovery and registration.

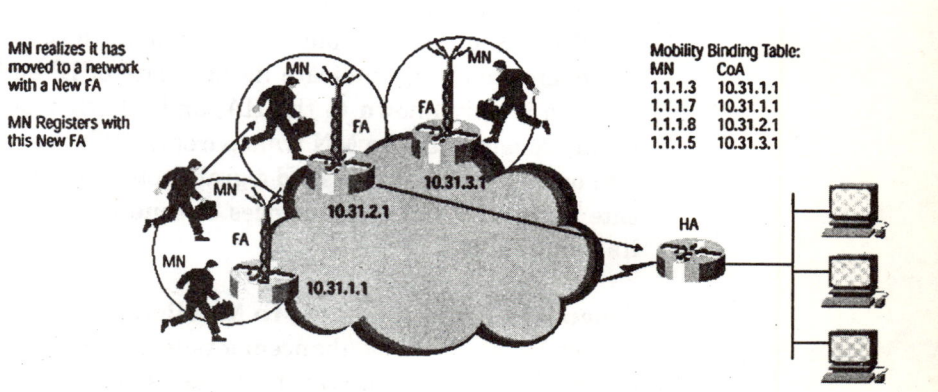

decides on its care-of option, it sends a registration request to its HA. In this request it lists the options it would like for its registration.

Tunneling to mobile nodes can be done via IP-in-IP encapsulation (RFC 2003) or generic routing encapsulation (GRE; specified in RFC 1701). Cisco IOS has also implemented tunnel "soft state," as described in RFC 2003, to aid in path maximum transmittable unit (MTU) discovery. Tunnel soft state allows the tunnel head to keep track of the tunnel path MTU and return this value to senders of larger packets via Internet Control Message Protocol (ICMP) type 4 responses. The registration requests and replies are required to have an authentication extension that includes a keyed MD5 hash of the registration packet, as well as a time-stamp to ensure the origination of the request and the time it was sent, in order to prevent replay attacks.

When the home agent receives a registration request, it determines whether the authentication hash is valid, if the time-stamp is within an acceptable range, and if it can honor the request in terms of resources as well as options. It then sends a reply to the mobile node. When the MN and the HA agree upon a set of service options, then a mobility binding is put into the HA's binding table and is used to associate the mobile node's home address with the care-of address. This binding will allow the mobile node to receive tunneled datagrams destined for its home address when it is not physically connected to that network. Since the HA is attached to the home LAN of the MN, it will merely accept and forward traffic destined for the registered MN.

When this binding is first added to the table, the HA sends a gratuitous ARP on the MNs' home LAN so that all directly connected devices can continue to communicate with the mobile node through the HA. While the mobile node is registered with the home agent, the home agent will proxy ARP for the home address of the mobile node and tunnel packets to it using the care-of address in its mobility binding. When the mobile node moves its point of attachment to the Internet, it will notify the home agent and indicate its new care-of IP address. This change in location is only known to the HA, and all other devices can continue to communicate with the MN transparently. When a mobile node returns to its home network, it will send a gratuitous ARP response in order to indicate its return and allow devices to send packets directly to the MN on its home subnet.

Cisco IOS Enhancements to Mobile IP The Cisco IOS implementation of Mobile IP has enhancements to ensure scalability, resiliency, and security. IOS platforms can function as HAs or FAs, or both simultane-

Mobile IP

Figure 6-7
Transparent reregistration.

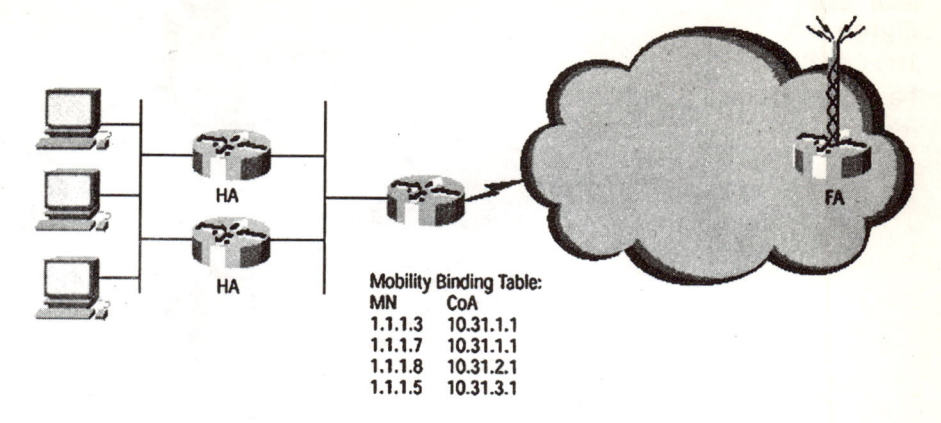

Mobility Binding Table:
MN	CoA
1.1.1.3	10.31.1.1
1.1.1.7	10.31.1.1
1.1.1.8	10.31.2.1
1.1.1.5	10.31.3.1

ously. Since it is possible for large numbers of devices to be mobile, the number of keys needed to perform the authentication function could become very large. For this reason, IOS software allows for the mobility keys to be stored on an authentication, authorization, and accounting (AAA) server that can be accessed via either TACACS+ or RADIUS. This allows for scalability to large numbers of potentially mobile users and provides a single place for maintenance. For security, IOS has the ability to use registration filters to restrict who is allowed to register. This mechanism can be used on both the FA and the HA to prevent certain MNs from registering and to prevent registration via some mobility agents. This provides the further ability to restrict usage only to areas where administrators have trusted relationships in place.

Because of many years of internetworking experience, Cisco recognized the fact that the Mobile IP architecture could benefit from additional built-in redundancy. The base specification could allow the failure of an HA to interrupt data flow to the mobile node. This is the case, since there is no "keep-alive" mechanism between the HA and registered MNs. If MNs fail to receive traffic tunneled from their home agent, it may be because there was no traffic. On the other hand, if there were some sort of failure on the HA due to a power failure or a software upgrade, the binding table could have been lost, and there is no mechanism to alert the MNs. Because of this situation, IOS software has implemented home agent redundancy, leveraging de facto Hot Standby Router Protocol (HSRP), as shown in Figure 6-8. This feature allows for one or more home agents to back one another up in the event of any kind of a failure. The active HA sends binding updates to the backup HA every time a new registration is entered into the binding table, which keeps the binding

Figure 6-8
The Cisco HSRP-based home agent redundancy.

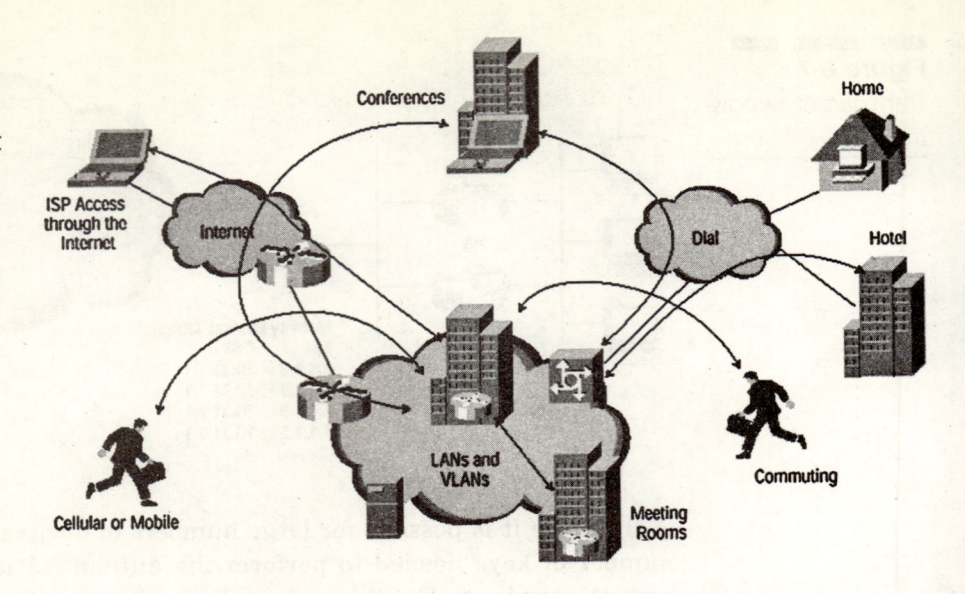

tables in sync. If a new HA boots up on the LAN, it can have the entire binding table loaded into its memory so that it can be ready in the event of any network failure. This enables the nonstop networking that customers have come to rely on from Cisco.

Standardization Status Mobile IP is the Internet proposed standard mechanism for dealing with mobility. It is outlined in RFCs 2002 to 2006:

- 2002—IP Mobility Support
- 2003—IP Encapsulation within IP
- 2005—Applicability Statement for IP Mobility Support
- 2006—The Definitions of Managed Objects for IP Mobility Support Using SMIv2

All of these RFCs are all in proposed-standard status with multivendor support. Cisco, as the market leader, has identified mobile data as one of the most significant emerging opportunities. Cisco IOS has the first implementation of IETF standard Mobile IP available on a router platform with the 12.0.1T release.

Other Important Issues

Security Concerns Security concerns are heightened whenever corporate network resources are accessed from beyond enterprise bounds.

Therefore, Cisco's implementation of Mobile IP has some additional security features. IOS software has support for the mandatory and both of the optional authentication parameters within Mobile IP. These are the mandated mobile-home authentication and the optional foreign-home and mobile-foreign authentications. The authentication procedures performed are keyed MD5 hashes, which cover all registration requests and replies. In addition, the registration requests and replies are all time-stamped to ensure that there can be no replay attack. Such attacks might occur if a registration packet is sniffed off the wire and then reused by an impostor in order to gain access to network resources. This time-stamp is also protected by the hash.

Cisco has implemented access list functionality to enable an administrator to permit the registration of certain users and prevent the registration via certain mobility agents. Reverse tunneling has been implemented in the home agent to allow for the optional tunneling of datagrams back to the home agent from the MN or the FA. This will allow for communication through firewalls, for example. Communication beyond a firewall can be an issue when ingress filtering is performed on firewalling devices or boundary routers. The logging of any type of Mobile IP security violation can be performed with IOS software as well, such as an attempt to register that fails authentication. In the future, it will be possible to utilize IPSec encryption with Mobile IP in IOS software. This will further ensure that corporate communications can remain private for mobile VPNs.

CHAPTER 7

Security of DHCP and Dynamic DNS

Security is often an afterthought in building a network, but you should be very concerned that your private (or even public) TCP/IP network can prevent unwanted access. This chapter will show how to refuse connections to the network so that no one with a notebook computer can walk in and grab your information (unless you want them to). One basic security issue is to make sure that you have the latest upgrades to your systems that are depended upon to provide network connectivity. All systems should be latest upgrades, but especially those that connect to the network. Manufacturers generally respond fairly quickly when crackers discover another hole in their software.

A good mailing list to be on for security issues is the Computer Emergency Response Team (CERT) list. You get notified of security holes as they are published. See *http://www.cert.org* to get on the mailing list, or *http://www.cert.org/advisories* for the latest information.

Security Trade-Off

For easy access and less procedure to hook up workstations, Dynamic Host Configuration Protocol (DHCP) is very convenient for both users and administrators. TCP/IP administrators will be relieved from the tedious work in assigning the IP address to a new request.

For a static IP address assignment, the administrator normally assigns the host name to the address. It will be treated like a memo; the host name would be *steven-king,* for example. The assigned host name is a kind of link to another document, which will have the actual name of the owner and phone number, and so on. However, the whole static TCP/IP itself has no security to prevent an unauthorized access to the IP network. By checking the existing workstation's configuration, people can find the unused IP addresses and required IP router address, then hook up their laptops, for example. (At least we can say it is not so easy to do all this work quickly.)

When a DHCP server is up and running, it provides a convenient environment for mobile users. Users can hook up their laptops and instantly gain access to a corporate network. In general, DHCP users are anonymous to the administrator. In a company where the basic TCP/IP security guard is required, the basic DHCP environment is not good.

That is probably the one reason why large customers are not eager to use DHCP servers. To break through this problem, there must be another mechanism in addition to DHCP. Presecured Dynamic Domain Name Service (DDNS) client and domain design is the answer to the security problem. The TCP/IP administrator might have slightly more workload than the static IP, but the result would be a well-protected dynamic IP network that is more secure.

RSA Public Key Authentication System

Dynamic DNS, as defined in RFC 2137, uses an RSA public key/private key authentication system to secure the Dynamic DNS update. A client has a set of keys stored on the hard disk. The key pair is dynamically generated by the client program or is generated by the administrator through the DDNS Administrator GUI called *DDNS Server*

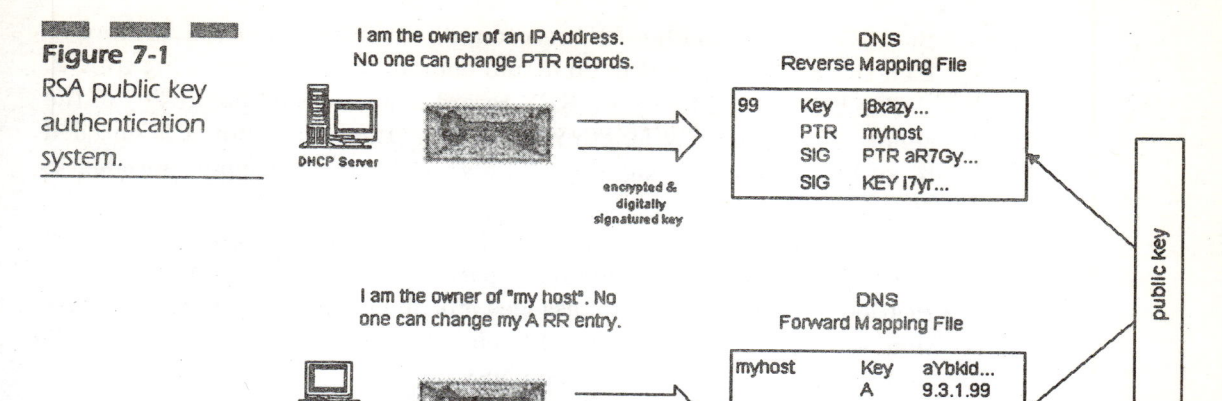

Security of DHCP and Dynamic DNS

Figure 7-1
RSA public key authentication system.

Top diagram:
"I am the owner of an IP Address. No one can change PTR records."
DHCP Server → encrypted & digitally signed key →

DNS Reverse Mapping File:
99	Key	j8xazy...
	PTR	myhost
	SIG	PTR aR7Gy...
	SIG	KEY l7yr...

Bottom diagram:
"I am the owner of "my host". No one can change my A RR entry."
→ encrypted & digitally signed key →

DNS Forward Mapping File:
myhost	Key	aYbkid...
	A	9.3.1.99
	SIG	Akjoj...
	SIG KEY 0Aor...	

→ public key

Administrator. Figure 7-1 illustrates how the DNS dynamic update is protected with the digital signature authentication.

A client owns the host name, so it authenticates the A RR (address resource record) in the DNS domain file. If the dynamic zone is created as a Dynamic Secured one, clients can dynamically register A RR at any time. That means the client generates an RSA key pair once at startup time and sends a registration request to a DNS server together with its public key (encoded) and its IP address. The important matter is that the client keeps the private key on a hard disk or a networked drive, and it should not be exposed.

The RSA key system depends on the fact that the digital signature can be verified with the client's public key and the private key cannot be discovered from either the public key, or the digital signature, or a combination of both. The client must generate a new digital signature each time an update request is sent to DNS. Once a host name is registered with the public key and the digital signature, the entry is verified or authenticated at each DHCP renewal time or when the DNS TTL (Time to Live) is expired.

If the dynamic zone is defined as a Dynamic Secured one, clients cannot add or update their host name dynamically. Since the administrator defines host names and generates key pairs for each host name, the client should import the specific key pair and must use it for further processing.

Figure 7-1 simplifies the record entries of both domain file (forward mapping file) and reverse file (reverse mapping file), but the basic procedure is that there are two SIG records and one SIG record authenticate the KEY record. Another SIG record authenticates either the A record or PTR record. This is part of an actual domain file is shown in Figure 7-2.

The highlighted field in a KEY record is an encoded public key of the client. The actual key length is 1024 bits (128 bytes), but it is encoded to 88 bytes. A digital signature is also 1024 bits but again encoded to 88 bytes.

You probably heard in the news that the U.S. government approved the 1024-bit RSA key system for export, since it is only used for authentication and not to encrypt messages. For the purpose of message encryption, the key length is restricted to 56 bits for the export version and 128 bits for the U.S. domestic version only.

There are two different Dynamic DNS zones:

- *Dynamic Secured.* The Dynamic Secured zone provides a great deal for a secured zone. Once a client's host name is dynamically registered in the DDNS database, it is protected and cannot be taken over by another client. The workstation with the DDNS client function can dynamically join the network and can register its name, and because of that, the DNS zone is open for all clients.

  The Dynamic Secured zone buys you tremendous flexibility, given the goal of an administratorless system, in that it requires no administrator intervention to get the DHCP clients registered, which is exactly the point of DHCP. The only shortcoming of this concept is that a malicious client could create useless names, but then, this shouldn't cause too much of a problem. However, be aware that any DDNS client could perform the very first registration and then all of a sudden would own a host name that might be rather critical.

- *Dynamic Presecured.* If you are looking for the perfect secured DNS zone you need to look at a so-called Dynamic Presecured zone. Clients joining the presecured domain must have the key pair generated by the administrator. This key can then be distributed to the client through a networked drive, through e-mail, or through a diskette.

Figure 7-2
Example of KEY, SIG, and A resource record.

```
client1  4660   IN  HINFO  "Ni0weDAwMDBlNTY4N2Y2MA==" "IBMDDNS-PROXY"              ;Cl=3
         4660   IN  SIG    A 1 4 4660 2147483647 893107703 0x6d25
                           client1.austin.cooking.net ulSD2P.....G5VK47mig== 2147483647 ;Cl=3
         4660   IN  SIG    HINFO 1 4 4660 2147483647 893107703 0x6d25
                           client1.austin.cooking.net Hxw7z........e4p+a/g== 2147483647 ;Cl=3
         4660   IN  SIG    KEY 1 4 4660 2147483647 893107703 0x6d25
                           client1.austin.cooking.net FFqsEa.......Yujelkw== 2147483647 ;Cl=3
         3600   IN  KEY    0x0000    0   1 AQPqq+gV....VuGWzJW3X                          ;Cl=3
         4660   IN  A      192.168.7.22    ;Cl=3
```

Security of DHCP and Dynamic DNS

Using this method, there is no chance for clients to (unlawfully) join the DNS space. The administrator would have perfect control over his or her DNS zone.

As for the client's public key, it is not a secret one. In fact, it is intended to be known by everyone. For example, the client's public key can be retrieved through the NSLOOKUP interface. Figure 7-3 is an example of the NSLOOKUP output, which provides all the information of *client1.austin.cooking.net*.

Figure 7-3
NSLOOKUP output returning public key.

```
Default Server: fajita.austin.cooking.net
Address:  192.168.7.10

> > Server:  fajita.austin.cooking.net
Address:  192.168.7.10

client1.austin.cooking.netCPU = Ni0weDAwMDB1NTY4N2Y2MA==OS = IBMDDNS-PROXY
client1.austin.cooking.net
Signature Record covering A RR's
Authentication Algorithm = 1 (MD5/RSA)  Labels = 4
Original TTL           = 4660 (1 hour 17 mins 40 secs)
Client SIG expiration = 2147483647, Mon Jan 18 21:14:07 2038
Time signed           = 893107703, Mon Apr 20 16:28:23 1998
Server SIG expiration = 2147483647, Mon Jan 18 21:14:07 2038
Key footprint = 0x6d25
Signer's name = client1.austin.cooking.net
Signature = u1SD2P0kC8Id1OHyelcqqZIRrMEkHQ3e2SdmwaaStBRRcSBC4DDRMSIRDwvgwcrA7wfDvY9
            QQEoOKG5VK47mig==
client1.austin.cooking.net
Signature Record covering HINFO RR's
Authentication Algorithm = 1 (MD5/RSA)  Labels = 4
Original TTL          = 4660 (1 hour 17 mins 40 secs)
Client SIG expiration = 2147483647, Mon Jan 18 21:14:07 2038
Time signed           = 893107703, Mon Apr 20 16:28:23 1998
Server SIG expiration = 2147483647, Mon Jan 18 21:14:07 2038
Key footprint = 0x6d25
Signer's name = client1.austin.cooking.net
Signature = HrwTzfLIGkvFfUmHwKr6aaHV/qO6RVc6uzItH9cYYQs1d1PRVgGrEN1QZscj2gwCY4Z
            B/LfBcH1fCVse4p+a/g==
client1.austin.cooking.net
Signature Record covering KEY RR's
Authentication Algorithm = 1 (MD5/RSA)  Labels = 4
Original TTL          = 4660 (1 hour 17 mins 40 secs)
Client SIG expiration = 2147483647, Mon Jan 18 21:14:07 2038
Time signed           = 893107703, Mon Apr 20 16:28:23 1998
Server SIG expiration = 2147483647, Mon Jan 18 21:14:07 2038
Key footprint = 0x6d25
Signer's name = client1.austin.cooking.net
Signature = FPqsEaYujelrDfRx1S77NxE5Om/1+OgvRUN/F2QLPiNIYa5S1FdNBttBi31OQRRs6eRje
            fwjJFB1IqqPVuX8kw==
client1.austin.cooking.net
flags = 0x0000 (HostKey) protocol = 0, algorithm = 1 (MD5/RSA)
public-key data = AQPqq+gVMx4td+vglqCjv3fknqVyNn++w/uAoNHA/t52qzVkyXOYAGftLS78gi
                  pWJtVpDGiqMWs71y3VuGWzJW3X
client1.austin.cooking.netinternet address = 192.168.7.22
austin.cooking.netnameserver = fajita.austin.cooking.net
fajita.austin.cooking.netinternet address = 192.168.7.10
>
```

Presecured Domain

The presecured domain is the most secured DNS name space available. For information on how to set up a presecured domain, refer to the software manual supplied by the vendor. You can set up a subdomain in the corporate root domain and make the subdomain work as a Dynamic Presecured domain using DDNS.

Two reasons for a higher security standard would be as follows:

- The DHCP client cannot register its host name without having an RSA key pair and the DDNS client code present.
- Without an RSA key pair, the PTR record for reverse mapping cannot be registered either. Therefore, reverse mapping would fail, and the administrator would be able to know which IP addresses are unofficial users. The administrator would also be able to determine the MAC address of those DHCP clients' LAN adapters. The administrator could then configure the DHCP server to exclude those unlawful clients through the server configuration GUI.

Just like a Lotus Notes administrator generates ID files for users and distributes them to users, the TCP/IP administrator generates them key files and passes them to clients.

ProxyArec Considerations

The ProxyArec function is desired by the industry, and several companies provide products that embrace ProxyArec. ProxyArec is based on the IETF Internet Draft called "Interaction between DHCP and DNS."

Besides the DHCP and DDNS servers, the NTS Shadow IPserver also provides a ProxyArec function. However, NTS Shadow IPserver does not support option 81, which tells the DHCP server that a DHCP/DDNS client wants to register/update its A RR by itself; so the DHCP server would not perform the ProxyArec function to update the DDNS table. Option 81 is discussed in the next section.

When the DHCP server is configured to enable the A resource record update in addition to the PTR resource record update, which is known as a Proxy Arec function, any DHCP client that carries the option 12 host name will register both A RR and PTR RR. Since the DHCP server uses its own RSA key for all DDNS update requests, there is no authentica-

Security of DHCP and Dynamic DNS

tion mechanism to validate that the client really is the client that has the original host name.

However, the ProxyArec function in other DHCP servers provides security. When the configuration file has the following statement, the client's MAC address will be used to memorize the ownership of the A RR:

```
ProxyArec Protected
```

To disable the MAC address identification, the statement should be as follows:

```
ProxyArec Standard
```

Then, the DHCP server will blindly update the A RR without comparing the MAC addresses at all.

From the DHCP Server Configuration GUI, the ProxyArec settings require you to complete two panels. First, you need to specify a domain name and a DDNS server IP address (or host name) in the DHCP Server Parameters window, as shown in Figure 7-4.

The Global Parameters window, as shown in Figure 7-5, is the only place where you would enable ProxyArec. You must have a Dynamic DNS server to enable dynamic A RR updates.

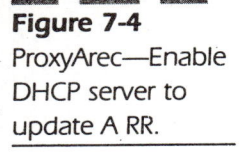

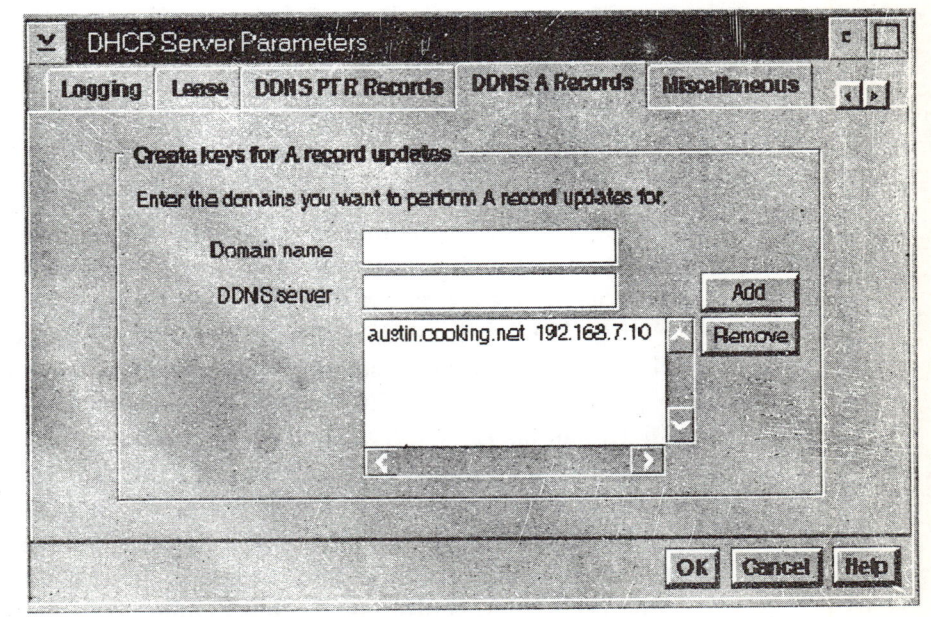

Figure 7-4
ProxyArec—Enable DHCP server to update A RR.

Figure 7-5
Enable ProxyArec and option for protection.

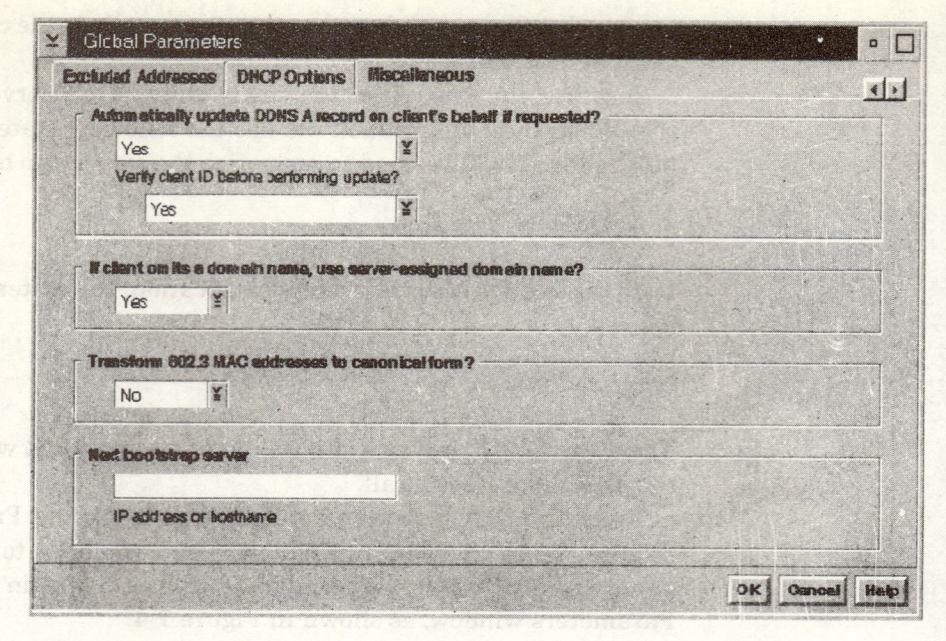

The question in Figure 7-5 that says *Automatically update DDNS A record on client's behalf if requested?* is defaulted to No. If you select Yes from the pull-down menu, the ProxyArec function is enabled. Another selection box, *Verify client ID before performing update?*, decides on the two modes of ProxyArec:

- Standard
- Protected

To enable protected ProxyArec, select Yes from the pull-down menu.

Remember that the main purpose of the ProxyArec function is to support non-DDNS clients to dynamically register/update host names where security is not a first priority. Configuring the DHCP server to use the client's MAC address to protect unauthorized update from a different client does not indicate security. Dynamic DNS name space is almost like a public space. Any DHCP client can register the host name with the DHCP option 12.

Windows 95 and NT handle option 12 in a different way than OS/2. Even though the Windows 95/NT client was provided with a host name in the TCP/IP DNS settings, the host name is not used. Instead, the *computername* definition is used as option 12. This is a unique (proprietary) Microsoft implementation of a host name. Traditionally, the computer-

Security of DHCP and Dynamic DNS

name, also know as the NetBIOS name, is not controlled by the IS department or TCP/IP administrators, so there might be a chance that people use the same computername in a TCP/IP network, which usually results in duplicated names. Duplicate names result in LAN adapters that won't open.

ProxyArec and Option 81

Having a ProxyArec DHCP server and standard DDNS clients in a same location is not recommended, because a DDNS client cannot use its own interface to the DDNS server. A RR will be owned by the DHCP server. However, in such a situation, the OS/2 DHCP/DDNS client can use a special DHCP option, option 81, which would disable the ProxyArec function for a requesting client.

Unfortunately, there is no graphical user interface where you could define option 81. You must manually add option 81 to the DHCP configuration file using HEX-translated FQDN (Fully Qualified Domain Name). This is shown in Figure 7-6.

Specifying an ASCII name rather than HEX code would be preferable; however, it would not work. The IETF document "Interaction between DHCP and DNS" defines option 81, as shown in Figure 7-7. The Flags field indicates the DHCP server to do the following:

00—Client wants to be responsible for updating the FQDN-to-IP address mapping.

Figure 7-6
DHCP configuration file example with option 81.

```
# Basic options required

clientid    MAC
interface   lan0

# Uncomment as desired for logging
numLogFiles    4
logFileSize    100
logFileName    dhcpcd.log
logItem        SYSERR
logItem        OBJERR
logItem        PROTERR
logItem        WARNING

option 12 tuna                              # Host name
option 81 HEX "00 00 00 74 75 6E 61 2E 61 75 73 74 69 6E 2E 63 6F 6F 6B 69 6E 67 2E 6E 65 74"
# Don't ProxyArec tuna.austin.cooking.net

updateDNSA   "nsupdate -h%s -d%s -s"d;a;*;a;a;%s;s;%s;3110400;q" -q"
updateDNSTxt "nsupdate.exe -h%s -s"d;txt;%s;a;txt;%s;s;%s;3110400;q""
```

Figure 7-7
IETF definition of option 81.

Code	Length	Flags	Rcode1	Rcode2	FQDN
81	n	00	00	00	

01—Client wants the server to be responsible for updating the FQDN-to-IP address mapping.

Rcode1 and Rcode2 define the response code area used by the DHCP server to check a DHCP client's response for Dynamic DNS updates.

Securing Lease Allocations

There is no one solution for controlling which clients can obtain a DHCP lease from a server, or if they should get a lease at all. However, there are some alternatives available to you:

- You can use classing (option 77) when configuring your address pools. Using classes requires you to visit each client and modify their configuration. Once you have your classes established, only devices that belong to the class will be allocated a lease. Be aware that not all clients can make use of option 77.

- At the server, you could allocate IP addresses to individual MAC addresses. This can be very labor-intensive, but it ensures that only machines with known MAC addresses will obtain a lease from a server.

- You may be able to find DHCP server software that allows you to list which MAC addresses the server will accept. DHCP servers that support roaming machines may be adapted for such use.

- If you want to ensure that clients are only served by a particular server, you could conceivably install one DHCP server per subnet. This is not a good solution, but if you choose to do this, ensure that your routers do not forward broadcast traffic and that there is no DHCP relay agent on the subnet. Keep in mind, however, that this solution does not stop any malicious user from connecting to the network and obtaining an IP address.

Preventing Access to Unauthorized Devices

The prevention of access to unauthorized devices would have to be done using a mechanism other than DHCP. Neither does DHCP prevent other

Security of DHCP and Dynamic DNS

clients from using the addresses it is set to hand out, nor can it distinguish between a computer's permanent MAC address and one set by the computer's user. DHCP can neither impose restrictions on what IP address can use a particular port nor control the IP address used by any client. You may, however, be able to use classing to limit leases to only those clients that belong to a valid class.

"Rogue" DHCP Servers

It is possible that a malicious or inexperienced user could create problems on your network by setting up an unofficial DHCP server. The initial problem is that the server could pass out IP addresses already belonging to some other computer, and you could end up with two or more devices with the same IP address, resulting in problems using the devices. These problems may be intermittent, or the devices may fail entirely, necessitating a restart.

Other problems are possible if the unofficial server gets a device to accept its lease offering, and then passes to the device its own (possibly incorrect) DHCP options. For example, if options 1 or 3 are incorrect, the device may not be able to communicate with devices outside its own subnet (or, in some cases, with devices on the same subnet). Another scenario to consider is a device that loads its operating system over the network using TFTP. If this device is directed to load a different file (possibly on a different server), it allows a perpetrator to take over the client. Given that boot parameters are often made to control many different things about the computers' operation and communication, many other scenarios are just as serious.

Note that by using BOOTP you are exposed to the same vulnerabilities.

Connecting to Untrusted Networks—Firewalls

There may come a time when you want to connect your private intranet to an untrusted network. What is an untrusted network? Well, the biggest example is the global public Internet (maybe it's time to have your own local mail or Web server rather than having your ISP host it for you). Another example may be one of your customers' networks. Say you are a consulting firm who wants to provide remote IS services for your clients. One way to do this is to connect your two corporate networks together. You would not want all your customers, and whomever they have logged onto their networks, to have access to all machines on your private network. You probably want them to have access to your Web server, and not much else. However, you need access to machines on their network so that you can do the appropriate maintenance, upgrades, monitoring, and so forth to perform your IS duties. There are many more examples of why you might want this kind of protected architecture between your private internet and other untrusted networks. This section will show you the how-to more than the why-to-do-it. Be aware that there are more methods to connect than the single one we are showing you.

To interconnect safely, you need a firewall. A firewall is not a panacea for security, and you should not treat it as such. Although firewalls can help provide security, there are many more issues beyond the firewall to keep in mind. Firewalls provide secure access from a company's internal TCP/IP network to the public Internet. Intruders are blocked and cannot access the internal network from the public network without authorization. Internal users, however, can still access resources on the public Internet. In combination with good security practices, firewalls can help keep private information on your network secure.

Several vendors produce high-quality, full-featured firewalls. Examples include IBM Firewall for AIX and Windows NT and LanOptics Guardian for Windows NT. Alternatively, many firms opt to contract for firewall services with their network providers to avoid having to learn the specialized skills required to manage network security.

Most firewalls can support two methods used by internal clients to access public Internet sites. SOCKS is the most modern method, and it can provide transparent access for all TCP/IP-based applications if the client operating system has a "SOCKSified" protocol stack. Some OSs, such OS/2 Warp and UNIX, have built-in SOCKS support; third parties provide SOCKS extensions for Windows 95 and Windows NT clients. Practically all Web browsers support SOCKS-based firewall access.

Proxy servers can also provide access to public sites through a firewall for internal clients. However, proxy servers can only handle HTTP, FTP, and Gopher protocols, so they are mainly of benefit to Web browsers. Caching proxy servers, such as IBM's Web Traffic Express, can even cut down on network traffic through the firewall by keeping frequently accessed Web pages and files on the proxy server itself.

In principle, a proxy server, such as IBM Web Traffic Express or Lotus Domino Go Webserver, can be used as a simple firewall solution when some degree of security is needed. A proxy server performing that role on Windows NT, for example, would need two network adapters (one for the internal network and one for the external network) and a proxy server software package installed and running. That server should have an `IPGATE OFF` command in AUTOEXEC.BAT so that TCP/IP traffic will not be forwarded from one LAN adapter to the other. (Otherwise, an intruder could access internal systems.) Also, it should not have any daemons running that may expose vulnerabilities. Nor should the proxy server have any LAN services bound to the adapter handling external network access. Moreover, the proxy server should not handle any requests from external users. Provided these conditions can be met, a proxy server can act as a simple firewall.

You may wish to download a 60-day evaluation version of IBM Web Traffic Express to learn how to set up a caching proxy server. Visit the following site to obtain a copy:

http://www.software.ibm.com/webservers/wte/index.htm

An evaluation copy of Lotus Domino Go Webserver can be found on the Internet at:

http://www.ics.raleigh.ibm.com/dominogowebserver

Connecting through Untrusted Networks—VPN

A virtual private network (VPN) is an extension of an enterprise's private intranet across a public network such as the Internet, creating a secure private connection, essentially through a private tunnel. VPNs securely convey information across the Internet, connecting remote users, branch offices, and business partners into an extended corporate network. Internet service providers (ISPs) offer cost-effective access to the Internet (via direct lines or local telephone numbers), enabling companies to eliminate their current, expensive leased lines, long-distance calls, and toll-free telephone numbers.

A 1997 VPN research report by Infonetics Research, Inc. estimates savings from 20 to 47 percent of wide area network (WAN) costs by replacing leased lines to remote sites with VPNs. And for remote access VPNs, savings can be 60 to 80 percent of corporate remote access dial-up costs. Additionally, Internet access is available worldwide, where other connectivity alternatives may not be available.

The technology to implement these virtual private networks, however, is just becoming standardized. Some networking vendors today are offering non-standards-based VPN solutions that make it difficult for a company to incorporate all its employees and/or business partners/suppliers into an extended corporate network. However, VPN solutions based on

IETF standards will provide support for the full range of VPN scenarios, with more interoperability and expansion capabilities.

The key to maximizing the value of a VPN is the ability for companies to evolve their VPNs as their business needs change and to easily upgrade to future TCP/IP technology. Vendors who support a broad range of hardware and software VPN products provide the flexibility to meet these requirements. VPN solutions today run mainly in the IPv4 environment, but it is important that they have the capability of being upgraded to IPv6 to remain interoperable with your business partner's and/or supplier's VPN solutions. Perhaps equally critical is the ability to work with a vendor who understands the issues of deploying a VPN. The implementation of a successful VPN involves more than technology. The vendor's networking experience plays heavily into this equation.

TFTP Security

If you decide to provide BootP services, remember that TFTP is inherently insecure. You can specify which client IP addresses have access to the TFTP directory. For example, say a TFT file contains the following lines:

```
C:\TFTPBOOT RO 192.168.6.17
C:\TMP RO 192.168.6.11
```

This means that the machines with the respective IP addresses have read-only access to the directories listed. Since we can preassign IP addresses based on the machines MAC address, this is fairly safe.

CHAPTER 8

Reliability

"I can't get on the network!"

Those six words should never be heard by a network manager. Yet with TCP/IP networks, they are, unfortunately, all too common. This chapter focuses on how to make your TCP/IP network super reliable, with connections always available and conflicts eliminated. If your TCP/IP network does not need to be reliable, please skip this chapter.

Battlefield Questions

To design a network for reliability, you might think of your network as a battlefield. The goal is to ensure that your messenger can travel from one end of the battlefield to another without getting blown up. In between are roads, bridges, highways, airways, rail lines, and other mechanisms used by your soldiers to communicate. If one (or more) of these conveyances gets blown up, your courier must still reach the destination.

In designing your network, you should ask yourself a series of "what if?" questions. What if the router shorts out? What if the DHCP server is buried by a mudslide? What if a remote office satellite link gets blocked because of sunspots?

Then, when you have examined the "what if?" questions, there are some more questions to answer:

- How likely are these events?
- How much reliability do I need? For whom?
- Where can I spend limited dollars to get the highest possible degree of reliability?
- If a failure does occur, will I know about it? How fast can I respond?
- Do I regularly rehearse how to respond to failures?
- Do I have a written plan of action to handle network outages?
- Am I measuring the frequency and severity of network problems so I can determine whether service improves?

If you're doing your job, these questions never have permanent answers. You should always regularly reexamine these issues, even if your network runs smoothly.

Failure Events

Datagrams can only travel across your network as long as every part of the link works, from end to end. Your network can only be as reliable as the weakest link.

Severed Connections

One obvious possible failure is a severed connection. Wires may be cut, cables inadvertently unplugged, or fiber optics dug up by a backhoe. TCP/IP can easily reroute around such failures provided another connection is available. An easy way to design redundancy into connections is to simply provide two (or more) separate lines or wires, preferably using different technologies. Another way is to structure the network as one unbroken ring (or circle). If one connection in the ring does break, traffic can still flow throughout the network because all points are still connected.

The U.S. Federal Aviation Administration, for example, discovered that their connection redundancy failed, and air traffic control services were disrupted for a time. (Fortunately, no one suffered any injury.) The FAA uses telephone lines to connect various facilities. These facilities each have multiple circuits, and switching equipment can quickly reroute network traffic over backup circuits. However, the FAA granted a single long-distance telephone company the contract to connect their facilities. When the telephone company's own network failed, the FAA had no backup, and the multiple circuits didn't matter. Now the FAA has contracted with a second long-distance telephone company to provide backup connections should they be needed.

In another example, PanAmSat's Galaxy IV satellite suffered a catastrophic failure in 1998. Amazingly, almost none of the U.S. paging services had any immediate backup satellite, so paging services were disrupted for days. Physicians, in particular, were hard hit, because they lost contact with hospitals and could not be called in by pager.

Facility Loss

Fires, floods, earthquakes, hurricanes, power outages, and other catastrophes can wreak havoc with a network by knocking out crucial servers, routers, bridges, switches, and other devices. Large parts of the Internet, for example, were disabled when the last San Francisco earthquake knocked down some key buildings.

Many companies do not properly plan for these contingencies. Your network may be required to handle these events, so try to avoid placing all your vital network devices in one location. In addition, an uninterruptable power supply (UPS) with a remote alerting mechanism can help keep critical network systems up and running. However, backup electrical power should be provided for all critical systems. It's easy to forget that routers, bridges, concentrators, hubs, servers, switches, and even clients all need backup power if they are to continue operating.

Router Outages

Subnets in a TCP/IP network can quickly become cut off from the rest of a network if a router fails. These devices should be extremely reliable, and many network designers choose dedicated pieces of industrial equipment from IBM, Bay Networks, Cisco, and other vendors instead of less-reliable PCs. Routers can also be installed in pairs.

DHCP Server Problems

DHCP can help provide added flexibility and convenience in managing a TCP/IP network. Static addresses can often conflict, locking systems out of a network. Also, static configurations can only be changed with a significant amount of work, making it difficult to deal with router outages, changes in subnet structures, and so forth. In other words, DHCP servers can actually help ensure reliability.

However, if a DHCP server fails, then a TCP/IP network can quickly run into trouble. DHCP servers must be reliable. Failures of DHCP relay agents can also prevent new systems from joining a TCP/IP network. Some TCP/IP experts recommend using DHCP relay agents sparingly. Instead, you may wish to have dedicated routers handle the task, with BootP relays as needed. If you do use DHCP relay agents, consider a more fault-tolerant solution, such as the one described later in this chapter.

Name Server Difficulties

Without name servers, your users will have to resort to numeric IP addresses, effectively making your network useful only to the most savvy technicians. DNS servers must also be active and reachable at all times.

TCP/IP clients, including Windows 95, can readily accept two or more name server addresses. If the first name server can't be reached, the client will attempt to contact the backup name server. Say you may want

Reliability

to take advantage of this simple feature and use two (or more) name servers on your mission-critical network.

Dynamic DNS servers also help minimize network problems. For example, if an important Web server fails, its name can be reassigned to another numeric IP address very quickly and easily with a DDNS server. In fact, this secure update may be triggered automatically when a server failure has been detected by network alerting tools.

Other Server Vulnerabilities

Server failures can prevent users from accessing important applications and databases. Technologies such as RAID can help cope with hard disk failures. Many vendors provide fault-tolerant server solutions, including IBM. Storage management software, such as IBM's ADSM, helps send backup copies of files across the network to off-site locations.

Yet with all these server technologies, it's important to remember that most failures occur because of software problems. All the RAID storage in the world won't help if your server suffers from the blue screen of death. Some operating systems can be vulnerable to failure, especially when intentionally induced. For example, in the late 1980s, Robert Morris at Cornell University discovered a security vulnerability in some versions of UNIX. He used this vulnerability to spread a worm that quickly infected numerous systems connected to the Internet. For several hours, the Internet essentially ground to a halt as system managers attempted to address the problem. Many could not even log on to their own servers, since the worm multiplied rapidly, consuming practically all the attention of each server's processors. More recently, some versions of Windows NT have been vulnerable to attacks using ping and/or Telnet.

You should keep close watch on your servers and regularly review software bug reports and other information in case others find additional problems that may affect you. Antivirus software, such as Norton AntiVirus, may detect and eradicate PC viruses on your servers. (Viruses can also cause network problems.)

Client Failures

Many network problems really relate to the fragility of traditional PC clients, which tend to break down all too often. It isn't hard to delete an important icon, modify a critical system file, or otherwise render a traditional PC unable to connect to the network. PC users then have to wait for time-consuming repairs to software, hardware, or both.

Various estimates peg the cost of managing a typical business PC (the annual total cost of ownership) at between $5,000 and $26,000. These costs appear to be rising despite (or perhaps because of) advances in technology. While that annual cost may be perfectly justified for many users, including programmers, engineers, heavy office suite users, hobbyists, and others, the high cost is not necessarily attractive to everyone. Yet, the benefits of PC applications, graphical user interfaces, and online help do make sense.

Many companies in the computing industry recognize these problems and are working to solve them through network computing. True network computing solutions provide most or all of the benefits of PC applications, with a total cost of ownership approaching that of a mainframe or UNIX terminal. Examples include network computers from IBM, Sun, Oracle, and others, along with Java and IBM's WorkSpace On-Demand for Intel-compatible systems. One of the key benefits is that users can log on from any station on the network and get access to individual documents, applications, and Web pages from anywhere. Consequently, network computing can improve the reliability of the whole network by providing access to it more often and with less complexity.

While some users do need the mainframe on a desk that the PC has become, you should seriously examine network computing solutions for many users. It is also recommendable to implement network computing solutions, even for PC users where they make sense, such as Web-delivered Java applications, to help promote reliability within your network.

AIX and UNIX Features

You may wish to opt for AIX-based servers as your need for a large, reliable, and stable network continues to grow. IBM's AIX can be made fault-tolerant by including clustering technology, such as High Availability Cluster Multi-Processing (HACMP). One suggestion is to have a pair of AIX machines running HACMP using a set of shared disks that the DHCP and DNS servers write their data to. The HACMP failover scripts on the secondary machine then need to be modified so that the DHCP and DNS servers are started in the event of a failure on the primary machine.

Reliability

Shadow IPserver Features

Shadow IPserver can be expanded into a cluster of peer servers to implement redundant DHCP, dynamic DNS, and NBNS services. The IPserver peers are independent servers that may be installed alongside each other or in different locations. Each server coordinates its activities with the other across the network.

The IPserver cluster architecture allows real-time data replication. Fully redundant data distribution to multiple IPservers provides high reliability, tolerance of hardware failure, and the ability to balance the client load across multiple servers.

CHAPTER 9

Performance

If you're looking to boost the performance and capacity of your TCP/IP network, this chapter should help. This chapter examines how to set lease times and minimize broadcast traffic, among other issues.

Leases

The lease time implemented in your network will vary depending on how your network is configured and by the nature of the clients that are attached to it. Here, we examine how you could determine what the lease time should be on your network.

What Is a Lease?

The lease time is the time that a DHCP client has to use the parameters supplied to it by a DHCP server. The time itself is one of the parameters passed. At the end of Chapter 2 are packet decodes that show the T1 and T2 parameters.

How Leases Work

When a client receives TCP/IP configuration parameters from a server, it receives as part of those parameters a lease time that defines how long a client is able to use the parameters. (See Appendix A.3.2, "Option 51: IP Address Lease Time.") On receipt and acceptance of the parameters, two timers, T1 and T2, start to count down. T1 will expire before T2, and T2 will expire before the end of the lease time. When T1 expires (at 0.5 times the total lease time), the client will try to extend its lease for the current configuration. If the DHCP server has not responded by the time T2 has expired (0.875 times the lease time), the client will then start broadcasting to try to obtain a new lease.

A client is able to terminate a lease without having to wait for the lease to expire, for example, when it is shutting down. This frees up the IP address at the DHCP server and makes it available for other clients

Choosing a Lease Time

There are no hard-and-fast rules for setting lease times. They can vary from site to site according to usage patterns, goals, service levels for the DHCP servers, and WAN stability. In determining the optimum lease time, ask yourself these questions:

- *Do I have more users than IP addresses?* For example, you may have many mobile users coming and going from your location. Each user

Dynamic IP Routing Protocols

that leaves your site can still have a valid lease.

- *How many clients do I have?* If you have a fairly short lease time and a large number of clients, you may begin to impact the performance of your DHCP server.

- *How long will it take to repair or restart a failed DHCP server?* If a DHCP server fails, clients trying to obtain a lease will encounter problems. Clients already active will have problems when their T2 timer expires.

- *Will I need to change IP parameters at the client?* Are there parameters that are likely to change that are needed by the clients to work correctly, such as a new default router?

- *How reliable are WAN connections?* The effects of a WAN outage on a client are the same as if the DHCP server itself has failed. The server may experience heavy loads when a failed WAN connection is reestablished and all the remote clients try to obtain leases.

- *Will I need to reclaim addresses?* Will you need to "get back" IP addresses so they can be statically assigned to new hosts, such as a new router?

NOTE: *As a rule of thumb, make the lease time twice as long as any potential outage of the DHCP server. Remember: The longer the lease, the longer it takes for changes in DHCP options to reach the clients.*

Example Lease Times Here's a list of example lease times, with the possible reasons you could use them:

15 minutes	Allows you to maximize available addresses when you have a dynamic environment with lots of mobile users and, therefore, a shortage of IP addresses.
6 hours	Allows you time to repair a failed DHCP server (3 hours).
12 hours	Allows you to distribute new IP parameters and reclaim an IP addresses overnight.
24 hours	Allows clients to continue working in the morning if a DHCP server has failed overnight.
3 days	Appears to be Microsoft's default value, so it is used by many locations.
6 days	Allows clients to continue working on Monday morning if a DHCP server has failed over a weekend.

1 year   If a client has not used the address for a year, they have probably left and the address can be reused.

Multiple Leases

With two or more DHCP servers on a network, clients that are moved around (for example, laptops) can end up with multiple and redundant leases. Consider a local network with two DHCP servers and a remote site also served by those servers. A mobile client initially connects to the local network and receives a lease from one of the two servers. It is then moved to the remote network without releasing the lease. When it attempts to use the address it already has, it is NAKed by the server, and the client will then receive an address appropriate for the remote network.

If the client is then moved back to the local network and tries to use the address allocated for the remote network, it will again be NAKed by the server. Now the client, rather than reusing the lease it originally had for the local network, will broadcast a DHCPDISCOVER to obtain an address. The server that holds the previous lease will offer the address back to the client, but there is no guarantee that the client will accept the address. Therefore, it is possible that the client will obtain an address from the other server and now hold two leases within the local network.

This problem can be eased by using only one DHCP server per network or location and also by using short lease times. If in your network DHCP servers are maintained by individual departments, offices, or individuals with their own small address pools, they can find that their addresses are being used by any device on the LAN that has been configured to use DHCP.

Monitoring and Troubleshooting

Most TCP/IP implementations come with a few standard tools that can be used in monitoring and debugging your IP network. Alternatively, you could use third-party applications and dedicated analyzers to do this more thoroughly. The following commands are included with most implementations of TCP/IP and can be used to check connectivity. Their usage may vary with other operating systems.

Dynamic IP Routing Protocols

The `ping` Command

By sending ICMP echo requests to specific IP addresses, the `ping` command (short for Packet Internet Groper) is used to verify connections between hosts. The syntax is as follows:

```
PING [-?drv] host [ size [ packets ] ]
```

where:

-?	Displays the syntax of the `ping` command
-d	Bypasses the normal routing tables
-v	Verbose output. Should include all ICMP packets received
host	A host's name, IP address or broadcast address
size	The size of data portion of the packet
packets	The number of echo request packets to send

For example:

```
C:\>PING banquet 56 2
PING banquet.AUSTIN.COOKING.NET: 56 data bytes
64 bytes from 192.168.6.1: icmp_seq=0. time=0. ms
64 bytes from 192.168.6.1: icmp_seq=1. time=0. ms
—banquet.AUSTIN.COOKING.NET PING Statistics—
2 packets transmitted, 2 packets received, 0% packet loss
round-trip (ms) min/avg/max = 0/0/0
```

The `traceroute` Command

The `traceroute` command (or `traceroute` on some other platforms) is used to trace the route an IP packet takes to reach a host on a remote subnet. It can tell you where and why a route is lost. The syntax is as follows:

```
TRACEROUTE [-dnrv] [-w wait] [-m max_ttl] [-p port#] [-q nqueries] [-t
tos] [-s src_addr] host [data_size]
```

where:

-d	Turns debug on
-n	Displays IP addresses instead of host names
-r	Disables routing of IP packets
-v	Turns verbose on
-w *wait*	Wait time in *wait* seconds between packets
-m *max_ttl*	Maximum Time to Live in *max_ttl* hops
-p *port#*	Destination port number *port#*

-q `nqueries`	`nqueries`, number of probes for each TTL
-t `tos`	`tos`, type of service
-s `src_addr`	Source IP address `src_addr`.
`host`	A host's name or IP address
`data_size`	The number of bytes of data used

For example:

```
C:\>traceroute 192.168.7.10
traceroute to 192.168.7.10 (192.168.7.10), 30 hops max, 38 byte pack-
ets
1 192.168.6.1 (192.168.6.1) 0 ms 0 ms 10 ms
2 brie (192.168.7.10) 0 ms 0 ms 0 ms
```

The `traceroute` command returns an indication as to errors encountered while trying to trace the route to the destination system. The indicators are as follows:

- `!`   Port unreachable, connection refused
- `!N` Network unreachable, no route to host
- `!H` Host unreachable, no route to host
- `!P` Protocol unreachable, connection refused
- `!F` Message too big
- `!S` No route to host

For example:

```
C:\>traceroute 192.168.10.1
traceroute to 192.168.10.1 (192.168.10.1), 30 hops max, 38 byte pack-
ets
1     192.168.6.1      (192.168.6.1)      10 ms    10 ms    0 ms
2     192.168.6.1      (192.168.6.1)       0 ms    !H       0 ms    !H
0 ms    !H
```

This indicates that our default router 192.168.6.1 has no routing information to reach the host 192.168.10.1.

The `iptrace` Command

The `iptrace` command is used to trace all packets received by and sent from a network interface. All data collected will be written to the IPTRACE.DMP file in the current directory. Depending on the platform, the dump file may be stored in a noneditable format. The `ipformat` command is used to view the dump file; in AIX use the `ipreport` command.

The syntax is as follows:

```
IPTRACE [-i] [interface]
```

where:

    `-i` Specifies that only IP packets should be traced.
`interface` Specifies an interface to be traced.

The arp Command

ARP is a mechanism to dynamically map IP addresses to the MAC addresses of other network adapters in the same local subnet and then cache them in memory for future reference. You can use the `arp` command to display and manually maintain the ARP cache. The syntax is as follows:

```
arp [-afds?] hostname [hardware_addr] [temp|pub]
```

where:
`hostname` A host's name or IP address.
   `-?` Show the online help.
   `-a` Print all ARP table entries.
   `-f` Flush all ARP table entries.
   `-d` Delete ARP table entry for the host `hostname`.
   `-s` Add ARP table entry for the host `hostname`.
  `temp` Timeout this entry if it is not used.
   `pub` Reply for other host.

The netstat Command

The `netstat` command displays the network status of the local workstation. It supplies information about routing, TCP connections, UDP statistics, IP statistics, memory buffers, and sockets. The syntax is as follows:

```
NETSTAT [ -? ] [-acghilmnprstu]
```

where:
a Displays addresses of network interfaces
c Displays ICMP statistics
g Displays IGMP statistics

h   Displays the resolved host name
i   Displays IP statistics
l   Displays information about the socket that is listening
m   Displays information about memory buffer usage
n   Displays information about LAN interfaces
p   Displays the contents of the ARP table
r   Displays the routing tables
s   Displays information about sockets
t   Displays information about TCP connections
u   Displays UDP statistics

For example, to dump the current routing table:

```
C:\>NETSTAT -r
destination     router        netmask         metric flags intrf
default         192.168.6.1   0.0.0.0         0      UGP   lan0
127.0.0.1       127.0.0.1     255.255.255.255 0      UH    lo
192.168.6       192.168.6.10  255.255.255.0   0      UC    lan0
192.168.7.10    192.168.6.1   255.255.255.255 0      UGHW3 lan0
192.168.9.10    192.168.6.4   255.255.255.255 0      UGHDM lan0
```

The `host` Command

The `host` command is used to ask a DNS server to resolve host names to IP addresses and vice versa. The syntax is as follows:

```
HOST <hostname>
```

where:
hostname A host's name or IP address

The `nslookup` Command

The `nslookup` command is used to query DNS servers in either an interactive or noninteractive fashion. The syntax is as follows:

```
NSLOOKUP    [-options]                  (Interactive mode using default server)
            [-options] -server          (Interactive mode using server)
            [-options] host             (Look up host using default server)
            [-options] host server      (Look up host using server)
```

where *[options]* are as follows:

all   Print options, current server and host.
[no]debug   Print debugging information.

`[no]d2`	Print exhaustive debugging information.
`[no]defname`	Append domain name to each query.
`[no]recurse`	Ask for recursive answer to query.
`[no]search`	Use the search list.
`[no]vc`	Always use a virtual circuit.
`domain=`*name*	Set default domain name to *name*.
`port=`*x*	Use TCP/IP port number *x*.
`srchlist=`*n1[/n2/.../ n6]*	Set domain to *n1* and search list to *n1*, *n2*, etc.
`root=`*name*	Set root server to *name*.
`retry=`*x*	Set number of retries to *x*.
`timeout=`*x*	Set initial timeout interval to *x* seconds.
`querytype=`*x* or `type=`*x*	Set query type, for example: `A`, `ANY`, `CNAME`, `NS`, `PTR`.
`class=`*x*	Set query class to one of `IN` (Internet), `CHAOS`, `HESIOD`, or `ANY`.

Troubleshooting TCP/IP Networks

Sooner or later you will encounter problems on your network. How quickly you can resolve these problems depends on your approach to troubleshooting. Here we examine ways to debug your network using the commands that come as standard with most implementations of TCP/IP.

Prerequisites for Troubleshooting

If you encounter connectivity problems with your network, it may take many steps to find the problem and, hence, the solution. When debugging a network problem, keep the following prerequisites in mind.

Understand TCP/IP. To solve an IP-related problem, it goes without saying that you have to have a high understanding of TCP/IP. TCP/IP is an open multivendor protocol. As such, there is a lot of publicly available information available—see your local bookstore.

Know Your Environment. As a network administrator, you should know what equipment and systems have been placed onto the network. Not only should you know what equipment is out there, you should know and understand their roles within the greater whole.

Any Information Can Help. Any symptom can be a clue to currently occurring problem, even if at first glance it appears to be unrelated.

Don't Believe What People Say. Don't believe what people have told you until it has been verified.

You Can Be Limited by the Person On-Site. Your current skill level is equal to that of the person on the other end of the phone. Unless you can talk that person through your diagnostic procedures, diagnosis may not start until you can actually get on-site.

A Bottom-Up Approach

Because protocols are divided into several layers and each layer's connectivity depends on the layer beneath it, it therefore is reasonable to start diagnosing network problems from the bottom and work up. TCP/IP does not match the OSI seven-layer model completely, but it is useful to use the following definitions. Each layer is explained from the bottom to the top.

Layer 1—Physical Layer The physical layer represents the media used within the network, such as fiber-optic or coaxial cable. It is only responsible for the transmission of data across the physical network.

Layer 2—Data Link Layer The data-link layer represents a communication link between two systems. Network types such as Ethernet, token ring, and FDDI are covered by this layer. The data processed in this layer is often called a *frame*.

In debugging the network layer, you will probably use the `arp` command as documented. Keep the following in mind:

- When arp fails, you cannot communicate.
- When arp succeeds, you don't have any hardware problems.
- When arp succeeds, but you still can't communicate, then you have a problem in a higher layer.

The `arp` command cannot be used to diagnose higher layers, but applications that use the higher layers (such as ping) can assist in diagnosing lower layers. In using arp for testing, use the following procedure:

1. Clear the ARP cache with the an `arp -f` command.
2. Check that the cache is empty with an `arp -a` command.

Dynamic IP Routing Protocols

3. Try to ping the host you are trying to connect to.
4. Then check the ARP cache again. If the ping was successful, and the host you pinged is on the same subnet, there will be an entry for the host in the table. If the host is on another subnet, there should be an entry for the router that would be used. (Note in the following example that an ARP entry for a name server with the address 192.168.6.5 was also added.)

```
C:\>arp -a
ARP table contents:
Interface    Hardware Address       IP Address      Minutes Since Last Use
lan0         0 :6 :29:b3:e :ed      192.168.6.1     0
lan0         8 :0 :5a:ce:ea:cb      192.168.6.5     0
```

If the ping was unsuccessful and the host is on the same subnet, try to ping other devices on the subnet. If the host being pinged is on a different subnet, try pinging the default router. By doing this, you can receive some indication as to where to next proceed.

Use arp when checking for duplicate IP addresses. If the ARP entry for an IP address is different when queried from different locations, then you know that you have a duplicate address.

Layer 3—Network Layer The network layer represents communication between multiple systems. In TCP/IP, IP and ICMP are network-layer protocols, but IP is the only protocol to carry user data. The data passed through this layer is often called a *packet*. (An IP packet is sometimes called an *IP datagram*.) The IP address is used to identify various systems within the network. This layer also allows for the connection between two systems, and between two systems by passing through other systems, through a process known as *routing*.

In debugging the network layer, there are several commands that can be useful.

USE THE `ping` COMMAND The `ping` command is documented earlier in this chapter. When using ping, keep the following in mind:

- When ping fails, you cannot communicate by using the IP protocol.
- When ping succeeds, you don't have hardware or network configuration problems.
- When ping succeeds, but communication still fails, there is an application problem.

If you cannot connect to a host, try the following ping sequence to help determine where the problem lies:

1. Ping the IP address 127.0.0.1 by issuing the command `ping 127.0.0.1`. As discussed above, 127.0.0.1 is the loopback IP address. If you can successfully ping this address, then you have proven that the IP stack on your host is working correctly.
2. Ping your own IP address. A ping to your own address will physically transmit out onto the network. If the ping is successful, then you know that your network adapter is working.
3. Ping the IP address of your default router. This will determine if your default router is connected to the network, but not that it is working correctly. It can also show if your subnet mask is correct.
4. Ping an IP address of a host on the same subnet of the host you want to connect to. This will determine if all routers between you and the host you want to connect to are working correctly.
5. Ping the IP address of the host you want to connect to.

In the above procedure, IP addresses only were used because any problems in communicating with your name server, or misconfigurations in your name server, can cause connectivity problems in general when you are trying to connect by name.

In the following example, we are trying to ping the machine called *hotdog*:

```
C:\>PING hotdog 56 2
PING hotdog.AUSTIN.COOKING.NET: 56 data bytes

----hotdog.AUSTIN.COOKING.NET PING Statistics----
2 packets transmitted, 0 packets received, 100% packet loss
```

As you can see, the `ping` command itself has failed, but the host name was successfully resolved by the name server. This proves that the name server is working, although the address supplied by the name server may not necessarily be correct.

USE THE `traceroute` COMMAND In Step 4 above, if you could not ping any hosts on the remote subnet, you can use the `traceroute` command as documented to determine where and why data is being lost.

USE THE `netstat` COMMAND Use the `netstat` command as documented. Use `netstat -i` to check IP statistics and `netstat -c` to

Dynamic IP Routing Protocols

Figure 9-1
Output from `netstat -i`.

```
[C:\]NETSTAT -i
total packets received 5548
checksum bad 0
packet too short 0
not enough data 0
ip header length < data size 0
ip length < ip header length 0
fragments received 0
frags dropped (dups, out of space) 0
fragments timed out 0
packets forwarded (
packets rcvd for unreachable dest 0
packets forwarded on same net 0
Unknown/Unsupported protocol  2
requests for transmission 4974
lost packets due to no bufs, etc 0
output packets discarded because no route could be found 0
input packets delivered successfully to user-protocols 5546
input packets with an unknown protocol 0
output packets successfully fragmented 0
output fragments created 0
fragmentation failed 0
successfully assembled packets 0
Packets received with version !=4 0
Raw ip packets generated 193
```

check ICMP statistics. Figure 9-1 shows output from the `netstat -i` command.

Look for unusual counters. If `output packets discarded because no route could be found` is not zero, you have a routing problem somewhere. If `netstat -c` gives a high source quench count, the host you are talking to (or the routers you are talking through) may be overloaded.

Layer 4—Transport Layer   This layer represents a connection between two processes. Any system can have multiple processes running on it, and TCO and UDP are the protocols used to achieve this connection. TCP data passed through this layer is often called a *segment*; UDP data is known as a *datagram*.

This layer also provides functionality for flow control and reliability (including retransmission). TCP provides these functions, while UDP does not.

To debug the transport layer, use the following command:

USE THE `netstat` COMMAND   Use the `netstat` command as documented previously. Use `netstat -t` to check TCP statistics and `netstat -u` to display UDP statistics. Additionally, use `netstat -s` to check socket

Figure 9-2
Output from `netstat -t`.

```
[C:\]NETSTAT -t
TCP STATISTICS
connections initiated              2
connections accepted               1
connections established            2
embryonic connections dropped      0
conn. closed (includes drops)      4
segs where we tried to get rtt    10
times we succeeded                 8
delayed acks sent                  8
conn. dropped in rxmt timeout      0
retransmit timeouts                0
persist timeouts                   0
keepalive timeouts                 0
keepalive probes sent              0
connections dropped in keepalive   0
total packets sent                23
data packets sent                  6
data bytes sent                   92
data packets retransmitted         0
data bytes retransmitted           0
ack-only packets sent             12
window probes sent                 0
packets sent with URG only         0
window update-only packets sent    1
```

information. Figure 9-2 shows part of the output from the `netstat -t` command.

Again, look for unusual counters. If packets received with `ccksum errs` is not zero, you are experiencing errors somewhere on your network.

Layer 5—Session Layer The session layer provides dialog sessions such as full- and half-duplex and synchronization points in the dialog. Within TCP/IP, there is no precise session layer, although some of its functionality is provided within TCP.

Layer 6—Presentation Layer The presentation layer provides for common data presentation between applications. Within TCP/IP, there is no precise presentation layer.

Layer 7—Application Layer The application layer represents the application entity, usually an application program. When diagnosing DNS issues, there are two commands that are useful.

USE THE host COMMAND The `host` command is used to query a DNS server and can be used to verify that your DNS configuration is correct. The `host` command can only be used for name-to-address and address-to-name resolution.

Dynamic IP Routing Protocols

USE THE `nslookup` COMMAND The `nslookup` command is used to query a DNS server and can be used to verify that your DNS configuration is correct. This section provides an overview of how to use nslookup. The information presented here should work for many UNIX versions of nslookup. Practically all Windows-based versions of nslookup are GUI programs and have different (and varying) usage. In addition to the material presented here, you should also read the *TCP/IP Command Reference* in the TCP/IP Information folder of Warp Server.

The `nslookup` command is a resolver that sends queries to name servers. This is the same task that your browser has to do when locating a particular Web page (if you entered the server name rather than the server IP address). By default, nslookup performs recursive queries. See Figure 9-3 for an example of how a name server resolves a recursive query. Resolvers make recursive queries, which causes the name server the most amount of work. Name servers themselves make nonrecursive queries. You can configure nslookup to do nonrecursive queries as well.

The `nslookup` command is useful while you are configuring your name servers and also for troubleshooting certain issues after configuration. For example, say you have configured one of your servers to provide zone transfers to only a specified group of machines (for example, by using the `secure_zones` option). It is probably prudent to use nslookup to try a zone transfer (using the `ls` subcommand) from a machine other than the trusted machines, rather than to wait for crackers to test your configuration for you. Most name servers, you will find, will not pass you zone information for security reasons.

Figure 9-3
Name resolution example.

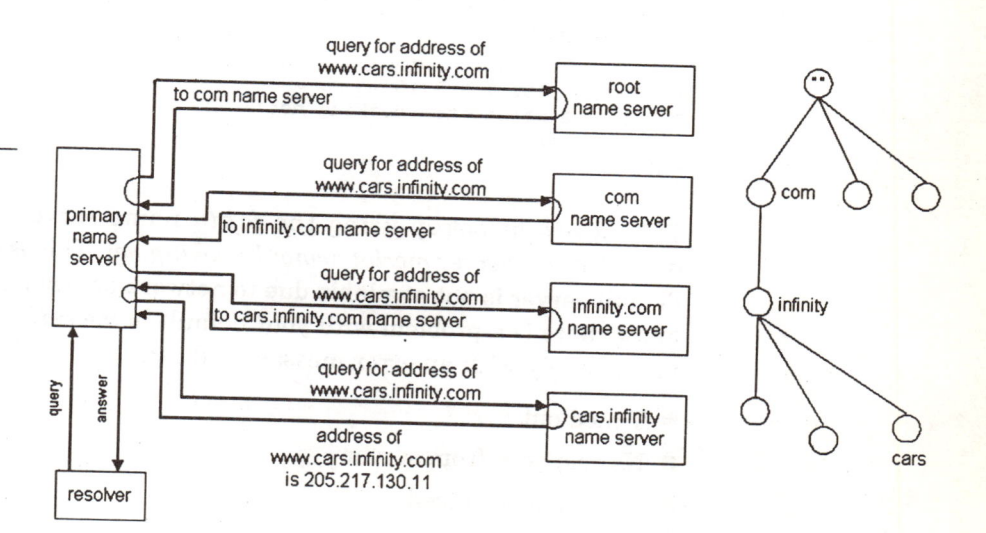

The `nslookup` command can be run interactively, or if you have a single query, you can type the query from the command line. When you start nslookup interactively, it is useful to enter the command `set all` to remind you of your default settings (particularly your default name server, domain, and search list, if any). To finish an interactive session, type `exit` or press CTRL+Z or CTRL+D (end of file on UNIX). For extra help during an interactive session, type `?` or `help` at the > prompt.

The `nslookup` command can be configured for recursive and nonrecursive queries by using the `set recur` and `set norecur` subcommands. You can start the program so that it uses the default name server, or you can direct it to use a specific name server for your session. The file %ETC%\RESOLV2 will contain the name of your default name server (if any) and your default domain. An example of %ETC%\RESOLV2 is shown below for a machine on the *newfairfield.cooking.net* subnet.

```
domain newfairfield.cooking.net
nameserver 192.168.6.10
```

You could include the line option's `debug`, which turns on debugging for nslookup. When you first start using nslookup, it may be useful to have debug on to better understand what is happening. With `debug` on (or `d2`), you will see just about as much DNS information as you would see if you were using a protocol analyzer. This discussion is not using debugging here because of the amount of information it creates. You should use debugging, though, while you are getting familiar with nslookup.

The nslookup syntax shows how to specify a particular name server to use. For example:

```
NSLOOKUP - 192.168.7.10
Server: fajita.austin.cooking.net
Address: 192.168.7.10
>exit
```

This starts nslookup using the *fajita* name server, rather than the default name server *merlot.armonk.cooking.net*. This is useful when your default server is not available due to network or other problems. You will know there is a problem with your default name server if nslookup exits immediately with an error message indicating:

- Timed out
- No response from server
- Connection refused

Dynamic IP Routing Protocols

- Server failure
- Default servers not available

If you do get errors like these, you probably want to start nslookup using a different name server until you can determine what is wrong that the default name server.

Do not confuse the previous errors with errors of the following type:

- Nonexistent domain (host or domain is not known to name server).
- Query refused (often because of security settings at name server).
- Format error (possible error in nslookup or network packet error; the name server thinks request packet is an improper format).
- No records (of the type you are requesting; change your querytype to `any` and try again).

You can also redirect some nslookup output to a file. For example, when in interactive mode if you wanted to create a file of all mail exchanger (MX) records (that is, mail hosts) for the domain *newfairfield.cooking.net,* you would do the following commands (the `t` is for recordtype):

```
nslookup
Server: fajita.newfairfield.cooking.net
Address: 192.168.6.10
> ls -t MX armonk.cooking.net > mailhost.txt
> view mailhost.txt
```

While records are still being read, you will see a series of # signs going across the screen; so you know something is happening. The `view` command shows you the file as if you were using the `more` command (which is what `view` uses). If you want to halt a long command, you can type CTRL+C during the command, which will bring you back to the > prompt. For example, if you entered the `ls -t MX` command on a large Internet domain, it would possibly generate pages of information.

The following command:

```
> ls -t any newfairfield.cooking.net
```

would show all records for the domain, which would, of course, give even more information than just the MX records. The record types that you can show individually are as follows:

A	Host name-to-IP address records.
ANY	All records available from name server.

CNAME	Canonical names for aliases. For example, we use *ns-updates* as an alias for the canonical name of *fajita.armonk.cooking.net*. Usually you will see *mail* or *www* as an alias for the fully qualified domain name of the server on which the mail server or Web server runs.
HINFO	Host information.
KEY	Public key information.
MB	Mailbox information.
MINFO	Mailbox or mail list information.
MX	Mail exchanger.
NS	Name server.
PTR	IP address-to-host name records.
SIG	List records with expiration time and signature information, such as A and KEY records.
SOA	Domain's start of authority.
TXT	Text records.
UINFO	User information. For example, will sometimes contain contact information of responsible person for a particular server.
WKS	Well-known services that the host advertises.

When you enter the querytype to `nslookup` subcommands, remember that they are case-insensitive. The `ls` subcommand causes zone transfers, and some hosts will not allow that (for security or because of the extra workload on the name server and network).

The `set` command is used when in the interactive mode to change default settings. For example, it can be useful to do a `set debug` or `set d2` (both of which turn on debugging) so that you can see how the name resolution is occurring when you make a query. You can change the default querytype for a single command. For example, to show all name server records for the *newfairfield.cooking.net* domain, enter:

```
C:\>NSLOOKUP -query=NS newfairfield.cooking.net
Server: fajita.newfairfield.cooking.net
Address: 192.168.6.10
newfairfield.cooking.net nameserver = fajita.armonk.cooking.net
newfairfield.cooking.net nameserver = ns-update
fajita.newfairfield.cooking.net internet address = 192.168.6.10
ns-update internet address = 192.168.6.10
```

Your default record querytype can be set to NS as opposed to the default of any records:

Dynamic IP Routing Protocols

```
C:\>NSLOOKUP -query=NS
Default Server: fajita.armonk.cooking.net
Address: 192.168.6.10
>
```

You are now in the interactive mode and can give more commands. To change the default name server, use the following:

```
> set root=192.168.7.10
>
```

To change the default querytype back to any, do the following:

```
> set q=any
```

You can abbreviate most subcommand arguments using the first unique character pattern of the name. Now you would be using the name server for the *austin.cooking.net* subnetwork. This could become confusing because the default domain is still *armonk.cooking.net,* so you might want to use a search list to include both domains:

```
> set srchlist=austin.cooking.net/armonk.cooking.net
```

Now, when the name resolution occurs, first *austin.cooking.net* will be appended to the name you are looking up, then *armonk.cooking.net* will be appended, then the name will be searched by itself with no appending. For example:

```
> jalapeno
```

Name resolution occurs as follows. When the `defname` and `search` options are both on (the default), nslookup uses the search list and successively appends each name in the list to any host query not ending in a dot (.) until the name resolution is successful (*jalapeno.austin.cooking.net* and then *jalapeno.armonk.cooking.net* would be searched). If no attempt is successful, nslookup tries the user-entered query as is. If you do not want the search list to be used, you can append a dot (.) to your command as follows:

```
> jalapeno.austin.cooking.net.
```

In this case, the name is used as is with no appending. Note that the name resolution stops when an address is found. If `search` is off and `defname` is on, nslookup does not use the search list but appends only the domain name (which is the first entry in the search list). Also, nslookup will only append this domain name to user queries that do not have dots in the name (rather than names that do not end in a dot, which was the case when `search` was on).

If `defname` is off, no domain is appended to the query. In this case, setting `search/nosearch` has no effect.

Tuning TCP/IP Networks

Once you have your network running reliably, you will probably want to tune it so that it runs to its greatest potential.

An Approach to Tuning Your Network

There is no set method to performance tuning, and as such, this section merely discusses one possible approach.

Gather Information Gather as much information as possible so that possible causes to your problem (in this case, poor performance) can be found. Some questions to ask yourself are as follows:

- Do all applications suffer from poor performance?
- Do all operations within an application suffer from poor performance?
- Do all systems within the network suffer from poor performance?
- When did the problem begin?
- Is the problem intermittent?
- Are there any error messages on either the console or logged-to file somewhere?

Understand Your Environment You have to know and understand the environment with which you are dealing. This includes all products—both hardware and software—and protocols that actively use the network. Check that all products are being used within specification. For example, most networking environments specify the maximum number of workstations and maximum cable lengths that can be used in a network segment. If additional workstations have been added to the network, this maximum may have been exceeded.

Is It Really a Problem? Are your users expecting too much? If they are used to loading files from a local file server, they may start to complain that it's too slow when downloading from the Internet. A T1 connection is not going to give the same throughput as a 16-Mb token ring.

Is It Really a Network Function? Don't forget that memory usage, disk, CPU, and I/O activity on both the source and target hosts can influence performance. Before you delve deeply into the network, confirm that these resources are not constrained on your hosts.

What Do You Want to Achieve? Are you trying to achieve a better response time, or greater throughput in general? Tuning the response time may entail tuning a particular application on a host, whereas to get better throughput, you might have to visit every workstation, host, and router.

TCP/IP Tuning Parameters

When tuning your network, there a several parameters that you may be able to manipulate to enhance network performance. The ability to change these parameters is dependent on the implementation of TCP/IP that you are using.

MTU and Fragmentation The maximum transfer unit is a very important parameter. Because TCP/IP works in almost all situations without modifying the default MTU, the MTU is not often tuned. By changing the MTU size, you can minimize the fragmentation that occurs on a packet as it travels through your IP network.

Consider the following:

- When you are sending small packets and there is no fragmentation:
    - More packets have to be sent; so there is an increased number of I/O operations to the network. This adds overhead.
    - There is lower throughput.
- When you are sending large packets and there is no fragmentation:
    - Fewer packet have to be sent; so there is a reduced number of I/O operations to the network. This reduces overhead.
    - There is higher thoughput.
- When you are sending large packets and there is fragmentation:
    - More packets have to be sent because the original data has been fragmented. This increases I/O operations to and from the network.

- There is lower throughput.
- More packets must be transmitted to recover from lost data packets.

Given the above, you can see that you should set the MTU size to be as large as possible so that a packet traveling through the network does not become fragmented.

In addition, you can use the ping and traceroute commands to determine the bottlenecks that occur on your network. Use traceroute to determine the IP addresses of the routers between you and the host you are connecting to. Then ping each IP address found with a range of packet sizes (use the same range for each address) and graph the results. Any bottlenecks with larger MTU sizes should be readily apparent.

Also, remember to make the MTU size on your workstation larger than the packet sizes you are using so that fragmentation does not occur before the data reaches the network. To change the MTU size, you would usually use the ifconfig command, although some implementations of TCP/IP may use configuration files to hold the MTU definition. For example, you could issue the commands:

```
IFCONFIG lan0 down
IFCONFIG lan0 mtu 4400
IFCONFIG lan0 up
```

This will set the MTU size to 4400 bytes. Now issue the command:

```
NETSTAT -n
```

This will confirm that the change has been made.

TCP Maximum Segment Size As stated previously, a unit of TCP transmission is known as a *segment*. IP and UDP datagrams each have a maximum length of 65,536 bytes. A TCP segment also has a maximum length, but it is determined when two systems connect. The maximum segment size, or MSS, is negotiated by both systems to guarantee connectivity.

The MSS is calculated using the MTU as follows:

1. Calculate variable A.

$$A = MTU - (TCP\ header\ size + IP\ header\ size)$$

2. Calculate variable B.

$$B = Socket\ Receive\ Buffer\ size\ /\ 2$$

Dynamic IP Routing Protocols

3. The smaller of A and B is used as the effective MSS.

Now consider the following scenario. Your workstation is connected to a token ring network and communicates with hosts also attached to the ring. To enhance performance, you are using a large MTU of 17,960 bytes. Later, you have to connect over a router to hosts attached to an Ethernet network. To avoid fragmentation at the router, you should set your MTU to 1500 bytes. But now you have an inefficiency when talking to hosts connected to the token ring.

How do you resolve this problem? Some stacks have MTU discovery enabled, thereby bypassing the issue. If they don't, you can use the `-mtu` option with the `route` command. The `-mtu` option allows you to configure the MTU for each route, not just for each interface. It allows you to give a specific value to only the traffic that is passing through a router.

For example, say there are workstations on 192.168.6 token ring network. They are using an MTU of 4400 bytes. If they need to connect to the 192.168.9 Ethernet network, you could issue the command:

```
route add -net 192.168.9 192.168.6.4 -mtu 1500
```

Here, it is assumed that 192.168.6.4 is the router to the 192.168.9 network. By adding this specific MTU size for traffic to the Ethernet network, you can now communicate efficiently with both local and remote hosts. Your MTU and MSS would be large, however, without fragmentation.

The IP Queue IP keeps a queue for incoming IP datagrams. The queue is only used for receiving datagrams, not sending. Since routing is done at the IP layer, the IP queue is important in a system configured as a router, because it is used when passing datagrams from one network to another. If a router receives a burst of IP datagrams, it is possible for the queue to overflow. Many implementations of TCP/IP do not allow you to set the queue size. AIX, however, does.

To set and check the IP queue, do the following:

1. To check the current queue size, issue the command:
    ```
    no -o ipqmaxlen
    ```

2. To set the IP queue length, issue the command:
    ```
    no -o ipqmaxlen=x
    ```
    Where x is the new size of the queue.

3. To check for IP queue overflows, issue the command:
    ```
    netstat -p ip
    ```

The following is an extract from the output, with the IP queue counter in bold type:

```
...
0 path MTU discovery memory allocation failures
0 ipintrq overflows
0 with illegal source
```

Note that a larger queue may require more CPU time to process; so don't make it too large. If you must increase it, make the increments moderate.

Buffers The buffers are temporary data storage used to store data sent between an application and the network. Some applications can set their buffer size (by using the `setsockopt()` function), but generally you cannot modify the buffer size.

You can check the buffers with the `netstat` command. `netstat -m` displays details for memory buffer usage. `netstat -c` displays ICMP statistics. When looking at the ICMP statistics, look for high source quench counters. If an ICMP source quench message is received from a router, it means that the router does not have the buffer space needed to queue the datagrams for output to the next network.

Bandwidth Efficiency

While the easiest solution to network performance problems may be to provide a faster connection, it's not always the most practical. After all, it might not be cost-effective to link every remote user or office with a T3 line. Sometimes it pays to closely examine the amount and nature of the network traffic flowing through your network connections to see if it's possible to use limited bandwidth more efficiently.

Broadcast Traffic

Be aware that your network may have multiple protocols running over it. Not all protocols are efficient in how they use the network. Some, like NetBEUI for example, introduce a large quantity of broadcast traffic.

Your environment may use combined bridge/routers (*brouters*) to interconnect remote locations. If these connections are maintained over relatively slow WAN links, your WAN link may be swamped with broadcast traffic. In extreme cases, connections that have timer-critical response times (for example, SNA) may fail.

It is possible to remove NetBEUI from your WAN connections entirely by implementing TCPBEUI. You can choose to still use NetBEUI within the local network where it is most efficient, but your WAN connections will have been freed up from carrying broadcast traffic.

RSVP

Unfortunately, TCP/IP has not had any standard method of prioritizing traffic until quite recently. Yet, in the real world, bank transactions can be much more important than casual e-mail. Unfortunately, most TCP/IP networks can't tell the difference between high-priority datagrams and lower-priority ones, so the bandwidth gets split more or less evenly between competing users.

RSVP (Resource Reservation Protocol) has been introduced as a way to solve the problem. If your network application has been programmed to take advantage of RSVP, and if the routers en route support RSVP, then TCP/IP datagrams can be prioritized according to their relative importance. Datagrams for bank transactions can be "tagged" by the application as high priority, while e-mail applications may tag their datagrams as lower priority. Intermediate network devices such as routers can then handle the traffic more intelligently, giving more bandwidth to the higher-priority traffic as needed.

There's one major downside to RSVP, at least at this point in time: Many applications and network devices do not yet support this protocol extension. Hopefully, the widespread adoption over time of IPv6 will help speed the implementation of RSVP as well. Nonetheless, if you have control over your own TCP/IP intranet and you can take advantage of the RSVP programming interfaces now becoming more and more common, you can design your own network and applications to take advantage of prioritization. Doing so can help you avoid buying more high-cost bandwidth.

For more information on RSVP, please consult RFC 2205.

Communications Server

Although TCP/IP has achieved tremendous popularity, it isn't necessarily the best protocol for all purposes. Other network protocols have particular strengths and weaknesses. You can take advantage of the strengths of other protocols while still preserving the universal reach of TCP/IP on your network.

For example, IBM's SNA (Systems Network Architecture) protocols work particularly well over WAN connections. If your network consists of remote offices, perhaps linked together with low-bandwidth connections, then you may be able to improve the performance of TCP/IP applications by encapsulating that traffic in SNA protocols across the WAN. Benchmark results indicate that you can get more TCP/IP traffic across low-bandwidth LAN connections if it's "wrapped" into SNA at one end and "unwrapped" at the other, particularly if you take advantage of SNA's end-to-end data compression.

IBM's Communications Server, available for a variety of platforms from PCs (Windows NT) to mainframes, can be placed at both ends of a WAN connection to encapsulate TCP/IP into SNA. For more information on IBM Communications Server, check out the following Web site:
http://www.software.ibm.com/enetwork/commserver

CHAPTER 10

Quality of Service

This chapter discusses the topic of traffic priority, or quality of service (QoS). It explains why QoS may be desirable in an intranet as well as on the Internet, and it presents two approaches to implementing QoS in TCP/IP networks:

- Integrated Services
- Differentiated Services

Why QoS?

On today's Internet and intranets, bandwidth is an important subject. More and more people are using the Internet for private and business reasons. The amount of data that must be transmitted through the Internet increases exponentially. New applications such as RealAudio, RealVideo, Internet phone software, and videoconferencing systems need a lot more bandwidth than the applications that were used in the early years of the Internet. Traditional Internet applications, such as WWW, FTP, or Telnet, cannot tolerate packet loss but are less sensitive to variable delays. Most real-time applications show just the opposite behavior: they can compensate for a reasonable amount of packet loss but are usually very critical toward high-variable delays.

This means that without any bandwidth control, the quality of these real-time streams depends on the bandwidth that is just available. Low bandwidth, or better, unstable bandwidth, leads to poor-quality real-time transmissions, for instance, dropouts and hangs. Even the quality of a transmission using the real-time protocol RTP depends on the utilization of the underlying IP delivery service.

Therefore, new concepts are necessary to guarantee a specific QoS for real-time applications on the Internet. A QoS is a set of parameters that describe the quality (for example, bandwidth, buffer usage, priority, CPU usage, etc.) of a specific stream of data. The basic IP protocol stack provides only one QoS, which is called *best-effort*. The packets are transmitted from point to point without any guarantee of a special bandwidth or minimum time delay. With the best-effort traffic model, Internet requests are handled with the first-come, first-served strategy. This means that all requests have the same priority and are handled one after the other. There is no possibility of making bandwidth reservations for specific connections or of raising the priority for special requests. As a consequence of these limitations, new strategies were developed to provide predictable services for the Internet.

Today, there are two main rudiments for bringing QoS to the Internet:

- Integrated Services
- Differentiated Services

Integrated Services bring enhancements to the IP Network Model to support real-time transmissions and guaranteed bandwidth for specific flows. In this case, a *flow* is defined as a distinguishable stream of related datagrams from a unique sender to a unique receiver that results from a single user's activity and requires the same QoS.

For example, a flow might consist of one video stream between a given host pair. To establish the video connection in both directions, two flows are necessary. Each application that initiates data flows can specify which QoS is required for this flow. If the videoconferencing tool needs a minimum bandwidth of 128 kbps and a minimum packet delay of 100 ms to assure a continuous video display, such a QoS can be reserved for this connection.

Differentiated Services mechanisms do not use per-flow signaling. Different service levels can be allocated to different groups of Internet users, which means that the whole traffic is split into groups with different QoS parameters. This reduces the maintenance overhead in comparison to Integrated Services. The following sections describe Integrated Services and Differentiated Services in more detail.

Integrated Services

The Integrated Services (IS) model was defined by an Internet Engineering Task Force (IETF) working group as being the keystone of the planned IS Internet. This Internet architecture model includes the currently used best-effort service and a new real-time service that provides functions for reserving bandwidth on the Internet.

IS was developed to optimize network and resource utilization for new applications, such as real-time multimedia, which require QoS guarantees. Because of routing delays and congestion losses, real-time applications do not work very well on the current best-effort Internet. Videoconferencing, video broadcast, and audio conferencing software needs a guaranteed bandwidth to provide video and audio in acceptable quality. Integrated Services makes it possible to divide the Internet traffic into the standard best-effort traffic for traditional uses and for application data flows with guaranteed QoS.

To support the Integrated Services model, an Internet router must be able to provide an appropriate QoS for each flow in accordance with the service model. The router function that provides different qualities of service is called *traffic control*. It consists of the following components:

Packet scheduler. The packet scheduler manages the forwarding of different packet streams in hosts and routers, based on their service class, using queue management and various scheduling algorithms. The packet scheduler must ensure that the packet delivery corresponds to the QoS parameter for each flow. A scheduler can also police or shape the traffic to conform to a certain level of service. The packet scheduler must be implemented at the point where packets are queued. This is typically the output driver level of an operating system and corresponds to the link layer protocol.

Packet classifier. The packet classifier identifies the packets of an IP flow in hosts and routers that will receive a certain level of service. To realize effective traffic control, each incoming packet is mapped by the classifier into a specific class. All packets that are classified in the same class get the same treatment from the packet scheduler. The choice of a class is based upon the source and destination IP address and port number in the existing packet header or an additional classification number that must be added to each packet. A class can correspond to a broad category of flows.

For example, all video flows from a videoconference involving several participants can belong to one service class. But it is also possible that only one flow belongs to a specific service class.

Admission control. The admission control contains the decision algorithm that a router uses to determine if there are enough routing resources to accept the requested QoS for a new flow. If there are not enough free routing resources, accepting a new flow would impact earlier guarantees, and the new flow must be rejected. If the new flow is accepted, the reservation instance in the router assigns to the packet classifier and the packet scheduler the task of reserving the requested QoS for this flow. Admission control is invoked at each router along a reservation path so as to make a local accept/reject decision at the time a host requests a real-time service. The admission control algorithm must be consistent with the service model.

[NOTE] Admission control is sometimes confused with policy control, which is a packet-by-packet function processed by the packet scheduler. Policy control ensures that a host does not violate its promised traffic characteristics. Nevertheless, to ensure that QoS guarantees are honored, the admission control is concerned with enforcing administrative policies on resource reservations. Some policies are used to check the user authentication for a requested reservation. Unauthorized reservation requests can be rejected. Admission control will play an important role in accounting costs for Internet resources in the future.

Figure 10-1 shows the operation of the Integrated Services model in a host and a router.

Quality of Service

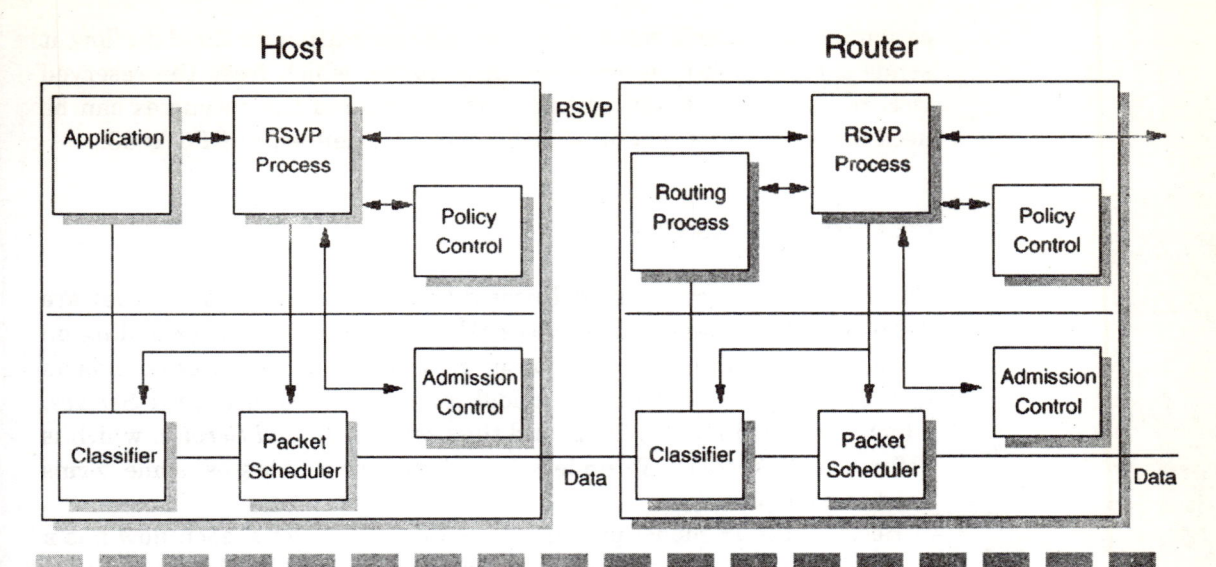

Figure 10-1 Integrated Services Model.

Integrated Services use the Reservation Protocol (RSVP) to signal the reservation messages. The IS instances communicate via RSVP to create and maintain flow-specific states in the endpoint hosts and in routers along the path of a flow. Please see the section, "The Reservation Protocol (RSVP)" later in this chapter for a detailed description of the RSVP protocol.

As shown in Figure 10-1, the application that wants to send data packets in a reserved flow communicates with the reservation instance RSVP. The RSVP protocol tries to set up a flow reservation with the requested QoS, which is accepted if the application fulfilled the policy restrictions and the routers can handle the requested QoS. RSVP advises the packet classifier and packet scheduler in each node to process the packets for this flow adequately. If the application now delivers the data packets to the classifier in the first node, which has mapped this flow into a specific service class complying with the requested QoS, the flow is recognized with the sender IP address and is transmitted to the packet scheduler. The packet scheduler forwards the packets, depending on their service class, to the next router or, finally, to the receiving host.

Because RSVP is a simplex protocol, QoS reservations are only made in one direction, from the sending node to the receiving node. If the application in our example wants to cancel the reservation for the data flow, it sends a message to the reservation instance, which frees the reserved QoS resources in all routers along the path, and the resources can be used for other flows. The IS specifications are defined in RFC 1633.

Service Classes

The Integrated Services model uses different classes of service that are defined by the Integrated Services IETF working group. Depending on the application, those service classes provide tighter or looser bounds on QoS controls. The current IS model includes the *Guaranteed Service,* which is defined in RFC 2212, and the *Controlled Load Service,* which is defined in RFC 2211. To understand these service classes, some terms need to be explained.

Because the IS model provides per-flow reservations, each flow has a flow descriptor assigned to it (see Figure 10-2). The flow descriptor defines the traffic and QoS characteristics for a specific flow of data packets. In the IS specifications, the flow descriptor consists of a filter specification (filterspec) and a flow specification (flowspec).

The filterspec is used to identify the packets that belong to a specific flow with the sender IP address and source port. The information from the filterspec is used in the packet classifier. The flowspec contains a set of parameters that are called the *invocation information.* It is possible to assort the invocation information into two groups:

- Traffic Specification (Tspec)
- Service Request Specification (Rspec)

Figure 10-2
Flow Descriptor.

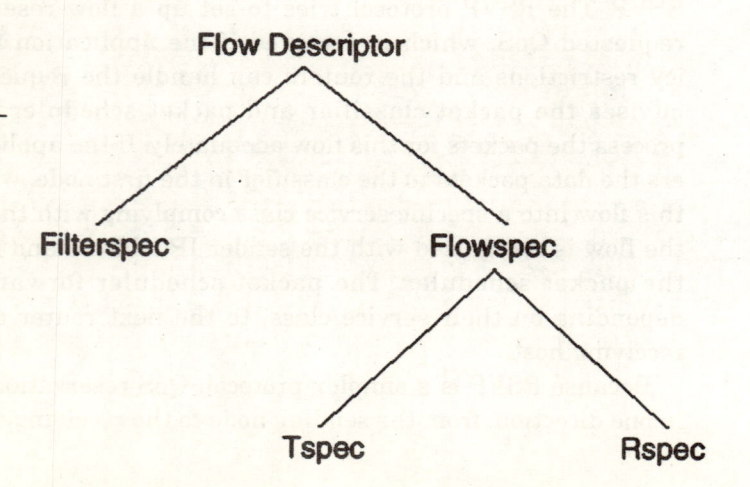

The Tspec describes the traffic characteristics of the requested service. In the IS model, this Tspec is represented with a *token bucket filter* (see Figure 10-3). This principle defines a data flow control mechanism that adds characters (tokens) in periodical time intervals into a buffer (bucket) and allows a data packet to leave the sender only if there are at least as many tokens in the bucket as the packet length of the data packet. This strategy makes possible a precise control of the time interval between two data packets on the network. The token bucket system is specified by two parameters: the *token rate* r, which represents the rate at which tokens are placed into the bucket, and the *bucket capacity* b. Both r and b must be positive.

The parameter r specifies the long-term data rate and is measured in bytes of IP datagrams per second. The value of this parameter can range from 1 byte per second to 40 terabytes per second. The parameter b specifies the burst data rate allowed by the system and is measured in bytes. The value of this parameter can range from 1 byte to 250 gigabytes. The range of values allowed for these parameters is intentionally large in preparation for future network technologies. The network elements are not expected to support the full range of the values. Traffic that passes the token bucket filter must obey the rule that over all time periods T, the amount of data sent does not exceed rT + b, where r and b are the token bucket parameters.

Two other token bucket parameters are also part of the Tspec: the *minimum policed unit* m and the *maximum packet size* M. The parameter m

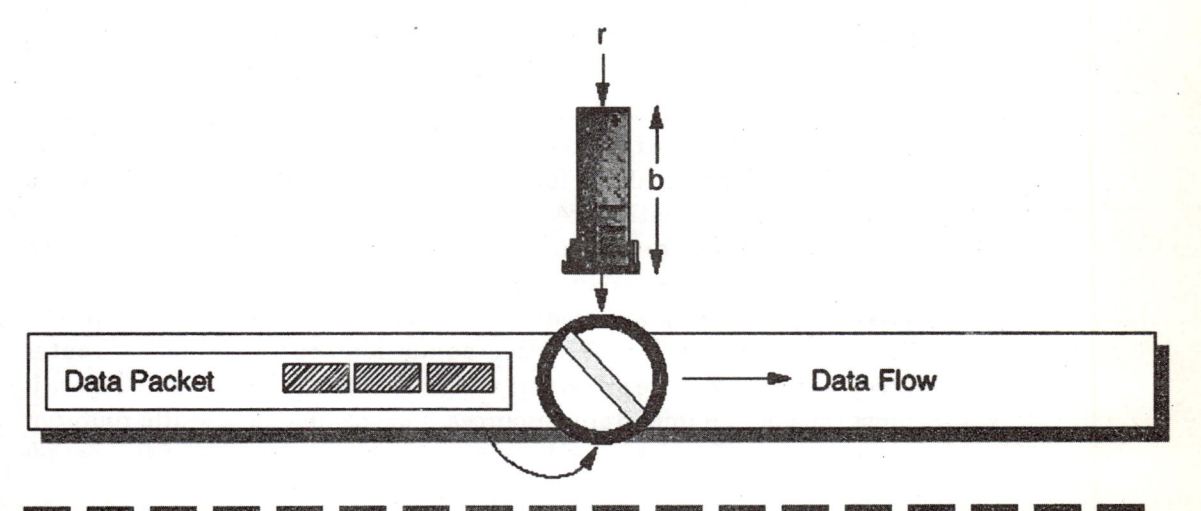

Figure 10-3 Token Bucket Filter.

specifies the minimum IP datagram size in bytes. Smaller packets are counted against the token bucket filter as being of size m. The parameter M specifies the maximum packet size, in bytes, that conforms to the Tspec. Network elements must reject a service request if the requested maximum packet size is larger than the MTU size of the link. To summarize, the token bucket filter is a policing function that isolates the packets that conform to the traffic specifications from those that do not.

The Service Request Specification (Rspec) specifies the QoS that the application wants to request for a specific flow. This information depends on the type of service and the needs of the QoS requesting application. It may consist of a specific bandwidth, a maximum packet delay, or a maximum packet loss rate. In the IS implementation, the information from Tspec and Rspec is used in the packet scheduler.

Controlled Load Service The Controlled Load Service is intended to support the class of applications that are highly sensitive to overloaded conditions in the Internet, such as real-time applications. These applications work well on unloaded networks but degrade quickly under overloaded conditions. If an application uses the Controlled Load Service, the performance of a specific data flow does not degrade if the network load increases.

The Controlled Load Service offers only one service level, which is intentionally minimal. There are no optional features or capabilities in the specification. The service offers only a single function. It approximates best-effort service over lightly loaded networks. This means that applications that make QoS reservations using Controlled Load Services are provided with service closely equivalent to the service provided to uncontrolled (best-effort) traffic under lightly loaded conditions. In this context, the term *lightly loaded conditions* means that a very high percentage of transmitted packets are successfully delivered to the destination, and the transit delay for a very high percentage of the delivered packets does not greatly exceed the minimum transit delay.

Each router in a network that accepts requests for Controlled Load Services must ensure that adequate bandwidth and packet processing resources are available to handle QoS reservation requests. This can be realized with active admission control. Before a router accepts a new QoS reservation, which is represented by the Tspec, it must consider all important resources, such as link bandwidth, router or switch port buffer space, and the computational capacity of the packet forwarding.

The Controlled Load Service class does not accept or make use of specific target values for control parameters such as bandwidth, delay, or loss. Applications that use Controlled Load Service must be proof against small amounts of packet loss and packet delays.

QoS reservations using Controlled Load Service need to provide a Tspec that consists of the token bucket parameters r and b as well as the minimum policed unit m and the maximum packet size M. An Rspec is not necessary because Controlled Load Service doesn't provide functions for reserving a fixed bandwidth or guaranteeing minimum packet delays. Controlled Load Service provides QoS control only for traffic that conforms to the Tspec that was provided at setup time. Hence, service guarantees only apply to packets respecting the token bucket rule that states for all time periods T, the amount of data sent cannot exceed $rT + b$.

Guaranteed Service Functions provided by the Guaranteed Service model assure that datagrams arrive within a guaranteed delivery time. Thus, every packet of a flow to the traffic specifications arrives at least at the maximum delay time specified in the flow descriptor. Guaranteed Service is used for applications that must have a guarantee for a datagram's arrival at the receiver no later than a certain time after it was transmitted by its source.

For example, real-time multimedia applications, such as video and audio broadcasting systems that use streaming technologies, cannot use datagrams that arrive after their proper playback time. Applications that have hard real-time requirements, such as the real-time distribution of financial data (share prices), will also require guaranteed service. Guaranteed Service does not minimize the jitter (the difference between the minimal and maximal datagram delays), but it controls the maximum queuing delay.

The Guaranteed Service model represents the extreme end of delay control for networks. Other service models providing delay control have much weaker delay restrictions. Therefore, Guaranteed Service is only useful if it is provided by every router along the reservation path.

Guaranteed Service gives applications considerable control over their delay. It is important to understand that the delay in an IP network has two parts: a fixed transmission delay and a variable queuing delay. The fixed delay depends on the chosen path, which is determined not by Guaranteed Service but by the setup mechanism. All data packets in an IP network have a minimum delay that is limited by the speed of light and the turnaround time of the data packets in all the routers on the routing path. The queuing delay is determined by Guaranteed Service, and it is controlled by two parameters: the token bucket (in particular, the bucket size b) and the bandwidth R that is requested for the reservation. These parameters are used to construct the *fluid model* for the end-to-end behavior of a flow that uses Guaranteed Service.

The fluid model specifies the service that would be provided by a dedicated link between sender and receiver that provides the bandwidth R. In the fluid model, the flow's service is completely independent of the service for other flows. The definition of Guaranteed Service relies on the following result: the fluid delay of a flow obeying a token bucket (r, b) and being served by a line with bandwidth R is bounded by b/R as long as R is not less than r. Guaranteed Service approximates this behavior with the service rate R, where R is now a share of bandwidth through the routing path and not the bandwidth of a dedicated line.

In the Guaranteed Service model, Tspec and Rspec are used to set up a flow reservation. The Tspec is represented by the token bucket parameters. The Rspec contains the parameter R that specifies the bandwidth for the flow reservation.

The Reservation Protocol (RSVP)

The Integrated Services model uses the Reservation Protocol (RSVP) to set up and control QoS reservations. RSVP is defined in RFC 2205 and has the status of a proposed standard. Because RSVP is an Internet control protocol and not a routing protocol, it requires an existing routing protocol to operate. RSVP runs on top of IP and UDP and must be implemented in all routers on the reservation path. The key concepts of RSVP are flows and reservations.

An RSVP reservation applies for a specific flow of data packets on a specific path through the routers. As described in the first section of this chapter, "Why QoS?", a flow is defined as a distinguishable stream of related datagrams from a unique sender to a unique receiver. If the receiver is a multicast address, a flow can reach multiple receivers. RSVP provides the same service for unicast and multicast flows. Each flow is identified from RSVP by its destination IP address and destination port. All flows have dedicated a flow descriptor that contains the QoS that a specific flow requires. RSVP does not understand the contents of a flow descriptor. It is carried as an opaque object by RSVP and is delivered to a router's traffic control functions (packet classifier and scheduler) for processing.

Quality of Service

Because RSVP is a simplex protocol, reservations are only done in one direction. For duplex connections, such as video and audio conferences where each sender is also a receiver, it is necessary to set up two RSVP sessions for each station.

RSVP is receiver-initiated. Using RSVP signaling messages, the sender provides a specific QoS to the receiver, which sends an RSVP reservation message back with the QoS that should be reserved for the flow from the sender to the receiver. This behavior considers the different QoS requirements for heterogeneous receivers in large multicast groups. The sender doesn't need to know the characteristics of all possible receivers to structure the reservations.

To establish a reservation with RSVP, receivers send reservation requests to the senders depending on their system capabilities. For example, a fast workstation and a slow PC want to receive a high-quality MPEG video stream with 30 frames per second that has a data rate of 1.5 Mbps. The workstation has enough CPU performance to decode the video stream, but the PC can only decode 10 frames per second. If the video server sends the messages to the two receivers to which it can provide the 1.5 Mbps video stream, the workstation can return a reservation request for the full 1.5 Mbps. But the PC doesn't need the full bandwidth for its flow because it cannot decode all frames. So the PC may send a reservation request for a flow with 10 frames per second and 500 kbps.

RSVP Operation A basic part of a resource reservation is the path. The path is the route a packet follows as it flows through the different routers from the sender to the receiver. All packets that belong to a specific flow use the same path. The path is determined when a sender generates RSVP path messages that travel in the same direction as the flow. Each sender host periodically sends a path message for each data flow it originates. The path message contains traffic information that describes the QoS for a specific flow. Because RSVP doesn't handle routing by itself, it uses the information from the routing tables in each router to forward RSVP messages.

When a path message reaches the first RSVP router, the router stores the IP address from the last hop field in the message, which is the address of the sender. Then the router inserts its own IP address into the last hop field, sends the path message to the next router, and the process repeats itself until the message has reached the receiver. At the end of this process, each router will know the address from the previous router, and the path can be accessed backward. Figure 10-4 shows the process of the path definition.

Figure 10-4
RSVP Path Definition Process.

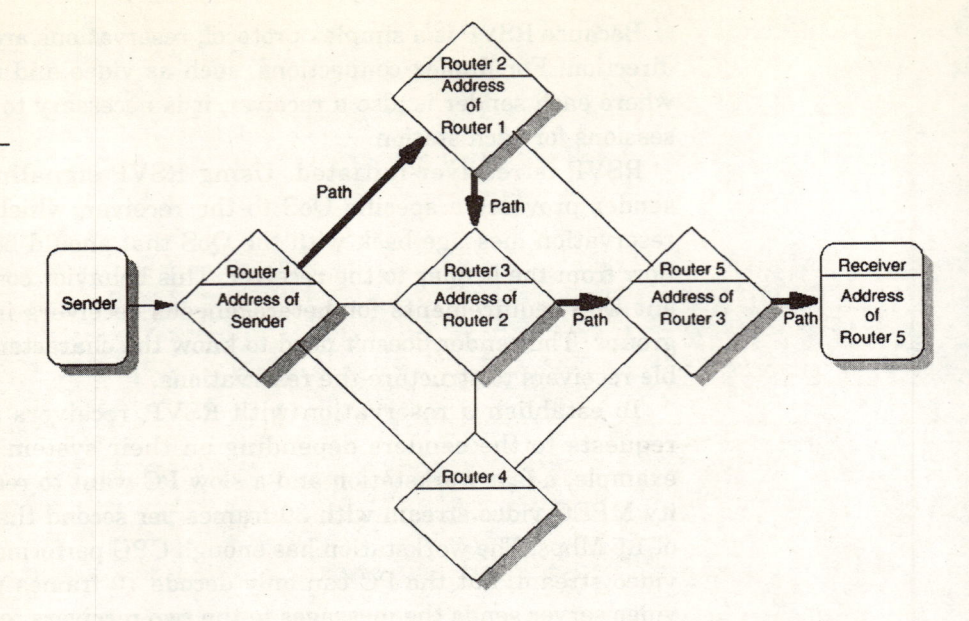

```
                        ┌─────────┐
                        │ Router 2│
                        │Address  │
                        │   of    │
                        │ Router 1│
                        └─────────┘
                       ↗           ↘
                   Path              Path
                  ↗                     ↘
┌──────┐   ┌─────────┐   ┌─────────┐   ┌─────────┐   ┌─────────┐   ┌────────┐
│Sender│ → │ Router 1│ → │ Router 3│ → │ Router 5│ → │Receiver│
│      │   │Address of│  │Address of│Path│Address of│Path│Address │
│      │   │ Sender  │   │ Router 2│   │ Router 3│   │   of   │
│      │   │         │   │         │   │         │   │Router 5│
└──────┘   └─────────┘   └─────────┘   └─────────┘   └────────┘
                        ↘           ↗
                         ┌─────────┐
                         │ Router 4│
                         └─────────┘
```

Routers that have received a path message are prepared to process resource reservations for a flow. All packets that belong to this flow take the same way through the routers, which is the way defined by the path messages.

The status in a system after sending the path messages is the following: All receivers know that a sender can provide a special QoS for a flow, and all routers know about the possible resource reservation for this flow.

If a receiver wants to reserve QoS for this flow, it sends a reservation (resv) message. The reservation message contains the QoS requested from this receiver for a specific flow and is represented by the filterspec and flowspec that form the flow descriptor. The receiver sends the resv message to the last router in the path specified by the address in the path message. Because every RSVP-capable device knows the address of the previous device on the path, reservation messages travel the path in reverse direction toward the sender and establish the resource reservation in every router. Figure 10-5 shows the flow of the reservation messages through the routers.

At each node, a reservation request initiates two actions:

1. *QoS reservation on this link.* The RSVP process passes the request to the admission control and policy control instance on the node. The admission control checks if the router has the necessary

Quality of Service

Figure 10-5
RSVP Resv Messages Flow.

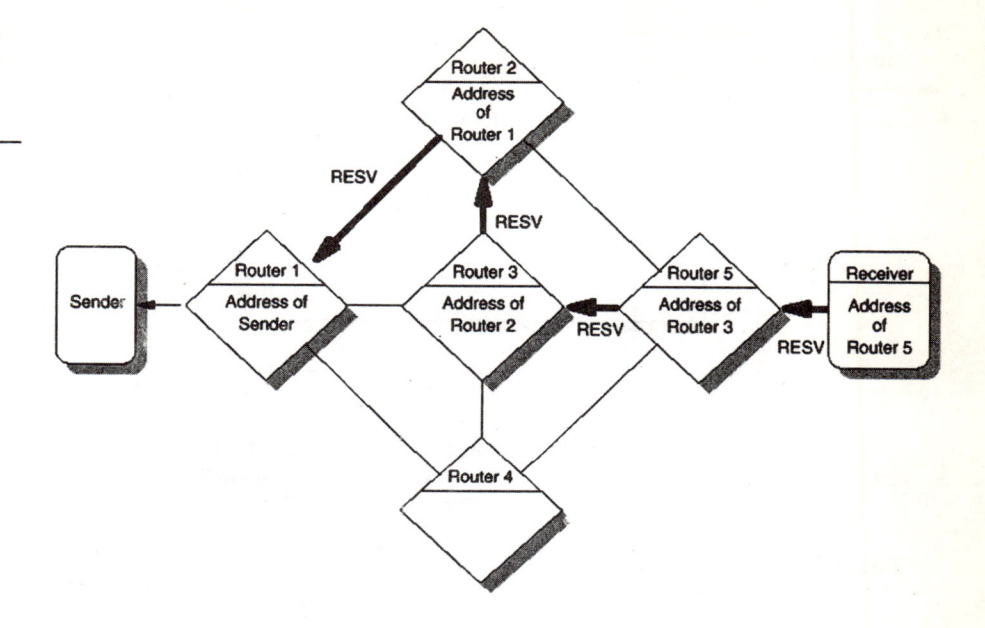

resources to establish the new QoS reservation, and the policy control checks if the application has the authorization to make QoS requests. If one of these tests fails, the reservation is rejected and the RSVP process returns a ResvErr error message to the appropriate receiver. If both checks succeed, the node uses the filterspec information in the resv message to set the packet classifier and the flowspec information to set the packet scheduler. After this, the packet classifier will recognize the packets that belong to this flow, and the packet scheduler will obtain the desired QoS defined by the flowspec.

Figure 10-6 shows the reservation process in an RSVP router.

2. *Forwarding of the reservation request.* After a successful admission and policy check, a reservation request is propagated upstream toward the sender. In a multicast environment, a receiver can get data from multiple senders. The set of sender hosts to which a given reservation request is propagated is called the *scope* of that request. The reservation request that is forwarded by a node after a successful reservation can differ from the request that was received from the previous hop downstream. One possible reason for this is that the traffic control mechanism may modify the flowspec hop by hop. Another more important reason is that in

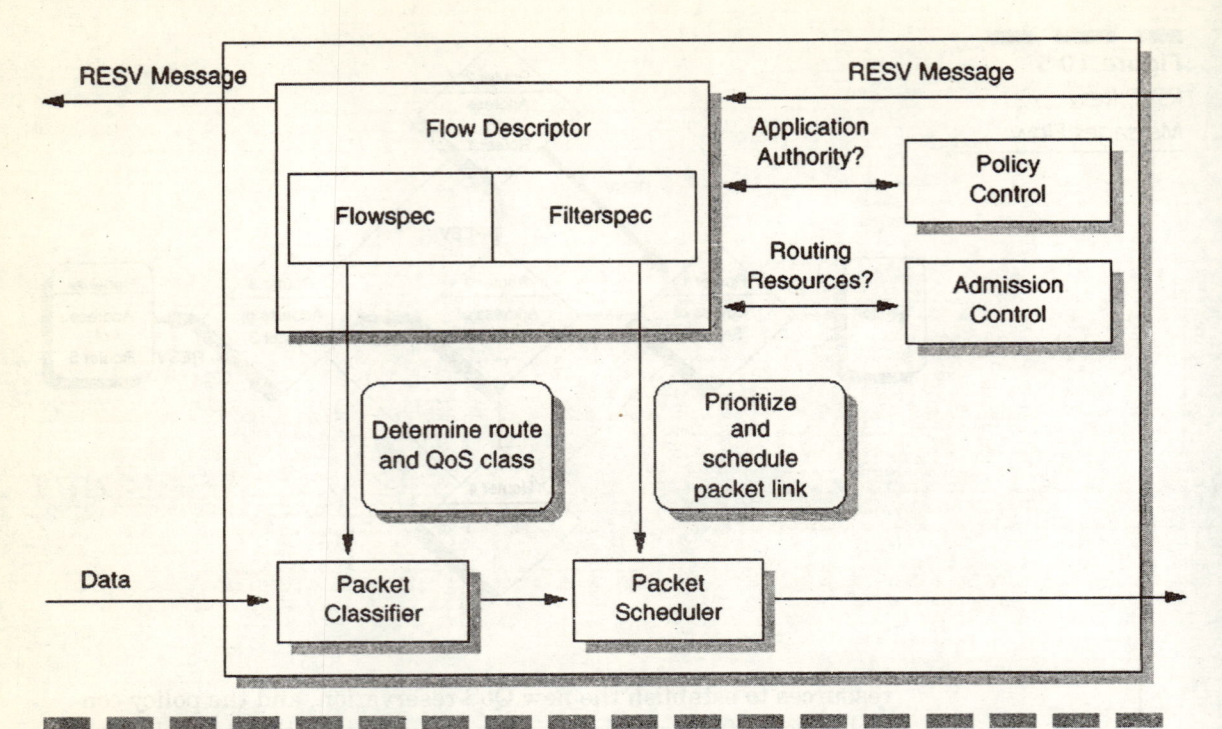

Figure 10-6 RSVP Reservation Process.

a multicast environment, reservations from different downstream branches but for the same sender are merged together as they travel across the upstream path. This merging is necessary to conserve resources in the routers.

A successful reservation request propagates upstream along the multicast tree until it reaches a point where an existing reservation is equal to or greater than that being requested. At this point, the arriving request is merged with the reservation in place and need not be forwarded further.

Figure 10-7 shows the reservation merging for a multicast flow.

If the reservation request reaches the sender, the QoS reservation has been established in every router on the path, and the application can start to send packets downstream to the receivers. The packet classifier and the packet scheduler in each router make sure that the packets are forwarded according to the requested QoS.

This type of reservation is only reasonable if all routers on the path support RSVP. Even if only one router doesn't support resource reservation, the service cannot be guaranteed for the whole path because of the

Quality of Service

Figure 10-7
RSVP Reservation Merging for Multicast Flows.

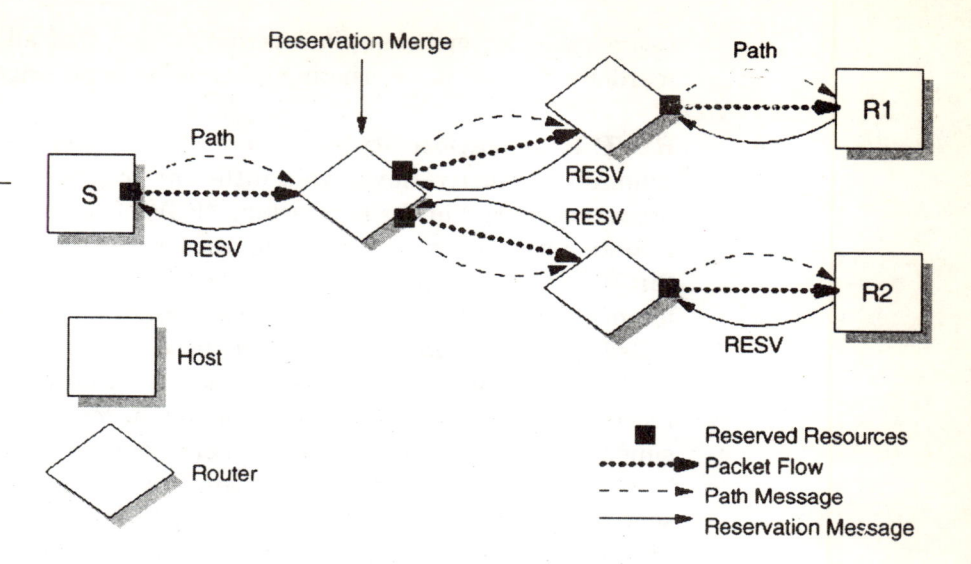

"best-effort" restrictions that apply for normal routers. A router on the path that doesn't support RSVP would be a bottleneck for the flow.

A receiver that originates a reservation request can also request a confirmation message that indicates that the request has been installed in the network. The receiver includes a confirmation request in the Resv message and gets a ResvConf message if the reservation has been established successfully.

RSVP resource reservations maintain a soft state in routers and hosts, which means that a reservation is canceled if RSVP doesn't send refresh messages along the path for an existing reservation. This allows route changes to occur without causing protocol overhead. Path messages must also be resent because the path state fields in the routers are reset after a timeout period.

Path and reservation states can also be deleted with RSVP teardown messages. There are two types of teardown messages:

- *PathTear messages.* PathTear messages travel downstream from the point of initiation to all receivers, deleting the path state as well as all dependent reservation states in each RSVP-capable device.
- *ResvTear messages.* ResvTear messages travel upstream from the point of initiation to all senders, deleting reservation states in all routers and hosts.

Teardown request can be initiated by senders, receivers, or routers that notice a state timeout. Because of the soft-state principle of RSVP reservations, it is not really necessary to explicitly tear down an old reservation. Nevertheless, it is recommended that all end hosts send a teardown request if a consisting reservation is no longer needed.

RSVP Reservation Styles Users of multicast multimedia applications often receive flows from different senders. In the reservation process described in the last section, "RSVP Operation," a receiver must initiate a separate reservation request for each flow it wants to receive. But RSVP provides a more flexible way to reserve QoS for flows from different senders. A reservation request includes a set of options that are called the *reservation style*. One of these options deals with the treatment of reservations for different senders within the same session. The receiver can establish a *distinct* reservation for each sender or make a single *shared* reservation for all packets from the senders in one session.

Another option defines how the senders for a reservation request are selected. It is possible to specify an *explicit* list or a *wild card* that selects the senders belonging to one session. In an explicit sender-selection reservation, a filterspec must identify exactly one sender. In a wild-card sender selection the filterspec is not needed. Figure 10-8 shows the reservation styles that are defined with this reservation option:

WILD-CARD-FILTER (WF) The Wild-Card-Filter style uses the option's shared reservation and wild-card sender selection. This reservation style establishes a single reservation for all senders in a session. Reservations from different senders are merged together along the path so that only the biggest reservation request reaches the senders.

A wild-card reservation is forwarded upstream to all sender hosts. If new senders appear in the session, for example, new members enter a videoconference, the reservation is extended to these new senders.

Figure 10-8 RSVP Reservation Styles.

Sender Selection	Distinct Reservation	Shared Reservation
Explicit	Fixed-Filter (FF) Style	Shared-Explicit (SE) Style
Wildcard	(Not Defined)	Wildcard-Filter (WF) Style

FIXED-FILTER (FF) The Fixed-Filter style uses the option's distinct reservations and explicit sender selection. This means that a distinct reservation is created for data packets from a particular sender. Packets from different senders that are in the same session do not share reservations.

SHARED-EXPLICIT (SE) The Shared-Explicit style uses the option's shared reservation and explicit sender selection. This means that a single reservation covers flows from a specified subset of senders. Therefore, a sender list must be included in the reservation request from the receiver.

Reservations established in shared style (WF and SE) are mostly used for multicast applications. For this type of application, it is unlikely that several data sources transmit data simultaneously, so it is not necessary to reserve QoS for each sender.

For example, in an audio conference that consists of five participants, every station sends a data stream with 64 kbps. With a Fixed-Filter style reservation, all members of the conference must establish four separate 64-kbps reservations for the flows from the other senders. But in an audio conference usually only one or two people speak at the same time. Therefore, it would be sufficient to reserve a bandwidth of 128 kbps for all senders because most audio conferencing software uses silence suppression, meaning that if a person doesn't speak no packets are sent. This can be realized if every receiver makes one shared reservation of 128 kbps for all senders.

Using the Shared-Explicit style, all receivers must explicitly identify all other senders in the conference. With the Wild-card-Filter style the reservation counts for every sender that matches the reservation specifications. If, for example, the audio conferencing tool sends the data packets to a special TCP/IP port, the receivers can make a Wild-card-Filter reservation for all packets with this destination port.

RSVP Messages Format Basically, an RSVP message consists of a common header followed by a body consisting of a variable number of *objects*. The number and the content of these objects depends on the message type. The message objects contain the information that is necessary to realize resource reservations (e.g., the flow descriptor or the reservation style). In most cases, the order of the objects in an RSVP message makes no logical difference. RFC 2205 recommends that an RSVP implementation should use the object order defined in the RFC but should also accept the objects in any permissible order. Figure 10-9 shows the common header of an RSVP message, which has the following fields:

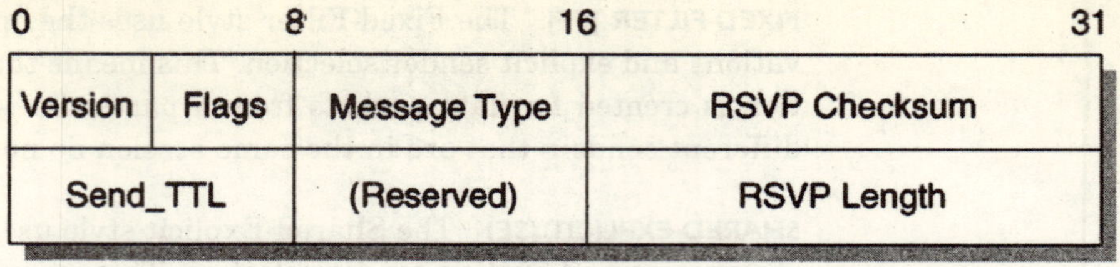

Figure 10-9
RSVP Common Header.

0	8	16	31
Version	Flags	Message Type	RSVP Checksum
Send_TTL		(Reserved)	RSVP Length

Version is a 4-bit RSVP protocol number. The current version is 1.

Flags is 4-bit field that is reserved for flags. No flags are defined yet.

Message Type is an 8-bit field that specifies the message type, which can be one of the following:

1. Path
2. Resv
3. PathErr
4. ResvErr
5. PathTear
6. ResvTear
7. ResvConf

RSVP Checksum is 16-bit field. The checksum can be used by receivers of an RSVP message to detect errors in the transmission of this message.

Send_TTL is an 8-bit field that contains the IP TTL value the message was sent with.

RSVP Length is a 16-bit field that contains the total length of the RSVP message, including the common header and all objects that follow. The length is counted in bytes.

The RSVP objects that follow the common header consist of a 32-bit header and one or more 32-bit words. Figure 10-10 shows the RSVP object header, which has the following fields:

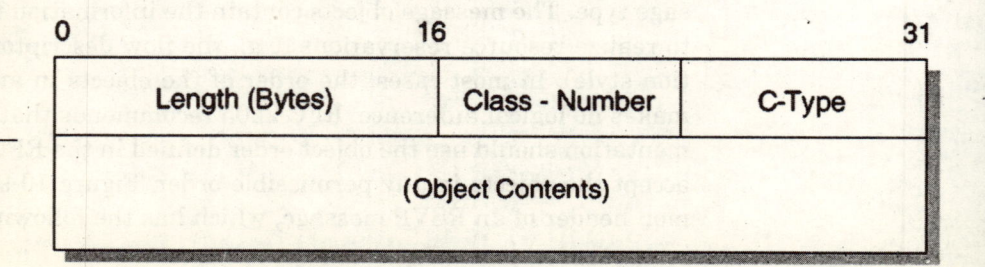

Figure 10-10
RSVP Object Header.

0	16	31
Length (Bytes)	Class - Number	C-Type
(Object Contents)		

Quality of Service

Length is a 16-bit field that contains the object length in bytes. This must be a multiple of four. The minimum length is 4 bytes.

Class-Number identifies the object class. The following classes are defined:

NULL

The NULL object has a Class-Number of zero. The length of this object must be at least four, but it can be any multiple of four. The NULL object can appear anywhere in the object sequence of an RSVP message. The content is ignored by the receiver.

Session

The session object contains the IP destination address, the IP protocol ID, and the destination port to define a specific session for the other objects that follow. The session object is required in every RSVP message.

RSVP_HOP

The RSVP_HOP object contains the IP address of the node that sent this message and a logical outgoing interface handle. For downstream messages (for example, path messages), the RSVP_HOP object represents a PHOP (previous hop) object, and for upstream messages (for example, resv messages) it represents an NHOP (next hop) object.

Time_Values

The Time_Values object contains the refresh period for path and reservation messages. If these messages are not refreshed within the specified time period, the path or reservation state is canceled.

Style

The style object defines the reservation style and some style-specific information that is not in flowspec or filterspec. The style object is required in every resv message.

Flowspec

This object specifies the required QoS in reservation messages.

Filterspec

The filterspec object defines which data packets receive the QoS specified in the flowspec.

Sender_Template

This object contains the sender IP address and additional demultiplexing information, which is used to identify a sender. The Sender_Template is required in every path message.

Sender_Tspec

This object defines the traffic characteristics of a data flow from a sender. The Sender_Tspec is required in all path messages.

Adspec

The adspec object is used to provide advertising information to the traffic control modules in the RSVP nodes along the path.

Error_Spec

This object specifies an error in a PathErr or ResvErr message or a confirmation in a ResvConf message.

Policy_Data

This object contains information that allows a policy module to decide whether an associated reservation is administratively permitted or not. It can be used in path, resv, PathErr, or ResvErr messages.

Integrity

The integrity object contains cryptographic data to authenticate the originating node and to verify the contents of an RSVP message.

Scope

The scope object contains an explicit list of sender hosts to which the information in the message is sent. The object can appear in a resv, ResvErr, or ResvTear message.

Resv_Confirm

This object contains the IP address of a receiver that requests confirmation for its reservation. It can be used in a resv or ResvConf message.

C-Type specifies the object type within the class number. Different object types are used for IPv4 and IPv6.

Object contents depend on the object type and have a maximum length of 65,528 bytes.

All RSVP messages are built from a variable number of objects. The recommended object order for the most important RSVP messages, the path and the resv message, are shown in the following. Figure 10-11 gives an overview of the format of the RSVP path message. Objects that can appear in a path message but that are not required are parenthesized.

If the integrity object is used in the path message, it must immediately follow the common header. The order of the other objects may differ

Quality of Service

Figure 10-11
RSVP Path Message Format.

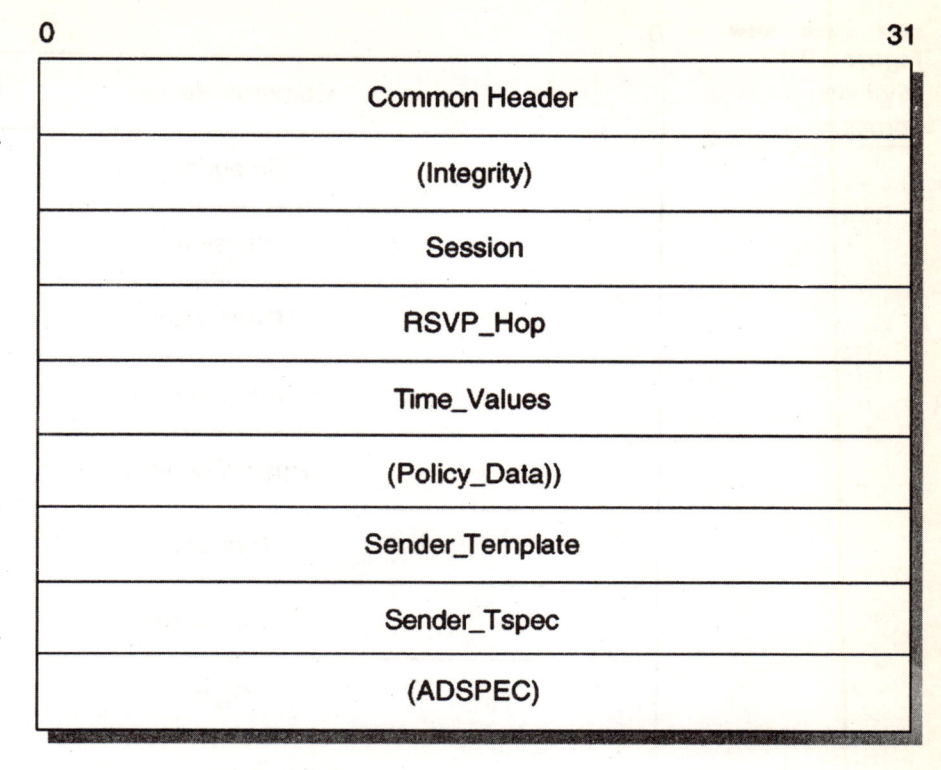

```
0                                                    31
┌─────────────────────────────────────────────────────┐
│                  Common Header                      │
├─────────────────────────────────────────────────────┤
│                    (Integrity)                      │
├─────────────────────────────────────────────────────┤
│                      Session                        │
├─────────────────────────────────────────────────────┤
│                     RSVP_Hop                        │
├─────────────────────────────────────────────────────┤
│                   Time_Values                       │
├─────────────────────────────────────────────────────┤
│                   (Policy_Data))                    │
├─────────────────────────────────────────────────────┤
│                  Sender_Template                    │
├─────────────────────────────────────────────────────┤
│                   Sender_Tspec                      │
├─────────────────────────────────────────────────────┤
│                     (ADSPEC)                        │
└─────────────────────────────────────────────────────┘
```

in different RSVP implementations, but the order shown in Figure 10-11 is recommended by the RFC.

The RSVP Resv messages looks similar to the path message. Figure 10-12 shows the objects used for reservation messages.

As in the path message, the integrity object must follow the common header if it is used. Another restriction applies for the style object and the following flow descriptor list. They must occur at the end of the message. The order of the other objects follows the recommendation from the RFC.

For a detailed description of the RSVP message structure and the handling of the different reservation styles in reservation messages, please consult RFC 2205.

The Future of Integrated Services

At the moment it is not known if the Integrated Services model will win recognition on the future Internet. More and more router manufacturers

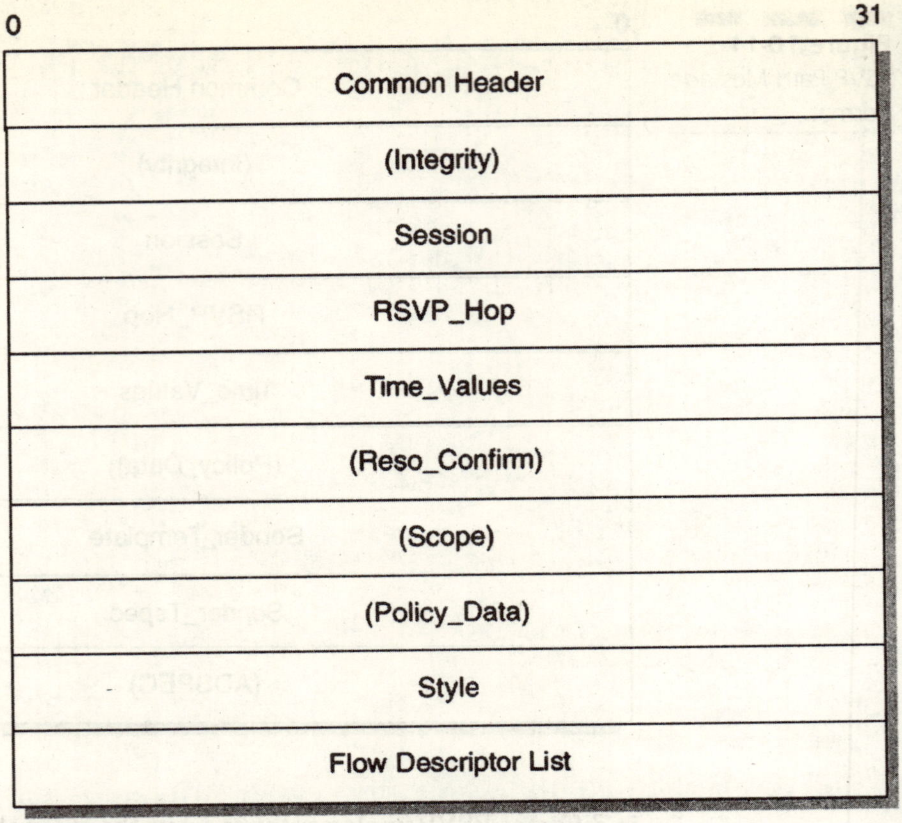

Figure 10-12
RSVP Resv Message Format.

```
0                                                               31
┌─────────────────────────────────────────────────────────────────┐
│                        Common Header                            │
├─────────────────────────────────────────────────────────────────┤
│                         (Integrity)                             │
├─────────────────────────────────────────────────────────────────┤
│                          Session                                │
├─────────────────────────────────────────────────────────────────┤
│                         RSVP_Hop                                │
├─────────────────────────────────────────────────────────────────┤
│                        Time_Values                              │
├─────────────────────────────────────────────────────────────────┤
│                       (Reso_Confirm)                            │
├─────────────────────────────────────────────────────────────────┤
│                          (Scope)                                │
├─────────────────────────────────────────────────────────────────┤
│                       (Policy_Data)                             │
├─────────────────────────────────────────────────────────────────┤
│                           Style                                 │
├─────────────────────────────────────────────────────────────────┤
│                    Flow Descriptor List                         │
└─────────────────────────────────────────────────────────────────┘
```

support RSVP in their routers. But to provide IS for a larger group of users, many Internet routers should support RSVP.

An important point that should be monitored by the router manufacturers is that the traffic control overhead in RSVP-capable routers may decrease the routing performance. The more data flows are passing a router, the more RSVP sessions must be handled by the RSVP daemon inside the router. Router manufacturers must make sure that in high-traffic situations a router is not blocked by having to manage RSVP sessions instead of routing data packets and keeping up with routing table updates.

Future extensions of the policy control module may implement a priority mechanism that allows users to send reservation requests that have higher priority than others. If the routers on the path run out of routing capacity, the high-priority requests will be favored. This may be coupled with a billing system that charges the user for high-priority reservation requests. If IS is supported on the Internet, it must be

Quality of Service

assured that the normal best-effort traffic is still served. It must not happen that some routers are blocked with RSVP reservations and can't handle any best-effort traffic. This may even be an economic policy decision for ISPs to make. A conceivable scenario is that one half of the routing capacity is used for RSVP flow reservations and the other half for the classic best-effort traffic.

It may be some time, if ever, before RSVP end-to-end services are deployed on the Internet. At the moment, IS is preferably used on corporate intranets to provide multimedia and other real-time data to the end users. For example, if all routers in an intranet support RSVP, a video transmission can be broadcasted for informational or educational reasons to all workstations in a company.

Differentiated Services

The Differentiated Services (DS) concept is currently under development at the IETF DS working group. The DS specifications are defined in some IETF Internet drafts, and there is no RFC available yet. This section gives an overview of the rudiments and ideas behind providing differentiation on the Internet. Because the concept is still under development, some of the specifications mentioned in this book may be changed in the final definition of Differentiated Services.

The goal of the DS development is to make it possible to provide differentiated classes of service for Internet traffic and to support various types of applications and specific business requirements. DS offers predictable performance (delay, throughput, packet loss, etc.) for a given load at a given time. The difference between Integrated Services (described in the section "Integrated Services" at the beginning of this chapter) and Differentiated Services is that DS provides scalable service discrimination on the Internet without the need for per-flow state and signaling at every hop. It is not necessary to perform a unique QoS reservation for each flow. With DS, the Internet traffic is split into different classes with different QoS requirements.

A central component of DS is the Service Level Agreement (SLA). The SLA is a service contract between a customer and a service provider that specifies the details of the traffic classifying and the corresponding forwarding service that a customer should receive. A customer may be a user organization or another DS domain. The service provider must ensure that the traffic of a customer with whom it has an SLA gets the contracted QoS. Therefore, the service provider's network administration must set up the appropriate service policies and measure the network performance to guarantee the agreed-upon traffic performance.

To distinguish the data packets from different customers in DS-capable network devices, the IP packets are modified in a specific field. A small bit pattern, called the DS byte, in each IP packet is used to mark the packets that receive a particular forwarding treatment at each network node. The DS byte uses the space of the TOS octet in the IPv4 IP header (shown in the section titled "IP Datagram Format" in Chapter 2) and the traffic class octet in the IPv6 header. All network traffic inside of a domain receives a service that depends on the traffic class that is specified in the DS byte.

To provide SLA conform services, the following mechanisms must be combined in a network:

- Setting bits in the DS byte (TOS octet) at network edges and administrative boundaries.
- Using those bits to determine how packets are treated by the routers inside the network.
- Conditioning the marked packets at network boundaries in accordance with the QoS requirements of each service.

The currently defined DS architecture only provides service differentiation in one direction and is therefore asymmetric. The development of a complementary symmetric architecture is a topic of current research. The following section describes the DS architecture in more detail.

Differentiated Services Architecture

Unlike in Integrated Services, in Differentiated Services QoS guarantees are static and stay long-term in routers. This means that applications using DS don't need to set up QoS reservations for specific data packets. All traffic that passes DS-capable networks can receive a specific QoS. The data packets must be marked with the DS byte, which is interpreted by the routers in the network.

The Per-Hop Behavior As mentioned earlier, the IETF DS working group has proposed redefining the structure of the IPv4 TOS byte and the IPv6 traffic class field and relabeling this field as the DS byte. The DS byte specifications supersede the IPv4 TOS octet definitions of RFC 1349. Figure 10-13 shows the structure of the newly defined DS byte.

Quality of Service

Figure 10-13
DS Byte.

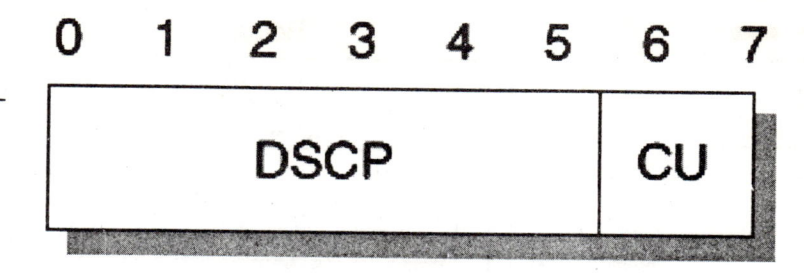

```
 0   1   2   3   4   5   6   7
+-----------------------+-------+
|         DSCP          |  CU   |
+-----------------------+-------+
```

Six bits of the DS field are used as a Differentiated Services CodePoint (DSCP) to select the traffic class that a packet experiences at each node. A two-bit currently unused (CU) field is reserved and can be assigned later.

Each DS-capable network device must have information on how packets with different DS bytes should be handled. In the DS specifications, this information is called the *Per-Hop Behavior* (*PHB*). It is a description of the forwarding treatment a packet receives at a given network node. The DSCP value in the DS byte is used to select the PHB that a packet experiences at each node. To provide predictable services, per-hop behaviors need to be available in all routers in a Differentiated Services-capable network. The PHB can be described as a set of parameters inside of a router that can be used to control how packets are scheduled onto an output interface. This can be a number of separate queues with settable priorities, parameters for queue lengths or drop algorithms, and drop preference weights for packets.

DS requires routers that support queue scheduling and management to prioritize outbound packets and control the queue depth so as to minimize congestion on the network. The traditional FIFO queuing in common Internet routers provides no service differentiation and can lead to network performance problems. The packet treatment inside of a router depends on the router's capabilities and its particular configuration. It is selected by the DS byte in the IP packet. For example, if a IP packet reaches a router with eight different queues that all have different priorities, the DS byte can be used to select which queue is liable for the routing of this packet (see Figure 10-14). The scale ranges from zero, for lowest priority, to seven, for highest priority.

Another example is a router that has a single queue with multiple drop priorities for data packets. It uses the DS byte to select the drop preference for the packets in the queue. A value of zero means "it is most likely to drop this packet," and seven means "it is least likely to drop this packet." Another possible configuration is four queues with two levels of drop preference in each.

Figure 10-14
DS Routing Example.

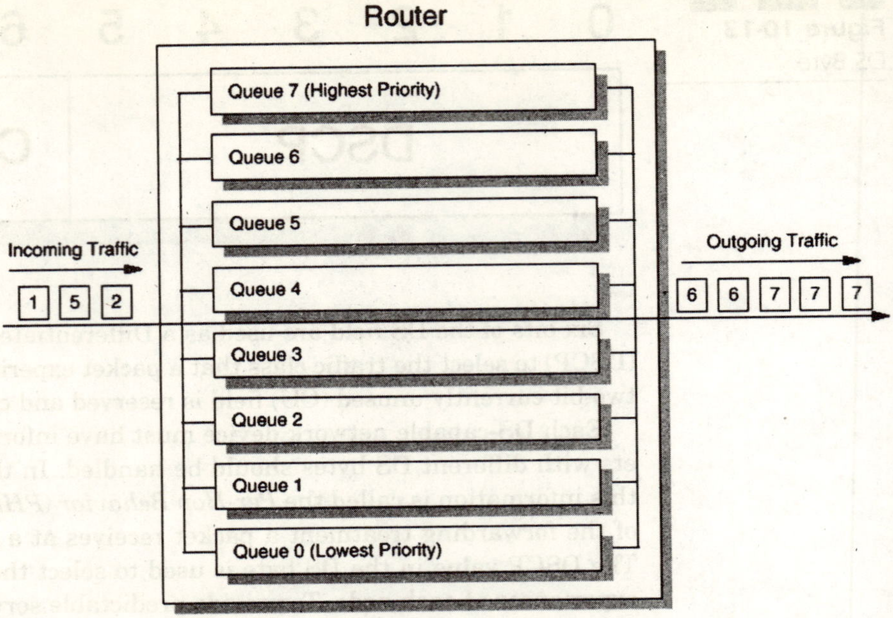
Router
Queue 7 (Highest Priority)
Queue 6
Queue 5
Queue 4
Queue 3
Queue 2
Queue 1
Queue 0 (Lowest Priority)
Incoming Traffic
1
5
2
Outgoing Traffic
6
6
7
7
7

To make sure that the per-hop behaviors in each router are functionally equivalent, certain common PHBs must be defined in future DS specifications to avoid the situation where the same DS byte value causes different forwarding behaviors in different routers of one DS domain. This means that in future DS specifications some unique PHB values must be defined that represent specific service classes. All routers in one DS domain must know which service a packet with a specific PHB should receive. The DiffServ working group will propose PHBs that should be used to provide Differentiated Services. Some of these proposed PHBs will be standardized; others may have widespread use, and still others may remain experimental.

PHBs will be defined in groups. A PHB group is a set of one or more PHBs that can only be specified and implemented simultaneously because of queue servicing or queue management policies that apply to all PHBs in one group. A default PHB must be available in all DS-compliant nodes. It represents the standard best-effort forwarding behavior available in existing routers. When no other agreements are in place, it is assumed that packets belong to this service level. The IETF working group recommends the use of the DSCP value 000000 in the DS byte to define the default PHB.

Quality of Service

Another PHB that is proposed for standardization is the Expedited Forwarding (EF) PHB. It is a high-priority behavior that is typically used for network control traffic such as routing updates. The value 101100 in the DSCP field of the DS byte is recommended for the EF PHB.

Differentiated Services Domains QoS guarantees are not set up for specific end-to-end connections but for well-defined Differentiated Services domains. The IETF working group defines a Differentiated Services domain as a contiguous portion of the Internet over which a consistent set of Differentiated Services policies are administered in a coordinated fashion. It can represent different administrative domains or autonomous systems; different trust regions; and different network technologies, such as cell or frame-based techniques, hosts, and routers. A DS domain consists of boundary components that are used to connect different DS domains to each other and interior components that are only used inside of the domains. Figure 10-15 shows the use of boundary and interior components for two DS domains.

A DS domain normally consists of one or more networks under the same administration. This can be, for example, a corporate intranet or an Internet service provider (ISP). The administration of the DS domain is responsible for ensuring that adequate resources are provisioned and reserved to support the SLAs offered by the domain. Network administrators must use appropriate measurement techniques to monitor whether the network resources in a DS domain are sufficient to satisfy all authorized QoS requests.

Figure 10-15 DS Domain.

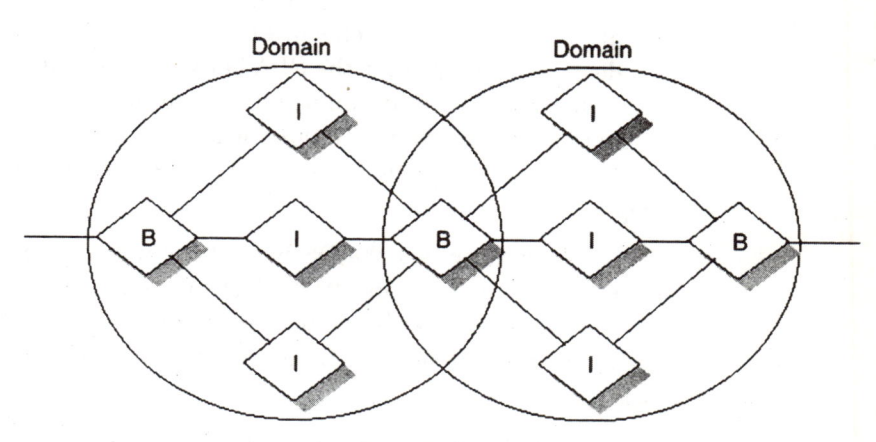

B = Boundary Component
I = Interior Component

DS Boundary Nodes All data packets that travel from one DS domain to another must pass a boundary node, which can be a router, a host, or a firewall. A DS boundary node that handles traffic leaving a DS domain is called an *egress node,* and a boundary node that handles traffic entering a DS domain is called an *ingress node.* Normally, DS boundary nodes act both as ingress node and egress node, depending on the traffic direction. The ingress node must make sure that the packets entering a domain receive the same QoS as in the domain the packets traveled through before. A DS egress node performs conditioning functions on traffic that is forwarded to a directly connected peering domain. The traffic conditioning is done inside of a boundary node by a *traffic conditioner.* It classifies, marks, and possibly conditions packets that enter or leave the DS domain. A traffic conditioner consists of the following components:

Classifier

A classifier selects packets based on their packet header and forwards the packets that match the classifier rules for further processing. The DS model specifies two types of packet classifiers:

1. Multi-field (MF) classifiers, which can classify on the DS byte as well as on any other IP header field, for example, the IP address and the port number, like an RSVP classifier.

2. Behavior Aggregate (BA) classifiers, which classify only on the bits in the DS byte.

Meter

Traffic meters measure whether the forwarding of the packets that are selected by the classifier correspond to the traffic profile that describes the QoS for the SLA between customer and service provider. A meter passes state information to other conditioning functions so as to trigger a particular action for each packet, which either does or does not comply with the requested QoS requirements.

Marker

DS markers set the DS byte of the incoming IP packets to a particular bit pattern. The PHB is set in the first six bits of the DS byte so the marked packets are forwarded inside of the DS domain according to the SLA between service provider and customer.

Shaper/Dropper

Packet shapers and droppers cause conformance to some configured traffic properties, for example, a token bucket filter as described in the

Quality of Service

section "Service Classes" earlier in this chapter. They use different methods to bring the stream into compliance with a traffic profile. Shapers delay some or all of the packets. A shaper usually has a finite-sized buffer, and packets may be discarded if there is not sufficient buffer space to hold the delayed packets. Droppers discard some or all of the packets. This process is know as "policing the stream." A dropper can be implemented as a special case of a shaper by setting the shaper buffer size to zero packets.

The traffic conditioner is mainly used in DS boundary components, but it can also be implemented in an interior component. Figure 10-16 shows the cooperation of the traffic conditioner components.

The traffic conditioner in a boundary component makes sure that packets that transit the domain are correctly marked to select a PHB from one of the PHB groups supported within the domain. This is necessary because different DS domains can have different groups of PHBs, which means that the same entry in the DS byte can be interpreted variably in different domains.

For example, in the first domain a packet traverses all routers have four queues with different queue priorities (0-3). Packets with a PHB value of three are routed with the highest priority. But in the next domain the packet travels through, all routers have eight different queues, and all packets with the PHB value of seven are routed with the highest priority. The packet that was forwarded in the first domain with high priority has only medium priority in the second domain. This may violate the SLA contract between customer and service provider. Therefore, the traffic conditioner in the boundary router that connects the two domains must assure that the PHB value is remarked from three to seven if the packet travels from the first to the second domain. Figure 10-17 shows an example of the remarking of data packets that travel through two different domains.

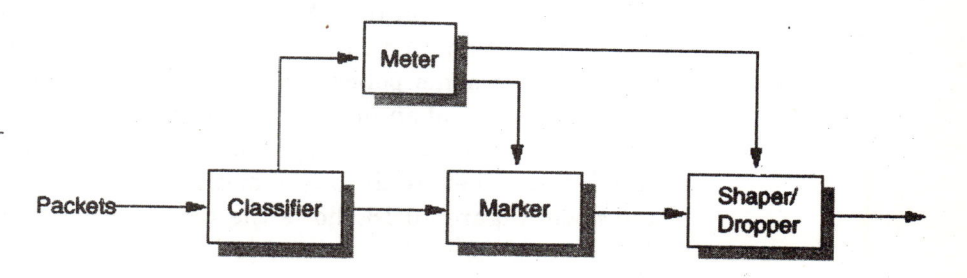

Figure 10-16
DS Traffic Conditioner.

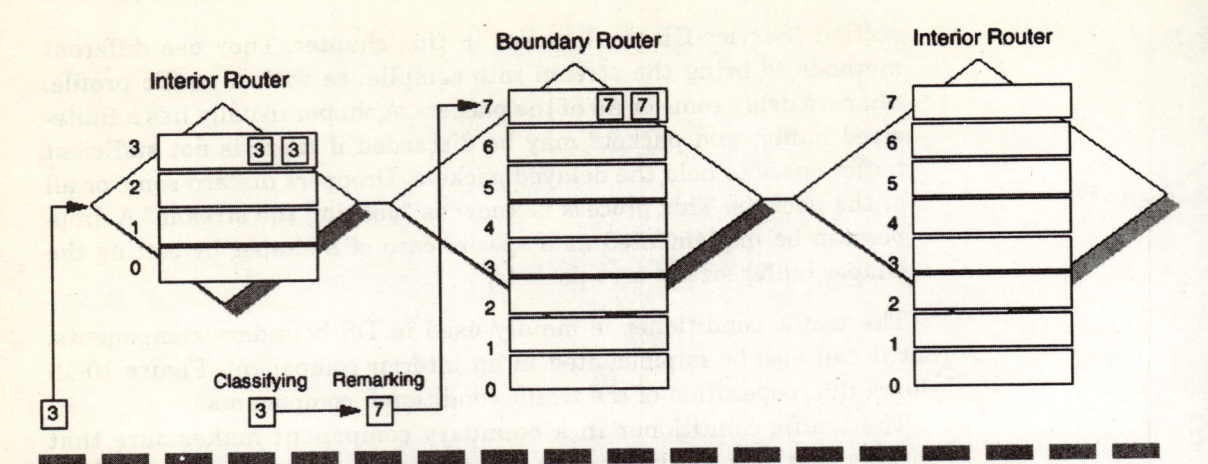

Figure 10-17 Remarking of Data Packets.

If a data packet travels through multiple domains, the DS byte can be remarked at every boundary component to guarantee the QoS that was contracted in the SLA. The SLA contains the details of the *Traffic Conditioning Agreement* (*TCA*) that specifies classifier rules and temporal properties of a traffic stream. The TCA contains information on how the metering, marking, discarding, and shaping of packets must be done in the traffic conditioner to fulfill the SLA. The TCA information must be available in all boundary components of a DS network to guarantee that packets passing different DS domains receive the same service in each domain.

DS Interior Components The interior components of a DS domain select the forwarding behavior for packets based on their DS byte. The interior component is usually a router that contains a traffic prioritization algorithm. Because the value of the DS byte normally doesn't change inside of a DS domain, all interior routers must use the same traffic forwarding policies to comply with the QoS agreement. Data packets with different PHB values in the DS byte receive different QoSs according to the QoS definitions for this PHB. Because all interior routers in a domain use the same policy functions for incoming traffic, the traffic conditioning inside of an interior node is done only by a packet classifier. It selects packets based on their PHB value or other IP header fields and forwards the packets to the queue management and scheduling instance of the node. Figure 10-18 shows the traffic conditioning in an interior node.

Quality of Service

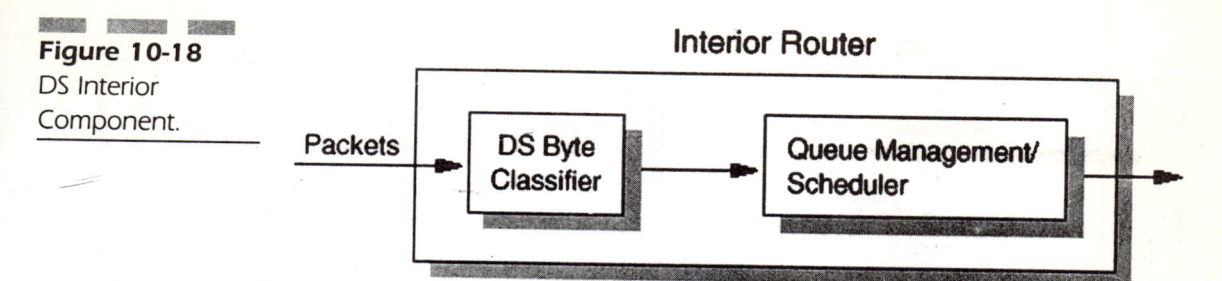

Figure 10-18
DS Interior Component.

[Diagram: Interior Router containing Packets → DS Byte Classifier → Queue Management/Scheduler]

Traffic classifying and prioritized routing is done in every interior component of a DS domain. After a data packet has crossed a domain, it reaches the boundary router of the next domain and may get remarked to cross this domain with the requested QoS.

Source Domains The IETF DS working group defines a source domain as the domain that contains one or more nodes that originate the traffic that receives a particular service. Traffic sources and intermediate nodes within a source domain can perform traffic classification and conditioning functions. The traffic that is sent from a source domain may be marked by the traffic sources directly or by intermediate nodes before leaving the source domain.

In this context, it is important to understand that the first PHB marking of the data packets is not done by the sending application itself. Applications do not notice the availability of Differentiated Services in a network. Therefore, applications using DS networks must not be rewritten to support DS. This is an important difference via-à-vis Integrated Services, where most applications support the RSVP protocol directly, making some code changes necessary.

The first PHB marking of packets that are sent from an application can be done in the source host or in the first router the packet passes. The packets are identified with their IP address and source port. For example, a customer has an SLA with a service provider that guarantees a higher priority for the packets sent by an audio application. The audio application sends the data packets through a specific port and can be recognized in multi-field classifiers. This classifier type recognizes the IP address and port number of a packet and can distinguish the packets from different applications. If the host contains a traffic conditioner with an MF classifier, the IP packet can be marked with the appropriate PHB value and consequently receives the QoSs that are requested by the customer. If the host doesn't contain a traffic conditioner, the initial marking of the packets is done by the first router in the source domain that

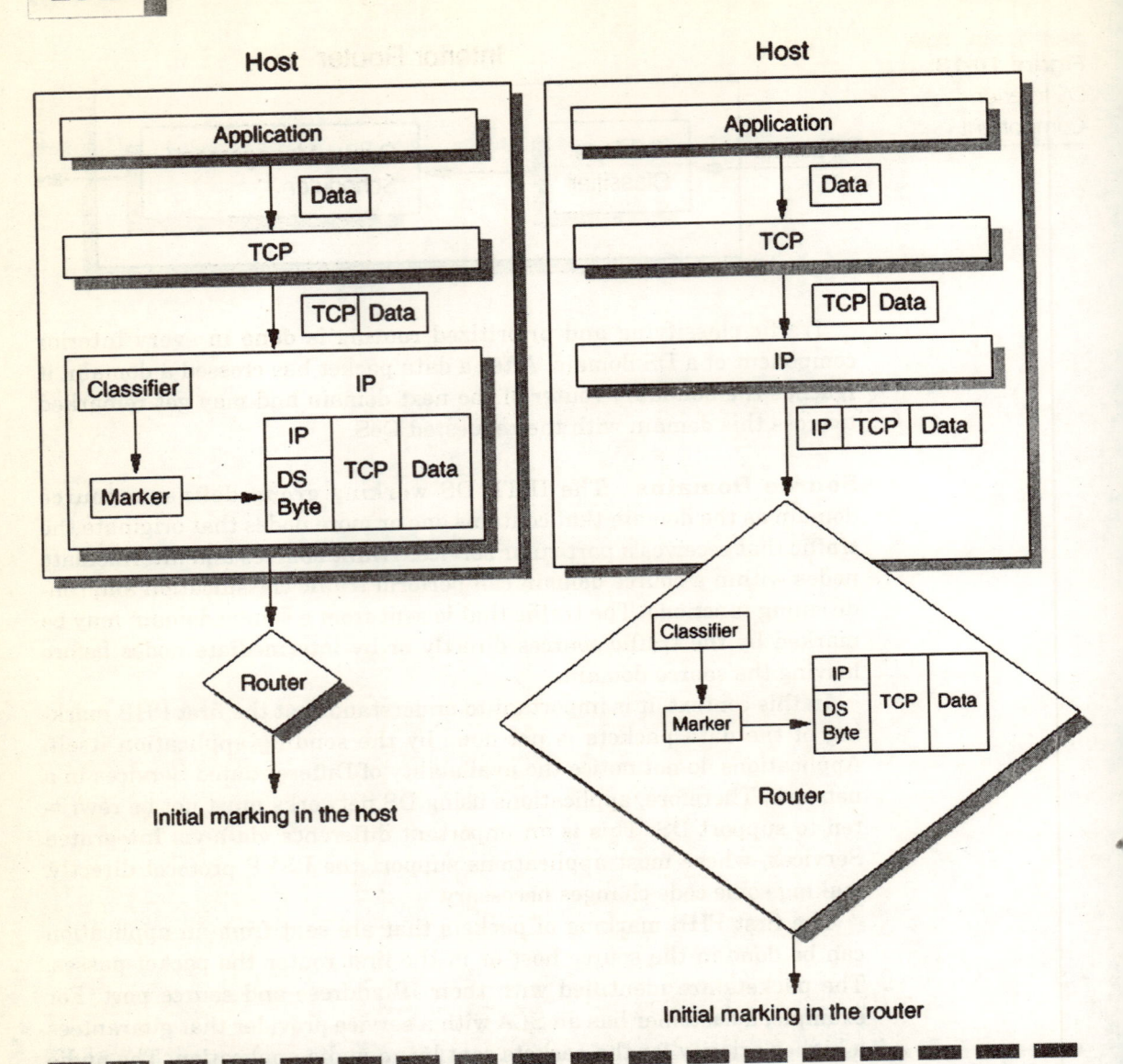

Figure 10-19 Initial Marking of Data Packets.

supports traffic conditioning. Figure 10-19 shows the initial marking of a packet inside of a host and a router.

In our example, the DS network has the policy that the packets from the audio application should have higher priority than other packets. The sender host can mark the DS field of all outgoing packets with a DS codepoint that indicates higher priority. Alternatively, the first-hop

Quality of Service

router directly connected to the sender's host may classify the traffic and mark the packets with the correct DS codepoint. The source DS domain is responsible for ensuring that the aggregated traffic toward its provider DS domain conforms to the SLA between customer and service provider. The boundary node of the source domain should also monitor that the provided service conforms to the requested service and may police, shape, or remark packets as necessary.

Using RSVP with Differentiated Services

The RSVP protocol, which is described in the section titled "The Reservation Protocol (RSVP)" above, enables applications to signal per-flow requirements to a network. Integrated Services parameters are used to quantify these requirements for the purpose of admission control. But RSVP and Integrated Services have some basic limitations that impede the deployment of these mechanisms on the Internet at large:

1. The reliance of RSVP on per-flow state and per-flow processing raises scalability concerns in large networks.
2. Today, only a small number of hosts generate RSVP signaling. Although this number is expected to grow dramatically, many applications may never generate RSVP signaling.
3. Many applications require a form of QoS but are unable to express these requirements using the IS model.

These disadvantages can be circumvented if Integrated Services is implemented only in intranets and it uses Differentiated Services on the Internet as a backbone. Figure 10-20 shows an imaginable network structure:

Two RSVP-capable customer intranets are connected to the DS Internet backbone. The routers R2 and R3 are boundary routers that can condition incoming and outgoing traffic at the interfaces of the DS network to the IS networks. In our example, the boundary routers are not required to run RSVP. They are expected to implement the policing functions of the DS ingress router. There must be a set of end-to-end services defined in the DS network that allow the mapping of RSVP flow reservations to an appropriate DS service class. The routers in the DS network must provide a set of per-hop behaviors (see the section, "The Per-Hop Behavior," earlier in this chapter), which provide the service of a true end-to-end connection. It must be possible for RSVP applications to invoke specific end-to-end service levels for their traffic flows in the DS

Figure 10-20
Using RSVP with Differentiated Services.

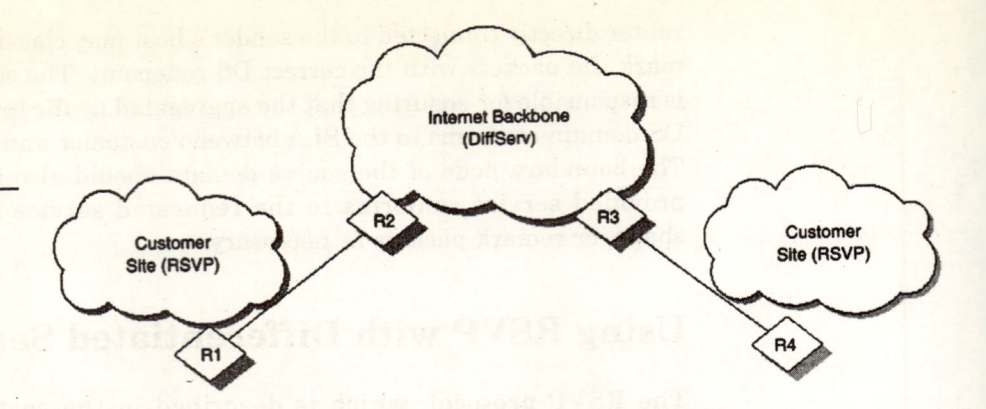

network. In this model, the IS intranets are customers of the DS Internet.

The edge routers R1 and R4 are special routers that work both in the RSVP/IS region of the network and the DS region of the network. These routers can be visualized as being split in two halves. One half supports standard RSVP, and it interfaces to the intranets. The other half supports DS and interfaces to the DS Internet. The RSVP half must be at least partially RSVP-capable. The router must be able to process path and resv messages, but it is not required to support packet classification and the storing of RSVP states. The DS half of the router provides the interface to the admission control function for the DS network. If the service agreement between the IS intranets and the DS Internet is static, the admission control service can be a simple table that specifies the QoS at each service level. If the service agreement is dynamic, admission control service communicates with counterparts within the DS network to make admission control decisions based on the capacity of the network.

In our model, RSVP signaling is used to provide admission control to specific service levels in the DS and the IS network. RSVP signaling messages carry an IS QoS description that specifies the type of service that should be provided in the IS regions of the network. At the boundary between the IS network and a DS network the edge routers map the requested IS QoS to an appropriate DS service level. After this, the edge router can provide admission control to the DS network by accepting or rejecting the QoS request based on the capacity available at the requested DS service level. If an RSVP reservation message from the IS network arrives at an edge router, the RSVP flow descriptor will be mapped to a PHB that represents the corresponding service level in the DS network. The edge router appends the PHB value to the RSVP resevation message, which is carried to the sending host. The sending host then marks all outgoing packets with this PHB value. This approach allows end-to-end QoS guarantees for RSVP applications in different intranets that use the DS Internet as backbone.

Configuration and Administration of DS Components with LDAP

In a Differentiated Services network, the service level information must be provided to all network elements to ensure the correct administrative control of bandwidth, delay, or dropping preferences for a given customer flow. All DS boundary components must have the same policy information for the defined service levels. This ensures that the packets marked with the DS byte receive the same service in all DS domains. If only one domain in the DS network has different policy information, it can happen that the data packets passing this domain don't receive the service that was contracted in the SLA between customer and service provider.

Network administrators can define different service levels for different customers and provide this information manually to all boundary components. This policy information remains statically in the network components until the next manual change. But in dynamic network environments it is necessary to enable flexible definitions of class-based packet handling behaviors and class-based policy control. Administrative policies can change in a running environment, making it is necessary to store the policies in a directory-based repository. The policy information from the directory can be distributed across multiple physical servers, but the administration is done for a single entity by the network administrator. The directory information must be propagated on all network elements, such as hosts, proxies, and routers, that use the policy information for traffic conditioning in the DS network.

In today's heterogeneous environments, it is likely that network devices and administrative tools are developed by different vendors. Therefore, it is necessary to use a standardized format to store the administrative policies in the directory server function and a standardized mechanism to provide the directory information to the DS boundary components that act as directory clients. These functions are provided by the *Lightweight Directory Access Protocol (LDAP)*, which is a simple, widely deployed industry protocol for accessing directories. Policy rules for different service levels are stored in directories as LDAP schema and can be downloaded to devices that implement the policies, such as hosts,

Figure 10-21
Administration of DS Components with LDAP.

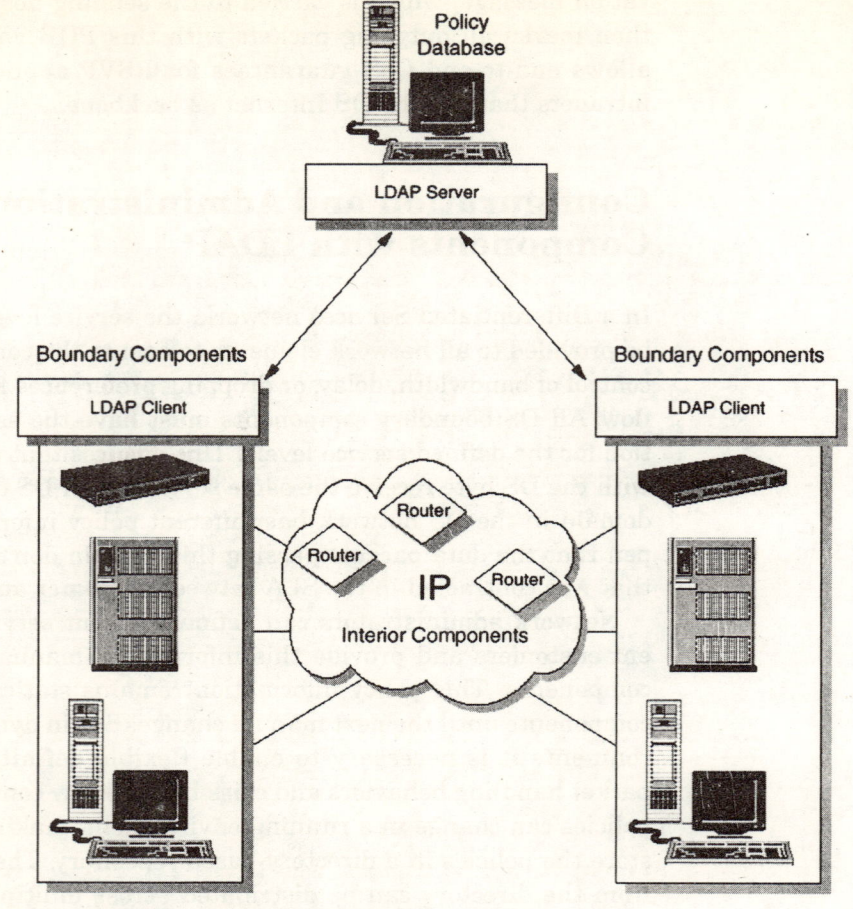

routers, policy servers, or proxies. Figure 10-21 shows the cooperation of the DS network elements with the LDAP server.

Using Differentiated Services with IPSec

The IPsec protocol does not use the DS field in an IP header for its cryptographic calculations. Therefore, the modification of the DS field by a

Quality of Service

network node has no effect on IPsec's end-to-end security because it cannot cause any IPsec integrity check to fail. This makes it possible to use IPsec-secured packets in DS networks.

IPsec's tunnel mode provides security for the encapsulated IP header's DS field. A tunnel mode IPsec packet contains an outer header that is supplied by the tunnel start point and an encapsulated inner header that is supplied by the host that has originally sent the packet.

The processing of the DS field in the presence of IPSec tunnels would then work as follows:

1. The node where the IPsec tunnel begins encapsulates the incoming IP packets with an outer IP header and sets the DS byte of the outer header according to the SLA in the local DS domain.
2. The secured packet travels through the DS network, and intermediate nodes modify the DS field in the outer IP header as appropriate.
3. If a packet reaches the end of an IPSec tunnel, the outer IP header is stripped off by the tunnel end node, and the packet is forwarded using the information contained in the inner (original) IP header.
4. If the DS domain of the original datagram is different from the DS domain where the IPSec tunnel ends, the tunnel end node must modify the DS byte of the inner header to match the SLA in its domain. The tunnel end node would then effectively act as a DS ingress node.
5. As the packet travels onward in the DS network on the other side of the IPSec tunnel, intermediate nodes use the original IP header to modify the DS byte.

Internet Drafts on Differentiated Services

The following Internet drafts were available on Differentiated Services at the time this chapter was written:

http://www.ietf.org/internet-drafts/draft-ietf-diffserv-arch-01.txt
http://www.ietf.org/internet-drafts/draft-nichols-dsopdef-00.txt
http://www.ietf.org/internet-drafts/draft-ietf-diffserv-header-02.txt
http://www.ietf.org/internet-drafts/draft-ietf-diffserv-framework-00.txt
http://www.ietf.org/internet-drafts/draft-ietf-diffserv-rsvp-00.txt
http://www.ietf.org/internet-drafts/draft-ietf-diffserv-phb-ef-00.txt

References

Please refer to the following RFCs for more information on QoS on the Internet:

- RFC 1349—*Type of Service in the Internet Protocol Suite*
- RFC 1633—*Integrated Services in the Internet Architecture: An Overview*
- RFC 2205—*Resource Reservation Protocol (RSVP)—Version 1 Functional Specification*
- RFC 2206—*RSVP Management Information Base Using SMIv2*
- RFC 2207—*RSVP Extensions for IPSEC Data Flows*
- RFC 2208—*Resource Reservation Protocol (RSVP)—Version 1 Applicability Statement*
- RFC 2209—*Resource Reservation Protocol (RSVP)—Version 1 Message Processing Rules*
- RFC 2210—*The Use of RSVP with IETF Integrated Services*
- RFC 2211—*Specification of the Controlled Load Network Element Service*
- RFC 2212—*Specification of Guaranteed Quality of Service*

CHAPTER 11

IP Version 6

The Internet is growing extremely rapidly. The latest Internet Domain Survey, conducted in January 1998, counted over 29.5 million hosts in more than 190 countries. The IPv4 addressing scheme, with a 32-bit address field, provides for over 4 billion possible addresses. It might therefore seem more than adequate for the task of addressing all of the hosts on the Internet since there appears to be room for a thousandfold increase before it is completely filled. Unfortunately, this is not the case for a number of reasons, including the following:

- The IP address is divided into a network number and a local part, which is administered separately. Although the address space within a network may be very sparsely filled, as far as the effective IP address space is concerned if a network number has been allocated then all addresses within that network are unavailable for allocation elsewhere.
- The address space for networks is structured into Class A, B, and C networks of differing sizes, and the space within each needs to be considered separately.
- The IP addressing model requires that unique network numbers be assigned to all IP networks whether or not they are actually connected to the Internet.
- It is anticipated that growth of TCP/IP usage into new areas outside the traditional connected PC will shortly result in a rapid explosion of demand for IP addresses. For example, widespread use of TCP/IP for interconnecting handheld devices, for electronic point-of-sale (POS) terminals or for Web-enabled television receivers, all devices that are now available, will enormously increase the number of IP hosts.

These factors mean that the address space is much more constrained than our simple analysis would indicate. This problem is called *IP Address Exhaustion*. Methods for relieving this problem are already being employed, but eventually the present IP address space will be exhausted. The Internet Engineering Task Force (IETF) set up a working group on *Address Lifetime Expectations* (ALE) with the express purpose of providing estimates of when the exhaustion of the IP will become an intractable problem. Their final estimates (reported in the ALE working group minutes for December 1994) were that the IP address space would be exhausted at some point between 2005 and 2011. Since then, the situation may have changed somewhat in that the use of CIDR (Classless Inter Domain Routing) and the increased use of DHCP may have relieved pressure on the address space, but on the other hand current growth rates are probably exceeding the expectations of December 1994.

Apart from address exhaustion, other restrictions in IPv4 also called for the definition of a new IP protocol:

1. Even with the use of CIDR, routing tables, primarily those in the IP backbone routers, are growing too large to be manageable.
2. Traffic priority, or class of service, is vaguely defined, scarcely used, and not at all enforced in IPv4, but it is highly desirable for modern real-time applications.

IP Version 6

In view of these issues, the IETF established an IPng (IP next generation) working group and published *RFC 1752—The Recommendation for the IP Next Generation Protocol.* Eventually, the specification for Internet Protocol, Version 6 (IPv6) was produced in RFC 1883.

IPv6 Overview

IPv6 offers the following significant features:

- A dramatically larger address space, said to be sufficient for the next 30 years
- Globally unique and hierarchical addressing, which is based on prefixes rather than address classes, to keep routing tables small and backbone routing efficient
- A mechanism for the autoconfiguration of network interfaces
- Support for encapsulation of itself and other protocols
- Class of service to distinguish types of data
- Improved multicast routing support (in preference to broadcasting)
- Built-in authentication and encryption
- Transition methods to migrate from IPv4
- Compatibility methods to coexist and communicate with IPv4

NOTE: IPv6 uses the term packet *rather than* datagram. *The meaning is the same, although the formats are different.*

IPv6 uses the term *node* for any system running IPv6, that is, a host or a router. An IPv6 host is a node that does not forward IPv6 packets that are not explicitly addressed to it. A router is a node that does forward IP packets not addressed to it.

The IPv6 Header Format

The format of the IPv6 packet header has been simplified from its counterpart in IPv4. The length of the IPv6 header is increased to 40 bytes (from 20 bytes) and contains two 16-byte addresses (source and destination) preceded by 8 bytes of control information, as shown in Figure 11-1. The IPv4 header (see Figure 20) has two 4-byte addresses preceded by 12 bytes of control information and possibly followed by option data. The reduction of the control information and the elimination of options in the header for most IP packets are intended to optimize the processing time per packet in a router. The infrequently used fields that have been removed from the header are moved to optional extension headers when they are required.

Vers   This is a 4-bit Internet Protocol version number 6.

Priority   This is a 4-bit priority value. See the section titled "Priority" later in this chapter.

Flow Label   This is a 28-bit field. See the section, "Flow Labels" later in this chapter.

Payload Length   This is the length of the packet in bytes (excluding this header) encoded as a 16-bit unsigned integer. If length is greater than

Figure 11-1
IPv6 header.

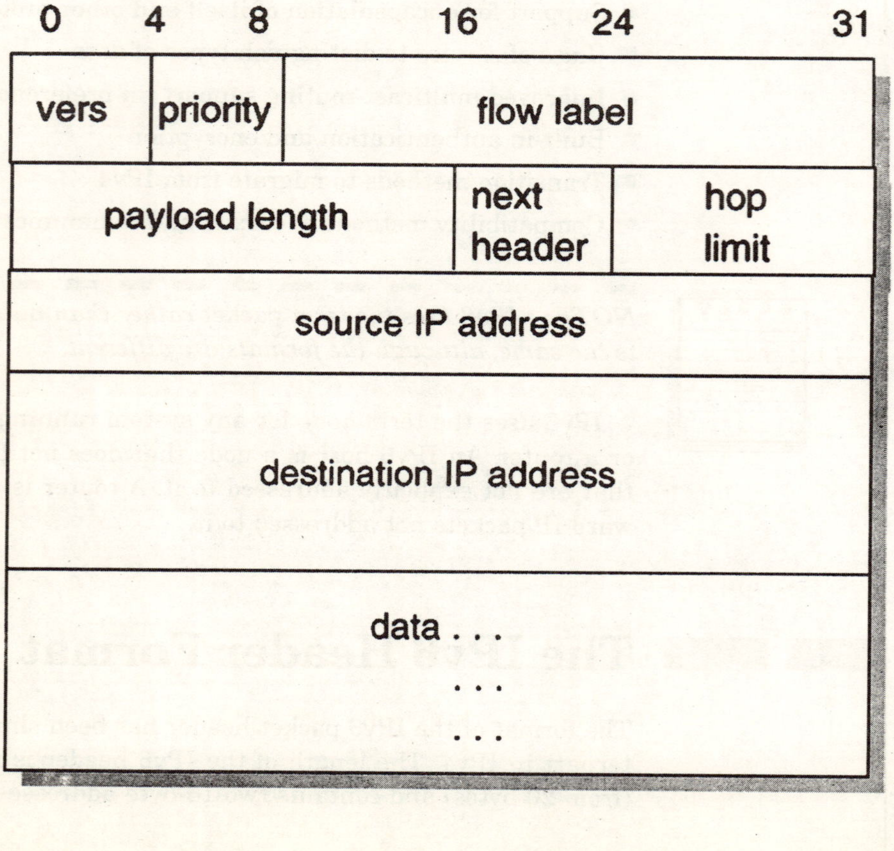

| 0 | 4 | 8 | 16 | 24 | 31 |

vers	priority	flow label		
payload length			next header	hop limit
source IP address				
destination IP address				
data				

IP Version 6

64 KB, this field is 0 and an option header (Jumbo Payload) gives the true length.

Next Header This indicates the type of header immediately following the basic IP header. It may indicate an IP option header or an upper layer protocol. The protocol numbers used are the same as those used in IPv4. The next header field is also used to indicate the presence of extension headers, which provide the mechanism for appending optional information to the IPv6 packet. The following values will appear in IPv6 packets, in addition to those mentioned for IPv4:

- 41 IPv6 Header
- 45 Interdomain Routing Protocol
- 46 Resource Reservation Protocol
- 58 IPv6 ICMP Packet

The following values are all extension headers:

- 0 Hop-by-Hop Options Header
- 43 IPv6 Routing Header
- 44 IPv6 Fragment Header
- 50 Encapsulating Security Payload
- 51 IPv6 Authentication Header
- 59 No Next Header
- 60 Destination Options Header

The different types of extension header are discussed in the section "Extension Headers" later in this chapter.

Hop Limit This is the IPv4 TTL field, but now it is measured in hops and not seconds. It was changed for two reasons:
- IP normally forwards datagrams faster than one hop per second, and the TTL field is always decremented on each hop, so in practice it is measured in hops and not seconds.
- Many IP implementations do not expire outstanding datagrams on the basis of elapsed time.

The packet is discarded once the hop limit is decremented to zero.

Source Address This is a 128-bit address. IPv6 addresses are discussed in the section "IPv6 Addressing" later in this chapter.

Destination Address This is a 128-bit address. IPv6 addresses are discussed in the section "IPv6 Addressing" later in this chapter.

A comparison between the IPv4 and IPv6 header formats shows that a number of IPv4 header fields have no direct equivalents in the IPv6 header.

Type of Service Type of service issues in IPv6 are handled by the *flow* concept, which is described in the section "Flow Labels" later in this chapter.

Identification, Fragmentation Flags, and Fragment Offset Fragmented packets have an extension header rather than fragmentation information in the IPv6 header. This reduces the size of the basic IPv6 header. Since higher-level protocols, particularly TCP, tend to avoid the fragmentation of datagrams, this reduces the IPv6 header overhead for the normal case. As noted later, IPv6 does not fragment packets en route to their destinations, only at the source.

Header Checksum Because transport protocols implement checksums and because IPv6 includes an optional authentication header that can also be used to ensure integrity, IPv6 does *not* provide checksum monitoring of IP packets.

Both TCP and UDP include a pseudo IP header in the checksums they use, so in these cases the IP header in IPv4 is checked twice.

TCP and UDP, and any other protocols that use the same checksum mechanisms running over IPv6, will continue to use a pseudo IP header although, obviously, the format of the pseudo IPv6 header will be different from the pseudo IPv4 header. ICMP and IGMP and any other protocols that do not use a pseudo IP header over IPv4 will use a pseudo IPv6 header in their checksums.

Options All optional values associated with IPv6 packets are contained in extension headers, which ensures that the basic IP header is always the same size.

NOTE: At the time this chapter was written, an Internet draft existed that proposes a change to the IPv6 header format. The draft specifies the replacement of the 4-bit priority field and 24-bit flow label with an 8-bit traffic class field followed by a 20-bit flow label. The 8-bit Traffic Class field in the IPv6 header is intended for use by originating nodes and/or forwarding routers to identify and distinguish between different classes or priorities of IPv6 packets. Currently, there are a number of experiments under way in the use of the IPv4 Type of Service and/or Precedence bits to provide various forms of Differentiated Service for IP packets, other than through the use of explicit flow setup. The Traffic Class field in the IPv6 header is intended to allow similar functionality to be supported in IPv6.

IP Version 6

For the latest information, please refer to the Internet draft at http://search.ietf.org/internet-drafts/draft-ietf-ipngwg-ipv6-spec-v2-02.txt.

Packet Sizes

All IPv6 nodes are expected to dynamically determine the maximum transmission unit (MTU) supported by all links along a path (as described in *RFC 1191—Path MTU Discovery*), and source nodes will only send packets that do not exceed the path MTU. IPv6 routers will therefore not have to fragment packets in the middle of multihop routes, and they will allow much more efficient use of paths that traverse diverse physical transmission media. IPv6 requires that every link supports an MTU of 576 bytes or greater.

Extension Headers

Every IPv6 packet starts with the basic header. In most cases, this is the only header necessary to deliver the packet. Sometimes, however, it is necessary for additional information to be conveyed along with the packet to the destination or to intermediate systems on route (information that would previously have been carried in the Options field in an IPv4 datagram). Extension headers are used for this purpose.

Extension headers are placed immediately after the IPv6 basic packet header and are counted as part of the payload length. Each extension header (with the exception of 59) has its own 8-bit *Next Header field* as the first byte of the header that identifies the type of the following header. This structure allows IPv6 to chain multiple extension headers together. Figure 11-2 shows an example of a packet with multiple extension headers.

The length of each header varies, depending on type, but is always a multiple of 8 bytes. There are a limited number of IPv6 extension headers, any one of which may be present only once in the IPv6 packet (with the exception of the Destination Options Header—60, which may appear more than once). IPv6 nodes that originate packets are required to place extension headers in a specific order (numeric order with the exception of 60), although IPv6 nodes that receive packets are not required to verify that this is the case. The order is important for efficient processing at

Figure 11-2
IPv6 packet containing multiple extension headers.

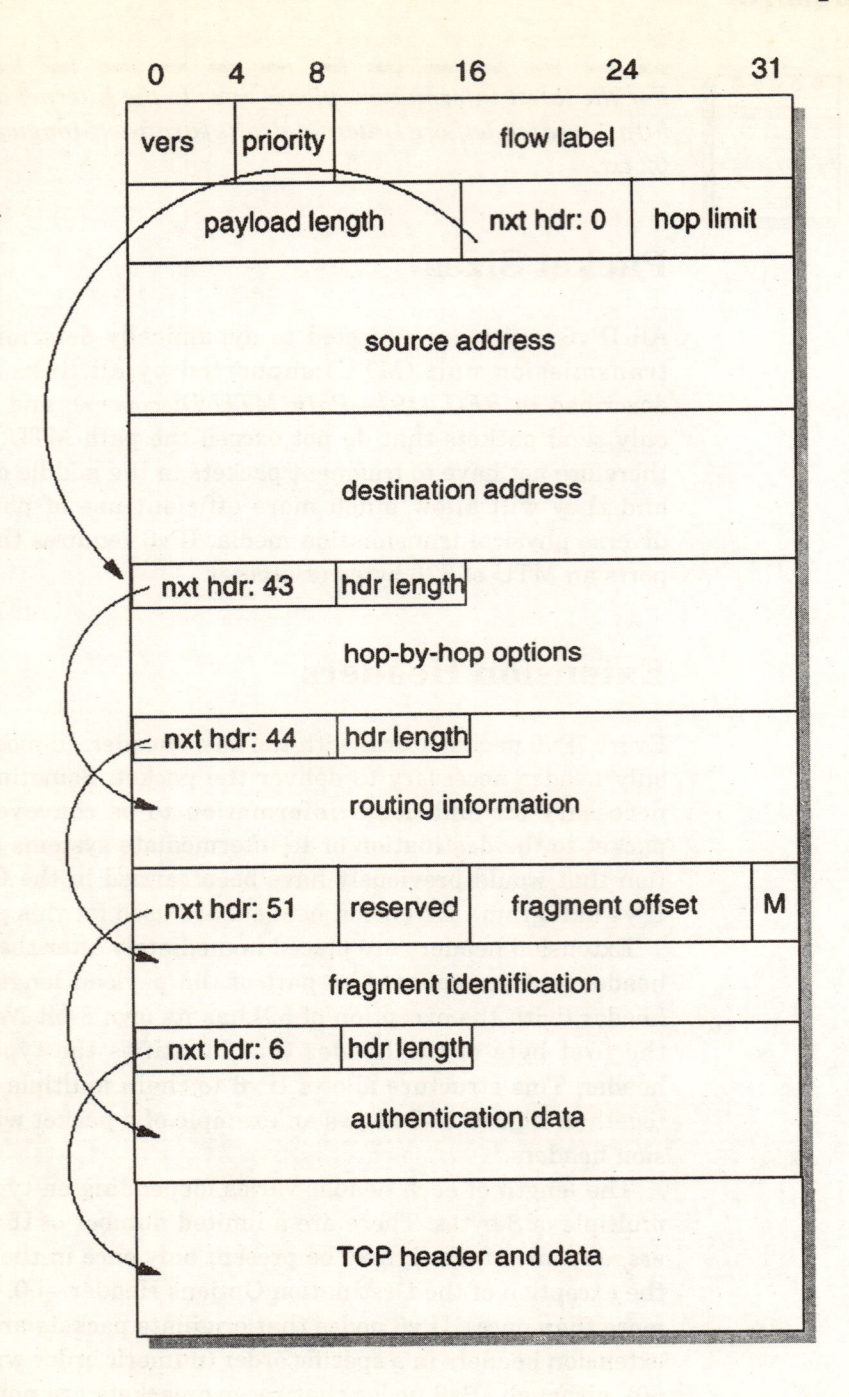

| 0 | 4 | 8 | 16 | 24 | 31 |

| vers | priority | flow label |
| payload length | nxt hdr: 0 | hop limit |
| source address |
| destination address |
| nxt hdr: 43 | hdr length |
| hop-by-hop options |
| nxt hdr: 44 | hdr length |
| routing information |
| nxt hdr: 51 | reserved | fragment offset | M |
| fragment identification |
| nxt hdr: 6 | hdr length |
| authentication data |
| TCP header and data |

intermediate routers. Routers generally only are interested in the hop-by-hop options and the routing header. Once the router has read this far, it does not need to read further in the packet and can forward immediately. When the Next Header field contains a value other than one for an extension header, this indicates the end of the IPv6 headers and the start of the higher-level protocol data.

IPv6 allows for encapsulation of IPv6 within IPv6 (known as "tunneling"). This is done with a Next Header value of 41 (IPv6). The encapsulated IPv6 packet may have its own extension headers. Because the size of a packet is calculated by the originating node to match the path MTU, IPv6 routers should not add extension headers to a packet but instead should encapsulate the received packet within an IPv6 packet of their own making (which may be fragmented, if necessary).

With the exception of the hop-by-hop header (which must immediately follow the IP header if present) and sometimes the Destination Options header (see the section "Destination Options Header" later in this chapter), extension headers are not processed by any router on the packet's path except the final one.

Hop-by-Hop Header A hop-by-hop header contains options that must be examined by every node the packet traverses as well as the destination node. It must immediately follow the IPv6 header if present and is identified by the special value 0 in the Next Header field of the IPv6 basic header. (This value is not actually a protocol number but a special case for identifying this unique type of extension header). Hop-by-hop headers contain different length options of the following format (this format is commonly known as the *Type-Length-Value* [*TLV*] format) (see Figure 11-3):

Type The type of the option. The option types all have a common format (see Figure 11-4):

- xx A 2-bit number indicating how an IPv6 node that does not recognize the option should treat it.
    - 0 Skip the option and continue.
    - 1 Discard the packet quietly.
    - 2 Discard the packet and inform the sender with an ICMP Unrecognized Type message.
    - 3 Discard the packet and inform the sender with an ICMP Unrecognized Type message unless the destination address is a multicast address.

Figure 11-3
IPv6 Type-Length-Value (TLV) option format.

```
  type   |  length  |  value  //
                              //
```

Figure 11-4
IPv6 Type-Length-Value (TLV) option type format.

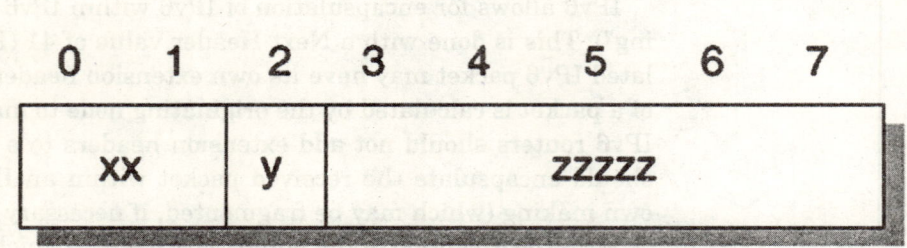

```
 0  1  2  3  4  5  6  7
|  xx  | y |   zzzzz    |
```

    y   If set, this bit indicates that the value of the option may change en route. If this bit is set, the entire Option Data field is excluded from any integrity calculations performed on the packet.

    zzzzz   The remaining bits define the option:

              0   Pad1
              1   PadN
              194 Jumbo Payload Length

    Length   The length of the option value field in bytes.

    Value   The value of the option. This is dependent on the type.

Hop-by-Hop Header Option Types You may have noticed that each extension header is an integer multiple of 8 bytes long so as to retain 8-byte alignment for subsequent headers. This is done not purely for "neatness" but because processing is much more efficient if multibyte values are positioned on natural boundaries in memory (and today's processors have natural word sizes of 32 or 64 bits).

In the same way, individual options are also aligned so that multibyte values are positioned on their natural boundaries. In many cases, this results in the option headers being longer than otherwise necessary, but it still allows nodes to process packets more quickly. To allow this alignment, two padding options are used in hop-by-hop headers:

Pad1   A X'00' byte used for padding a single byte. Longer padding sequences should be done with the PadN option.

IP Version 6

PadN An option in the TLV format described earlier. The length byte gives the number of bytes of padding after the minimum two that are required.

The third option type in a hop-by-hop header is the *Jumbo Payload Length* (see Figure 11-5). This option is used to indicate a packet that has a payload size in excess of 65,535 bytes (which is the maximum size that can be specified by the 16-bit Payload Length field in the IPv6 basic header). When this option is used, the payload length in the basic header must be set to zero, and this option carries the total packet size, less the 40-byte basic header.

Routing Header The path that a packet takes through a network is normally determined by the network itself. Sometimes, however, the source may wish to have more control over the route taken by a packet. It may wish, for example, for certain data to take a slower but more secure route than would normally be taken. The routing header allows a path through the network to be predefined (see Figure 11-6). The routing header is identified by the value 43 in the preceding Next Header field. It has its next header field as the first byte and a single-byte routing type as the second. The only type defined initially is type 0—Strict/Loose Source Routing, which operates much like source routing in IPv4.

Next Hdr The type of header after this one.

Hdr Length Length of this routing header, not including the first 8 bytes.

Type The type of the routing header. Currently, this can only have the value 0, meaning Strict/Loose Source Routing.

Addresses Left The number of intermediate nodes still to be visited on route to the final destination. Maximum allowed value is 23.

Reserved This is initialized to zero for transmission and ignored on reception.

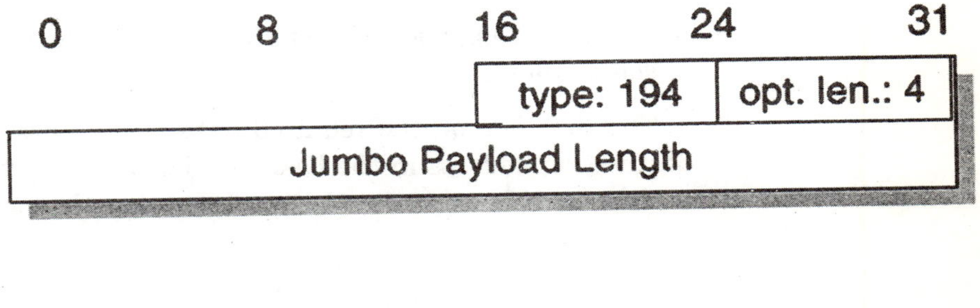

Figure 11-5
Jumbo Payload Length option.

0	8	16	24	31
		type: 194	opt. len.: 4	
		Jumbo Payload Length		

Figure 11-6
IPv6 routing header.

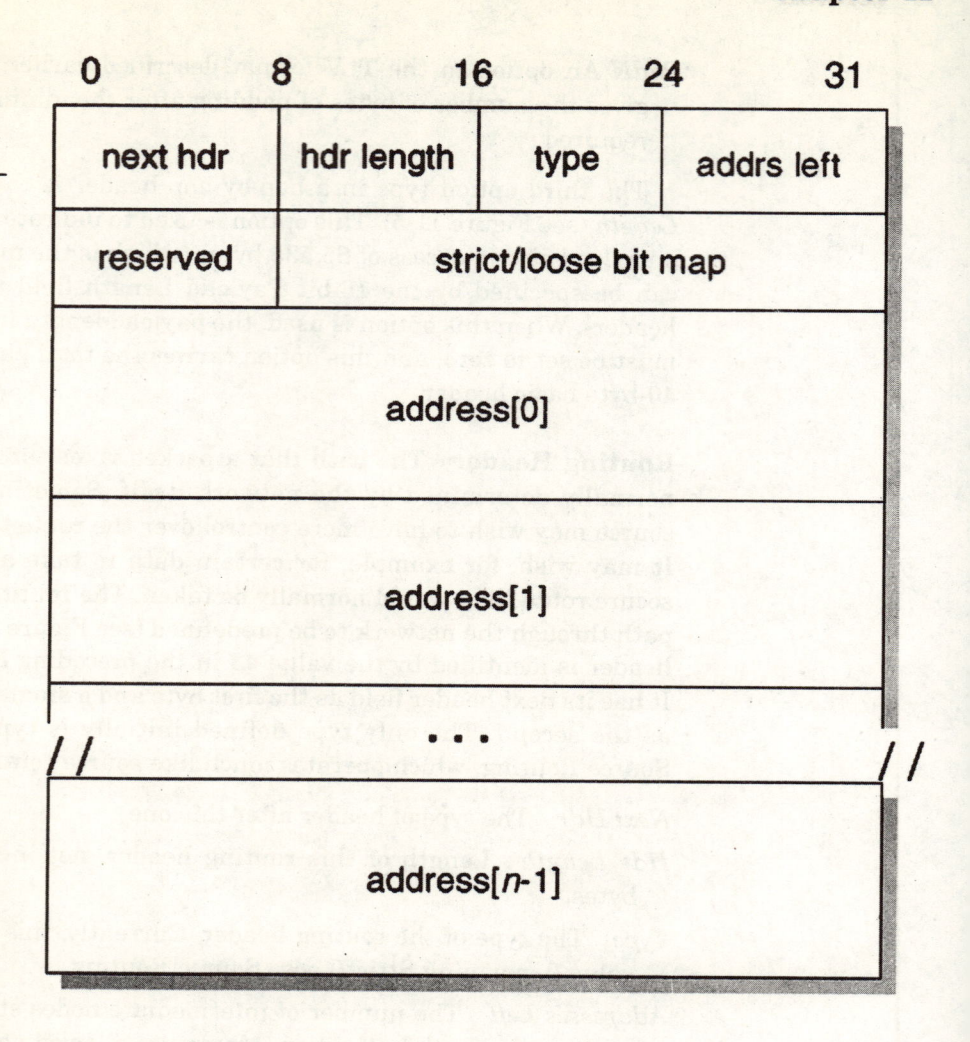

0	8	16	24	31
next hdr	hdr length	type	addrs left	

reserved	strict/loose bit map

address[0]

address[1]

...

address[n-1]

Strict/Loose bit map   This is a 24-bit series that indicates for each segment of the route whether the next address must be a neighbor of the preceding address (1, strict) or whether the packet is allowed to pass through intermediate routers on the way to the next destination address (2, loose).

Address n   This is a series of 16-byte IPv6 addresses that comprise the source route.

The first hop on the required path of the packet is indicated by the destination address in the basic header of the packet. When the packet arrives at this address, the router swaps the next address from the

IP Version 6

router extension header with the destination address in the basic header. The router also decrements the addresses left field by one, then forwards the packet.

Fragment Header As discussed in the section "Packet Sizes" earlier in this chapter, the source node determines the MTU for a path before sending a packet. If the packet to be sent is larger than the MTU, the packet is divided into pieces, each of which is a multiple of 8 bytes and carries a fragment header (see Figure 11-7). The fragment header is identified by the value 44 in the preceding Next Header field and has the following format:

Nxt Hdr This is the type of the next header after this one. It is an 8-bit reserved field—initialized to zero for transmission and ignored on reception.

Fragment Offset This is a 13-bit unsigned integer giving the offset, in 8-byte units, of the data that follows relative to the start of the original data before it was fragmented.

Res This is a 2-bit reserved field—initialized to zero for transmission and ignored on reception.

M This means more flag. If set it indicates that this is not the last fragment.

Fragment Identification This is an unambiguous identifier used to identify fragments of the same datagram. This is very similar to the IPv4 Identifier field, but it is twice as wide.

Authentication Header The authentication header is used to ensure that a received packet has not been altered in transit and that it really came from the claimed sender. The authentication header is identified by the value 51 in the preceding Next Header field. The format of the

Figure 11-7
IPv6 fragment header.

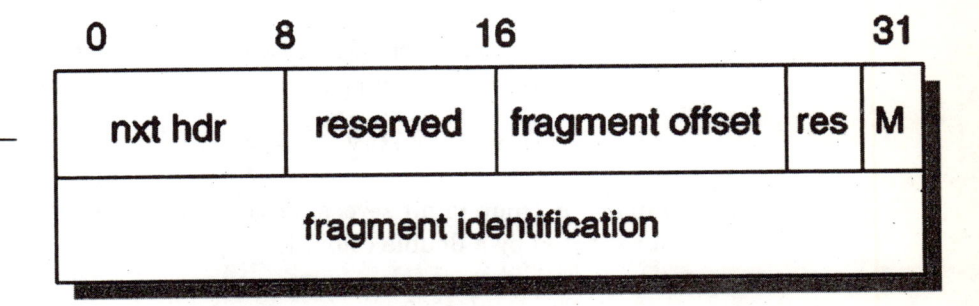

authentication header and further details on authentication can be found in the section "Authentication Header (AH)" in Chapter 5.

Encapsulating Security Payload The Encapsulated Security Payload (ESP) is a special extension header, in that it can appear anywhere in a packet between the basic header and the upper layer protocol. All data following the ESP header is encrypted.

Destination Options Header This has the same format as the hop-by-hop header, but it is only examined by the destination node(s). Normally, the destination options are only intended for the final destination, and the destination options header is immediately before the upper layer header. However, destination options can also be intended for intermediate nodes, in which case they must precede a routing header. A single packet may therefore include two destination options headers. Currently, only the Pad1 and PadN types of options are specified for this header (see the section "Hop-by-Hop Header" earlier in this chapter). The value for the preceding Next Header field is 60.

IPv6 Addressing

The IPv6 address model is specified in *RFC 2373—IP Version 6 Addressing Architecture*. IPv6 uses a 128-bit address instead of the 32-bit address of IPv4. That theoretically allows for as many as 340,282,366,920,938,463,463,374,607,431,768,111,456 addresses. Even when used with the same efficiency as today's IPv4 address space, that would still allow for 50,000 addresses per square meter of land on Earth.

IPv6 addresses are represented in the form of eight hexadecimal numbers divided by colons, for example:

`FE80:0000:0000:0000:0001:0800:23e7:f5db`

To shorten the notation of addresses, leading zeroes in any of the groups can be omitted, for example:

`FE80:0:0:0:1:800:23e7:f5db`

Finally, a group of all zeroes, or consecutive groups of all zeroes, can be substituted by a double colon, for example:

`FE80::1:800:23e7:f5db`

IP Version 6

> **NOTE:** The double colon shortcut can be used only once in the notation of an IPv6 address. If there are more groups of all zeroes that are not consecutive, only one may be substituted by the double colon; the others would have to be noted as 0.

The IPv6 address space is organized using format prefixes, similar to telephone country and area codes, that logically divide it in the form of a tree so that a route from one network to another can easily be found. The prefixes that have been assigned so far are shown in Table 11-1.

IPv6 defines the following types of addresses: unicast, global unicast, multicast, and anycast which are described in the following sections.

Unicast Address A unicast address is an identifier assigned to a single interface. Packets sent to that address will only be delivered to that interface. Special-purpose unicast addresses are defined as follows:

Loopback address (::1) This address is assigned to a virtual interface over which a host can send packets only to itself. It is equivalent to the IPv4 loopback address 127.0.0.1.

Allocation	Prefix (bin)	Start of Address Range (hex)	Mask Length (bits)	Fraction of Address Space
Reserved	0000 0000	0:: /8	8	1/256
Reserved for NSAP	0000 001	200:: /7	7	1/128
Reserved for IPX	0000 010	400:: /7	7	1/128
Aggregatable Global Unicast Addresses	001	2000:: /3	3	1/8
Link-local Unicast	1111 1110 10	FE80:: /10	10	1/1024
Site-local Unicast	1111 1110 11	FEC0:: /10	10	1/1024
Multicast	1111 1111	FF00:: /8	8	1/256
Total Allocation				15%

TABLE 11-1 IPv6—Format Prefix Allocation

Unspecified address (::) This address is used as a source address by hosts while performing autoconfiguration. It is equivalent to the IPv4 unspecified address 0.0.0.0.

IPv4-compatible address (::<IPv4_address>) Addresses of this kind are used when IPv6 traffic needs to be tunneled across existing IPv4 networks. The endpoint of such tunnels can be either hosts (automatic tunneling) or routers (configured tunneling). IPv4-compatible addresses are formed by placing 96 bits of zero in front of a valid 32-bit IPv4 address. For example, the address 1.2.3.4 (hex 01.02.03.04) becomes ::0102:0304.

IPv4-mapped address (::FFFF:<IPv4_address>) Addresses of this kind are used when an IPv6 host needs to communicate with an IPv4 host. This requires a dual stack host or router for header translations. For example, if an IPv6 node wishes to send data to a host with an IPv4 address of 1.2.3.4, it uses a destination address of ::FFFF:0102:0304.

Link-local address Addresses of this kind can be used only on the physical network that a host's interface is attached to.

Site-local address Addresses of this kind cannot be routed into the Internet. They are the equivalent of IPv4 networks for private use (10.0.0.0, 1711.16.0.0-1711.31.0.0, 192.168.0.0-192.168.255.0).

Global Unicast Address Format The global unicast address format, as specified in *RFC 2374—An IPv6 Aggregatable Global Unicast Address Format* is expected to become the predominant format used for IPv6 nodes connected to the Internet. The aggregatable address can be split into three sections that relate to the three-level hierarchy of the Internet, namely:

Public Topology This topology is for providers and exchanges that provide public Internet transit services.

Site Topology This topology is local to an organization that does not provide public transit service to nodes outside of the site.

Interface Identifiers These identify interfaces on links.

The global unicast address format is designed for the infrastructure shown in Figure 11-8. P1, P2, and P3 are long-haul providers. P4 is a smaller provider that obtains services from P2. Exchanges (X1 and X2), which are analogous to exchanges in a telephone network, allocate addresses. Subscribers (S1-S6) have the choice of connecting directly to a

IP Version 6

Figure 11-8
Global unicast address format: Three-level hierarchy.

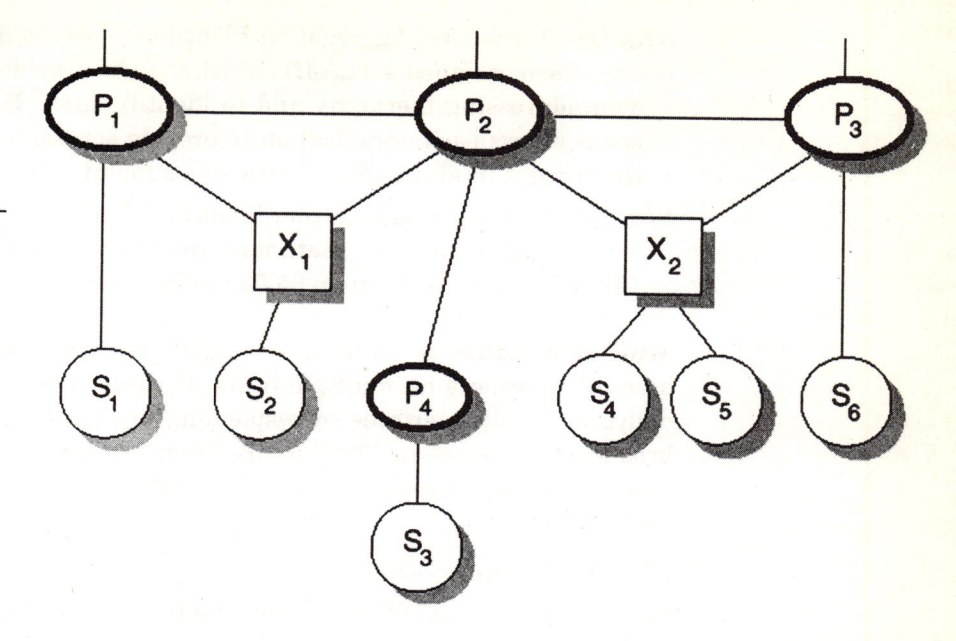

provider or to an exchange (in which case they must also subscribe to a provider for long-haul service). Organizations connecting via an exchange have the flexibility to be able to change their long-haul provider without having to change their IP addresses.

The format of the aggregatable global unicast address is shown in Figure 11-9.

FP   Format Prefix (001).

TLA ID   Top-Level Aggregation Identifier. These are the top level in the routing hierarchy. Internet top-level routers will need a routing table entry for every active TLA ID. This will be a maximum of 8,192 entries, which compares with around 50,000 entries in today's IPv4 top-level routers.

RES   Reserved for future use. This will allow growth in the number of either TLA IDs or NLA IDs in the future if that becomes necessary.

Figure 11-9
Global unicast address format.

NLA ID   Next-Level Aggregation Identifier. Used by organizations that have been assigned a TLA ID (which may be providers) to create their own addressing hierarchy and to identify sites. The 24-bit NLA ID space allows each organization to provide service to as many sites as the current total number of networks supported by IPv4.

SLA ID   Site-Level Aggregation Identifier. This field is used by an individual organization to create its own local addressing hierarchy. The 16-bit field allows for up to 65,535 individual subnets.

Multicast Address   A multicast address is an identifier assigned to a set of interfaces on multiple hosts. Packets sent to that address are delivered to all interfaces corresponding to that address. There are no broadcast addresses in IPv6 because their function has been superseded by multicast addresses. Figure 11-10 shows the format of an IPv6 multicast address.

FP   Format Prefix—1111 1111.

Flags   This is a set of four flag bits. Only the low-order bit currently has any meaning, which is as follows:

0000   Permanent address assigned by a numbering authority.

0001   Transient address. Addresses of this kind can be established by applications as required. When the application ends, the address will be released by the application and can be reused.

Scope   This is a 4-bit value that indicates the scope of the multicast. Possible values are as follows:

0   Reserved
1   Confined to interfaces on the local node (node-local)
2   Confined to nodes on the local link (link-local)
5   Confined to the local site
8   Confined to the organization
E   Global scope
F   Reserved

Group ID   This identifies the multicast group.

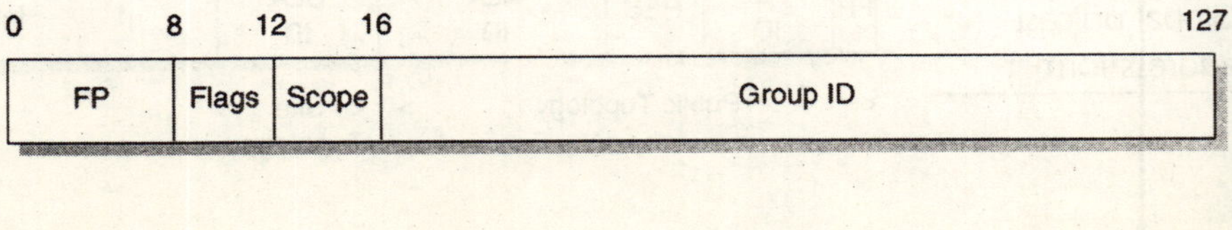

Figure 11-10
IPv6 multicast address format.

IP Version 6

For example, if the NTP servers group is assigned a permanent multicast address with a group ID of X'101, then:

FF02::101 means all NTP servers on the same link as the sender.

FF05::101 means all NTP servers on the same site as the sender.

Certain special-purpose multicast addresses are predefined as follows:

FF01::1   All interfaces node-local—Defines all interfaces on the host itself.

FF02::1   All nodes link-local—Defines all systems on the local network.

FF01::2   All routers node-local—Defines all routers local to the host itself.

FF02::2   All routers link-local—Defines all routers on the same link as the host.

FF05::2   All routers site-local—Defines all routers on the same site as the host.

FF02::B   Mobile agents link-local.

FF02::1:2   All DHCP agents link-local.

FF05::1:3   All DHCP servers site-local.

A more complete listing of reserved multicast addresses may be found in *RFC 2375—IPv6 Multicast Address Assignments*. This RFC also defines a special multicast address known as the *solicited node address*, which has the format FF02::1:FFxx:xxxx, where xx xxxx is taken from the last 24 bits of a node's unicast address. For example, the node with the IPv6 address of 4025::01:800:100F:7B5B belongs to the multicast group FF02::1:FF 0F:7B5B. The solicited node address is used by ICMP for neighbor discovery and to detect duplicate addresses. See the section "Internet Control Message Protocol Version 6 (ICMPv6)" later in this chapter for further details.

Anycast Address An anycast address is a special type of unicast address that is assigned to interfaces on multiple hosts. Packets sent to such an address are delivered to the nearest interface with that address. Routers determine the nearest interface based upon their definition of distance, for example, hops in case of RIP or link state in case of OSPF.

Anycast addresses use the same format as unicast addresses and are indistinguishable from them. However, a node that has been assigned an anycast address must be configured to be aware of this fact. RFC 2373 currently specifies the following restrictions on anycast addresses:

- An anycast address must not be used as the source address of a packet.
- Any anycast address may only be assigned to a router.

A special anycast address, the *subnet-router address,* is predefined. This address consists of the subnet prefix for a particular subnet followed by trailing zeros. This address may be used when a node needs to contact a router on a particular subnet and it does not matter which router is reached (for example, when a mobile node needs to communicate with one of the mobile agents on its "home" subnet).

Priority

The 4-bit priority field allows applications to specify a certain priority for the traffic they generate, thus introducing the concept of *Class of Service.* IPv4-based routers normally treat all traffic equally, whereas IPv6-based routers now must act on such prioritized packets in the following way:

1. For priorities 0 to 7, start dropping packets when the network becomes congested (congestion-controlled).
2. For priorities 8 to 15, try to forward packets even when the network is becoming congested by dropping packets with lower priority (noncongestion-controlled). Real-time applications would opt for this range of priority. For a comparison of the ways priority traffic may be handled in an IPv4 network, see the section entitled "Why QoS?" in Chapter 10.

Flow Labels

IPv6 introduces the concept of a *flow,* which is a series of related packets from a source to a destination that requires a particular type of handling by the intervening routers, for example real-time service. The nature of that handling can either be conveyed by options attached to the datagrams (that is, by using the IPv6 hop-by-hop options header) or by a separate protocol (such as resource reservation protocol; see the section "The Reservation Protocol (RSVP)" in Chapter 10). The handling requirement for a particular flow label is known as the *state information*; this is cached at the router. When packets with a known flow label arrive at the router, the router can efficiently decide how to route and forward the packets without having to examine the rest of the header for each packet.

There may be multiple active flows between a source and a destination, as well as traffic that is not associated with any flow. Each flow is distinctly labeled by the 24-bit flow label field in the IPv6 packet. See RFC 1883 and RFC 1809 for further details on using the flow label.

Internet Control Message Protocol Version 6 (ICMPv6)

The Internet Protocol concerns itself with moving data from one node to another. However, in order for IP to perform this task successfully, there are many other functions that need to be carried out: error reporting, route discovery, and diagnostics, to name but a few. All these tasks are carried out by the Internet Control Message Protocol (ICMP). ICMP version 6.0 also carries out the tasks of conveying multicast group membership information, a function that was previously performed by the IGMP protocol in IPv4, and of address resolution, which was previously performed by ARP.

ICMPv6 messages and their use are specified in *RFC 1885—Internet Control Message Protocol (ICMPv6) for the Internet Protocol Version 6 (IPv6) Specification* and *RFC 1970—Neighbor Discovery for IP Version 6 (IPv6)*. Both RFCs are proposed standards with a status of elective.

Every ICMPv6 message is preceded by an IPv6 header (and possibly some IP extension headers). The ICMPv6 header is identified by a Next Header value of 58 in the immediately preceding header. ICMPv6 messages all have a similar format, which is shown in Figure 11-11.

Type There are two classes of ICMPv6 messages. Error messages have a Type of 0 to 127. Informational messages have a Type of 128 to 255. The error message types are as follows:

1   Destination Unreachable

2   Packet Too Big

3   Time (Hop Count) Exceeded

4   Parameter Problem

Figure 11-11
ICMPv6 general message format.

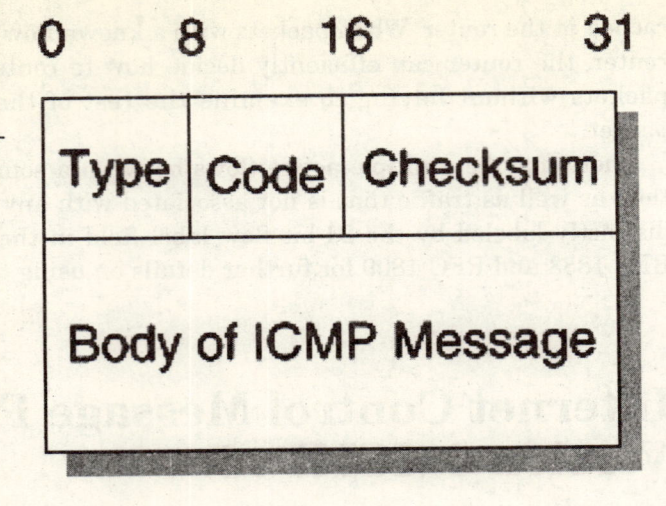

```
 0        8         16                    31
┌─────────┬─────────┬──────────────────────┐
│  Type   │  Code   │      Checksum        │
├─────────┴─────────┴──────────────────────┤
│                                          │
│         Body of ICMP Message             │
│                                          │
└──────────────────────────────────────────┘
```

128 Echo Request
129 Echo Reply
130 Group Membership Query
131 Group Membership Report
132 Group Membership Reduction
133 Router Solicitation
134 Router Advertisement
135 Neighbor Solicitation
136 Neighbor Advertisement
137 Redirect Message

Code   This varies according to message type.

Checksum   This is used to detect data corruption in the ICMPv6 message and parts of the IPv6 header.

Body of Message   This varies according to message type.

For full details on ICMPv6 messages for all types, please refer to RFC 1885 and RFC 1970.

Neighbor Discovery

Neighbor discovery is an ICMPv6 function that enables a node to identify other hosts and routers on its links. The node needs to know of at least one router so it knows where to forward packets if a target node is not on its local link. Neighbor discovery also allows a router to redirect a node to use a more appropriate router if the node has initially made an incorrect choice.

Address Resolution Figure 11-12 shows a simple Ethernet LAN segment with four IPv6 workstations.

Workstation A needs to send data to workstation B. It knows the IPv6 address of workstation B, but it does not know how to send a packet because it does not know its MAC address. To find this information, it sends a *neighbor solicitation* message of the format shown in Figure 11-13.

Notice the following important fields in the IP header of this packet:

Next 58 (for the ICMP message header that follows).

Hops Any solicitation packet that does *not* have hops set to 255 is discarded; this ensures that the solicitation has not crossed a router.

Destination address This address is the *solicited node address* for the target workstation. Every workstation *must* respond to its own solicited node address, but other workstations will simply ignore it. This is an improvement over ARP in IPv4, which uses broadcast frames that have to be processed by every node on the link.

In the ICMP message itself, notice the following:

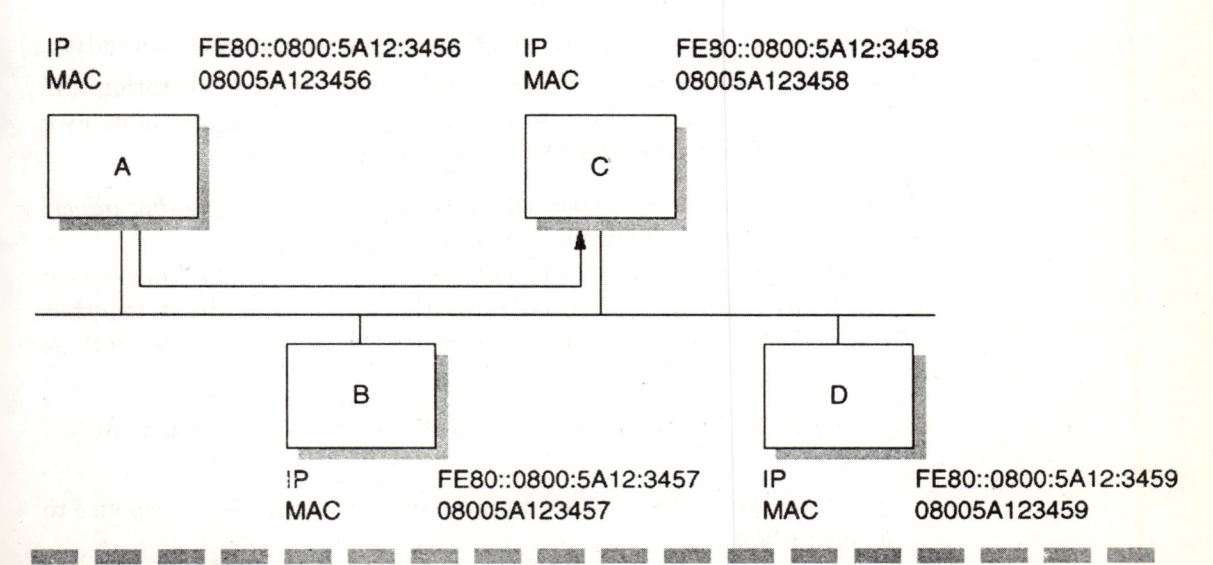

```
IP    FE80::0800:5A12:3456        IP    FE80::0800:5A12:3458
MAC   08005A123456                MAC   08005A123458

         A                                 C


                  B                                D

         IP    FE80::0800:5A12:3457        IP    FE80::0800:5A12:3459
         MAC   08005A123457                MAC   08005A123459
```

Figure 11-12 IPv6 address resolution.

Figure 11-13
Neighbor solicitation message format.

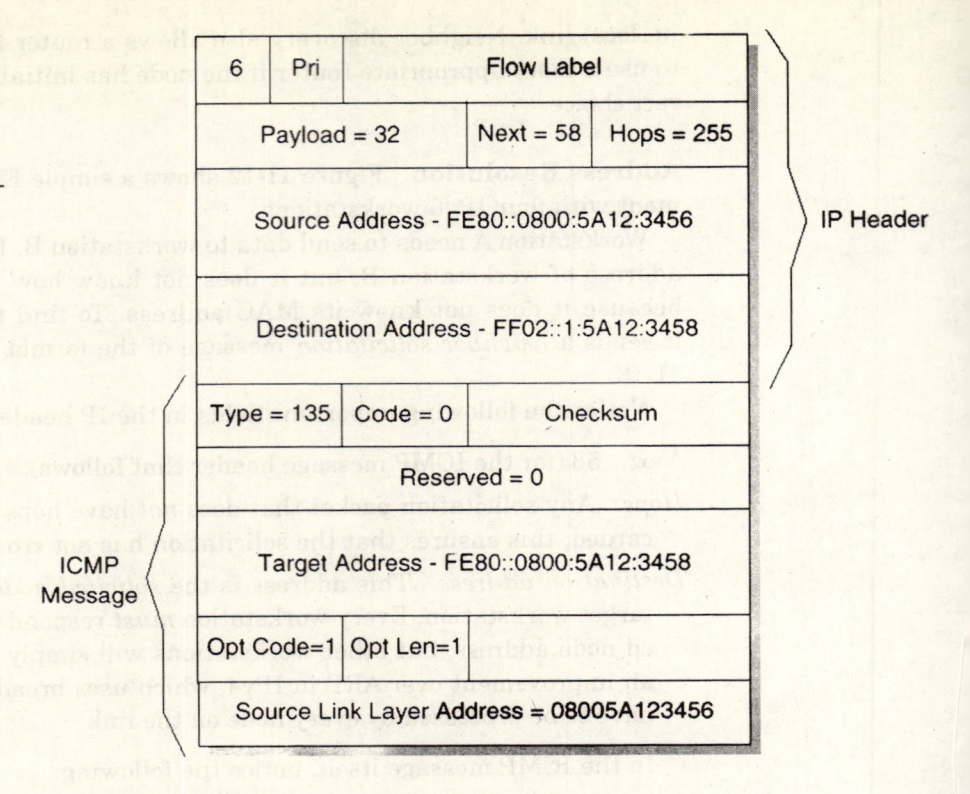

```
                    IP Header
┌─────┬─────┬───────────────────────┐
│  6  │ Pri │     Flow Label        │
├─────┴─────┴─────┬─────────┬───────┤
│ Payload = 32    │ Next=58 │Hops=255│
├─────────────────┴─────────┴───────┤
│ Source Address - FE80::0800:5A12:3456 │
├───────────────────────────────────┤
│ Destination Address - FF02::1:5A12:3458│
└───────────────────────────────────┘

                    ICMP Message
┌──────────┬─────────┬──────────────┐
│Type = 135│Code = 0 │  Checksum    │
├──────────┴─────────┴──────────────┤
│         Reserved = 0              │
├───────────────────────────────────┤
│ Target Address - FE80::0800:5A12:3458│
├──────────┬────────┬───────────────┤
│Opt Code=1│Opt Len=1│              │
├──────────┴────────┴───────────────┤
│Source Link Layer Address = 08005A123456│
└───────────────────────────────────┘
```

Type 135 (Neighbor Solicitation).

Target address This is the known IP address of the target workstation.

Source link layer address This is useful to the target workstation and saves it from having to initiate a neighbor discovery process of its own when it sends a packet back to the source workstation.

The response to the neighbor solicitation message is a *neighbor advertisement*, which has the format shown in Figure 11-14.

The neighbor advertisement is addressed directly back to Workstation A. The ICMP message option contains the target IP address together with the target's link layer (MAC) address. Note also the following flags in the advertisement message:

R   *Router Flag*. This bit is set on if the sender of the advertisement is a router.

S   *Solicited Flag*. This bit is set on if the advertisement is in response to a solicitation.

O   *Override Flag*. When this bit is set on, the receiving node must update an existing cached link layer entry in its neighbor cache.

IP Version 6

Figure 11-14
Neighbor advertisement message.

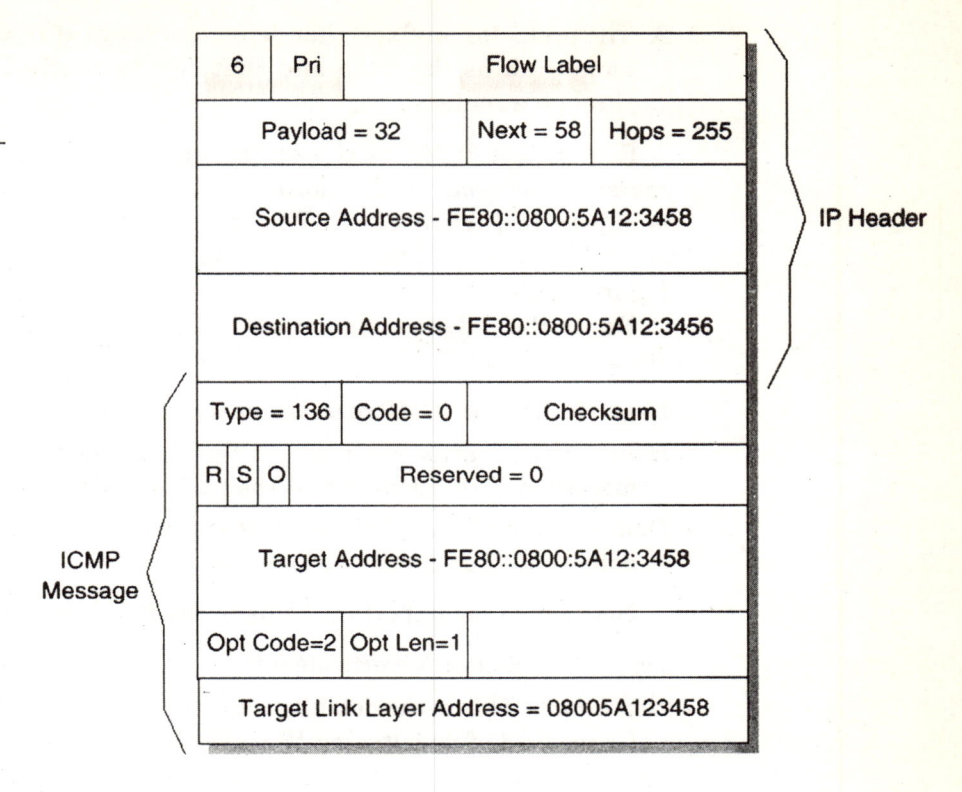

```
                    IP Header
  ┌─────────────────────────────────────────────┐
  │ 6 │ Pri │         Flow Label                │
  ├───┴─────┼──────────────┬─────────┬──────────┤
  │ Payload = 32           │ Next=58 │ Hops=255 │
  ├────────────────────────┴─────────┴──────────┤
  │  Source Address - FE80::0800:5A12:3458      │
  ├─────────────────────────────────────────────┤
  │  Destination Address - FE80::0800:5A12:3456 │
  └─────────────────────────────────────────────┘

                    ICMP Message
  ┌──────────────┬──────────┬──────────────────┐
  │ Type = 136   │ Code = 0 │    Checksum      │
  ├───┬───┬──────┴──────────┴──────────────────┤
  │ R │ S │ O │        Reserved = 0            │
  ├───┴───┴───┴────────────────────────────────┤
  │ Target Address - FE80::0800:5A12:3458      │
  ├──────────────┬─────────────┬───────────────┤
  │ Opt Code=2   │ Opt Len=1   │               │
  ├──────────────┴─────────────┴───────────────┤
  │ Target Link Layer Address = 08005A123458   │
  └────────────────────────────────────────────┘
```

Once Workstation A receives this packet, it commits the information to memory in its neighbor cache, then forwards the data packet that it wanted to send to Workstation C originally. Neighbor advertisement messages may also be sent by a node to force updates to neighbor caches if one of them becomes aware that its link layer address has changed.

Router and Prefix Discovery Figure 11-12 shows an example of a very simple network. In a larger network, particularly one connected to the Internet, the neighbor discovery process is used to find nodes on the same link in exactly the same way. However, it is more than likely that a node will need to communicate, not just with other nodes on the same link, but with nodes on other network segments, which may be anywhere in the world. In this case, there are two important pieces of information that a node needs to know:

1. The address of a router that the node can use to reach the rest of the world

2. The prefix (or prefixes) that define the range of IP addresses on the same link as the node and that can be reached without going through a router

Routers use ICMP to convey this information to hosts by means of *router advertisements*. The format of the router advertisement message is shown in Figure 11-15. The message generally has one or more attached options; all three possible options are shown in the example in Figure 11-15.

Notice the following important fields in the IP header of the packet shown in Figure 11-15.

Next 58 (for the ICMP message header that follows).

Hops Any advertisement packet that does *not* have hops set to 255 is discarded. This ensures that the packet has not crossed a router.

Destination address This address is the special multicast address that defines all systems on the local link.

Notice also the important fields in the ICMP message itself:

Type 134 (Router Advertisement).

Hop Limit This is the default value that a node should place in the Hop Count field of its outgoing IP packets.

M This is the 1-bit Managed Address Configuration Flag (see the section "Stateless Address Autoconfiguration" later in this chapter).

O 1-bit Other Stateful Configuration Flag (see the section "Stateless Address Autoconfiguration").

Router Lifetime This is how long the node should consider this router to be available. If this time period is exceeded and the node has not received another router advertisement message, the node should consider this router to be unavailable.

Reachable Time This sets a parameter for all nodes on the local link. It is the time in milliseconds that the node should assume a neighbor is still reachable after having received a response to a neighbor solicitation.

Retransmission Timer This sets the time in milliseconds that nodes should allow between the retransmission of neighbor solicitation messages if no initial response is received.

The three possible options in a router advertisement message are as follows:

Option 1 (source link address) This allows a receiving node to respond directly to the router without having to do a neighbor solicitation.

IP Version 6

Figure 11-15
Router advertisement message format.

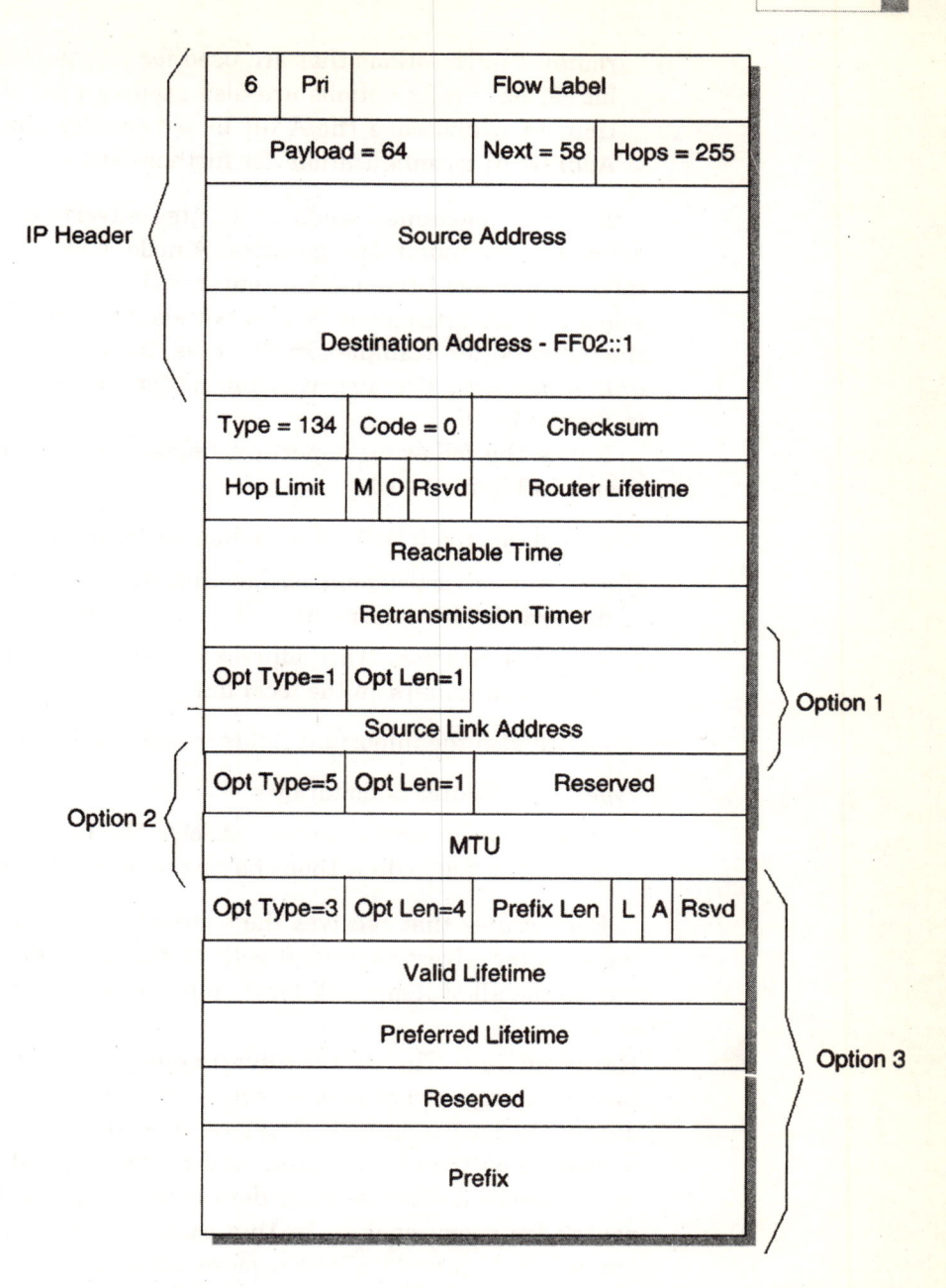

```
IP Header:
  6 | Pri | Flow Label
  Payload = 64 | Next = 58 | Hops = 255
  Source Address
  Destination Address - FF02::1

  Type = 134 | Code = 0 | Checksum
  Hop Limit | M | O | Rsvd | Router Lifetime
  Reachable Time
  Retransmission Timer

Option 1:
  Opt Type=1 | Opt Len=1
  Source Link Address

Option 2:
  Opt Type=5 | Opt Len=1 | Reserved
  MTU

Option 3:
  Opt Type=3 | Opt Len=4 | Prefix Len | L | A | Rsvd
  Valid Lifetime
  Preferred Lifetime
  Reserved
  Prefix
```

Option 5 (MTU) This specifies the maximum transmission unit size for the link. For some media, such as Ethernet, this value is fixed, so this option is not necessary.

Option 3 (Prefix) This defines the address prefix for the link. Nodes use this information to determine when they do, and do not, need to use a router. Prefix options that are used for this purpose have the L (link) bit set on. Prefix options are also used as part of address configuration, in which case the A bit is set on. See the section "Stateless Address Autoconfiguration" for further details.

A router constantly sends unsolicited advertisements at a frequency defined in the router configuration. A node, however, may wish to obtain information about the nearest router without having to wait for the next scheduled advertisement (a new workstation that has just attached to the network, for example). In this case, the node can send a *router solicitation message*. The format of the router solicitation message is shown in Figure 11-16.

Notice the following important fields in the IP header of the packet shown in Figure 11-16:

Next 58 (for the ICMP message header that follows).

Hops Any advertisement packet that does *not* have hops set to 255 is discarded. This ensures that the packet has not crossed a router.

Destination address This address is the special multicast address that defines all routers on the local link.

Notice also the important fields in the ICMP message itself:

Type 133 (Router Solicitation)

Option 1 (source link address) Allows the receiving router to respond directly to the node without having to do a neighbor solicitation.

Each router that receives the solicitation message responds by sending a router advertisement *directly* to the node that sent the solicitation (not to the all-systems link-local multicast address).

Redirection The router advertisement mechanism ensures that a node is always aware of one or more routers through which it is able to connect to devices outside of its local links. However, in a situation where a node is aware of more than one router, it is likely that the default router selected when sending data may not always be the most suitable router for every packet. In this case, ICMPv6 allows for *redirection* (shown in Figure 11-17) to a more efficient path for a particular destination.

Consider the simple example shown in Figure 11-17. Node X is aware of routers A and B, having received router advertisement messages from both. Node X wishes to send data to Node Y. By comparing Node Y's IP

IP Version 6

Figure 11-16
Router solicitation message format.

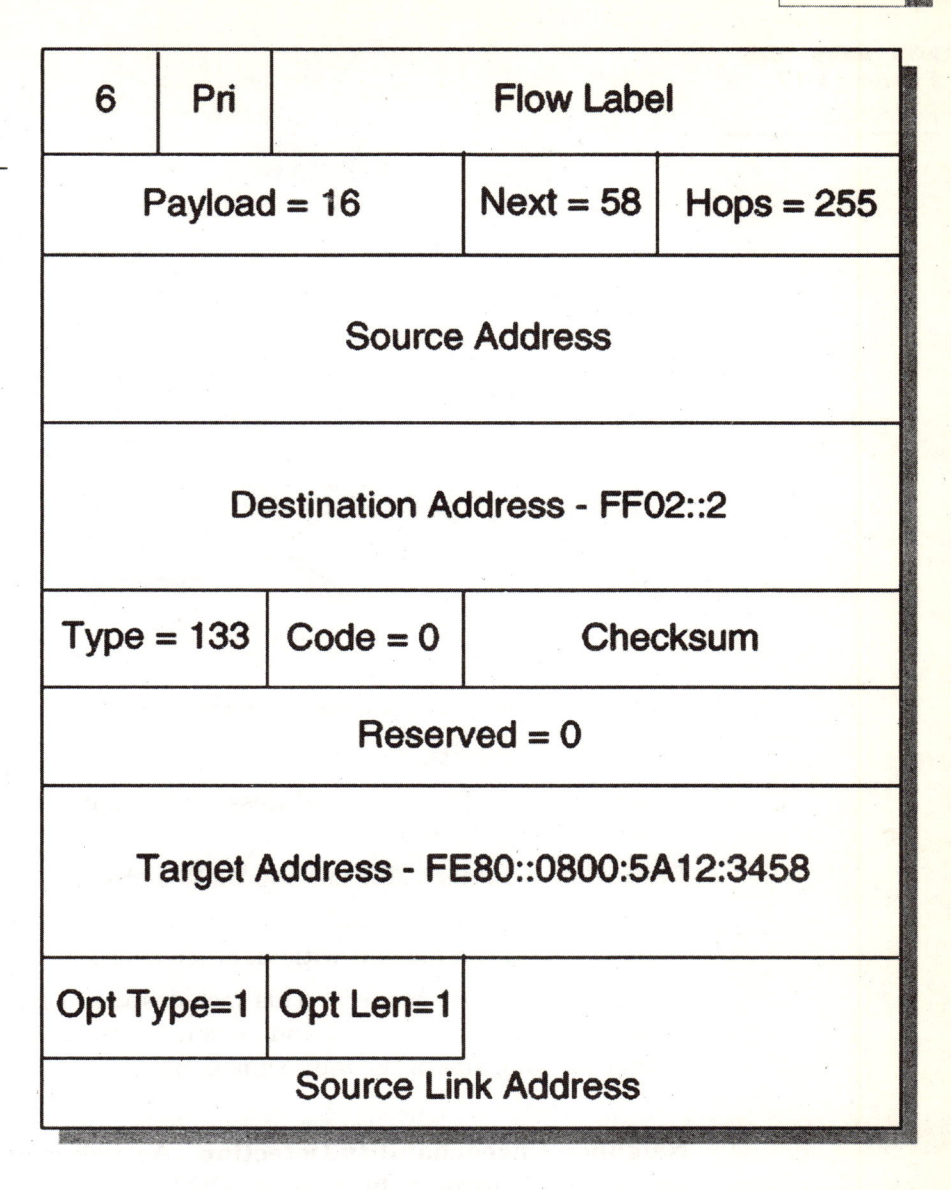

6	Pri	Flow Label

Payload = 16	Next = 58	Hops = 255

Source Address

Destination Address - FF02::2

Type = 133	Code = 0	Checksum

Reserved = 0

Target Address - FE80::0800:5A12:3458

Opt Type=1	Opt Len=1

Source Link Address

address against the local link prefix, Node X knows that Node Y is not on the local link and that it must therefore use a router. Node X selects router A from its list of default routers and forwards the packet. Obviously, this is not the most efficient path to Node Y. As soon as router A has forwarded the packet to Node Y (via router B), router A sends a *redirect message* to Node X. The format of the redirect message (complete with IP header) is shown in Figure 11-18.

Figure 11-17
Redirection.

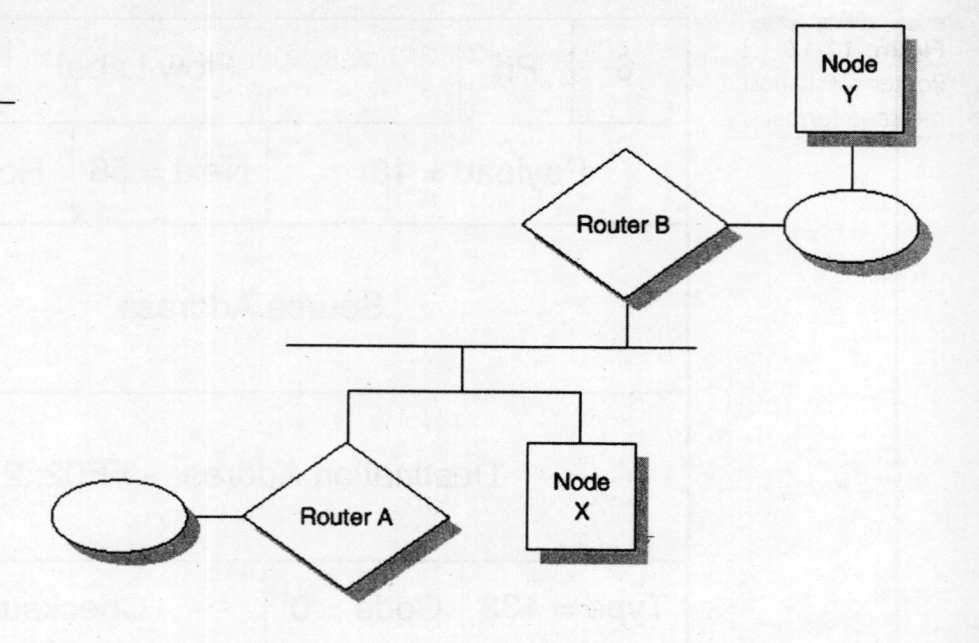

The fields to note in the message are as follows:

Type   137 (Redirect).

Target Address   This is the address of the router that should be used when trying to reach Node Y.

Destination Address   This is Node Y's IP address.

Option 2 (target link layer address)   This gives the link address of router B so Node X can reach it without a neighbor solicitation.

Option 4 (redirected header)   This includes the original packet sent by Node X, the full IP header, and as much of the data that will fit, such that the total size of the redirect message does not exceed 576 bytes.

Neighbor Unreachability Detection   An additional responsibility of the neighbor discovery function of ICMPv6 is *neighbor unreachability detection* (NUD).

A node actively tracks the reachability state of the neighbors to which it is sending packets. It may do this in two ways: either by monitoring the upper-layer protocols to see if a connection is making forward progress (for example, TCP acknowledgments are being received) or by issuing specific neighbor solicitations to check that the path to a target host is still available. When a path to a neighbor appears to be failing,

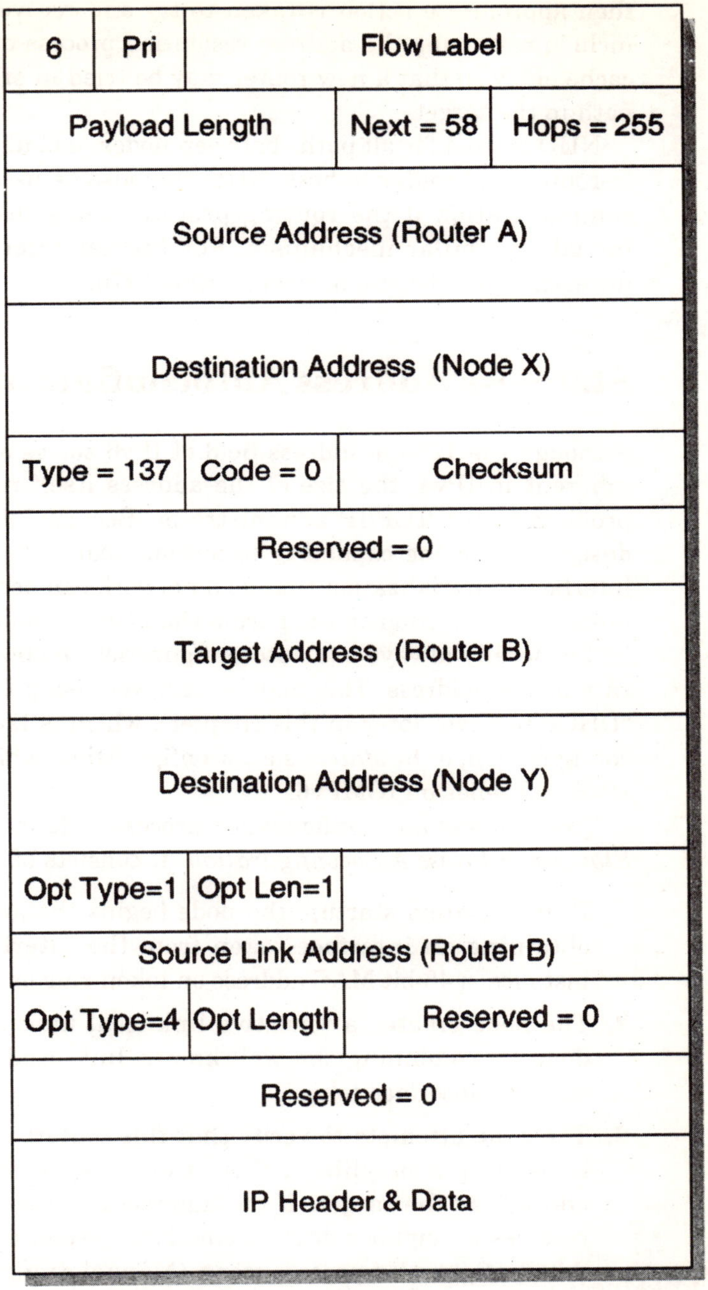

IP Version 6

Figure 11-18
Redirect message format.

6	Pri	Flow Label

Payload Length	Next = 58	Hops = 255

Source Address (Router A)

Destination Address (Node X)

Type = 137	Code = 0	Checksum

Reserved = 0

Target Address (Router B)

Destination Address (Node Y)

Opt Type=1	Opt Len=1	

Source Link Address (Router B)

Opt Type=4	Opt Length	Reserved = 0

Reserved = 0

IP Header & Data

then appropriate action is taken to try and recover the link. This may include restarting the address resolution process or deleting a neighbor cache entry so that a new router may be tried in order to find a working path to the target.

NUD is used for all paths between nodes, including host-to-host, host-to-router, and router-to-host. NUD may also be used for router-to-router communication if the routing protocol being used does not already include a similar mechanism. For further information on neighbor unreachability detection, refer to RFC 1970.

Stateless Address Autoconfiguration

Although the 128-bit address field of IPv6 solves a number of problems inherent in IPv4, the size of the address itself represents a potential problem to the TCP/IP administrator. Because of this, IPv6 has been designed with the capability to automatically assign an address to an interface at initialization time so a network can become operational with minimal to no action on the part of the TCP/IP administrator. IPv6 nodes will generally always use autoconfiguration to obtain their autoconfiguration IPv6 address. This may be achieved using DHCP (see the section "DHCP in IPv6" later in this chapter), which is known as *stateful* autoconfiguration, or by *stateless* autoconfiguration, which is a new feature of IPv6 and relies on ICMPv6.

The stateless autoconfiguration process is defined in *RFC 1971—IPv6 Stateless Address Autoconfiguration*. It consists of the following steps:

1. During system startup, the node begins the autoconfiguration by obtaining an interface token from the interface hardware, for instance, a 48-bit MAC address on token-ring or Ethernet networks.

2. The node creates a tentative link-local unicast address. This is done by combining the well-known link-local prefix (FE80::/10) with the interface token.

3. The node attempts to verify that this tentative address is unique by issuing a neighbor solicitation message with the tentative address as the target. If the address is already in use, the node receives a neighbor advertisement in response, in which case the autoconfiguration process stops. (Manual configuration of the node is then required.)

4. If no response is received, the node assigns the link-level address to its interface. The host then sends one or more router solicitations to

IP Version 6

the all-routers multicast group. If there are any routers present, they will respond with a router advertisement. If no router advertisement is received, the node should attempt to use DHCP to obtain an address and configuration information. If no DHCP server responds, the node continues using the link-level address and can communicate with other nodes only on the same link.

5. If a router advertisement *is* received in response to the router solicitation, then this message contains several pieces of information that tell the node how to proceed with the autoconfiguration process (see Figure 11-15). They are as follows:

   M flag Managed address configuration. If this bit is set, the node should use DHCP to obtain its IP address.

   O flag Other stateful configuration. If this bit is set then the node uses DHCP to obtain other configuration parameters.

   Prefix Option If the router advertisement has a prefix option with the A bit (autonomous address configuration flag) set on, then the prefix is used for stateless address autoconfiguration.

6. If stateless address configuration is to be used, the prefix is taken from the router advertisement and added to the interface token to form the global unicast IP address, which is assigned to the network interface.

7. The working node continues to receive periodic router advertisements. If the information in the advertisement changes, the node must take appropriate action.

Note that it is possible to use both stateless and stateful configuration simultaneously. It is quite likely that stateless configuration is used to obtain the IP address, but DHCP is used to obtain further configuration information. However, plug-and-play configuration is possible in both small and large networks without requiring DHCP servers.

The stateless address configuration process, together with the fact that more than one address can be allocated to the same interface, also allows all the nodes on a site (for example, if a switch to a new network provider necessitates new addressing) to be gracefully renumbered without disrupting the network. For further details, refer to RFC 1971.

Multicast Listener Discovery (MLD)

The process used by a router to discover the members of a particular multicast group is known as *Multicast Listener Discovery* (MLD). MLD is a subset of ICMPv6 and provides the equivalent function of IGMP for IPv4. This information is then provided by the router to whichever multicast routing protocol is being used, so that multicast packets are correctly delivered to all links where there are nodes listening for the appropriate multicast address.

MLD uses ICMPv6 messages of the format shown in Figure 11-19.

Note the following fields in the IPv6 header of the message of Figure 11-19:

Next   58 (for the ICMPv6 message header that follows).
Hops   Always set to 1.
Source Address   A link-local source address is used.

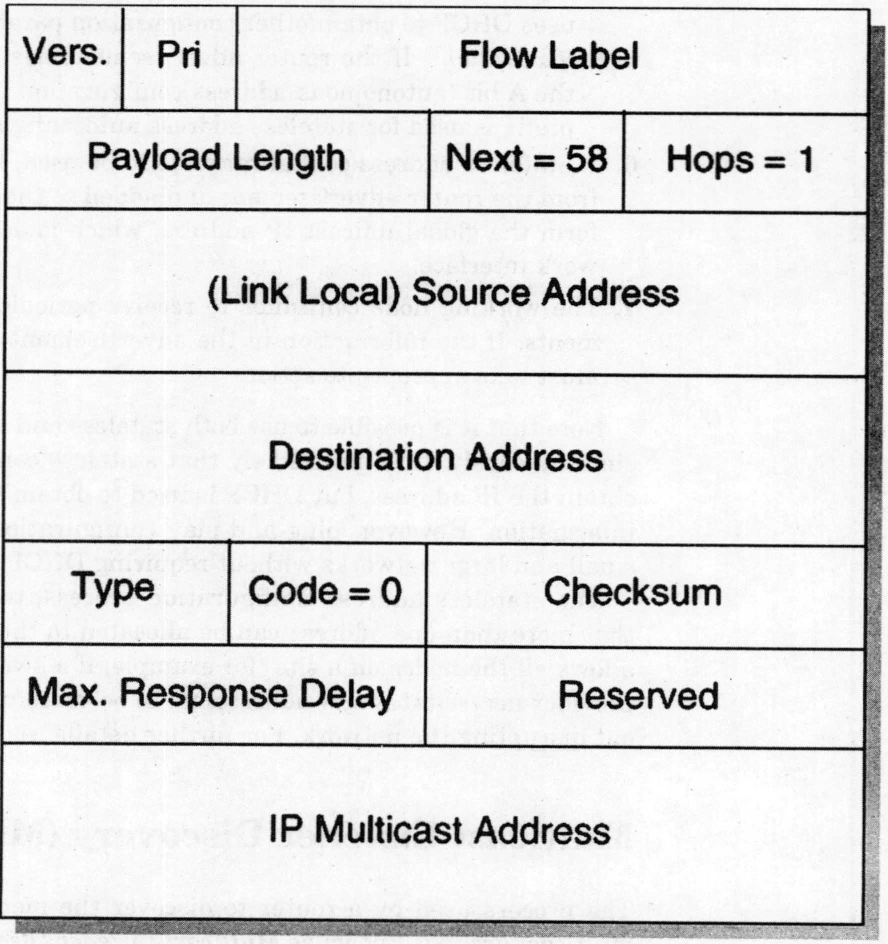

Figure 11-19
MLD message format.

Vers.	Pri	Flow Label	
Payload Length		Next = 58	Hops = 1
(Link Local) Source Address			
Destination Address			
Type	Code = 0	Checksum	
Max. Response Delay		Reserved	
IP Multicast Address			

In the MLD message itself, notice these fields:

Type   There are three types of MLD messages:

130   Multicast Listener Query
                There are two types of queries: general query, which is used to find which multicast addresses are being listened for on a link, and multicast-address-specific query, which is used to find if any nodes are listening for a specific multicast address on a link.

131   Multicast listener report
                This is used by a node to report that it is listening to a multicast address.

132   Multicast listener done
                This is used by a node to report that it is ceasing to listen to a multicast address.

Code   Set to 0 by sender and ignored by receivers.

Max Response Delay   This sets the maximum allowed delay before a responding report must be sent. This parameter is only valid in query messages. Increasing this parameter can prevent sudden bursts of high traffic if there a lot of responders on a network.

Multicast Address   In a query message, this field is set to zero for a general query or set to the specific IPv6 multicast address for a multicast-address-specific query.

In a response or done message, this field contains the multicast address being listened for.

A router users MLD to learn which multicast addresses are being listened for on each of its attached links. The router only needs to know that nodes listening for a particular address are present on a link; it does not need to know the unicast address of those listening nodes or how many listening nodes are present.

A router periodically sends a General Query on each of its links to the all-nodes link-local address (FF02::1). When a node listening for any multicast addresses receives this query it sets a delay timer (which may be anything between 0 and the maximum response delay) for each multicast address for which it is listening. As each timer expires, the node sends a *multicast listener report* message containing the appropriate multicast address. If a node receives another node's report for a multicast address while it has a timer still running for that address, then it stops its timer and does not send a report for that address. This prevents duplicate reports from being sent and, together with the timer mechanism, prevents excess or bursty traffic from being generated.

The router manages a list of, and sets a timer for, each multicast address it is aware of on each of its links. If one of these timers expires without a report being received for that address, the router assumes that no nodes are still listening for that address, and the address is removed from the list. Whenever a report *is* received, the router resets the timer for that particular address.

When a node has finished listening to a multicast address, if it was the last node on a link to send a report to the router (that is, its timer delay was not interrupted by the receipt of another node's report), then it sends a *multicast listener done* message to the router. If the node *was* interrupted by another node before its timer expired, then it assumes that other nodes are still listening to the multicast address on the link and therefore does not send a done message.

When a router receives a done message, it sends a multicast-address-specific message on the link. If no report is received in response to this message, the router assumes that there are no nodes still listening to this multicast address and removes the address from its list. MLD is not currently specified in an RFC, but it is the subject of an Internet draft, *Multicast Listener Discovery for IPv6.* For further information, please refer to the latest draft at http://www.ietf.org/internet-drafts/draft-ietf-ipngwg-mld-00.txt

DNS in IPv6

With the introduction of 128-bit addresses, IPv6 makes it even more difficult for one network user to be able to identify another network user by means of the IP address of his or her network device. Using the Domain Name Service, therefore, becomes even more of a necessity.

A number of extensions to DNS are specified to support the storage and retrieval of IPv6 addresses. These are defined in *RFC 1886—DNS Extensions to Support IP Version 6,* which is a proposed standard with elective status. However, there is also work in progress on usability enhancements to this RFC, which are described in an Internet draft of the same name.

The following extensions are specified:

- A new resource record type, AAAA, which maps the domain name to the IPv6 address

- A new domain, which is used to support address-to-domain name lookups
- A change to the definition of existing queries so they correct process on both A and AAAA record types

Format of IPv6 Resource Records

RFC 1886 defines the format of the AAAA record as being similar to an A resource record but with the 128-bit IPv6 address encoded in the data section and a Type value of 28 (decimal).

A special domain, IP6.INT, is defined for inverse (address-to-host name) lookups (similar to the *in-addr.arpa* domain used in IPv4). As in IPv4, the address must be entered in reverse order, but hexadecimal digits are used rather than decimal notation. For example, the inverse domain name entry for the IPv6 address

```
11-122:0:1:2:3:4:5678:9abc
```

is as follows:

```
c.b.a.9.8.7.11.5.4.0.0.0.3.0.0.0.2.0.0.0.1.0.0.0.0.0.0.0.2.2.2.2.IP6.INT.
```

So, if the above address relates to the node ND1.test.com, the following entries should appear in the name server zone data:

```
$origin test.com.
ND1 99999 IN AAAA 11-122:0:1:2:3:4:5678:9abc
cba9876540003000200010000000011-122.IP6.INT. IN PTR ND1*
```

Proposed Changes to Resource Records The IPv6 addressing system has been designed to allow for multiple addresses on a single interface and to facilitate address renumbering (for example, when a company changes one of its service providers). Using the AAAA resource record format specified in RFC 1886 would require a major administrative effort in the event of a renumbering change. The work in progress in the current Internet draft *DNS Extensions to Support IP Version 6* proposes changes to the format of the AAAA resource record to simplify network renumbering.

---

*All characters that make up the reversed IPv6 address in this PTR entry should be separated by a period (.). These have been omitted in this example for clarity.

The proposed format of the data section of the AAAA record is as shown in Figure 11-20.

IPv6 Address   128-bit address (contains only the lower bits of the address)

P   Prefix Length (0-128)

Domain Name   The domain name of the prefix

To see how this format works, consider the example shown in Figure 11-21.

Site X is multihomed to two providers, PROV1 and PROV2. PROV1 gets its transit services from top-level provider TOP1. PROV2 gets its service from TOP2. TOP1 has the top-level aggregate (TLA ID + format prefix) of 11-11 (see Figure 11-9). TOP2 has the TLA of 11-122.

TOP1 has assigned the next-level aggregate (NLA) of 00AB to PROV1. PROV2 has been assigned the NLA of 00BC by TOP2. PROV1 has assigned the subscriber identifier 00A1 to site X. PROV2 has assigned the subscriber identifier 00B1 to site X. Node ND1, at site X, which has the interface token of 10005A111-2456, is therefore configured with the following two IP addresses:

```
11-11:00AB:00A1::1000:5A12:3456
11-122:00BC:00B1::1000:5A12:3456
```

Site X is represented by the domain name test.com. Each provider has its own domain: top1.com, top2.com, prov1.com, and prov2.com. In each of these domains is created an IP6 subdomain that is used to hold prefixes. The node ND1 can now be represented by the following entries in the DNS:

```
ND1.TEST.COM AAAA ::1000:5A12:3456 80
IP6.TEST.COM

IP6.TEST.COM AAAA 0:0:00A1:: 32 IP6.PROV1.COM
IP6.TEST.COM AAAA 0:0:00B1:: 32 IP6.PROV2.COM

IP6.PROV1.COM AAAA 0:00AB:: 16 IP6.TOP1.COM

IP6.PROV2.COM AAAA 0:00BC:: 16 IP6.TOP2.COM
```

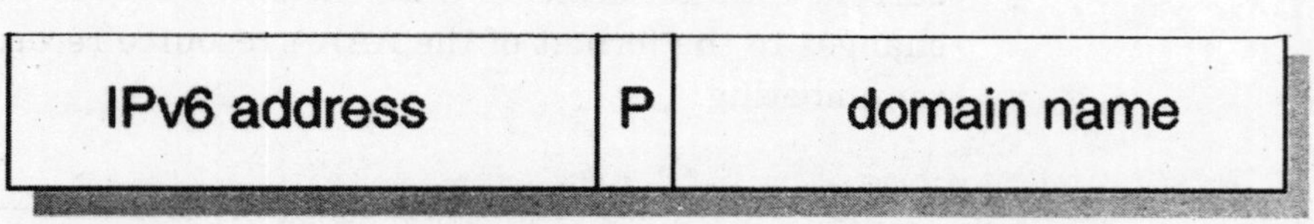

Figure 11-20
AAAA resource record—proposed data format.

IPv6 address	P	domain name

Figure 11-21
Prefix numbering example.

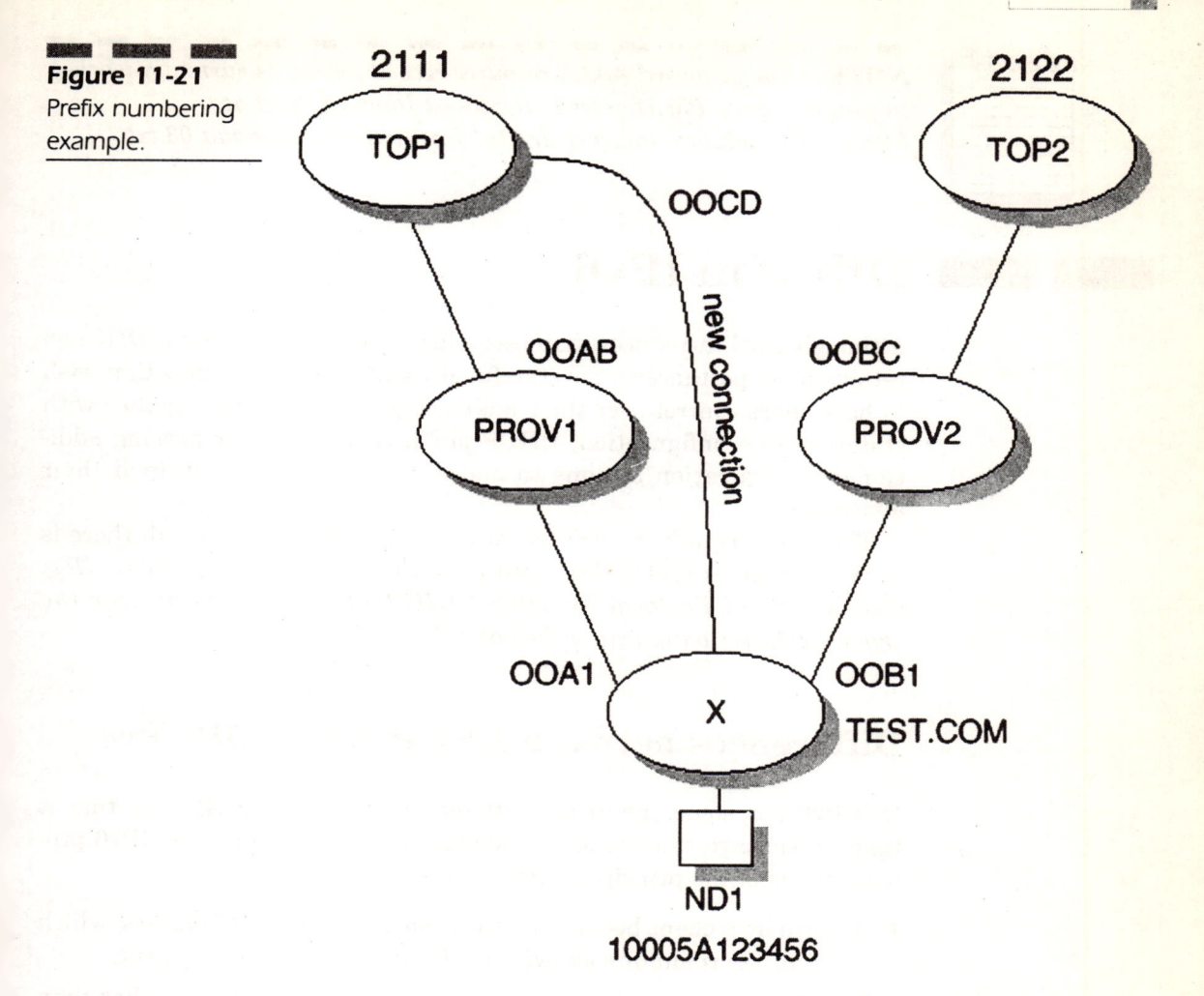

```
IP6.TOP1.COM AAAA 11-11::
IP6.TOP2.COM AAAA 11-122::
```

This format simplifies the job of the DNS administrator considerably and makes renumbering changes much easier to implement. Say, for example, site X decides to stop using links from providers PROV1 and PROV2 and invests in a connection direct from the top-level service provider TOP1 (who allocates the next-level aggregate 00CD to site X). The only change necessary in the DNS would be for the two IP6.TEST.COM entries to be replaced with a single entry as follows:

```
IP6.TEST.COM AAAA 0:00CD:: 16 IP6.TOP1.COM
```

> **NOTE:** The proposed AAAA resource record format is currently work-in-progress only. Please refer to the latest Internet draft at http://www.ietf.org/internet-drafts/draft-ietf-ipngwg-aaaa-03.txt.

DHCP in IPv6

Although IPv6 introduces stateless address autoconfiguration, DHCPv6 retains its importance as the stateful alternative for those sites that wish to have more control over their addressing scheme. Used together with stateless autoconfiguration, DHCP provides a means for passing additional configuration options to nodes once they have obtained their addresses.

There is currently no RFC covering DHCP in IPv6, although there is work in progress that is described in two Internet drafts, *Dynamic Host Configuration Protocol for IPv6 (DHCPv6)* and *Extensions for the Dynamic Host Configuration Protocol for IPv6*.

Differences between DHCPv6 and DHCPv4

DHCPv6 has some significant differences vis-à-vis DHCPv4, in that it takes advantage of some of the inherent enhancements of the IPv6 protocol. Some of the principal differences are as follows:

- As soon as a client boots, it already has a link-local IP address, which it can use to communicate with a DHCP server or a relay agent.
- The client uses multicast addresses to contact the server, rather than broadcasts.
- IPv6 allows the use of multiple IP addresses per interface, and DHCPv6 can provide more than one address when requested.
- Some DHCP options are now unnecessary. Default routers, for example, are now obtained by a client using IPv6 neighbor discovery.
- DHCP messages (including address allocations) appear in IPv6 message extensions rather than in the IP header as in IPv4.
- There is no requirement for BOOTP compatibility.
- There is a new reconfigure message, which is used by the server to send configuration changes to clients (for example, the reduction in an

address lifetime). Clients must continue to listen for reconfigure messages once they have received their initial configuration.

DHCPv6 Messages

The following DHCPv6 messages are currently defined:

DHCP Solicit   This is an IP multicast message. The DHCP client forwards the message to FF02::1:2, the well-known multicast address for all DHCP agents (relays and servers). If received by a relay, the relay forwards the message to FF05::1:3, the well-known multicast address for all DHCP servers.

DHCP Advertise   This is a unicast message sent in response to a DHCP Solicit. A DHCP server responds directly to the soliciting client, if it is on the same link, or via the relay agent, if the DHCP Solicit was forwarded by a relay. The advertise message may contain one or more extensions (DHCP options).

DHCP Request   Once the client has located the DHCP server, the DHCP request (unicast message) is sent to request an address and/or configuration parameters. The request must be forwarded by a relay if the server is not on the same link as the client. The request may contain extensions (options specified by the client) that may be a subset of all the options available on the server.

DHCP Reply   This is an IP unicast message sent in response to a DHCP request (it may be sent directly to the client or via a relay). Extensions contain the address and/or parameters committed to the client.

DHCP Release   This is an IP unicast sent by the client to the server, informing it of resources that are being released.

DHCP Reconfigure   This is an IP unicast or multicast message, sent by the server to one or more clients, to inform them that there is new configuration information available. The client must respond to this message with a DHCP request to request these new changes from the server.

For further details on DHCPv6, refer to the latest Internet drafts. Note that the exact numbering of the drafts is subject to change:

http://www.ietf.org/internet-drafts/draft-ietf-dhc-dhcpv6-13.txt
http://www.ietf.org/internet-drafts/draft-ietf-dhc-v6exts-10.txt

Mobility Support in IPv6

At the time this was written, there was no RFC covering mobility support in IPv6, although there is work in progress on the subject, which is described in a current Internet draft, *Mobility Support in IPv6*.

Certain enhancements in the IPv6 protocol lend themselves particularly well to the mobile environment. For example, unlike Mobile IPv4, there is no requirement for routers to act as "foreign agents" on behalf of the mobile node, as neighbor discovery and address autoconfiguration allow the node to operate away from home without any special support from a local router. Also, most packets sent to a mobile node while it is away from its home location can be tunneled by using IPv6 routing (extension) headers rather than a complete encapsulation, as is used in Mobile IPv4. This reduces the overhead of delivering packets to mobile nodes.

For further information on mobility support in IPv6, please refer to the latest Internet draft at http://www.ietf.org/internet-drafts/draft-ietf-mobileip-ipv6-06.txt

Internet Transition: Migrating from IPv4 to IPv6

If the Internet is to realize the benefits of IPv6, then there will have to be a period of transition when new IPv6 hosts and routers will need to be deployed alongside existing IPv4 systems. *RFC1933—Transition Mechanisms for IPv6 Hosts and Routers* and *RFC11-85—Routing Aspects of IPv6 Transition* define a number of mechanisms to be employed that ensure both compatibility between old and new systems and a gradual transition that does not impact the functionality of the Internet. These techniques are sometimes collectively termed *Simple Internet Transition (SIT)*. The transition employs the following techniques:

- Dual-stack IP implementations for hosts and routers that must interoperate between IPv4 and IPv6.
- Embedding of IPv4 addresses in IPv6 addresses. IPv6 hosts will be assigned addresses that are interoperable with IPv4, and IPv4 host addresses will be mapped to IPv6.
- IPv6-over-IPv4 tunneling mechanisms for carrying IPv6 packets across IPv4 router networks.

- IPv4/IPv6 header translation. This technique is intended for use when implementation of IPv6 is well advanced and only a few IPv4-only systems remain.

These techniques are also adaptable to other protocols, notably Novell IPX, which has similar internetwork layer semantics and an addressing scheme that can be mapped easily to a part of the IPv6 address space.

Dual IP Stack Implementation: The IPv6/IPv4 Node

The simplest way to ensure that a new IPv6 node maintains compatibility with existing IPv4 systems is to provide a dual IP stack implementation. An IPv6/IPv4 node can send and receive either IPv6 packets or IPv4 datagrams, depending on the type of system with which it is communicating. A node has both a 128-bit IPv6 address and a 32-bit IPv4 address, which do not necessarily need to be related. Figure 11-22 shows a dual stack IPv6/IPv4 system communicating with both IPv6 and IPv4 systems on the same link.

The IPv6/IPv4 node may use stateless or stateful autoconfiguration to obtain its IPv6 address. It may also use any method to obtain its IPv4 address, such as DHCP, BOOTP, or manual configuration. However, if the node is to perform automatic tunneling, then the IPv6 address must be an IPv4-compatible address, with the low-order 32-bits of the address serving as the IPv4 address. (See "IPv6 Addressing" earlier in this chapter.)

Conceptually, the dual-stack model envisages a doubling up of the protocols only in the internetwork layer. However, related changes are obvi-

Figure 11-22 IPv6/IPv4 dual stack system.

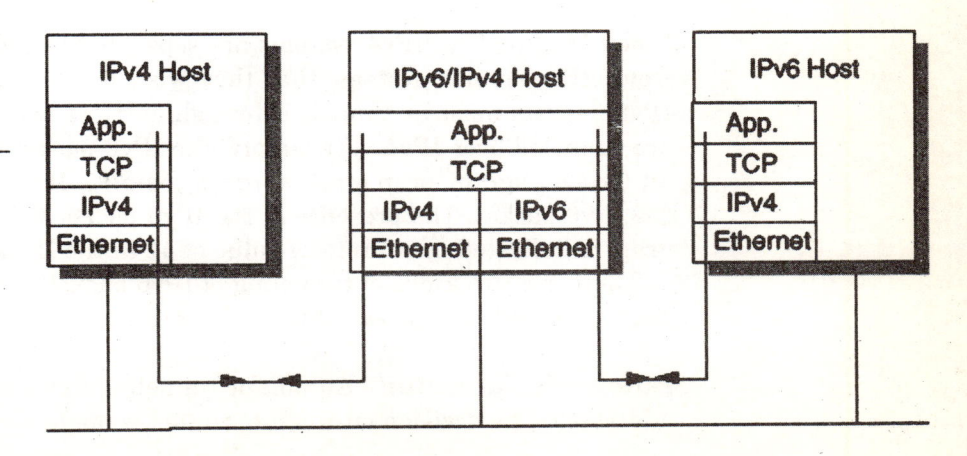

ously needed in all transport-layer protocols in order to operate using either stack and possibly in applications as well if they are to exploit IPv6 capabilities, such as longer addresses.

When an IPv6/IPv4 node wishes to communicate with another system it needs to know the capabilities of that system and which type of packet it should send. The DNS plays a key role here. As described in the section "DNS in IPv6" earlier in the chapter, a new resource record type, AAAA, is defined for mapping host names to IPv6 addresses. The results of a name server lookup determine how a node attempts to communicate with that system. The records found in the DNS for a node depend on which protocols it is running:

- IPv4-only nodes have only A records containing IPv4 addresses in the DNS.
- IPv6/IPv4 nodes that can interoperate with IPv4-only nodes have AAAA records containing IPv4-compatible IPv6 addresses and A records containing the equivalent IPv4 addresses.
- IPv6-only nodes that cannot interoperate with IPv4-only nodes have only AAAA records containing IPv6 addresses.

Because IPv6/IPv4 nodes make decisions about which protocols to use based on the information returned by the DNS, the incorporation of AAAA records in the DNS is a prerequisite for interoperability between IPv6 and IPv4 systems. Note that name servers do not necessarily need to use an IPv6-capable protocol stack, but they must support the additional record type.

Tunneling

When IPv6 or IPv6/IPv4 systems are separated by older IPv4 networks from other similar systems that they wish to communicate with, then IPv6 packets must be tunneled through an IPv4 network. IPv6 packets are tunneled over IPv4 very simply: the IPv6 packet is encapsulated in an IPv4 datagram, or in other words, a complete IPv4 header is added to the IPv6 packet. The presence of the IPv6 packet within the IPv4 datagram is indicated by a Protocol value of 41 in the IPv4 header.

There are two kinds of tunneling of IPv6 packets over IPv4 networks: *automatic* and *configured*. They are described in the following sections.

Automatic Tunneling Automatic tunneling relies on IPv4-compatible addresses. The decision on when to tunnel is made by an IPv6/IPv4 host that has a packet to send across an IPv4-routed network area, and it follows the following rules:

- If the destination is an IPv4 or an IPv4-mapped address, send the packet using IPv4 because the recipient is not IPv6-capable.
- If the destination is on the same subnet, send it using IPv6 because the recipient is IPv6-capable.
- If the destination is not on the same subnet but there is at least one default router on the subnet that is IPv6-capable, or there is a route configured to an IPv6 router for that destination, then send it to that router using IPv6.
- If the address is an IPv4-compatible address, send the packet using automatic IPv6-over-IPv4 tunneling.

If none of the preceding conditions apply then,

- The destination is a node with an IPv6-only address that is connected via an IPv4-routed area, which is not also IPv6-routed. Therefore, the destination is unreachable.

NOTE: *The IP address must be IPv4-compatible for tunneling to be used. Automatic tunneling cannot be used to reach IPv6-only addresses because they cannot be addressed using IPv4. Packets from IPv6/IPv4 nodes to IPv4-mapped addresses are not tunneled to because they refer to IPv4-only nodes.*

The preceding rules emphasize the use of an IPv6 router in preference to a tunnel for three reasons:

- There is less overhead because there is no encapsulating IPv4 header.
- IPv6-only features are available.
- The IPv6 routing topology is used when it is deployed in preference to the preexisting IPv4 topology.

A node does not need to know whether it is attached to an IPv6-routed or an IPv4-routed area; it always uses an IPv6 router if one is configured on its subnet, and it uses tunneling if one is not (in which case it can infer that it is attached to an IPv4-routed area).

Automatic tunneling may be either host-to-host, or it may be router-to-host. A source host sends an IPv6 packet to an IPv6 router if possible, but that router may not be able to do the same and have to perform automatic tunneling to the destination host itself. Because of the preference for using IPv6 routers rather than tunneling, the tunnel is always as "short" as possible. However, the tunnel always extends all the way to the destination host. Because IPv6 uses the same hop-by-hop routing paradigm, a host cannot determine if a packet will eventually emerge into an IPv6-complete area before it reaches the destination host. To use a tunnel that does not extend all the way to the recipient, configured tunneling must be used.

The mechanism used for automatic tunneling is very simple:

- The encapsulating IPv4 datagram uses the low-order 32 bits of the IPv6 source and destination addresses to create the equivalent IPv4 addresses and sets the protocol number to 41 (IPv6).

- The receiving node's network interface layer identifies the incoming packets (or packets if the IPv4 datagram was fragmented) as belonging to IPv4 and passes them upward to the IPv4 part of the dual IPv6/IPv4 internetwork layer.

- The IPv4 layer then receives the datagram in the normal way, reassembling fragments if necessary; notes the protocol number of 41; and then removes the IPv4 header and passes the original IPv6 packet "sideways" to the IPv6 part of the internetwork layer.

- The IPv6 code then processes the original packet as it would normally. Since the destination IPv6 address in the packet is the IPv6 address of the node (an IPv4-compatible address matching the IPv4 address used in the encapsulating IPv4 datagram) the packet is at its final destination. IPv6 then processes any extension headers as normal and passes the packet's remaining payload to the next protocol listed in the last IPv6 header.

Figure 11-23 shows two IPv6/IPv4 nodes separated by an IPv4 network. Both workstations have IPv4-compatible IPv6 addresses. Workstation A sends a packet to workstation B, as follows:

1. Workstation A has received router solicitation messages from an IPv6-capable router (X) on its local link. It forwards the packet to this router.

2. Router X adds an IPv4 header to the packet, using IPv4 source and destination addresses derived from the IPv4-compatible addresses. The packet is then forwarded across the IPv4 network, all the way to workstation B. This is router-to-host automatic tunneling.

IP Version 6

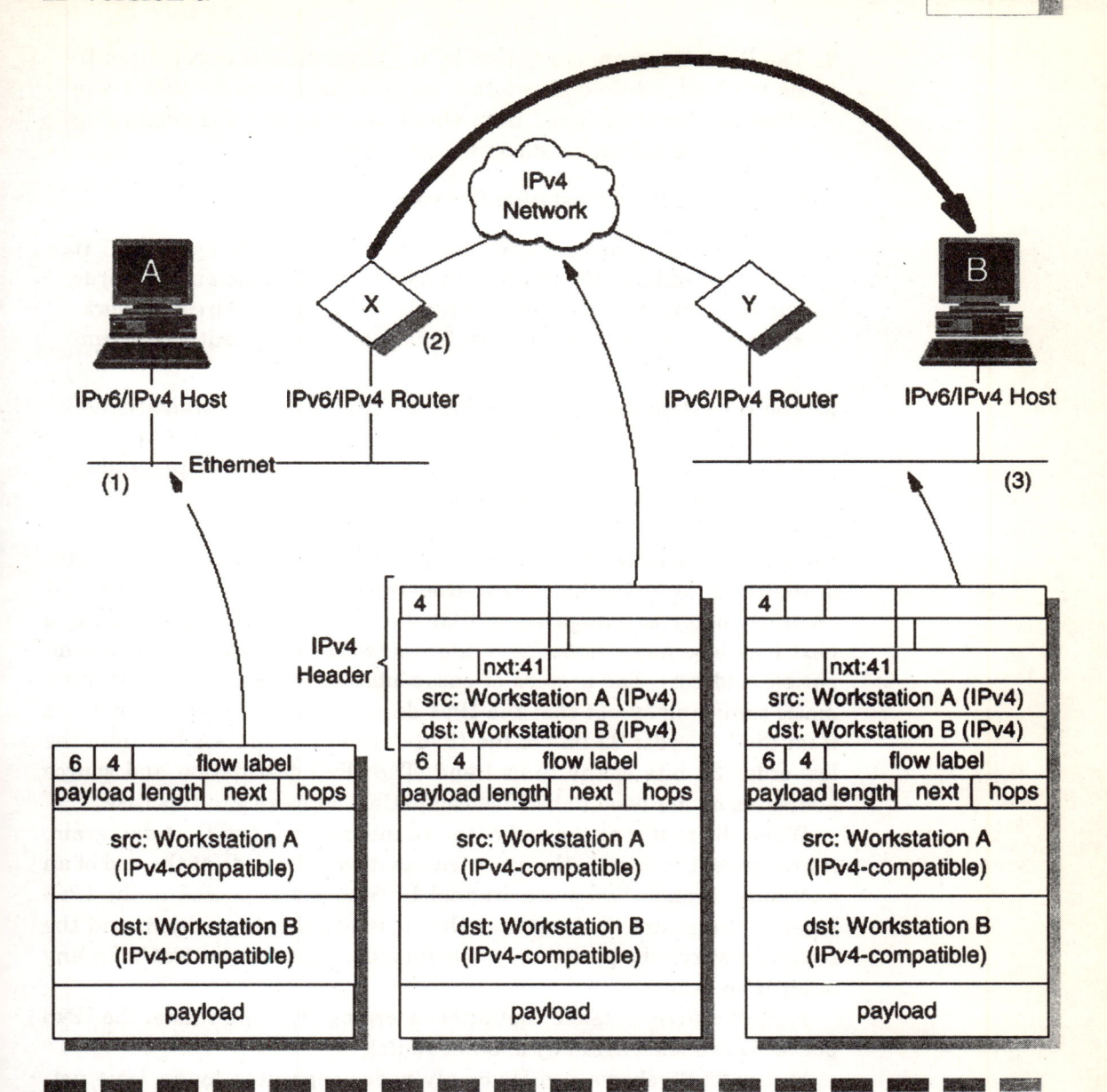

Figure 11-23 Router-to-host automatic tunneling.

3. The IPv4 datagram is received by the IPv4 stack of workstation B. As the Protocol field shows that the next header is 41 (IPv6), the IPv4 header is stripped from the datagram, and the remaining IPv6 packet is then handled by the IPv6 stack.

In Figure 11-24, workstation B responds as follows:

1. Workstation B has no IPv6-capable router on its local link. It therefore adds an IPv4 header to its own IPv6 frame and forwards the resulting IPv4 datagram directly to the IPv4 address of workstation A via the IPv4 network. This is host-to-host automatic tunneling.

2. The IPv4 datagram is received by the IPv4 stack of workstation A. As the Protocol field shows that the next header is 41 (IPv6), the IPv4 header is stripped from the datagram, and the remaining IPv6 packet is then handled by the IPv6 stack.

Configured Tunneling Configured tunneling is used for host-router or router-router tunneling of IPv6-over-IPv4. The sending host or the forwarding router is configured so that the route, in addition to having a next hop, also has a *tunnel end* address (which is always an IPv4-compatible address). The process of encapsulation is the same as for automatic tunneling except that the IPv4 destination address is not derived from the low-order 32 bits of the IPv6 destination address but from the low-order 32 bits of the tunnel end. The IPv6 destination and source addresses *do not* need to be IPv4-compatible addresses in this case.

When the router at the end of the tunnel receives the IPv4 datagram, it processes it in exactly the same way as it would a node at the end of an automatic tunnel. When the original IPv6 packet is passed to the IPv6 layer in the router, it recognizes that it is not the destination, and the router forwards the packet on to the final destination as it would for any other IPv6 packet.

It is, of course, possible that after emerging from the tunnel the IPv6 packet is tunneled again by another router.

Figure 11-25 shows two IPv6-only nodes separated by an IPv4 network. A router-to-router tunnel is configured between the two IPv6/IPv4 routers X and Y:

1. Workstation A constructs an IPv6 packet to send to workstation B. It forwards the packet to the IPv6 router advertising on its local link (X).

IP Version 6

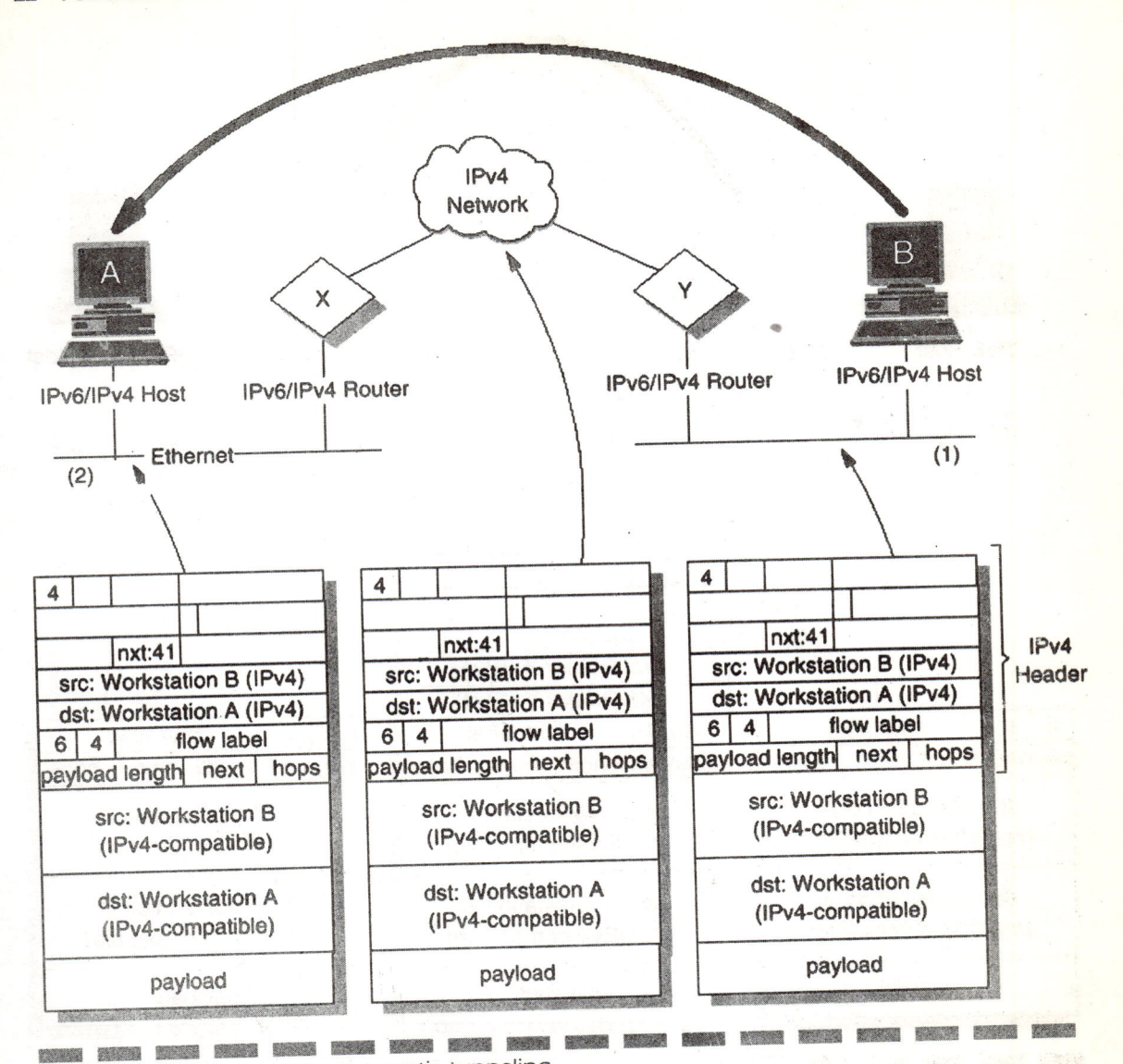

Figure 11-24 Host-to-host automatic tunneling.

2. Router X receives the packet but has no direct IPv6 connection to the destination subnet. However, a tunnel has been configured for this subnet. The router therefore adds an IPv4 header to the packet, with a destination address of the tunnel end (router Y) and forwards the datagram over the IPv4 network.

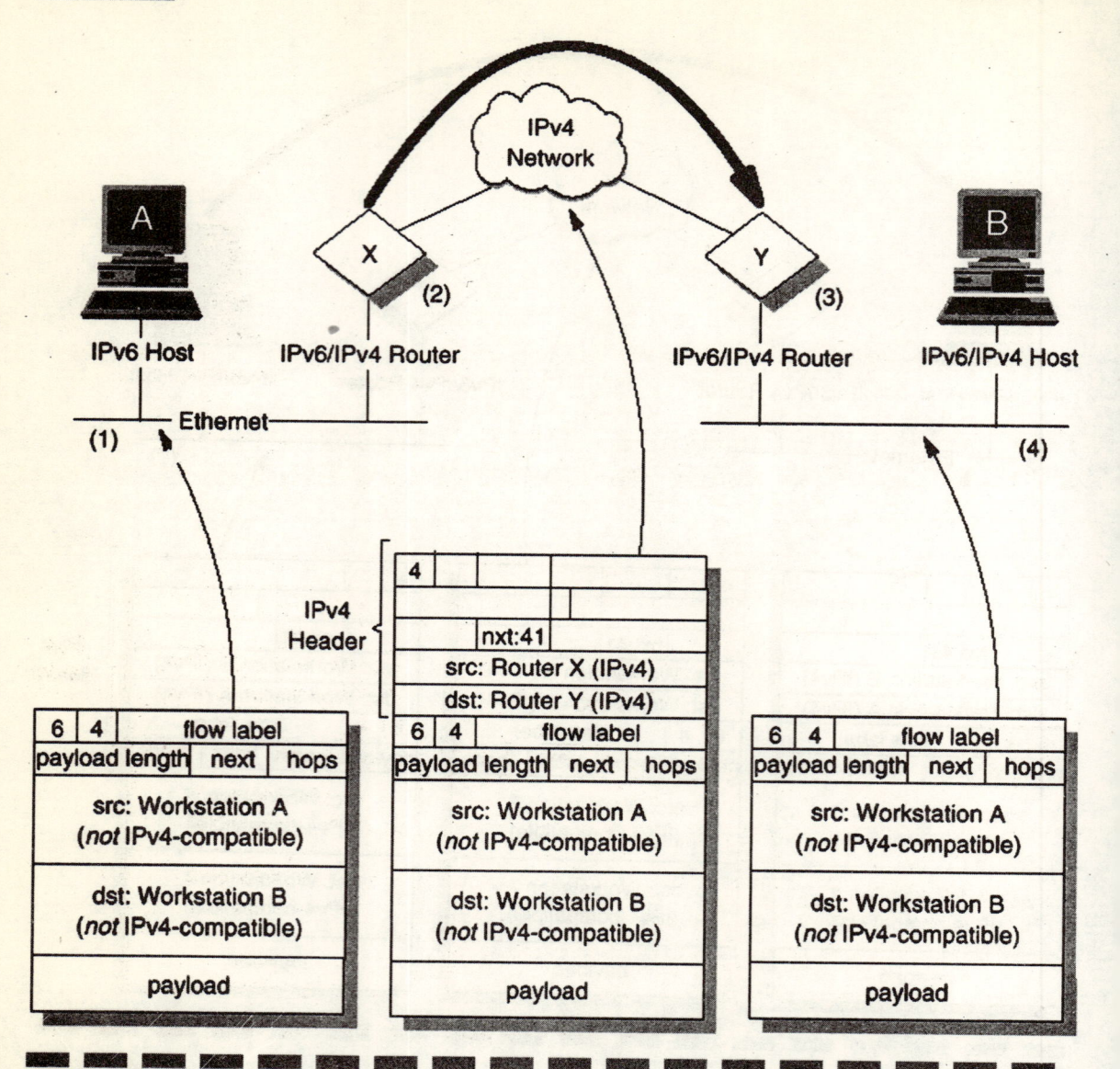

Figure 11-25 Router-to-router configured tunnel.

3. The IPv4 stack of router Y receives the frame. Seeing the Protocol field value of 41, it removes the IPv4 header and passes the remaining IPv6 packet to its IPv6 stack. The IPv6 stack reads the destination IPv6 address and forwards the packet.

4. Workstation B receives the IP6 packet.

Header Translation

Installing IPv6/IPv4 nodes allows for backward compatibility with existing IPv4 systems. However, when the migration of networks to IPv6 reaches an advanced stage, it is likely that new systems being installed will be IPv6 only. There will therefore be a requirement for IPv6-only systems to communicate with the remaining IPv4-only systems. Header translation is required in order for IPv6-only nodes to interoperate with IPv4-only nodes. Header translation is performed by IPv6/IPv4 routers on the boundaries between IPv6 routed areas and IPv4 routed areas.

The translating router strips the header completely from IPv6 packets and replaces it with an equivalent IPv4 header (or the reverse). In addition to correctly mapping between the fields in the two headers, the router must convert source and destination addresses from IPv4-mapped addresses to real IPv4 addresses (by taking the low-order 32 bits of the IP address). In the reverse direction, the router adds the ::FFFF /96 prefix to the IPv4 address to form the IPv4-mapped address. If either the source or the destination IPv6 address is IPv6 only, the header cannot be translated.

Note that for a site that has even just one IPv4 host, every IPv6 node with which it needs to communicate must have an IPv4-mapped address.

Interoperability Summary

Whether two nodes can interoperate depends upon their capabilities and their addresses. An IPv4 node can communicate with the following nodes:

- Any IPv4 node on the local link
- Any IPv4 node via an IPv4 router
- Any IPv6 node with IPv4-mapped address via a header translator

An IPv6 node (IPv6-only address) can communicate with the following nodes:

- Any IPv6 node on the local link
- Any IPv6 node via an IPv6 router on the local link (this may require tunneling through IPv4 network from the router)

An IPv6 node (IPv4-mapped address) can communicate with these nodes:

- Any IPv6 node on the local link
- Any IPv6 node via an IPv6 router on the local link (this may require tunneling through IPv4 network from the router)
- Any IPv4 node via a header translator

An IPv6/IPv4 node (IPv4-compatible address) can communicate with the following nodes:

- Any IPv4 node on the local link
- Any IPv4 node via an IPv4 router on the local link
- Any IPv6 node on the local link
- Any IPv6 node via an IPv6 router on the local link (this may require tunneling through IPv4 network from the router)
- Any IPv6/IPv4 node (IPv4-compatible address) via host-to-host tunnel

The Drive toward IPv6

The drivers for the introduction of IPv6 networks are likely to be requirements for new facilities that need IPv6 or the exhaustion of the IPv4 address space. Which of these is deemed more important will vary among organizations. For example, commercial organizations with large, long-established internal IPv4 networks are unlikely to be keen to upgrade thousands of working IPv4 hosts and routers unless they have a problem with the address space within their own networks. They will, however, be likely to invest in IPv6 deployment if new business-critical applications require facilities that are only available on IPv6 or if they require connectivity to other organizations that are using IPv6-only addresses.

Businesses that are implementing IP networks for the first time, however, may be interested in some of the capabilities of IPv6, such as the address autoconfiguration. However, anyone thinking of implementing IPv6 today needs to be aware that the protocol is still, as of today, very much under development. It may be said that IPv4 is also still under development since new RFCs and Internet drafts are constantly being produced, but for IPv6 certain key protocols, such as DHCP, at least at the time of writing are still at Internet draft stage only. The Internet backbone today consists of IPv4 routers and, until the IPv6 protocols have been widely used and tested, the owners of these production routers are unlikely to put them at risk by upgrading them to IPv6.

One offshoot of the IETF IPng (next generation) project was the development of the 6Bone, which is an Internetwide IPv6 virtual network layered on top of the physical IPv4 Internet. The 6Bone consists of many islands supporting IPv6 packets and linked by tunnels across the existing IPv4 backbone. The 6Bone is widely used for testing IPv6 protocols and products. It is expected that as confidence grows in IPv6 and more products with IPv6 capability become available the 6Bone will eventually be replaced by a production backbone of ISP and user network IPv6-capable routers.

References

The following RFCs contain detailed information on IPv6:

RFC 1752—*The Recommendation for the IP Next Generation Protocol*

RFC 1883—*Internet Protocol, Version 6 (IPv6)*

RFC 1191—*Path MTU Discovery*

RFC 2373—*IP Version 6 Addressing Architecture*

RFC 2374—*An IPv6 Aggregatable Global Unicast Address Format*

RFC 2375—*IPv6 Multicast Address Assignments*

RFC 1885—*Internet Control Message Protocol (ICMPv6) for the Internet Protocol Version 6 (IPv6) Specification*

RFC 1970—*Neighbor Discovery for IP Version 6 (IPv6)*

RFC 1971—*IPv6 Stateless Address Autoconfiguration*

RFC 1886—*DNS Extensions to Support IP Version 6*

RFC 1933—*Transition Mechanisms for IPv6 Hosts and Routers*

RFC 11-85—*Routing Aspects of IPv6 Transition*

CHAPTER 12

Dynamic DNS Review

Cisco DNS/DHCP Manager

Product Overview

The Cisco DNS/DHCP Manager is a suite of TCP/IP management applications that manage domain names and synchronize IP (Internet Protocol) addresses between a Domain Name System (DNS) server and a Dynamic Host Configuration Protocol (DHCP). The Cisco DNS/DHCP Manager includes the Domain Name Manager—a graphical DNS management tool—and a DHCP server that dynamically updates DNS with IP addresses assigned to DHCP clients. The Cisco DNS/DHCP Manager also includes a DNS server, a TFTP server, a NTP server, and a syslog server.

Managing a large TCP/IP network requires maintaining accurate and up-to-date IP address and domain name information. Today, organizations are forced to manage IP address and domain name information by manually modifying several databases. Organizations maintain IP address and domain name information in DNS servers' text-based configuration files. DHCP servers further complicate the situation by dynamically assigning domain names and IP addressees to nodes on the network. Organizations are therefore forced to manually synchronize the configuration of DNS and DHCP servers. Incorrect IP addresses and domain names can cause problems for people using the World Wide Web, a network file system (NFS), FTP, and e-mail. The Cisco DNS/DHCP Manager eliminates the need for manually configuring and synchronizing DNS and DHCP servers.

The Cisco DNS/DHCP Manager is designed for the following applications:

Managing DNS. Organizations currently manage DNS by editing configuration files that have a complex syntax. This process is time-consuming and subject to error. The Domain Name Manager browser reduces common configuration errors by checking the syntax of each new entry. The Domain Name Manager is easy to learn, and more people in an organization can use it to manage DNS.

The Cisco DHCP server automatically updates the Domain Name Manager with the IP address and domain name of the new nodes on the network. The Domain Name Manager then propagates this information to DNS servers on the network. The Domain Name Manager replaces an organization's existing primary DNS server and becomes the source of DNS information for the entire network.

DHCP in a switched network. The Cisco DHCP server allows organizations to use DHCP in a large switched network. The depletion of IP addresses on the Internet has forced organizations to use Classless Inter-Domain Routing (CIDR) blocks or groups of Class C network numbers to build physical networks with more than 256 nodes. This has created a problem for network administrators who want to use DHCP on large switched networks with more than 256 nodes.

Organizations building large switched networks with TCP/IP assign multiple logical IP networks on a single physical switched network. At the same time, organizations want to take advantage of DHCP to dynamically configure a large number of PCs on their network. The Cisco DHCP server supports address pools that contain multiple logical networks on the same physical network.

TCP/IP servers for Windows NT. The Cisco DNS/DHCP Manager has a complete range of TCP/IP services used to build and maintain a TCP/IP network. The Cisco DNS/DHCP Manager provides a DNS server for name service, an NTP server for time synchronization, TFTP to load binary images and configuration files to network devices (including Cisco routers and switches), and a syslog server for logging error messages from network devices over the network. All of these services are easily configured with a graphical user interface.

Key Features and Benefits

Cisco DNS/DHCP Manager provides the following features and benefits:

DNS easier to manage. Today, DNS is managed by editing text files on a UNIX system. The syntax of the text files, known as *zone files,* is cumbersome and prone to errors, and most organizations have one person who has spent months becoming the DNS expert.

The Cisco DNS/DHCP Manager has a graphical DNS management tool that eliminates the need to edit zone files. All entries in the DNS are checked for proper syntax and duplicate IP addresses, and PTR records for the "reverse lookup" are automatically generated. Because a graphical user interface is used, administrators learn DNS management quickly.

Improved security and reliability. Many TCP/IP services—the World Wide Web, NFS, RLOGIN, and FTP—use information in DNS to verify that incoming connections are from a legitimate computer. If both an A record and a PTR record are registered for the incoming client, the server assumes that a responsible network administrator has assigned this name and address. If the information in the DNS is incomplete or missing, many servers will reject connections from the client.

When adding a new node to DNS, the Cisco Domain Name Manager automatically adds the PTR record. The PTR record is the mapping between an IP address and a DNS name and is also known as "reverse mapping." Forgetting to add the PTR record is one of the most common mistakes when managing a DNS server.

TCP/IP network easier to configure. The DHCP protocol allows managers to add new nodes to a network without statically defining IP addresses for every node. Nodes, particularly PCs, use the DHCP protocol to dynamically get configuration information, including the IP address, domain name, default router, and subnet mask, from a DHCP server.

Dynamic updates to DNS. The Cisco DHCP server dynamically updates DNS with the domain name and the IP address allocated to the DHCP client.

DHCP server in a switched network. Today, many organizations are building large, flat networks with switching and routing technology. This has caused problems with the deployment of DHCP and the use of multiple logical networks on the same physical network. The Cisco DHCP server can combine pools of IP addresses from multiple networks into a single large pool of addresses. The DHCP server also supports BootP to enable you to manage BootP and DHCP from one server.

Enhanced TCP/IP services for Windows NT and UNIX. The Cisco DNS/DHCP Manager ships additional network services that efficiently maintain a TCP/IP network:

- A DNS server for name service
- NTP for times synchronization
- TFTP to load binary images and configuration files to network devices including routers
- A syslog server to log error messages from network devices over the network.

All of these services are configured with an easy-to-use graphical user interface.

Specifications

Hardware

The Cisco DNS/DHCP Manager is available for the following platforms:

- Sun Solaris 2.4. or greater (SPARC)
- HP-UX 10.0 or greater
- IBM AIX 4.1.3 or greater (Power2 and PowerPC)
- Windows NT 3.51 or greater (Intel)

NOTE: *Windows NT is supported in version 1.1 and later releases of the Cisco DNS/DHCP Manager and Cisco Server Suite 1000. The Cisco DNS/DHCP Manager will include licenses for the Domain Name Manager and the Cisco Server Suite 1000. The Domain Name Manager is licensed based on the number of DNS nodes managed. You can upgrade a license to the next tier.*

Cisco DNS/DHCP Manager Overview

This section introduces the Cisco DNS/DHCP Manager (CDDM) and the Cisco Server Suite 1000 (CSS1000). The CDDM is a suite of servers and tools that:

- Simplifies DNS management (see the next section, "Simplifying DNS Management with the Cisco Domain Name Manager Server").
- Automatically updates the DNS when DHCP and BootP clients boot off the network (see "Updating DNS Via the Cisco DHCP/BootP Server" later in the chapter).
- Supports DHCP and BootP clients on multiple logical networks that reside on a single physical network segment (see "Supporting Multiple Logical Networks on the Same Physical Network" later in the chapter).
- Simplifies network service management (see "Service Management" later in the chapter).

Simplifying DNS Management with the Cisco Domain Name Manager Server

The cornerstone of the CDDM is the Domain Name Manager (DNM) Server, which lets you manage zone data—typically, host names and addresses—dynamically from across a network. Traditionally, zone data originates as ASCII text files called zone files, which primary name servers read when they start and propagate to "secondary" name servers via zone transfers (see Figure 12-1). Many network managers choose to advertise only their secondary name servers and dedicate their primary name servers to perform zone transfers. The CDDM supports this approach by assigning zone transfer and name resolution to separate servers.

The DNM server takes over the role of zone transfers (see Figure 12-2) but leaves the role of name resolution to DNS servers. DNS servers configured as "secondary" name servers can obtain zone transfers from a DNM, but the DNM must not be advertised as a name server with NS (name server) records because it does not resolve names. Every time you modify the DNM server's database, the DNM server increments the appropriate zone serial numbers so that the corresponding secondary

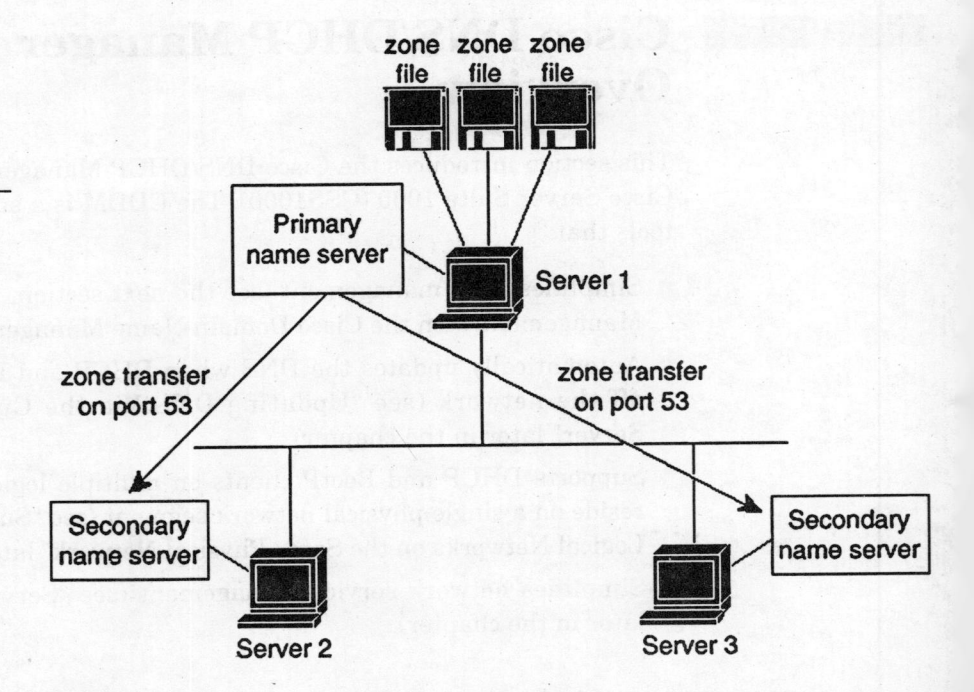

Figure 12-1
Using a primary name server for zone transfers.

Dynamic DNS Review

Figure 12-2
Using a DNM server for zone transfers.

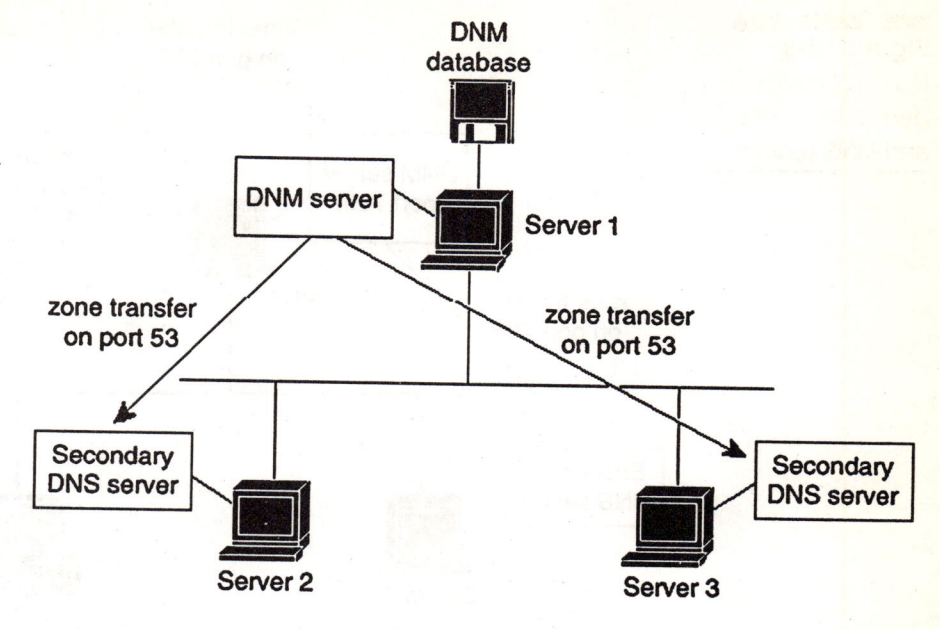

name servers can detect a change in the zones for which they are authoritative and request zone transfers.

Normally, you could not run a DNM server and a DNS server on the same host because both servers listen on port 53 for zone transfer requests. The CDDM, however, includes an enhanced DNS server that can request zone transfers over any port. The Cisco DNS server is based on BIND (Berkeley Internet Name Daemon) 4.9.3, so you can both use existing zone files and receive new zone data from your DNM server.

If you configure the DNM server to perform zone transfers on port 705, any host running the Cisco DNS server can obtain zone transfers on that port, and DNS resolvers can still obtain name service from the DNS server running on port 53. For example, in Figure 12-3, Server 1 is running the DNM server configured to provide zone transfers over port 705. The co-resident DNS server is configured to be secondary for zones in the DNM database and obtains zone transfers on port 705 for those zones. Because Server 1's DNM server only performs zone transfers on port 705, Server 2's DNS server must also be configured to obtain zone transfers from Server 1 on port 705.

DNM Clients Editing zone files manually can take a long time, and making mistakes along the way can cause DNS servers to stop working. Typical mistakes include syntax errors and incorrect, unnecessary, or missing entries.

Figure 12-3
Running co-resident Cisco DNM and DNS servers.

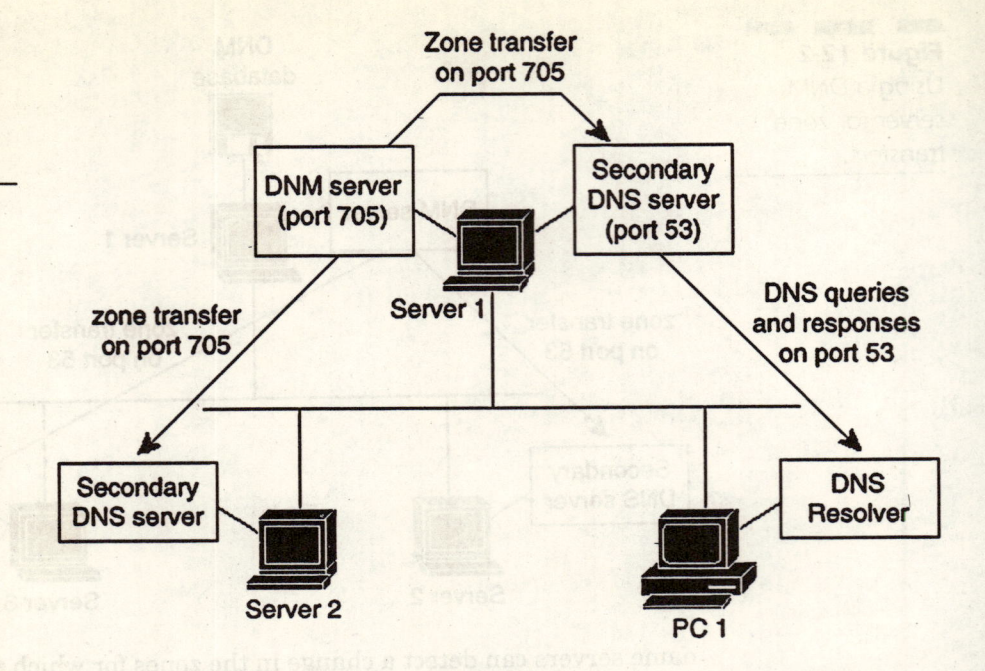

The DNM server maintains a single database instead of multiple zone files. Instead of editing the database manually with a text editor, you can manage the DNM server's database via a DNM client program. The DNM client and server communicate via a proprietary, operating-system-independent protocol, so you can manage any DNM server from any host running a DNM client.

DNM Browser The CDDM and CSS1000 include a client called the DNM Browser that simplifies everyday DNS management tasks such as adding new hosts or changing host addresses and lets you configure DNM servers from remote hosts. The DNM Browser presents a view of the domain name space in an outline-style layout that makes it easy to browse through domains.

Specifically, the DNM Browser does the following:

- Automatically modifies inverse mappings when you add new hosts and propagates name server and "glue" records when you create subdomains
- Checks for domain name conflicts
- Finds available IP addresses on specified networks
- Imports existing DNS zone files and exports zone files and UNIX-style host tables

On UNIX platforms, the DNM Browser is an X client. On Windows NT, the DNM Browser is a native Windows application. You can install the DNM Browser without installing the CDDM or CSS1000. In addition, the DNM Browser does not require a license key, so you can install the DNM Browser on multiple hosts.

DHCP/BootP Server   The Cisco DNS/DHCP Manager includes a DHCP/BootP server that can be configured to behave as a DNM client. When the DHCP/BootP server starts, it automatically updates the DNM server with IP addresses and host names for dynamic hosts such as diskless workstations and mobile computers. The DHCP/BootP server also tells the DNM server to create a special DHCP-only subdomain for the dynamic hosts. If the DHCP-only subdomain already exists, the DNM server deletes the old domain and creates an entirely new domain using the new DHCP information.

DNM Users   To manage a DNM server's database from a DNM client, you must have a DNM server account. When you connect to a DNM server, you must supply a valid user name and password. If you use the DNM Browser, you enter your account information when prompted. If you use the DHCP/BootP server to manage the DNM server, you must configure the DHCP/BootP server with valid account information. (For information on creating DNM user accounts, see the *Cisco DNS/DHCP Manager Administrator's Guide*.)

Cisco Server Suite 1000   Your site may require a relatively low number of DNM servers to serve your site's DNS and DHCP/BootP servers. To take full advantage of Cisco's DNS and DHCP servers, Cisco offers the Cisco Server Suite 1000, which provides all of the CDDM's features except for the DNM server.

You can install Cisco Server Suite 1000's enhanced TCP/IP services and manage DNS from your UNIX and Windows hosts, while maintaining a central DNS database on your Cisco DNS/DHCP Managers. Figure 12-4 illustrates how you can combine CDDM and CSS1000 systems.

Updating DNS Via the Cisco DHCP/BootP Server

By configuring the Cisco DHCP/BootP server to behave as a DNM client, you can update DNS when the DHCP/BootP server starts. Note that the

Figure 12-4
Combining Cisco DNS/DHCP Manager and Cisco Server Suite 1000 hosts.

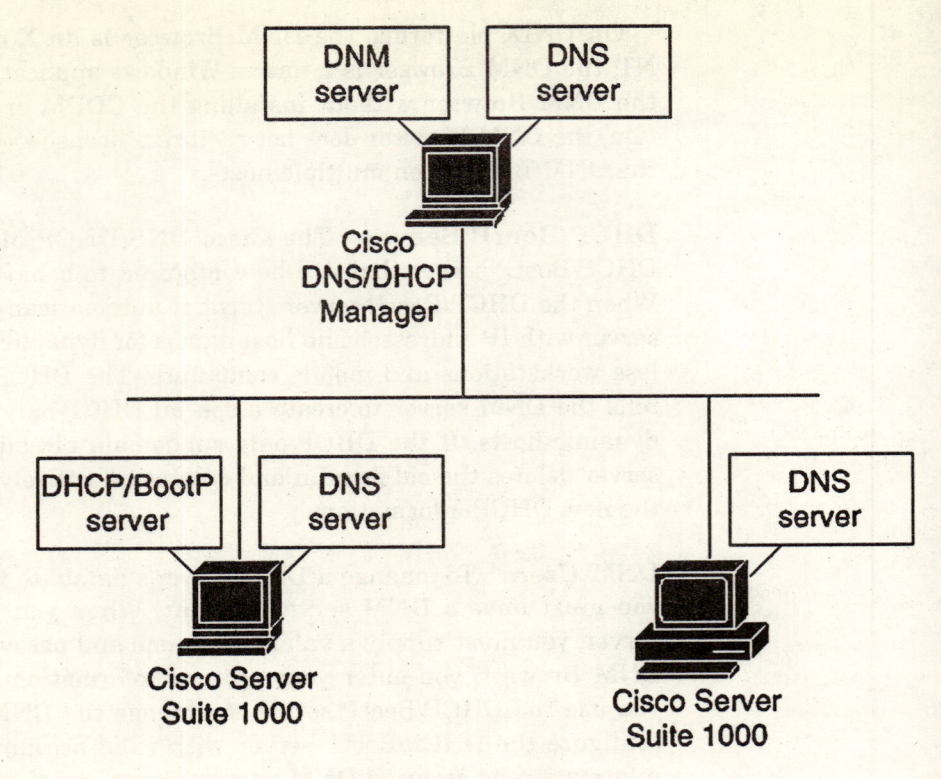

DHCP/BootP server can only update the DNM server with information from its DHCP database. The DHCP/BootP server does not propagate information from its BootP database to the DNM server.

Traditionally, DHCP and BootP databases are managed independently of the DNS (see Figure 12-5). With most DHCP and BootP servers, every time you add a host entry to the DHCP database, you must also add corresponding domain names for the host: one in the parent domain and another in the *in-addr.arpa* domain. Failure to update DNS when you update a DHCP database will prevent hosts from reaching DHCP clients by host name.

The Cisco DHCP/BootP server eliminates the need to manually coordinate the DNS with your DHCP or BootP databases by dynamically updating zones dedicated to your DHCP clients. Figure 12-6 illustrates how to use a Cisco DNM server to automatically link a DHCP database with an authoritative name server.

The DHCP/BootP server supports a new ub tag that lets you define which database entries it needs to propagate to DNS via the DNM server. When the DHCP/BootP server starts, the DHCP/BootP server

Dynamic DNS Review

Figure 12-5
Coordinating DHCP and DNS databases manually.

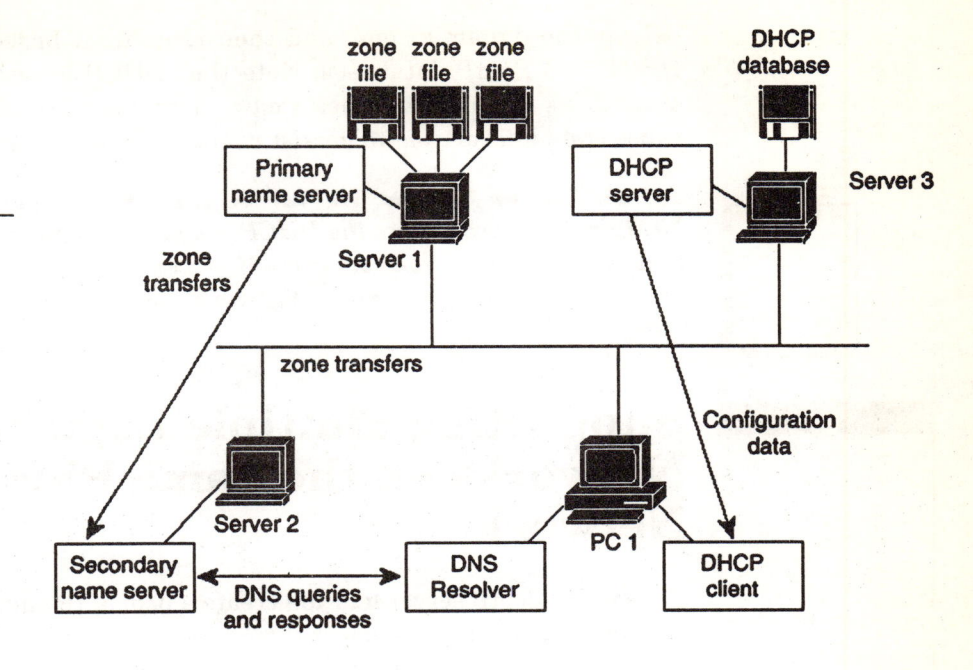

Figure 12-6
Coordinating DHCP and DNS databases via a DNM server.

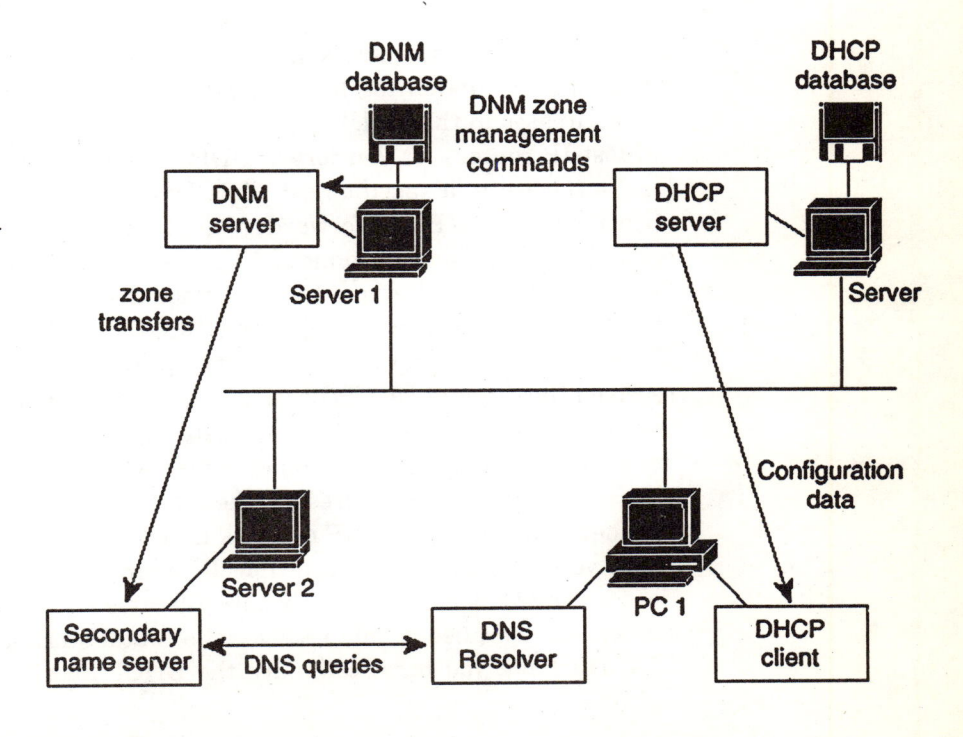

deletes the dynamic zone, and then rebuilds it based on the current DHCP and BootP databases. Note that DHCP leases IP addresses to other hosts when existing hosts move from one net to another. This may cause stale information to persist in the DNM database for a short time.

> *NOTE:* If you configure the DHCP/BootP server to automatically update a "dynamic" zone via a DNM server, make sure no other DHCP server is configured to manage the same zone.

Supporting Multiple Logical Networks on the Same Physical Network

The DHCP/BootP server lets you create a pool of IP addresses that spans multiple logical subnets, using the sc (subnet continuation) option tag, a functional extension of DHCP. This option tag is useful when you need to pool addresses from different networks, such as two Class C networks or a Class B and a Class C network. For example, suppose you need to offer a pool of 400 addresses and your network is composed of two Class C networks. The sc option tag lets you combine the two subnets and put all 400 addresses in the pool.

Most IP routers let you forward DHCP/BootP requests received on a local interface to a specific host. This forwarding feature is often called "BootP helper" or "BootP forwarder." On Cisco routers, BootP forwarding is controlled by the IOS command ip helper-address. When routers forward DHCP/BootP requests, they place their own IP addresses in the DHCP/BootP packet in a field called "GIADDR." The router inserts the IP address of the interface (called the "primary" interface) on which it received the original DHCP/BootP request. The DHCP/BootP server uses the address in the GIADDR field to determine the IP subnet from which the request originated so it can determine which pool of addresses to use before allocating an IP address to the DHCP/BootP client.

When you run multiple IP network numbers on the same physical network, you typically assign multiple IP addresses to a router interface. Because the DHCP/BootP server only allocates addresses on the primary subnet, and because it only receives the router's primary address in the GIADDR field, you must configure the DHCP/BootP server to associate the other network addresses with the primary address using the new `sc` tag. You can specify an arbitrary number of secondary address pools in the DHCP configuration, to make all addresses in the primary and secondary entries available to DHCP clients on the corresponding network segments. DHCP entries that contain `sc` tags must appear after the entry for the primary subnet in the DHCP configuration editor's entry list.

You must also add `sc` option tags to entries for "static" hosts (that is, entries for hosts with specific hardware addresses) on subnets that are part of the conceptual subnet. Static host entries require `sc` option tags to indicate to the DHCP server that the static IP address is actually on the network segment that the GIADDR field indicates.

Service Management

All CDDM servers are controlled by a "master" server called NetControl. You can use NetControl alongside the master server provided with your computer's operating system (for example, `inetd` on UNIX platforms), but you must make sure no servers requiring the same port are running under the master server and Cisco's NetControl simultaneously. For example, to use the Cisco DNS server on HP/UX, you must disable `named` (the DNS server supplied with HP/UX).

Supporting Servers

The Cisco DNS/DHCP Manager and Cisco Server Suite 1000 include the following "supporting" servers:

- NTP server
- TFTP server
- SYSLOG server

Service Configuration Manager

The Cisco DNS/DHCP Manager and Cisco Server Suite 1000 provide a configuration utility called the Service Configuration Manager (SCM) that lets you configure and manage all CDDM servers that run under NetControl. The SCM provides a graphical interface to configuration parameters that you would otherwise have to modify manually with a text editor.

On UNIX platforms, the SCM is an X client. On Windows NT, the SCM is a native Windows application. For details on managing and configuring the CDDM servers, see the *Cisco DNS/DHCP Manager Administrator's Guide*.

Ultimately, you will configure CDDM servers with the SCM and continue to configure all other native servers with the tools provided by your operating system. If your network already relies on a server that CDDM replaces, you probably will not want to stop the existing server until the new server is configured and tested. To simplify the migration from existing servers, you can configure CDDM servers to either use existing configuration files (for example, standard NTP configuration files) or import data from existing files (such as BIND zone files) before saving the data in a new format.

Competitive Automation's JOIN BootP, DHCP, and DDNS

BooTP

This section describes options for configuring BootP services with JOIN. BootP options include:

- Traditional BooTP—Using an existing booptab file to add static BootP clients to a network
- Dynamic BootP—allocating permanent addresses from a pool for BootP clients
- Finite BootP—Time-limited leasing of IP addresses to BootP clients

The technical aspects of BootP and DHCP overlap in significant ways. JOIN DHCP Server software takes advantage of the technical similarities between BootP and DHCP while protecting existing investments in both areas. JOIN DHCP Servers support a variety of BootP options that add flexibility to network administration in the following LAN environments:

- Networks using traditional BootP
- Networks with mobile and short-term BootP client machines
- Networks with BootP machines in transition to DHCP

Traditional BootP

JOIN provides both DHCP and BootP services in a single process. This service takes the place of an existing BootP server, and JOIN's BootP service can be customized to accommodate special requirements.

NOTE: By default, BootP is not enabled. To enable BootP service, select `BootP compatibility` *in the Server/Security dialog of the GUI.*

Basic Service   The JOIN DHCP server seamlessly takes the place of an existing BootP server while adding DHCP functionality to the network for those clients capable of using it. Just as BootP server software consults the bootptab file for IP addresses and other configuration information, JOIN uses a configuration file called dhcpcap for the same purpose.

A sample entry in the dhcpcap file for a BootP client that is configured with the IP address 192.245.139.199 is shown below:

```
bootpclient:\
:ht=1:\
:ha=aabbbbbbbbaa:\
:ip=192.245.139.199:\
:bf=/bootfilename:\
:gw=192.245.139.254:
```

Use of a common file structure simplifies the administration of legacy BootP equipment with JOIN. For instance, to completely migrate current clients from a BootP server to the JOIN server, the only configuration required is to rename the bootptab file to dhcpcap when initially configuring JOIN. Preexisting bootptab files can be appended to the dhcpcap file at any time, provided there is no conflict (overlap) between DHCP IP ranges and the IP addresses found in the bootptab file. The administrator must not allow IP addresses intended for BootP clients to appear in any IP ranges defined for DHCP clients.

Dynamic BootP

Traditional BootP service is based on a static file of hardware address-to-IP address mappings, where clients are expected to remain on a particular network. The `Check BOOTP Client Net` **parameter eliminates the** possibility of an invalid IP address being allocated to a roving BootP client, but it does not allow the assignment of an IP address to a client that has moved away from its "home" network.

NOTE: *For detailed descriptions of BootP service parameters, refer to "BootP Service: Details" coming up in this chapter.*

Competitive Automation offers a Dynamic BootP feature that permits a BootP client to be configured with an available IP address that is appropriate for the network to which the client is connected. With Dynamic BootP, the BootP client requests an address in the usual manner. If the JOIN server finds that an appropriate static BootP entry for the device does not exist in its dhcpcap file, it examines the list of available IP addresses for the network and replies with the first available address from that pool. A permanent lease is then added to the JOIN database for the client that requested BootP service. This is much different than in the case of a static BootP client, for which no entry appears in the lease database.

If a static address is defined in dhcpcap, but the client appears on a different net, the client will not be given an address from the pool.

Finite BootP

The server can use Dynamic BootP in a way that mimics DHCP. With Finite BootP, the entry added to JOIN's database for Dynamic BootP clients is a temporary lease that expires after the lease time applicable for that node, subnet, group, or the default as configured in the server.pcy file.

A BootP client is incapable of renewing its lease except by reboot, so eventually, the lease expires. When the lease time expires, the BootP client's IP address is available for reuse by another client (either DHCP or BootP). Should the address be required by the server for allocation to another device, the server will ping the BootP client's address to check if it is still in use. If a reply is received before ping timeout, the server reactivates the client's address in its database by extending the lease. The lease is extended according to the value assigned to the BootP client lease extension (`bp_auto_extension`) parameter.

NOTE: *When the* `bp_auto_extension` *is set to 0, finite BootP is disabled and Dynamic BootP requests are given permanent leases.*

BootP Service: Details

The JOIN DHCP Server can be modified to accommodate special requirements. These BootP service parameters descriptions suggest how you customize BootP service to control server responses.

Minimum BootP Packet Size A significant number of BootP client implementations can be expected on a single network. The `Minimum BOOTP Packet Size` parameter is used to selectively ignore requests based on their size. This parameter sets a size threshold to control the size of incoming BootP packets. The default size is 300 bytes.

Expand BootP Packet The `Expand BOOTP Packet` parameter is used to respond to BootP clients with a configurable packet size. Typically, a returned packet is 300 bytes or the same size as the request packet. By default, the BootP packet returned to the client is the same size as the request packet. The `Expand BOOTP Packet` parameter can be toggled on and off to expand the reply to full size, or 548 bytes. The default setting is `off`.

Check BootP Client Net The `Check BOOTP Client Net` parameter is used to ensure the IP address is consistent with the server-configured network structure. When the `Check BOOTP Client Net` parameter is enabled, the server checks that the client is connected to the logical network for which the address is valid. This prevents the server from giving a BootP client currently connected to subnet X an administrator-specified IP address for subnet Y. If an address is inconsistent, the following entry is made to the JOIN log file:

```
client aa:bb:bb:bb:bb:aa is on net X inconsistent
with static BootP IP address Y
```

`Check BOOTP Client Net` requires that the netmasks file contain the network numbers and masks for any non-standard IP networks.

Provisional TTL (Time-To-Live) The `Provisional TTL` parameter is used to configure the server to ignore repeated BootP requests by creating a "blackout" period. In the context of BootP service, TTL is interpreted as the time period following the reply during which the server will ignore further client requests. Modifying `Provisional TTL` saves the server from processing repeat requests and reduces network traffic.

Ping BootP Clients When first allocating an address to a DHCP client, JOIN sends an ICMP echo request or ping. By default, however, the server does not ping BootP clients. To extend this functionality to BootP service, enable the `Ping BOOTP Clients` parameter.

BootP Client Lease Extension If `BOOTP Client Lease Extension` is nonzero, the request is processed with a special kind of Dynamic BootP service called *Finite BootP*. The initial lease time for this client is that configured for the network, but upon lease expiration, the server can renew the lease with a lifetime specified by this parameter. The lease extension occurs only if the IP address is required by another client, and the server receives a ping response that indicates the original BootP client is still using the IP address.

BootP Address from Pool The `BOOTP Address from Pool` parameter is used to provide BootP clients with an address from an IP address range rather than from a static entry in the dhcpcap file.

Server Logic

How JOIN selects a New IP Address When a DHCP DISCOVER message is received by the server, JOIN's first action is to determine from what network the client has broadcast its request. The client is assumed to be on the same network as the interface on which the discover packet arrived—unless the packet was received from a relay agent. In the latter case, the relay agent will include in the message the IP address of the interface on which it received the client's DHCP DISCOVER. Either way, the server then computes the subnet using information in the etc/join/netmasks file.

Once the subnet number has been determined, JOIN is able to begin constructing a "DHCP offer" for the client. The offer is assembled in two steps:

1. An available IP address is obtained.
2. Client configuration parameters are resolved.

Obtaining an IP Address To get an IP address for the client, JOIN consults its "free list" of available addresses for the client subnet. A free list (by default, 8 elements long) is maintained in memory for every subnet for which an IP range has been specified. If the first IP address is in use, as indicated by a response to a ping, the next available address is used.

How JOIN Resolves a Client Configuration

IP address selection is based only on the subnet of the client. The remaining configuration can also be determined by subnet, optionally in combination with other information provided by the client. Other fields include Client Identifier and Client Class. Only the Client Identifier is provided by popular PC clients. Network computers (NCs) issue both the Client Identifier and Client Class. Competitive Automation's DHCP client for UNIX supports the client class.

DHCP parameters are most conveniently manipulated using xjoin's Subnets, Nodes, and Groups (SNG) dialogs. As described in Chapter 7, "Subnets, Nodes, and Groups," of the *JOIN Server Administrator's Guide*, typical assignment of parameters falls along membership in one of the following sets: a node corresponds to a particular client identifier, a subnet corresponds to a client network, and a group corresponds to a collection of nodes, subnets, or other group objects.

In a more abstract sense, an SNG dialog defines a set of parameters. Each group of parameters has a key. A key is a single field, or combination of fields, that identifies a particular scope of validity for those parameters.

The following list describes the keys that are used to resolve a configuration, including the client class:

`client identifier-subnet` The parameters are valid for the particular client machine on that particular network. The parameters are not valid for a different client on the network or for the specific client on a different network.

`subnet-client class` The parameters are valid for the specific class of machine on the specific network.

`client identifier` The parameters are valid for the client, regardless of the network, unless overridden by a `client identifier-net` combination.

`client class` The parameters are valid for the class, regardless of the network.

`net` The parameters are valid for the network, regardless of the client identifier.

`no key` Do not use a key when you want to factor out parameters with identical values. For example, assume a configuration where all networks use the same domain name and the same name servers. If you name an entry with these two data items, that name can be referenced from all other records that require those values.

Dynamic Naming

How Dynamic Naming Works Part of JOIN's flexibility is the ability for the network administrator to select the naming mechanism of the client name/IP address association. System naming conventions vary with the operating system (NT differs from UNIX), the user organization, and administrative preferences. JOIN performs two main functions with respect to naming:

- JOIN supplies a name to the client when requested.
- JOIN updates the name service with that name (and IP address).

The network administrator can set the following parameters to direct name-related functions:

Function	Parameter
Supply a name to the client	Assign Name by HW Address
	Assign Name by IP Address
	Accept Client Name
	Ignore Name Owner
Update the name service	Name Service
	Name Service Updatable

For example, the most common pairing of these parameters is as follows:

```
Assign Name by HW Address = true
Name Service = DNS
```

Naming the Client

JOIN server software tracks, maps, and validates client names using the `Assign Name by HW Address`, the `Assign Name by IP Address`, and the `Accept Client Name` parameters. The following sections describe the dynamics of these parameters in the role of naming a client.

Assign Name by Hardware Address Using the `Assign Name by HW Address` parameter, JOIN can track the mapping of the client identifier (CID) to the client name. In this case, a client retains the same name unless it changes domain. JOIN's ability to track mapping within a domain is needed for DHCP clients that have shareable resources. Domain changes occur only if the domain implied by the dhcpcap file changes (e.g., because it has been edited or because the client has moved to a different network that is not in the previous domain). JOIN cannot track a name across domains. If a domain changes, JOIN does not remember the name in the previous domain.

Assign Name by IP Address   Using the `Assign Name by IP address` parameter, JOIN determines an IP address for a client. The assigned IP address is looked up in the underlying name service, and the corresponding name is given to the client. This binding of names to IP addresses is fixed. Because of the name service lookup, there is no need for a dynamically updateable name service. This configuration is simpler than assigning a name by hardware address.

Clients change their names when they get a different IP address from the server, and name changes occur frequently with DHCP. When clients share resources on the network, this constant changing of names severely impairs referencing. The `Assign Name by IP Address` parameter is effective for networks where DHCP clients do not share resources with the network.

Accept Client Name   If `Accept Client Name` is set to `true` and the client sends a name, JOIN checks that the proposed assignment does not contradict the policy. If the name is not valid, the name will be ignored. Both `Assign Name by Hardware Address` and `Assign Name by IP Address` are complicated by the fact that the DHCP protocol allows the client to suggest its own name. A client name may have been hand-configured by a system administrator or user. Or, it may have been remembered from a previous invocation of the DHCP protocol. See Figure 12-7 for a logical view of this process.

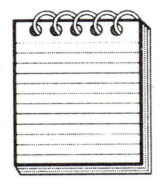

NOTE: All names and domains must be in lowercase. If a name is sent from the client, it will be converted to lowercase.

If both the `Accept Client Name` and `Assign Name by Hardware Address` parameters are set to `true`, JOIN will use the suggested client name if it is valid and it does not belong to another client.

Figure 12-7
Logical view of dynamic naming.

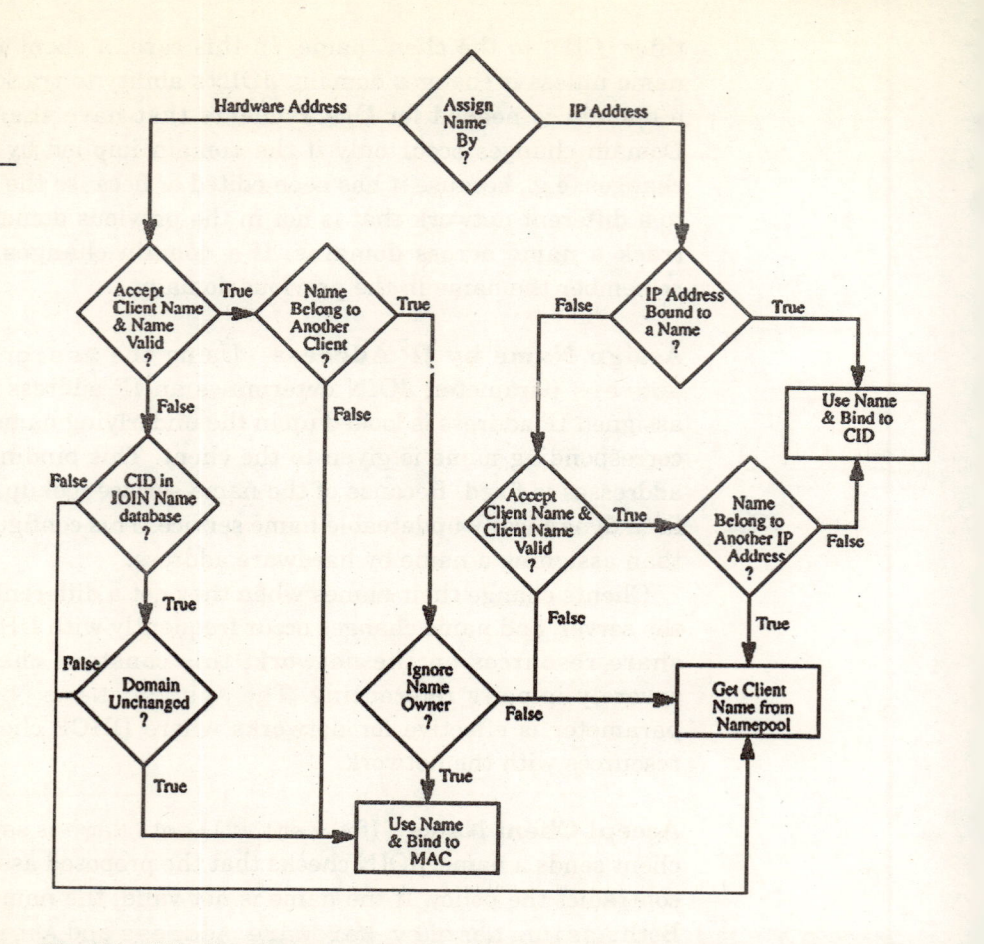

[Flowchart: Assign Name By? → Hardware Address branch: Accept Client Name & Name Valid? → True → Name Belong to Another Client? → False → CID in JOIN Name database? → True → Domain Unchanged? → True → Use Name & Bind to MAC. IP Address branch: IP Address Bound to a Name? → True → Use Name & Bind to CID; False → Accept Client Name & Client Name Valid? → True → Name Belong to Another IP Address? → True → Get Client Name from Namepool. Ignore Name Owner? branches feed into Use Name & Bind to MAC and Get Client Name from Namepool.]

> **NOTE:** Normally, a name sent by a client will match the name in the JOIN database. If it does not match, the first name remains "owned" by that client, even when JOIN assigns a new name. The old name will not be attached to any IP address, and it will not show up in the JOIN graphical user interface.

New Client A new client will have a CID that is not in any server database, but the server must determine the name. If the JOIN server does not get a client name from the settings described above, it will get a name from the `namepool` database. Names in the `namepool` are available on a per-domain, per-server basis. Once a name has been used from the pool, it will not be used again. Database f (`dbf.btr`) tracks the status of names in the pool and ensures they are used precisely once.

Updating the Name Service To authenticate route, address, and perform naming-related functions for other computers on the network, JOIN supports three different name services and one pseudo-name service. The following sections describe the dynamics of these services in the role of updating the name service database.

JOIN-supported name services include:

- DNS
- NIS
- NIS+
- /etc/hosts (known as "Local" in the JOIN GUI)

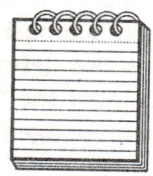

NOTE: The Local name service indicates that /etc/hosts is the repository of the name-address bindings.

In principle, a client may have a name that is different for each of the three name services. However, the DHCP protocol only allows one name to be returned. The name that JOIN returns is the one defined by the name service defined in the server.pcy file by the parameter `name service`.

Together with the name-domain, the name defines a unique identifier for a client, the fully qualified domain name (FQDN). Just as the name may be different in each of the first three name services, so may the domain. Unlike the name, DHCP provides a mechanism for returning three separate domain names.

When the name service is described as being name service updateable, JOIN will perform the update synchronously with its other operations. However, if the name service cannot be updated dynamically, then the system administrator must perform this task. The jdbdump utility is available to extract name and IP address assignments in a form suitable for use with UNIX-style filters.

JOIN's Internal Name-Address Database JOIN maintains its own local database that it uses to track the association of names with IP addresses and CIDs. JOIN does not act as a name service. The JOIN database cannot be queried by entities that wish to resolve names to IP addresses. The JOIN database is used to perform the following services:

- Track the association of names to CIDs
- Track the association of names to IP addresses
- Provide a local database for efficient lookup

The jdbmod utility is available for preloading or reloading the JOIN database with names. Keep in mind that jdbmod does not update name services. Instead, it assumes that name-IPA bindings originated from an authoritative source such as a name service or from a previous invocation of jdbdump.

VLSM

The JOIN DHCP server uses variable-length subnet masks (VLSM) to interpret the netmasks file. The netmasks file defines where, in a binary representation of an IP address, to partition between the network and the host portions of the address. For example, using a bit comparison of a target IP address against its own netmask, a client can determine whether that destination can be reached directly (i.e., is on the "local" network) or must instead be transported to an intermediate agent that will attempt to complete the delivery.

From a DHCP server perspective, the topology of a network, for which it offers configurations, is determined by JOIN's netmasks file. Using the information in /etc/join/netmasks, the server calculates whether a DHCP request comes from a network over which it has administrative authority. The netmasks file also defines the default subnet mask to return to clients when a request is filled.

The subnet masks in JOIN's netmasks file use VLSM as opposed to a "fixed-length" subnet mask. The subnetworks implied by a given netmasks entry depend upon the bit pattern of the network number itself.

Fixed Length vs. VLSM

Routing technologies that are created for large, widely distributed networks require a mechanism for distinguishing between local and remote destinations. In IPv4 routing, this fundamental concept is implemented via a 32-bit netmask.

Fixed Length Fixed-length subnet masking refers to the practice of establishing a network/host partition that is independent, or nearly independent, of the actual decimal value used to label the logical networks. This concept is evident in the Class A/B/C structure imposed early in the history of TCP/IP internetworking. The class of an IP address is determined by its first octet. This octet implies a subnet mask that provides for 8, 16, or 24 bits of network identifier, independent of the actual decimal address within the class.

As an example, consider two "natural" Class B networks: 156.64.0.0 and 139.117.0.0. For practical reasons, it may be useful to divide these networks into subnets using the mask 255.255.255.0. Application of a fixed-length subnet mask to these two networks implies only that each net is subdivided into 256 subnetworks, each capable of supporting 256 host addresses. Subnets such as 156.64.114.0 and 139.117.54.0 are examples.

Network numbers 156.64.0.0 and 139.117.0.0 are treated identically under fixed-length subnet masking. In each case, the subnets implied by the mask are those enumerated in the third octet of the network number. The partition between the network and hosts portion of the address is shifted from its implied position, between the second and third octets (determined by the 2-byte, or 16-bit fixed-length netmask), to a position between the third and fourth octets.

VLSM The artificial dividing point, on the byte boundary, was advocated largely for the convenience of network administrators. However, there are inefficiencies associated with this convenience, and the growth of the Internet has forced TCP/IP users to economize in matters dealing with routing and subnet masks. For these reasons, VLSM has become widely supported. The following examples illustrate how JOIN interprets the netmasks file.

Consider two networks, 156.64.0.0 and 139.117.0.0:

```
139.117.0.0     255.255.255.0
156.64.0.0      255.255.255.0
```

JOIN uses VLSM to interpret the first entry in the netmasks file and creates 256 subnetworks (each containing 256 addresses). However, the second entry implies 16,384 subnetworks (each containing 256 addresses). The difference between the two entries is determined by the bit pattern for 117 compared to that for 64 (0111 0101 compared to 0100 0000). The VLSM binary representation of the network number determines where the original partition between network and host portions of the bitfield actually lies.

We'll refer to the following examples as netmasks file entries (A) and (B):

```
140.213.164.0   255.255.255.128  (A)
140.213.165.0   255.255.255.128  (B)
```

A completely different set of networks is implied by a file containing (A) or (B). Entry (A) implies the following networks:

```
140.213.164.0
140.213.164.128
140.213.165.0
140.213.165.128
140.213.166.0
140.213.166.128
140.213.167.0
140.213.167.128
```

Entry (B) implies a smaller set of networks:

```
140.213.165.0
140.213.165.128
```

To understand how this structure results from entry (A), ignore the leading 2-octet "prefix" and consider the remaining bit pattern of the next 2 octets in both the network number and the mask:

```
164.0 = 10100100.0000 0000   255.128 = 1111 1111.1000 0000
```

VLSM means that with this mask we can use 3 bits in the above example as part of the network number: 2 bits "left over" from the third octet in the original IP network number, and the first bit of the fourth octet. This differs from traditional subnet masks, which would "waste" the last 2 bits of the third octet because of the artificial byte boundary. Possible networks are obtained by considering the additional 2^3 (= 8) different values of the 3 bits, resulting in the dotted-decimal values

Entry (B) is interpreted as follows:

```
165.0 = 1010 0101.0000 0000   255.128. = 1111 1111.1000 0000
```

In this example, 1 bit is available for the network definitions.

Addrmask

Addrmask is a utility program that calculates an IP address subnet and mask given a netmasks file. The network administrator uses addrmask to verify the desired assignment of host IP addresses to subnets.

As an example, consider the following netmasks file, which is "cached" in memory when the server or the utility addrmask is run:

Dynamic DNS Review

```
Net             Mask
10.0.0.0        255.255.255.0
10.119.28.0     255.255.255.192
10.119.32.0     255.255.255.192
10.119.34.0     255.255.255.0
10.119.36.0     255.255.255.0
10.119.37.0     255.255.255.192
10.119.38.0     255.255.255.192
```

We wish to know to which subnet(s) the IP addresses 10.119.35.132, 10.119.36.132, 10.119.37.132, and 10.119.38.132 belong. To use addrmask, include the IP addresses of interest as arguments, as shown in the following example:

```
#addrmask 10.119.35.132 10.119.36.132 10.119.37.132
10.119.38.132
Cache is:
Net             Mask
10.0.0.0        255.255.255.0
10.119.28.0     255.255.255.192
10.119.32.0     255.255.255.192
10.119.34.0     255.255.255.0
10.119.36.0     255.255.255.0
10.119.37.0     255.255.255.192
10.119.38.0     255.255.255.192
=================================================
10.119.35.132   mask=0xffffff00=255.255.255.0    subnet=10.119.35.0
10.119.36.132   mask=0xffffff00=255.255.255.0    subnet=10.119.36.0
10.119.37.132   mask=0xffffffc0=255.255.255.192  subnet=10.119.37.128
10.119.38.132   mask=0xffffffc0=255.255.255.192  subnet=10.119.38.128
```

This output of addrmask tells us that 10.119.37.132 is on the network 10.119.37.128, and a client that is offered this address will by default also be offered the netmask 255.255.255.192.

Note that the default client netmask can be overridden by including a different netmask as part of a subnet, node, or group definition. This is useful if the "client's view" of the network is different than the server's, such as may be the case in a switched network.

JOIN DHCP/DDNS Features

JOIN DHCP/DDNS features the following:

- Secondary addressing
- Support for BootP clients
- Dynamic BootP and finite BootP
- Security against unknown clients

- NIS/NIS+ updates
- Secure/nonsecure automatic DNS update
- Supports VLSM
- Supports Windows 95 and NT clients
- Supports RAS servers
- Reporting
- Fault tolerance
- TCP/IP and ATM networks
- Multithreaded server
- Proprietary database
- Y2K and RFC 2131-2 compliancy

Platforms

JOIN DDNS is available for Solaris 2.5/2.6, Solaris x86, HP-UX 10, SunOS, and Digital UNIX 3.2 and 4.0b.

Lucent QIP Enterprise 5.0

Automating IP Services Management

The momentum in communications network development continues to swing in the direction of Internet Protocol (IP) networks. Enterprises of all types and sizes are seeing dramatic increases in data traffic and eagerly anticipate emerging services, such as IP telephony. But growth—in the number of users, the volume of traffic, the number of addresses—must be well managed. Unmanaged growth can lead to breakdowns in network availability and quality of service, or in unacceptable delays.

Lucent Technologies answers the need for IP services management in mid- to large-scale enterprises with Lucent QIP Enterprise 5.0. Since its introduction, QIP Enterprise 5.0 has quickly become a leading method of automating and planning the management of IP name and address services across enterprisewide intranet and global internet systems.

QIP Enterprise 5.0 delivers a user interface that streamlines operations and allows you to plan, model, and build an IP network in ways that truly reflect your corporation's needs, structure, and goals. Because it is designed for high volume/high availability, mission-critical environments, some of the world's largest IP networks have selected QIP Enterprise 5.0 as their strategic solution to automate and manage IP name and address services.

Regulate User Access with Innovative Profiling Capabilities

With QIP Enterprise 5.0, creating a base of network user and device information is an easily executed operation that allows for policy-based network services. Lightweight Directory Access Protocol-enabled (LDAP) Domain Name System (DNS) and Dynamic Host Configuration Protocol (DHCP) servers allow organizations to leverage key information across a common directory services-based network, streamlining administration and improving integration of differing network applications.

Eliminate Major Causes of Network Failure

The underlying architecture of QIP Enterprise 5.0 offers among the most robust set of capabilities available for mid- to large-scale organizations. The DNS and DHCP servers are fully integrated to synchronize updates in real time and run autonomously. This provides maximum flexibility in configuring and deploying services across a distributed network. In addition, the extensive suite of command-line interfaces is a valuable tool for developing custom scripts and workflows. With its highly available DHCP services, LDAP-enabled DNS and DHCP servers, and multimaster database replication capabilities for centralized databases, QIP Enterprise 5.0 virtually eliminates IP service outages—a crucial feature for organizations that demand fault-tolerant, distributed, scalable IP services. QIP Enterprise 5.0's architecture has been fine-tuned in high-volume environments and has proven itself in some of the world's most demanding networks.

Exceed Industry Standards with High-Performance Servers

The QIP DNS Server To provide maximum throughput, performance, and real-time updates with minimal bandwidth consumption, the QIP

DNS Server is multithreaded, fully integrating with the QIP DHCP Server to optimize the synchronization process. The QIP DNS Server runs autonomously from the centralized management function and database server. Together with its support for primary and secondary DNS servers, it delivers a high degree of availability. Remote configuration and management capabilities allow organizations to reduce the DNS technical expertise required at the local administrator level. The QIP DNS Server is standards-compliant, runs on Microsoft Windows NT, Sun Solaris, and Hewlett-Packard HP-UX platforms, and supports implementations of both BIND 4.9.x and BIND 8.x, providing customers with among the greatest deployment options. The QIP DNS Server interoperates with other vendors' BIND 4.9.x- or 8.x-compliant DNS servers. The QIP DNS Server also supports both disk and LDAP-based modes of operation.

The QIP DHCP Server The QIP DHCP Server is also multithreaded to optimize performance. To eliminate any single point of failure and help ensure that services are delivered to the user, it is designed with a failover capability. This many-to-one failover minimizes network configuration hardware requirements and simplifies administration. Updates to DHCP lease information are automatically sent to the appropriate primary and secondary QIP DNS Servers and to QIP Enterprise 5.0's centralized database for audit, reporting, and recovery purposes. The Lucent server is compliant with RFCs 2131 and 2132 and is available on Microsoft Windows NT, Sun Solaris, and Hewlett-Packard HP-UX platforms. The QIP DHCP Server supports both disk and LDAP-based modes of operation. Statistics reporting for tracking server loads is also supported.

Centralize Network Configuration and Planning

QIP Enterprise 5.0 helps enable your entire network to be defined by a set of rules and policies. These include both physical and logical relationships for network objects and users. In this way, QIP Enterprise 5.0 helps ensure network integrity and accessibility on a worldwide basis, as well as a consistent enforcement of administrative and operational procedures. The centralized definition of the network model and the subsequent registration of all devices is the core of QIP Enterprise 5.0's ability to provide effective management of the address space.

Lucent Advantage: QIP Enterprise 5.0

QIP Enterprise 5.0 offers the following features:

- *Flexibility.* Lucent offers a comprehensive suite of IP services that allows network architecture to be tailored to a particular corporation's goals and objectives.
- *Open Design.* Allows easy integration into an existing system.
    - Cross-platform support allows QIP Enterprise 5.0 to operate within heterogeneous environments.
    - LDAP access to directory services.
    - Support for third-party DHCP and DNS services.
    - Integrated into network management systems.
    - Ability to integrate with Microsoft WINS.
    - Extensive suite of CLIs and the API Toolkit.
- *High Performance.* The Windows NT DHCP server can handle 15,000 requests per minute.
- *High Availability.* The QIP Enterprise 5.0 architecture eliminates any single point of failure, delivering uninterrupted IP services to the end user.
- *Scalability.* Manages millions of IP addresses, including some of the largest, distributed IP networks in the world.
- *Industry Leader.* Over 20 percent of the Fortune 500 companies are QIP customers, including 70 percent of Fortune 500 pharmaceutical companies, 50 percent of Fortune 500 telecommunications companies, 33 percent of Fortune 500 diversified financials companies, and the top six commercial Fortune 500 banks.
- *Standards-based.* QIP Enterprise 5.0 is fully RFC compliant.
- *Cost savings.* According to Lucent Technologies, QIP can reduce name and address management costs by 45 percent.

User Profile Management and Class of Service The database within QIP Enterprise 5.0 has been significantly extended to incorporate user-based information, allowing for delivery of network services to each user based on their class of service (see Figure 12-8). The Registration Manager provides an automated process to validate users and assign network access. A user can belong to a single group or multiple groups. The user is allocated a temporary address and then directed to a Web site to self-register. If the user is approved, a valid address is assigned

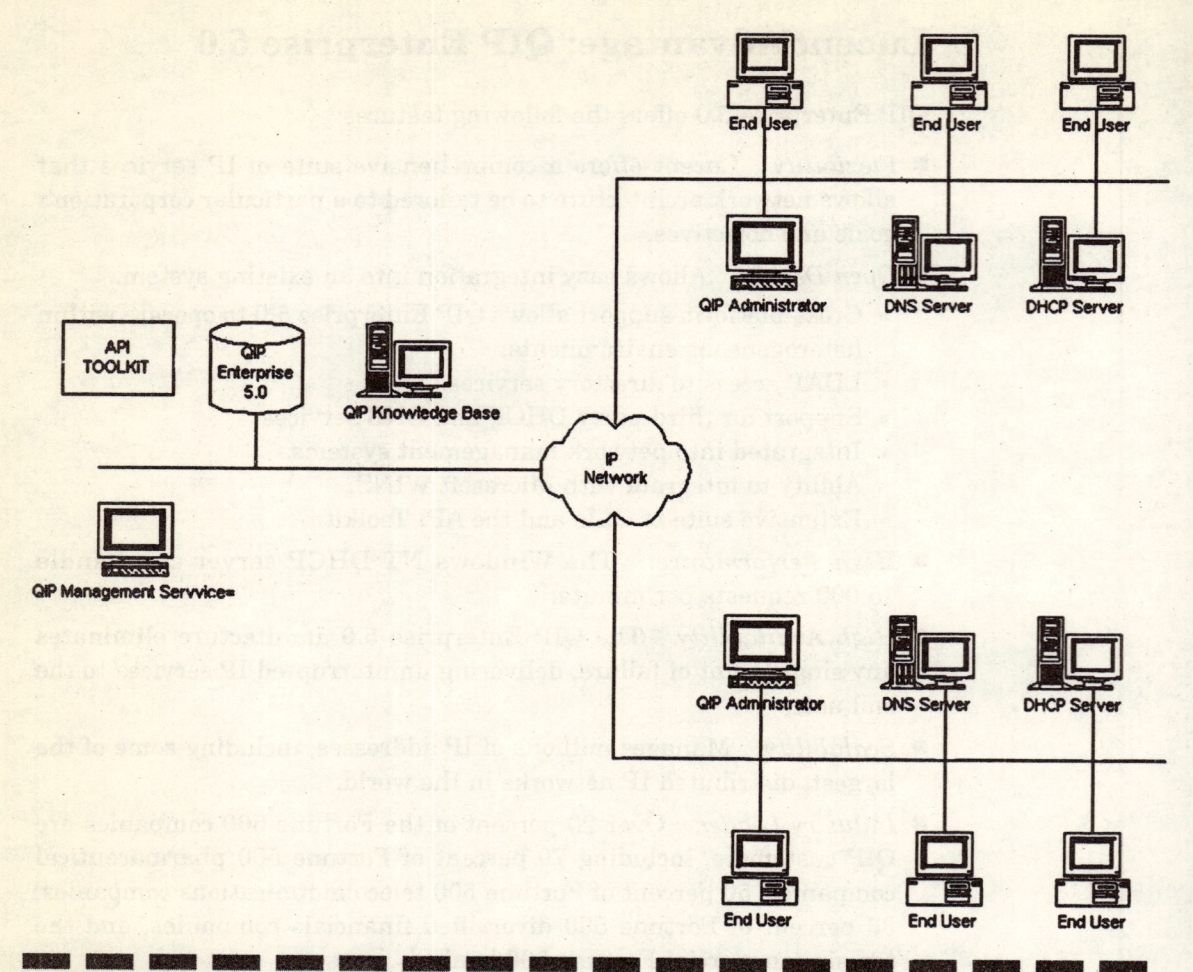

Figure 12-8 QIP Enterprise 5.0 integration.

based on the user's class of service. During the process, the machine access code (MAC) is captured and associated with the user, creating an audit trail to track activities.

Directory Services for Greater Flexibility QIP Enterprise 5.0 integrates leading directory services offerings via the LDAP gateway to directory servers from Novell, IBM, Netscape, or the University of Michigan, and, when available, Microsoft's Active Directory Server. Managers can utilize directory servers to hold configuration and lease information that simplifies administration, offers better control of services, and provides a more fault-tolerant environment. An easy-to-access

Dynamic DNS Review

(via LDAP) common data repository of configuration and binding information simplifies integration to other applications. By allowing directory-based and RDBMS-based data repositories to coexist, QIP Enterprise 5.0 gives administrators complete flexibility to migrate to a directory services model when desired.

Flexible Subnet Management   Today's networks must be updated constantly to keep up with frequent moves, mergers, and reorganizations that cause address spaces to become fragmented. The Subnet Organizer function within QIP Enterprise 5.0 handles true variable-length subnet masking (VLSM) so subnets can be split up easily or joined with other noncontiguous subnets. It also provides a customizable management framework that can assign IP address space to specific administrators or groups of administrators across domains, networks, and subnets. QIP Enterprise 5.0 makes changes and reconfigurations quickly and seamlessly, passing DHCP and DNS inheritances to the newly configured subnets. Thresholds can also be set that, if exceeded, will automatically generate warning messages.

Multi-Master Database Replication   QIP Enterprise 5.0 can scale from low-end to high-end network installations. The new Multi-Master Database Replication feature enhances scalability and reliability, as well as redundancy, and allows you to replicate key centralized IP data across multiple servers. This feature helps ensure uninterrupted workflow across wide area networks. QIP Enterprise 5.0 also allows organizations to optimize transaction performance by balancing transaction loads and application functions across replicated servers. QIP Enterprise 5.0 initially supports replication on the Sybase database running on UNIX.

Multivendor DNS/DHCP Services   QIP Enterprise 5.0 is able to configure and manage DNS and DHCP services from third-party vendors, including IBM and Microsoft. By integrating a greater range of DNS and DHCP servers, QIP Enterprise 5.0 is able to offer more flexibility than other IP services management solutions. In addition, it supports a WINS gateway from the QIP DNS Server running on either a UNIX or a Windows NT Server. Integration modules expedite the installation of QIP Enterprise 5.0 into existing Microsoft DHCP-enabled networks.

Across-Platform Integration   The QIP Enterprise 5.0 solution can be deployed across Microsoft Windows NT, Hewlett-Packard HP-UX, Sun Solaris, and IBM AIX server platforms. The centralized database can utilize either Sybase or Oracle (with some restrictions to platform), while the remote services can run using a flat-file data structure or an LDAPv3-enabled directory services schema using directory server engines from Novell, Netscape, IBM, or the University of Michigan. Plus, QIP Enterprise 5.0 supports IP services from third-party vendors such as Microsoft and IBM. This overall combination provides the highest level of investment protection and flexibility for organizations deploying QIP.

Multiple User Interfaces Network managers and administrators can utilize their tool of choice to work with QIP Enterprise 5.0. A comprehensive graphical user interface running on either Windows NT/95/98 or UNIX Motif may be selected. Or, QIP Enterprise 5.0's customizable Web interface may be used as the preferred interface for ubiquitous, secure access.

Customizable User Fields and Views QIP Enterprise 5.0 is designed to be customized to meet different needs. For instance, you can use the user-definable fields capability to collect information within QIP Enterprise 5.0, which can be used to influence QIP processes or to integrate the product with other critical network applications. Another key feature tailors how network hierarchy diagrams are displayed. These user-definable views improve ease of use by providing customer-specific representations of network objects.

Logical Address Grouping Logical address groupings are a critical feature for service providers who manage space for multiple customers, as well as for organizations that are active in mergers and acquisitions. QIP Enterprise 5.0 can manage multiple logical address grouping (i.e., multiple net 10s) within a single QIP Enterprise 5.0 database. QIP Enterprise 5.0 streamlines this process by allowing an address scheme to have an organization-level designation.

Value-Added Modules Lucent offers a number of value-added modules that are licensed as options to QIP Enterprise 5.0:

- *Registration Manager.* Streamlines network administration and enhances address tracking by identifying each user and dynamically allocating an IP address based on a profile that details levels of service to which the user is entitled.

- *Provisioning Manager.* Automates the creation of subnets and is ideal for organizations defining and deploying large numbers of sub-

Dynamic DNS Review

nets, such as service providers, outsourcers, or large enterprises. By using the Provisioning Manager's rule-based logic, subnets are created that minimize address space usage and optimize utilization of all available address space.

- *Services Manager.* Allows network managers to monitor and control IP services running on servers distributed throughout the network from a single remote location. It enables network managers to define enterprise policies, set performance thresholds, and define conditions when the system issues an alert. This capability means proactive steps can be taken to avoid problems and failures and to help correct failures before they become network outages. The Services Manager even simplifies the process of detecting and stopping rogue DHCP servers that issue IP addresses not in conformance with network policies.

- *API Toolkit.* Offers an extensive set of C/C++ application programming interfaces that can be used to extend and integrate the QIP Enterprise 5.0 system into other critical network applications. These extensions can also be used to create scripts that perform repetitive tasks and eliminate manual intervention.

- *Audit Manager.* Enables network managers and network security personnel to track the history of an address. Whether statically assigned through the database or dynamically assigned by a DHCP server, all history information is available for analysis.

Additional Compatibility Benefits

Following are additional benefits of the QIP Enterprise 5.0 system:

- The QIP DHCP Server can update both primary and secondary DNS servers with resource record information as DHCP leases are granted and deleted.

- QIP Enterprise 5.0 can configure and manage Microsoft's DHCP Server running under Windows NT 4.0.

- QIP's 4.9.x DNS Server running under NT and UNIX supports a WINS gateway.

- QIP's 8.x DNS Server fully supports Incremental Zone File Transfer (RFC 1995; IXFR) across UNIX and NT platforms.

- LDAP-enabled DHCP and DNS servers provide lower maintenance, since configuration and lease information is stored in a directory server. The QIP DHCP and DNS Servers also allow for hot failover to another directory server if the primary cannot be contacted.

IP Management Tools As your IP network continues to grow and diversify, you need automated and scalable management tools to keep pace. Your organization has already made a substantial investment in an IP infrastructure, and the more you grow, the more critical effective management becomes. The Lucent QIP Enterprise 5.0 product family delivers a management platform that provides the building blocks you need to run IP networks efficiently—server, database, and directory access; user profiling; improved security; addressing; and cross-platform interoperability. QIP Enterprise 5.0 is a complete management package, fully customizable and optimized for automated operation.

System Requirements

The QIP Enterprise Server is a central repository for all IP addresses, host names, and machine access code (MAC) address information. The Network Server provides an architected solution that allows communication between the QIP Enterprise Server and other DNS and DHCP servers across a network.

Platforms Supported

QIP Enterprise Server or Network Server:

- Microsoft Windows NT Server 4.0 (Service Pack 3 or higher)
- Hewlett-Packard HP-UX 10.10, 10.20
- Sun Microsystems Solaris 2.5, 2.5.1, 2.6
- IBM AIX 4.1, 4.2

Clients:

- Motif (Solaris 2.5, 2.5.1, 2.6, HP-UX 10.10, 10.20 IBM AIX 4.1, 4.2)
- Microsoft Windows NT Server 4.0 (Service Pack 3 or higher)
- Microsoft Windows NT Workstation 4.0
- Microsoft Windows 95 (4.00.950B or above)
- Microsoft Windows 98
- Web interfaces:
  - Netscape Navigator
  - Microsoft Internet Explorer 3.0 or above
- Command-line interfaces:
  - UNIX
  - Windows NT

Dynamic DNS Review

Hardware Requirements

QIP Enterprise Server for UNIX:

- 75 MHz RISC-based processor or better
- 128 MB memory minimum
- 256+ MB memory recommended
- 350 MB of disk space

Examples:

- Sun Microsystems SPARC Ultra 1
- Hewlett-Packard 9000, Series 800, Model D250

The above requirements will manage up to 100,000 addresses.

Enterprise Server for NT:

- 200 MHz Pentium Processor or better
- 128 MB memory minimum
- 256 MB memory minimum
- 250 MB of disk space (more based on number of objects managed)

Examples:

- Compaq ProSignia
- HP NetServer
- Dell PowerEdge
- IBM POWERServer

QIP for NT will manage up to 30,000 addresses. If more addresses need to be managed, the UNIX Enterprise Server should be considered.

Network Server for UNIX:

- 45 MHz RISC-based processor or better
- 32 MB memory
- 30 MB of disk space

Examples:

- Sun Microsystems SPARC 5
- Hewlett-Packard 9000, Series 800

Network Server for Windows NT:

- 120 MHz Pentium processor or better

- 32 MB memory minimum
- 20 MB of disk space

Examples:

- Compaq Deskpro
- Dell PowerEdge 2200
- HP Vectra
- IBM POWERserver

Clients

Windows NT Workstation or Server:

- 75 MHz Pentium processor or better
- 48 MB of memory minimum
- 64 to 80 MB of memory recommended
- 15 MB of disk space

Windows 95:

- 486 Intel processor or better
- 16 MB of memory minimum
- 32 MB recommended
- 15 MB of disk space

Windows 98:

- 75 MHz Pentium processor or better
- 48 MB of memory minimum
- 64 to 80 MB of memory recommended
- 15 MB of disk space

Motif:

- Same hardware and platform requirements as the network requirements as the network servers for UNIX

Web:

- Servers supported:
  - NCSA's Mosaic (UNIX)
  - Netscape FastTrack and Enterprise
  - UNIX and NT (2.0 or higher)

Dynamic DNS Review

- Microsoft IIS (3.0 and higher)
- Apache HTTP server (UNIX and NT)
- Browsers supported:
  - Netscape Navigator 2.0 and above
  - Microsoft Internet Explorer 3.0 and above

Databases Supported

- Sybase 11.5 (a runtime version is included in the QIP Enterprise 5.0 distribution)
- Oracle 7.3

DNS Servers Supported

QIP DNS (4.9.7 BIND compliant):

- Microsoft Windows NT Server 4.0 (Service Pack 3 or higher)
- Hewlett-Packard HP-UX 10.10, 10.20
- Sun Solaris 2.5, 2.5.1, 2.6

QIP DNS (8.1.2 BIND-compliant):

- Microsoft Windows NT Server (Service Pack 3 or higher)
- Hewlett-Packard HP-UX 10.10, 10.20
- Sun Solaris 2.5, 2.5.1, 2.6

BIND 4.8.x- and 4.9.x-compliant DNS server running on the following platforms:

- Hewlett-Packard HP-UX 10.10, 10.20
- Microsoft Windows NT Server 4.0 (Service Pack 3 or higher)
- IBM AIX 4.1, 4.2
- Sun Solaris 2.5, 2.5.1, 2.6

NOTE: *Additional DNS platforms not listed above can be supported by creating the DNS files on the Enterprise Server, and then transferring to the DNS Server.*

DHCP Servers Supported

QIP DHCP (conforms to RFCs 2131 and 2132) available on:

- Sun Solaris 2.5, 2.5.1, 2.6

- Hewlett-Packard HP-UX 10.10, 10.20
- Windows NT Server 4.0 (Service Pack 3 or higher)
- IBM's DHCP on AIX 4.1, 4.2
- IBM's DHCP on NT (Service Pack 3 or higher)
- Microsoft DHCP Windows NT Server 4.0 (Service Pack 4.0 only)

Bay Networks' NetID

NetID is a solution from Bay Networks, a Nortel Networks Business, for powerful, scalable, fault-tolerant Internet Protocol (IP) addressing, and DNS and DHCP management. NetID automates and integrates IP addressing, as well as DNS and DHCP management. Today, IP networks provide the foundation for business; business is no longer conducted in the boardroom, but over IP—through intranets, extranets, and electronic commerce. As more business applications are deployed over IP, businesses come to depend on the network for more than just e-mail.

Errors in IP addressing and DNS and DHCP management are a major source of downtime in IP networks. As businesses continue to optimize around IP and begin exploring strategies for policy-enabled networking, the elimination of these errors increases in importance. No one wants to run mission-critical applications on a network whose reliability is, at the best of times, unpredictable.

Simplifying IP addressing is at the core of NetID functionality. Providing an overall view of an organization's IP address architecture, NetID removes the major technical barriers to DHCP implementations by enabling dynamic DNS updates and DHCP redundancy, and by implementing full redundancy at every level of the product.

From a central management platform, NetID manages both static and dynamic addresses, and all NetID DNS and DHCP Servers. NetID automates complex management tasks, reducing the time a network manager traditionally has to devote to IP and to DNS and DHCP management (not to mention the time spent solving the problems that result from mistakes in the management of these IP services).

Benefits

Simplifies IP Address Management Tracking IP addresses, maintaining DNS and DHCP services, and performing manual configuration tasks is time-consuming and prone to error. NetID automates these tasks and integrates services that, in the past, network administrators had to perform and maintain manually. With NetID, IP address tracking and DNS and DHCP management become simple administrative tasks.

Provides Enterprisewide DHCP with Dynamic DNS Updates The difficulty in synchronizing DNS and DHCP services has deterred many organizations from taking advantage of the administrative savings DHCP offers. By integrating DNS and DHCP services, NetID enables dynamic DNS updates and overcomes this barrier. NetID support of Berkeley Internet Name Daemon (BIND) 8.1.1 and 8.1.2 (UNIX only) enables standards-based dynamic DNS updates (RFC 2136 and RFC 1996). Therefore, when a NetID DHCP server issues an address to a client, it updates the NetID database and the NetID DNS servers in parallel.

Offers High Network Availability NetID takes an active approach to IP management. Built-in fault tolerance at every level of the NetID solution allows system administrators to intercept problems on the network before they escalate to major network outages. At the database level, NetID supports database replication, ensuring that a backup copy of IP addressing information is always available. Alternate Server Managers can also be configured to maintain an open connection to the database.

In the event of a WAN or database outage, each component of NetID continues to function independently. NetID DNS and DHCP servers operate using their local configurations and update the database once it becomes available. Additionally, NetID DNS and DHCP servers generate alarms and warnings that administrators can view from the NetID Management Console. In the event, however, of an isolated server outage, NetID's support of DHCP redundancy, and its fault-tolerant DNS server, provides backup. This means that isolated outages remain virtually transparent to end users.

Enables Centralized Control with Distributed Management Flexible NetID access controls enable distributed management of IP addressing. Users can be granted access rights down to the subnet, subdomain, and range level, so that access is provided only to those IP addresses under their direct responsibility. NetID also allows for the creation of user groups, which saves time by assigning a common set of access privileges to multiple users.

Open, Scalable, Robust Architecture With a published application programming interface (API) and a published database schema, NetID is a commercial tool that accommodates an organization's many complex needs, especially when it comes to IP management. Organizations can develop their own unique application against NetID, customizing the product's functionality to their environment.

Extensive Platform Support With a Java-enabled interface, NetID can be integrated into an organization's existing infrastructure, regardless of the standard platform. Administrative functionality is provided through a Web browser, so administrators can perform all management tasks—from adding an IP address, to configuring a range of dynamic addresses—from any frames and Java 1.1-capable Web browser.

Ease of Use The NetID Management Console provides an intuitive and familiar platform for management. The browser interface organizes information hierarchically and provides administrators with a graphical overview of the organization's entire IP addressing structure. Also, DNS configuration can be viewed by zone and DHCP configuration by server or subnet.

Comprehensive Management Platform While the NetID Management Console provides a simplified view of an IP address space, it also provides a single point of management for all IP addressing information, as well as DNS and DHCP configuration and management. It is a platform for the administrator to disseminate IP addresses and DNS and DHCP information to the network; at the same time, it acts as a collection point for alarms and warnings.

Eliminates Custom Solutions Many organizations have developed in-house solutions to manage their IP addresses—often a custom database application. Custom solutions, however, have limited functionality, are labor- and capital-intensive, and require highly centralized maintenance. Consequently, a custom solution is not viable for an enterprise network. NetID surpasses the functionality of these solutions in a supported product.

Features

DHCP Redundancy The prospect of DHCP server outages has deterred many organizations from implementing DHCP across their networks. Through DHCP redundancy, NetID helps ensure high availability

Dynamic DNS Review

of DHCP services. With a primary and backup DHCP server serving the same address ranges, DHCP clients on these ranges will always be able to obtain an IP address. Primary and backup servers communicate through a server-to-server protocol; thus, if the backup detects that the primary is unavailable, it automatically begins serving ranges for the failed server.

Integrated IP Address, DNS and DHCP Management The NetID Management Console provides a platform for complete IP address and DNS and DHCP management. Intuitive NetID commands facilitate basic management tasks, such as moving IP addresses, entering domain names, and adding new subnets. Configuration parameters for DNS and DHCP servers are also defined from the interface. Servers obtain their configuration from the NetID database through the Server Manager, providing a single configuration point for servers across the network instead of on a single-server basis.

Active Server Management The NetID Active Server Management feature provides a complete platform not only for configuring NetID DNS and DHCP Servers, but also for monitoring server status and viewing alarms on a per-server basis. DNS and DHCP servers generate alarms and warnings that the Server Manager transmits to the database. From the NetID Management Console, alarms for every NetID DNS and DHCP Server across a network can be viewed. This provides a view of the configuration and the real-time status of every DNS and DHCP server on a network. Alarms also generate Simple Network Management Protocol (SNMP) traps that can be viewed from a network management platform.

Web-Based Management Console With a Java-enabled interface, platform support for the NetID Management Console is significantly extended. Moreover, the interface provides an intuitive, user-friendly platform for IP address management, and DNS and DHCP management. Customizable views allow network administrators to view information according to the fields they want displayed. For instance, instead of viewing objects by IP addresses, devices can be viewed by name, or by any other custom field defined in NetID. Also, DNS configuration can be viewed by zone, while DHCP configuration can be viewed by server or subnet.

IP Services API The complete functionality of NetID is available through an API that provides a fully supported library of C++ functions.

The API can be used to develop custom functionality on top of NetID, to integrate NetID with applications such as billing and provisioning.

Dynamic DNS Updates NetID's support of BIND 8.1.1 and BIND 8.1.2 (UNIX only) enables standards-based dynamic DNS updates. Additionally, updated domain name information is relayed from the DHCP server to the central database.

Extended Support for Dynamic Addressing NetID controls the allocation of DHCP addresses through the association of pools of client IDs, or Media Access Control (MAC) addresses with a DHCP range. Only members of the client pool are allowed to receive an address from a DHCP range associated with a client pool. The DHCP server's multi-threaded, nonblocking architecture enables it to respond to simultaneous DHCP requests from multiple clients, so there are no response delays for clients requesting IP addresses. Users view the configuration of individual servers from the NetID Management Console, providing easy access to information that has historically been difficult to track, yet is extremely useful for troubleshooting.

Support for DHCP Migration DHCP migration functionality facilitates an organization's migration from static to dynamic addressing. Users can convert dynamic DHCP clients to static DHCP and create dynamic ranges that overlap static addresses. Since ranges no longer have to be exclusively static or dynamic, the migration to DHCP can be a transitional process.

IP Audit Tool Through the NetID IP Audit Tool, network administrators can compare addresses stored in the database with those currently in use. Since NetID checks all data as it is entered, the IP Audit Tool provides an extra level of data verification. Administrators can optionally delete or retrieve unused addresses for reassignment, or automatically add newly detected addresses to the database.

Automated VLSM Design With NetID, it is easy to design or maintain VLSM address architecture. Subnets can be partitioned or joined through a series of mouse clicks. NetID automatically calculates subnet masks, eliminating the common errors associated with VLSM design and architecture.

User-Defined Custom Fields Custom fields track user-defined information—such as location identifiers—against IP addresses. This functionality enables NetID to be adapted to individual environments, tracking any required information against networks, subnets, or IP addresses. From the main IP address view in the Management Console, users can view custom field information, sort IP addressing data by custom fields, and enforce mandatory custom fields.

Automatic DNS Updates DNS updates are automatic with the NetID DNS Server. When the NetID Server Manager detects a change made to domain name information in the NetID database, it sends the incremental changes to the appropriate DNS servers.

Personal Views Personal Views extend NetID's hierarchical access rights, so that the NetID system administrator can limit not only the information that NetID users can modify but also the information they can see. The Personal Views feature prevents users from seeing areas of the network to which they do not have access. The only information the users can see is the information that the NetID system administrator has placed in their personal view. This new functionality enhances NetID's existing access features so users can see only the information to which they have been granted access. For a service provider looking to offer additional services (such as DNS hosting to clients), or for the enterprise with many distributed administrators, this feature offers additional control.

Imports/Exports Flexible importing and exporting options ensure that NetID is up and running quickly, and allow administrators to easily leverage information stored in the central database. NetID imports information from any of the following standard file formats: DNS configuration files, UNIX host files, and BootP configuration files. The database can also be populated using text files with user-defined formats. NetID supports the same standard exporting formats.

NetID Architecture

Database For an illustration of a typical NetID architecture, indicating the relationships between the NetID servers, server managers, and the NetID database, see Figure 12-9. Multiple users access IP addressing

Figure 12-9
NetID architecture.

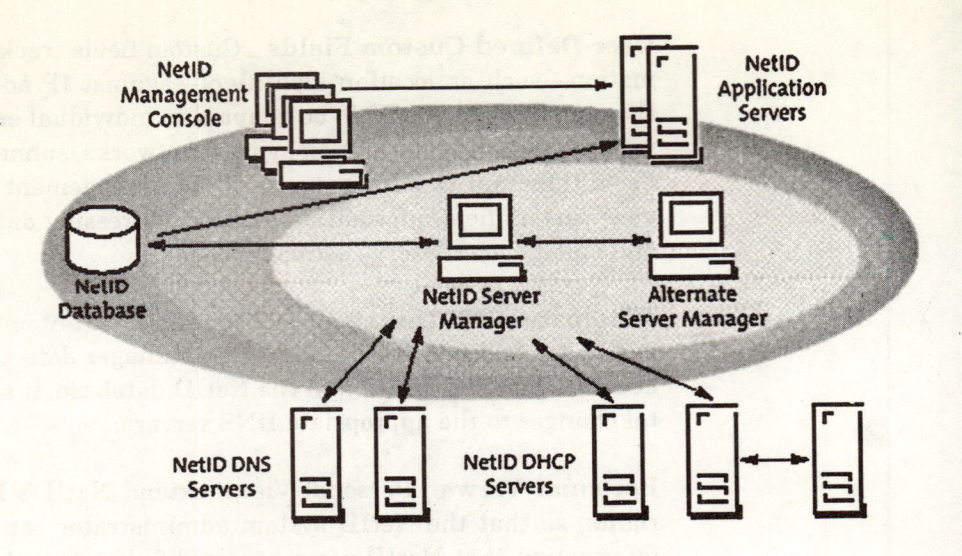

information stored in the NetID database (central Sybase or Oracle database) from the NetID Management Console.

Management Console The Management Console provides a complete platform for managing IP addresses, DNS, and DHCP. The Java interface allows administrators to access the central database from any Web browser. Views can be customized so administrators view networking information according to the fields they want displayed. For example, DHCP configuration can be viewed either by server or subnet.

Application Server The NetID Application Server serves Java applets for the NetID Management Console. Users manage network, subnet, host, DNS, and zone information with the NetID Management Console. The NetID Application Server receives this information from the NetID Management Console and sends it to the NetID database.

Server Manager The NetID Server Manager is the interface between the NetID DNS and DHCP Servers, and the central database. Along with providing the servers with their initial configuration, it sends incremental configuration changes out to servers across the network.

DNS Server The NetID DNS Server is a domain name server that is dynamically linked to the database by the Server Manager, allowing for automatic DNS updates and dynamic DNS reconfiguration (changing server policy and zone structure). Since the NetID DNS Server is based

Dynamic DNS Review

on BIND 8.1.1 and BIND 8.1.2 (UNIX only), it supports standards-based dynamic DNS updates, and will interoperate with other BIND-compliant DNS servers.

DHCP Server The NetID DHCP Server is a BootP/DHCP server that is configured from the Management Console. It updates the NetID DNS Server, enabling dynamic DNS updates.

System Requirements

See Table 12-1 for the NetID system requirements.

MetaInfo's Meta IP

To keep track of increasing numbers of static addresses, spreadsheets or free DHCP services that come bundled with server packages have traditionally been used. But these options have limitations: They involve many hours of clerical work for maintenance; establishing where an

TABLE 12-1 NetID System Requirements.

Product	Disk Space	Memory	Platform	Hardware
NETID Management Console	As required by Web browser	As required by Web browser	Netscape Internet Explorer Java 1.1 compatible	As required by Web browser
NetID DNS Server	25 MB	64 MB for 10,000 DNS entries	Windows NT 4.0 Solaris 2.5, 2.6 HP-UX 10.x	Pentium 166 Sun UltraSPARC HP 9000/700
NetID DHCP Server	25 MB	64 MB	Windows NT 4.0 Solaris 2.5, 2.6 HP-UX 10.x	Pentium 166 Sun UltraSPARC HP 9000/700
NetID Application Server	25 MB	64 MB	Windows NT 4.0 Solaris 2.5, 2.6 HP-UX 10.x	Pentium 166 Sun UltraSPARC HP 9000/700
Oracle Server	500 MB + 2 KB per IP address	64 MB (Oracle recommends a 128 MB)	Oracle 7.x and 8.0	As supported by database vendor
Sybase Server	500 MB + 2 KB per IP address	64 MB	Sybase 11.0-11.5	As supported by database vendor

address conflict lies is difficult (which would present time-consuming difficulties when a network is down); and identification of users isn't often easy (problematical when those users are monopolizing a particular bandwidth).

With Meta IP, IP addresses and the IP name space are centrally managed across an entire network. It integrates DHCP, DNS, and other IP services, and enables them to be administered through a single interface. Addressing with Meta IP is fully audited, easily administered, and purportedly fail-safe.

Fail-Safe Addressing and Naming

- Effectively eliminate the potential for conflicts.
- Ensure fault-tolerant services for every user and device on the network through redundant failover capability.
- Extend IP services to remote users via support for RADIUS protocol.

Complete Auditing and Reporting

- Accurately track and audit IP address assignments by MAC address and device name
- Correlate lease assignments with login names through the User-to-Address Mapping service.
- View address assignments, names, and other status information in real time.

Centralized, Automated Management

- Centrally administer the whole system, or delegate specified tasks to others on the network.
- Control IP services running on other servers including UNIX, Novell, and Windows NT.
- Administer all services via a password-protected Web interface.
- Set up the system quickly and make changes with re-entrant administration wizards.

Features and Benefits of Meta IP

Key Benefits

- Bring IP services into one centralized management policy.
- Ensure reliability of IP-dependent, mission-critical applications.

Dynamic DNS Review

- Eliminate timely, error-prone manual configuration of network services and end-user desktops.
- Simplify management and configuration of IP network services throughout the enterprise.
- Leverage existing network services through open standards to extend ROI.
- Lay foundation for policy-based management of IP networks.

Key Features

- Manage standards-based network services on heterogeneous platforms from a single management interface.
- Track individual users to IP address leases.
- Simplify name space management with Dynamic DNS support.
- Scale from one-site installations to worldwide distributed networks.
- Integrate IP network services into Directory Services through LDAP.
- Distribute administrative tasks throughout the enterprise.
- Manage remotely across heterogeneous platform with Java-based interface.
- Build fault tolerance into the IP Infrastructure.
- Integrate with network management products through SNMP.

DHCP Failover Meta IP's DHCP extends the reference code to provide redundant failover through a secondary DHCP service, which is aware of all lease information the primary service holds and can seamlessly replace the primary in the event of failure. In contrast, most DHCP services achieve failover through "splitting a lease pool," which is dividing the available IP addresses between two DHCP services. If one fails, all DHCP clients will attempt to renew leases from the other DHCP service. This will create a spike in network resource usage and may result in the inability to obtain an IP address.

Track IP Address to Users (UAM™ Service) The innovative User-to-Address Mapping (UAM) service associates a user login name with a host name, IP address, MAC address, domain, and login time, providing a highly tunable method for tracking and reporting the usage of IP address leases. The UAM integrates with all critical IP network services in the Meta IP system to create an active association between user names and IP addresses. By collecting IP address leases issued from the

DHCP services and matching them to user login names, administrators can determine which particular employee or user has been issued a particular IP address at any given time. As well as through the UAM database, the data is available via an RPC interface, allowing organizations to build solutions using this unique technology.

LDAP Data Store The Meta IP System utilizes an LDAP-based data schema and data store to house information critical to the network's operation. Utilizing an open data store based on the LDAP enables integration with any LDAP-compliant database, including Microsoft's Active Directory, NDS, or Netscape SuiteSpot, thereby avoiding third-party database installation and management issues.

Remote User Authentication (RADIUS) Since mobile remote computing has become more common and necessary, the Meta IP System integrates a standards-based commercial implementation of the Remote Authentication Dial-In User Service (RADIUS) for the support of remote and dial-in users. The RADIUS service supports the authentication and configuration of dial-in users to client communications servers and easily integrates into network authentication services for configuration on a per-user basis.

Auditing and Reporting Meta IP has the ability to generate reports based on information from the Admin Console. Represented in any of the PNG Multiview formats, the report data easily can be exported for use by third-party reporting tools such as Microsoft Excel. Meta IP is centrally managed and fully automated.

Meta IP brings an organization's entire IP address and name space under one unified interface, with the ability to manage standards-based services across multiple platforms. Granular access controls enable network managers to grant differing levels of access control and permissions on a by-user or by-group basis. This also includes the ability to enable managers to access the entire network site or a singular service or server.

Third-Party Integration (SNMP) Each of the services within the Meta IP System integrates SNMP to report and monitor activity in the system. The SNMP monitoring capabilities also allow for the integration of other SNMP-based network monitoring tools, such as HP OpenView, into the network systems enhancing flexibility.

Database Replication The management data in the Meta IP System is replicated across the distributed system with hubs that control each set of network services and distributed data. With a distributed system such as Meta IP, each service can work independently, providing backup to offline services in the system and aiding the retention configuration and management of data. This enables the IP Management System to run with a minimum of downtime.

Extending Security

With User-to-Address Mapping (UAM) capabilities, Meta IP gives network managers:

- Increased security
- Accountability for shared machines
- IP address troubleshooting

By integrating the Meta IP UAM service with FireWall-1, Check Point offers a solution to enforce security policies by user in a dynamic addressing environment. This dynamic firewall capability allows IS departments to:

- More easily create and enforce user profiles
- Create comprehensive internal security policies
- Apply and track security policies by user
- Improve security between departments
- Enable seamless connectivity for local and remote users

Meta DHCP

As corporations expand their networks to increase connectivity and communications both inside and outside their organizations, the traditional manual method of assigning and tracking IP addresses and computer names no longer meets the demands placed on it. Manually assigning and tracking IP addresses requires network administrators to configure each desktop and DNS service as a point solution. It is time-consuming, prone to error, and expensive.

Meta IP solves this problem with its DHCP service, an extended implementation of the reference ISC code, DHCPD. With Meta IP's

DHCP, an administrator can establish automated IP addressing and configuration policies for the entire organization (see Figure 12-10).

IP Address Allocation Meta IP's strict standards-based approach gives network administrators the ability to use DHCP to automatically assign IP addresses to any computer or other network device with a standards-compliant DHCP client. Additionally, the Meta IP DHCP service supports BootP clients for backward compatibility. With DHCP's automatic IP address allocation, an enterprise can minimize the time devoted

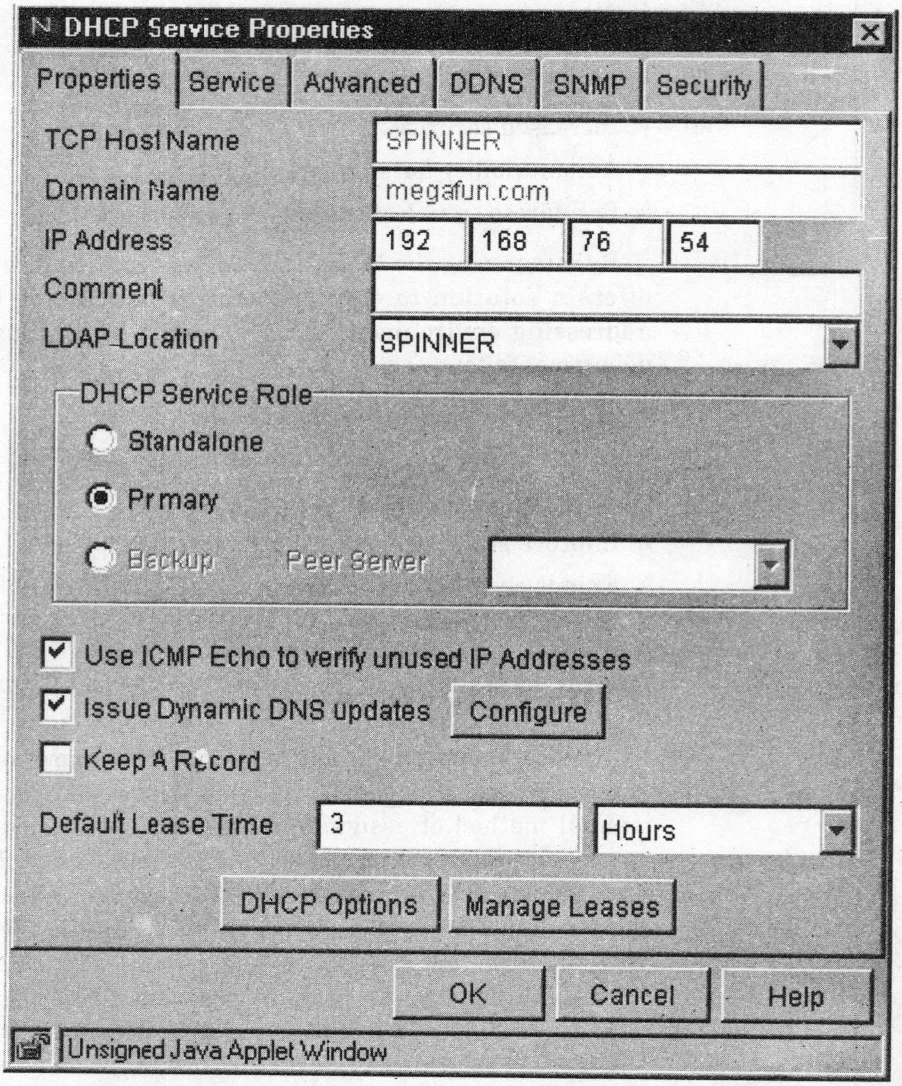

Figure 12-10
DHCP service properties.

to manually configuring each desktop with an IP address and maximize usage of the limited resource of IP addresses.

After issuing a DHCP lease, the Meta IP DHCP is able to automatically update any DNS service capable of receiving Dynamic DNS updates with the proper IP address and host name information. By tying the DHCP and DNS together through dynamic updates, an organization can be assured of keeping its name space directory up-to-date, enabling IP-dependent applications, such as document sharing, to function properly.

Reliability and Fault Tolerance Meta IP's DHCP extends the reference code to provide redundant failover through a secondary DHCP service, which is aware of all lease information the primary service holds and can seamlessly replace the primary in the event of failure. In contrast, most DHCP services achieve failover through "splitting a lease pool," which is dividing the available IP addresses between two DHCP services. If one fails, all DHCP clients will attempt to renew leases from the other DHCP service. This will create a spike in network resource usage and may result in the inability to obtain an IP address.

User-Based Auditing and Tracking In conjunction with Meta IP's User-to-Address Mapping technology, the DHCP service enables system administrators to track IP address leases to the end user rather than the usual hardware-based MAC address. Because of the UAM's ability to relate DHCP leases to a user's login name, a corporation implementing DHCP can now troubleshoot problems and create a IP address logging policy based on a user's identity rather than by hardware address.

Remote Desktop TCP/IP Configuration With the implementation of Meta IP's DHCP service, network administrators can easily propagate network configurations to users. Meta IP allows network configurations to be changed centrally in the DHCP configuration files and then pushed out to computers and devices as DHCP address leases are renewed. By allowing administrators to set a computer's DNS services, default router, and other options from one location, Meta IP enables network managers to implement changes to the infrastructure in a timely, accurate, cost-efficient manner.

Meta DNS

A DNS service is critical to enabling users to find and utilize resources on the Internet and company's intranet. As these network resources and applications become more central to a corporation's mission, Meta IP will provide the reliability for accurate and reliable IP address resolution with its Meta DNS service.

Meta DNS is a direct port of BIND 8.1.2, the Internet Software Consortium's reference implementation of the Domain Name System. It supports secure DNS extensions and Dynamic DNS updates, improving security and enabling full integration into a comprehensive IP Infrastructure Management System. Because of its adherence to standards, Meta DNS is able to interoperate in a heterogeneous environment with other standards-based DNS services, giving network administrators a high level of flexibility in how they deploy their IP address management solution. In conjunction with Meta IP's Service Manager Clients (SMCs), this standards-based approach allows administrators to bring an enterprise's entire name space under one central management interface.

Figure 12-11 shows the Meta IP Admin Console.

Assigning IP Addresses More Efficiently When used in conjunction with Meta IP's DHCP service, Meta DNS is able to accept dynamically assigned IP addresses and host names and automatically update the correct configuration files. Dynamic DNS allows network administrators to use DHCP to establish an IP addressing policy in an ever-changing environment. This functionality saves administrators from the time-consuming, expensive, and error-prone task of manually updating every desktop and DNS configuration file.

Table 12-2 shows the features of Meta DNS, along with their benefits.

RFC Compliance

RFC 974—Mail Routing and Domain System

RFC 1034—Domain Names: Concepts and Facilities

RFC 1035—Domain Names: Implementation and Specifications

RFC 1183—New DNS RR Definitions

RFC 1884—IP version 6 Addressing Architecture

RFC 1886—DNS Extensions to Support IP Version 6

RFC 1996—A Mechanism for Prompt Notification of Zone Changes (DNS Notify)

RFC 2052—A DNS RR for Specifying the Location of Services (DNS SRV)

RFC 2065—Domain Name System Security Extensions

RFC 2136—Dynamic Updates in the Domain Name Systems (DNS Update)

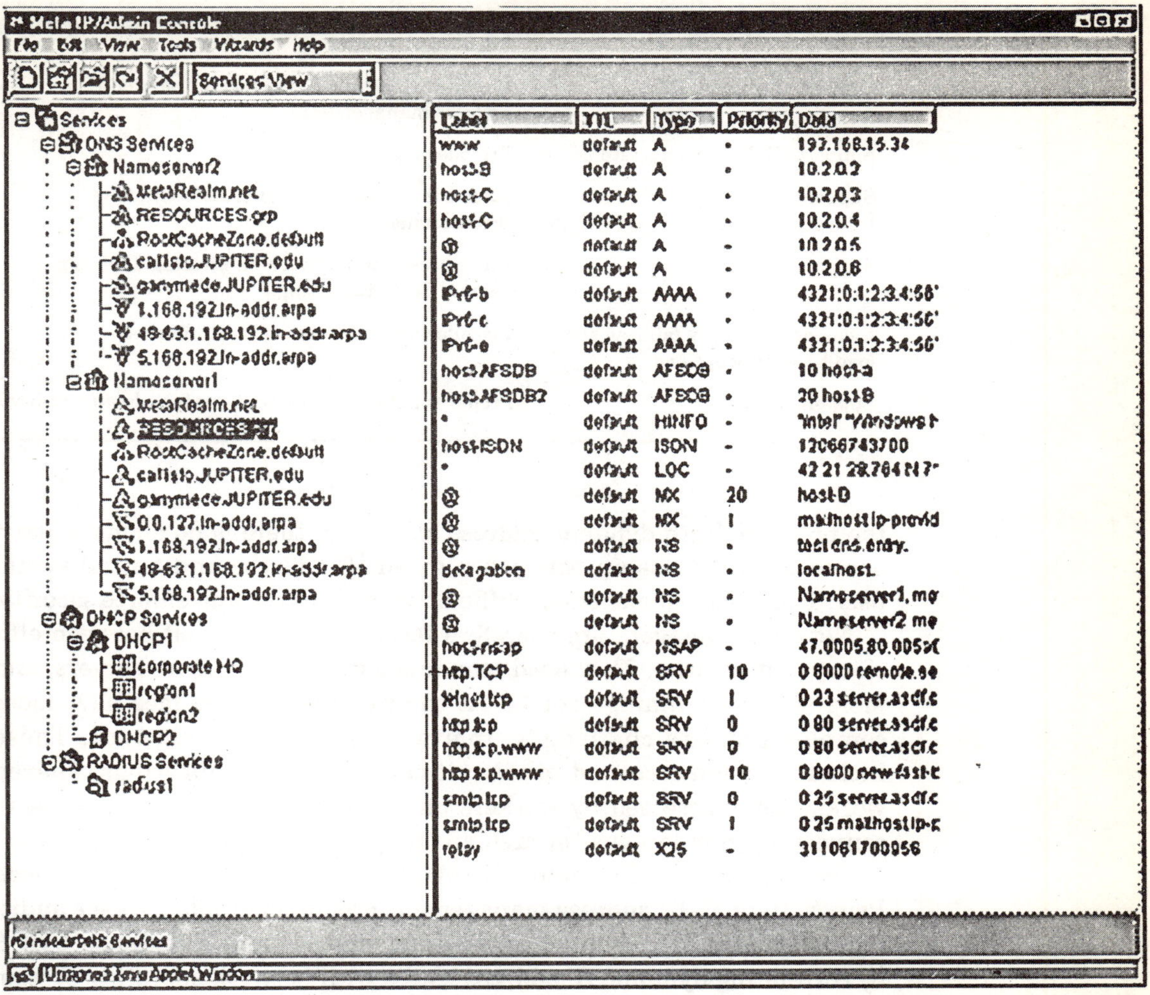

Dynamic DNS Review

Figure 12-11 Meta IP Admin Console.

RFC 2137—Secure Domain Name System Dynamic Update

User-to-Address Mapping

As networks grow exponentially, the traditional method of assigning static addresses and manually tracking them in spreadsheets becomes unreliable and cumbersome. Dynamic addressing via DHCP relieves much of the clerical overhead, but DHCP alone does not completely solve

TABLE 12-2

Features and Benefits of Meta DNS.

Features	Benefits
Supports Dynamic DNS	Works with DHCP to provide automated IP address management.
Supports DNS security extensions	Provides high level of security
Supports Microsoft's Windows Internet Naming Service (WINS)	Allows integration into Microsoft Windows Environment
Supports SNMP	Integrates with Network Monitoring Tools for Service State Reporting
Includes secondary failover and load-balancing options	Provides several levels of fault tolerance
Supports IPv6	Prepares network infrastructure for adoption of IPv6

the problem. With dynamic address allocation, there is no longer a strict one-to-one relationship between a given IP address and an individual user. This makes it extremely difficult to track usage and enforce security.

Network managers are therefore faced with a trade-off between efficiency and security. They need to manage more nodes, more servers, and more services running over IP. At the same time, they face new, more complex security challenges from within their own network. These include e-commerce and other critical business applications, shared workstations accessed by workers on business trips, and remote users connecting from laptops through virtual private networks (VPNs).

User-to-Address Mapping (UAM), a technology exclusive to Check Point's Meta IP IP address management product, permits by-user auditing and control in a dynamic addressing environment. It extends DHCP by correlating dynamic IP address leases with network operating system logins. UAM consolidates information including:

- Login name
- Login time
- MAC address
- IP address
- Host name

It stores the information in a database and logs it over time. Unlike other solutions, UAM tracks information not merely by machine, but by the authenticated user. UAM adds tracking and reporting, for monitoring network usage and troubleshooting IP addressing issues.

UAM also paves the way for managing IP networks on a per-user rather than a per-address basis. Its architecture is accessible to Check Point security products and to solutions from third parties. A new generation of firewalls, VPN solutions, routers, and other network equipment can use the UAM information to enforce security and provision services by user.

Table 12-3 details the benefits of UAM.

Multiplatform Support

Enterprise networks today are complex mixtures of platforms, operating systems, protocols, and legacy systems. Meta IP is designed not only to fit easily into these environments but to leverage existing infrastructure to simplify management, decrease costs, and improve return on investment. Central to this goal is Meta IP's Service Manager Client (SMC) architecture, which allows the Meta IP Service Manager to easily manage IP services on multiple platforms. It can export configuration files to other standards-based DNS services on nonsupported platforms as well. In addition, Meta IP adheres strictly to industry standards, giving its management components and services the ability to interoperate with existing network management systems and services.

Standards-based DNS services can be managed on the following:

- Windows NT
- Solaris 2.6.x
- SunOs 4.1.4
- HP-UX 10.2.x

TABLE 12-3
Benefits of UAM.

Benefit	Description
Transparent to the end user	UAM makes User-to-Address Mapping without separate authentication.
Enhanced auditing and reporting	Administrators can receive detailed information on which user has been assigned which IP address, both in real time and historically.
Enhanced Security and Integration with FireWall-1	The UAM, when combined with Fire-Wall-1, provides transparent single sign-on and user-based security.

- AIX 4.3.x
- Linux 2.x

Meta IP Solutions

Check Point provides two configurations of its IP address management product to meet the diverse needs of networks: Meta IP Standard and Meta IP Enterprise. Meta IP Standard is designed for smaller networks looking for an IP address management solution to work on Windows NT. Meta IP Enterprise is architected for the demands placed upon mid- to enterprise-sized networks.

Meta IP Standard   Designed for small networks, Meta IP Standard is a Windows NT-based solution for IP address management. With Meta IP, an organization can run up to two DNS and DHCP services each and manage up to 1000 dynamically assigned addresses. It includes the User-to-Address Mapping service to extend and enhance security.

Specifically, Meta IP Standard features the following:

- *User-to-Address Mapping Service.*   Enhances auditing and tracking of IP address usage to employees
- *Centralized Management Interface.*   Provides simpler, more complete management of DNS and DHCP services than that available from free network services
- *Integration with FireWall-1.*   Integrates with FireWall-1 to provide enhanced security in a dynamic addressing environment, including a single sign-on solution and user-based security policies.
- *Two DNS/Two DHCP.*   Provides the standards-based services necessary for your small business
- *Manage up to 1000 addresses*   Scales as your network grows

Meta IP Enterprise   Including all the features of Meta IP Standard, Meta IP Enterprise meets the specific requirements of enterprise-scale networks. Its modular architecture extends IP address management across multiple platforms and distributed management sites.

Meta IP Enterprise features the following:

- *User-to-Address Mapping Service.*   Enhances auditing and tracking of IP address usage to employees

Dynamic DNS Review

- *Unlimited DNS and DHCP services.* Designed to scale as a network grows
- *Management of standards-based DNS services on multiple platforms.* Incorporates existing network services into a centralized IP address management solution
- *Distributed, replicated management sites.* Enhances management fault tolerance by providing multiple management sites, all with replicated LDAP data stores
- *Delegated tasks.* Logically assign tasks to administrators best able to deal with them

Comparison of Meta IP Solutions

Table 12-4 compares the features of Meta IP Standard and Meta IP Enterprise.

TABLE 12-4

Meta IP Solutions

Meta IP System Features	Standard	Enterprise
Centralized Management	X	X
Remote Administration	X	X
Import/Export Capabilities	X	X
Dynamic DNS and DHCP	X	X
User-to-Address Mapping	X	X
FireWall-1 Integration	X	X
LDAP Data Schema	X	X
Multiview Interface	X	X
SNMP Support	X	X
Service Manager Clients		X
Distributed Management Sites		X
Task Delegation		X
RADIUS Service		X

System Requirements

Operating Systems:

Interface	Java Enabled Browser or Win32
Meta IP Management Server	Windows NT 4.0
	Intel Pentium
	32 MB RAM minimum
	64 MB RAM minimum
Meta IP Services	Windows NT 4.0
	Intel Pentium
	32 MB RAM minimum per service

Standards-based DNS Services Managed on:

- Windows NT 4.0
- Linux 2.x
- Solaris 2.x
- SunOs 4.1.4
- HP-UX 10.x
- vAIX 4.x

RFCs Supported:

Dynamic DNS	974, 1034, 1035, 1183, 1884, 1886, 1996, 2052, 2065, 2136, 2137
DHCP	951, 2131, 2132
RADIUS	2138

APPENDIX A

DHCP OPTIONS (RFC 2132)

The Internet Engineering Task Force (IETF) publishes the official documents describing Internet standards, including DHCP. DHCP provides several different options. This appendix, based on RFC 2132, includes a complete list of those options, along with information on which options are supported by popular server and client operating systems.

DHCP provides a framework for passing configuration information to hosts on a TCP/IP network. Configuration parameters and other control information are carried in tagged data items that are stored in the Options field of the DHCP message. The data items themselves are also called "options."

RFC 1497 was published previously and included vendor information extensions. These extensions are also described in this appendix, and RFC 1497 should now be considered obsolete. In addition, all the DHCP options described here, except those specific to DHCP in section A, "DHCP (Only) Options," may be used as BootP vendor information extensions.

For the latest, official list of DHCP options please visit *ftp://ds.internic.net/rfc/rfc2132.txt*.

A.1 Introduction

DHCP options have the same format as the BootP "vendor extensions" defined in RFC 1497. Options may be fixed length or variable length. All options begin with a tag octet, which uniquely identifies the option. Fixed-length options without data consist of only a tag octet. Only options 0 and 255 are fixed length. All other options are variable length with a length octet following the tag octet. The value of the length octet does not include the two octets specifying the tag and length. The length octet is followed by *length* octets of data. With some variable length options, the length field is a constant but must still be specified. Any options defined in a future version of this standard must contain a length octet even if the length is fixed or zero.

Options containing NVT ASCII data should not include a trailing null. However, the receiver of such options must be prepared to delete trailing nulls if they exist. The receiver must not require that a trailing null be included in the data.

Option codes 128 to 254 (decimal) are reserved for your own use.

A.2 DHCP and BootP Options

This section introduces all DHCP and BootP options that can be defined at the DHCP server and delivered to requesting DHCP and BootP clients. Be aware that although most DHCP servers can deliver all options illustrated here to requesting DHCP and BootP clients, there are platform-specific dependencies that determine whether or not requesting DHCP and BootP clients can actually make use of all delivered information.

A.2.1 Options 0 and 255: Pad and End

Originally described in RFC 1497, options 0 and 255 help provide vendor extensions to the DHCP standard. Option 0, the Pad option, can be used to cause subsequent fields to align on word boundaries. Its length is one octet. The End option, option 255, marks the end of valid information in the Vendor field. (Subsequent octets should be filled with pad options.) Its length is also one octet.

A.2.2 Option 1: Subnet Mask

Option 1 specifies the client's subnet mask per RFC 950. If both the subnet mask and the router (option 3) are specified in a DHCP reply, the Subnet Mask option must be first. The code for the Subnet Mask option is 1, and its length is 4 octets.

```
Code   Length        Subnet Mask
+-----+-----+-----+-----+-----+-----+
|  1  |  4  | m1  | m2  | m3  | m4  |
+-----+-----+-----+-----+-----+-----+
```

DHCP Options (RFC 2132)

A.2.3 Option 2: Time Offset

The Time Offset field specifies the offset, in seconds, of the client's subnet from Coordinated Universal Time (UTC). The offset is expressed as a two's complement 32-bit integer. A positive offset indicates a location east of the zero meridian, and a negative offset indicates a location west of the zero meridian.

The code for the Time Offset option is 2, and its length is 4 octets.

```
 Code   Length        Time Offset
+-----+-----+-----+-----+-----+-----+
|  1  |  4  | n1  | n2  | n3  | n4  |
+-----+-----+-----+-----+-----+-----+
```

A.2.4 Option 3: Router

The Router option specifies a list of IP addresses for routers on the client's subnet. Routers should be listed in order of preference.

The code for the router option is 3, and the minimum length for the router option is 4 octets. The length must always be a multiple of 4.

```
 Code   Length    Address 1                  Address 2 [...]
+-----+-----+-----+-----+-----+-----+-----+-----+-----+
|  3  |  n  | a1  | a2  | a3  | a4  | a1  | a2  | [...]
+-----+-----+-----+-----+-----+-----+-----+-----+-----+
```

A.2.5 Option 4: Time Server

The Time Server option specifies a list of RFC 868 time servers available to the client. Servers should be listed in order of preference.

The code for the time server option is 4, and the minimum length for this option is 4 octets. The length must always be a multiple of 4.

```
 Code   Length    Address 1                  Address 2 [...]
+-----+-----+-----+-----+-----+-----+-----+-----+-----+
|  4  |  n  | a1  | a2  | a3  | a4  | a1  | a2  | [...]
+-----+-----+-----+-----+-----+-----+-----+-----+-----+
```

A.2.6 Option 5: IEN 116 (Old) Name Server

The Name Server option specifies a list of IEN 116 name servers available to the client. Servers should be listed in order of preference. (Option

5 is provided for compatibility with old-style name servers. Use Option 6 for modern domain name servers.)

The code for the name server option is 5, and the minimum length for this option is 4 octets. The length must always be a multiple of 4.

```
 Code   Length    Address 1              Address 2 [...]
+-----+-----+-----+-----+-----+-----+-----+-----+-----+
|  5  |  n  | a1  | a2  | a3  | a4  | a1  | a2  | [...]
+-----+-----+-----+-----+-----+-----+-----+-----+-----+
```

A.2.7 Option 6: Domain Name Server

The Domain Name Server option specifies a list of Domain Name System (RFC 1035) servers available to the client. Servers should be listed in order of preference.

The code for the domain name server option is 6, and the minimum length for this option is 4 octets. The length must always be a multiple of 4.

```
 Code   Length    Address 1              Address 2 [...]
+-----+-----+-----+-----+-----+-----+-----+-----+-----+
|  6  |  n  | a1  | a2  | a3  | a4  | a1  | a2  | [...]
+-----+-----+-----+-----+-----+-----+-----+-----+-----+
```

A.2.8 Option 7: Log Server

The Log Server option specifies a list of MIT-LCS UDP log servers available to the client. Servers should be listed in order of preference.

The code for the log server option is 7, and the minimum length for this option is 4 octets. The length must always be a multiple of 4.

```
 Code   Length    Address 1              Address 2 [...]
+-----+-----+-----+-----+-----+-----+-----+-----+-----+
|  7  |  n  | a1  | a2  | a3  | a4  | a1  | a2  | [...]
+-----+-----+-----+-----+-----+-----+-----+-----+-----+
```

A.2.9 Option 8: Cookie Server

The Cookie Server option specifies a list of RFC 865 cookie servers available to the client. Servers should be listed in order of preference.

The code for the log server option is 8, and the minimum length for this option is 4 octets. The length must always be a multiple of 4.

```
 Code   Length     Address 1               Address 2 [...]
+-----+-----+-----+-----+-----+-----+-----+-----+-----+-----+
|  8  |  n  | a1  | a2  | a3  | a4  | a1  | a2  |[...]
+-----+-----+-----+-----+-----+-----+-----+-----+-----+-----+
```

A.2.10 Option 9: LPR Server

The LPR Server option specifies a list of RFC 1179 print servers available to the client. Servers should be listed in order of preference.

The code for the LPR Server option is 9, and the minimum length for this option is 4 octets. The length must always be a multiple of 4.

```
 Code   Length     Address 1               Address 2 [...]
+-----+-----+-----+-----+-----+-----+-----+-----+-----+-----+
|  9  |  n  | a1  | a2  | a3  | a4  | a1  | a2  |[...]
+-----+-----+-----+-----+-----+-----+-----+-----+-----+-----+
```

A.2.11 Option 10: Impress Server

The Impress Server option specifies a list of Imagen Impress servers available to the client. Servers should be listed in order of preference.

The code for the Impress Server option is 10, and the minimum length for this option is 4 octets. The length must always be a multiple of 4.

```
 Code   Length     Address 1               Address 2 [...]
+-----+-----+-----+-----+-----+-----+-----+-----+-----+-----+
| 10  |  n  | a1  | a2  | a3  | a4  | a1  | a2  |[...]
+-----+-----+-----+-----+-----+-----+-----+-----+-----+-----+
```

A.2.12 Option 11: Resource Location Server

This option specifies a list of RFC 887 resource location servers available to the client. Servers should be listed in order of preference.

The code for this option is 11, and the minimum length for this option is 4 octets. The length must always be a multiple of 4.

```
 Code   Length     Address 1               Address 2 [...]
+-----+-----+-----+-----+-----+-----+-----+-----+-----+-----+
| 11  |  n  | a1  | a2  | a3  | a4  | a1  | a2  |[...]
+-----+-----+-----+-----+-----+-----+-----+-----+-----+-----+
```

A.2.13   Option 12: Host Name

This option specifies the name of the client. The name may or may not include the full local domain name. (See E.2.16, "Option 15: Domain Name," in RFC 1497 for the preferred method of obtaining the domain name.) RFC 1035 explains the restrictions concerning which characters can be used in the host name.

The code for this option is 12, and its minimum length is 1.

```
Code   Length     Host Name
+-----+-----+-----+-----+-----+-----+-----+-----+-----+
| 12  |  n  | h1  | h2  | h3  | h4  | h5  | h6  |[...]|
+-----+-----+-----+-----+-----+-----+-----+-----+-----+
```

A.2.14   Option 13: Boot File Size

This option specifies the length, in 512-octet blocks, of the default boot image file for the client. The file length is specified as an unsigned 16-bit integer.

The code for this option is 13, and its length is 2.

```
Code   Length   File Size
+-----+-----+-----+-----+
| 13  |  2  | 11  | 12  |
+-----+-----+-----+-----+
```

A.2.15   Option 14: Merit Dump File

This option specifies the filename (with path) of a file where the client's core image should be dumped in the event the client crashes. The path is formatted as a string consisting of characters from the NVT ASCII character set.

The code for this option is 14, and its minimum length is 1.

```
Code   Length     Dump Path/File Name
+-----+-----+-----+-----+-----+-----+-----+
| 14  |  n  | n1  | n2  | n3  | n4  |[...]|
+-----+-----+-----+-----+-----+-----+-----+
```

A.2.16   Option 15: Domain Name

This option specifies the default domain name that the client should use when resolving host names using the Domain Name System. The code for this option is 15, and its minimum length is 1.

DHCP Options (RFC 2132)

```
 Code   Length        Domain Name
+-----+-----+-----+-----+-----+-----+-----+
|  15 |  n  |  d1 |  d2 |  d3 |  d4 | ... |
+-----+-----+-----+-----+-----+-----+-----+
```

A.2.17   Option 16: Swap Server

This option specifies the IP address of the client's swap server. The code for this option is 16, and its length is 4.

```
 Code   Length  Swap Server Address
+-----+-----+-----+-----+-----+-----+
|  16 |  n  |  a1 |  a2 |  a3 |  a4 |
+-----+-----+-----+-----+-----+-----+
```

A.2.18   Option 17: Root Path

This option specifies the path name that contains the client's root directory. The path is formatted as a string consisting of characters from the NVT ASCII character set.

The code for this option is 17, and its minimum length is 1.

```
 Code   Length     Root Disk Pathname
+-----+-----+-----+-----+-----+-----+-----+
|  17 |  n  |  n1 |  n2 |  n3 |  n4 | ... |
+-----+-----+-----+-----+-----+-----+-----+
```

A.2.19   Option 18: Extensions Path

This option specifies the path and name of a file, retrievable through TFTP, that contains information to be interpreted in the same way as the 64-octet vendor extension field within the BootP response. The following exceptions apply:

- The length of the file is not limited.
- All references to Tag 18 (instances of the BootP Extensions Path field) within the file are ignored.

The code for this option is 18, and its minimum length is 1.

```
 Code   Length     Extensions Path/File Name
+-----+-----+-----+-----+-----+-----+-----+
|  18 |  n  |  n1 |  n2 |  n3 |  n4 | ... |
+-----+-----+-----+-----+-----+-----+-----+
```

A.2.20 Option 19: IP Forwarding Enable/Disable

This option specifies whether the client should configure its IP layer for packet forwarding. A value of 0 means disable IP forwarding, and a value of 1 means enable IP forwarding.

The code for this option is 19, and its length is 1.

```
Code   Length Value
+-----+-----+-----+
|  19 |  1  |  n  |
+-----+-----+-----+
```

A.2.21 Option 20: Non-Local Source Routing Enable/Disable

This option specifies whether the client should configure its IP layer to allow forwarding of datagrams with non-local source routes. A value of 0 means disallow forwarding of such datagrams, and a value of 1 means allow forwarding.

The code for this option is 20, and its length is 1.

```
Code   Length Value
+-----+-----+-----+
|  20 |  1  |  n  |
+-----+-----+-----+
```

A.2.22 Option 21: Policy Filter

This option specifies policy filters for non-local source routing. The filters consist of a list of IP addresses and masks that specify destination/mask pairs with which to filter incoming source routes. Any source routed datagram whose next hop address does not match one of the filters should be discarded by the client.

The code for this option is 21, and the minimum length of this option is 8. The length must be a multiple of 8.

```
Code   Length     Address 1                   Mask 1
+-----+-----+-----+-----+-----+-----+-----+-----+-----+-----+
|  21 |  n  | a1  | a2  | a3  | a4  | m1  | m2  | m3  | m4  |
+-----+-----+-----+-----+-----+-----+-----+-----+-----+-----+
```

```
                       Address 2                  Mask 2
+-----+-----+-----+-----+-----+-----+-----+-----+-----+
|  a1 |  a2 |  a3 |  a4 |  m1 |  m2 |  m3 |  m4 | [...]
+-----+-----+-----+-----+-----+-----+-----+-----+-----+
```

A.2.23   Option 22: Maximum Datagram Reassembly Size

This option specifies the maximum-size datagram that the client should be prepared to reassemble. The size is specified as a 16-bit unsigned integer. The minimum legal value is 576.

The code for this option is 22, and its length is 2.

```
 Code   Length    Size
+-----+-----+-----+-----+
|  22 |  2  |  s1 |  s2 |
+-----+-----+-----+-----+
```

A.2.24   Option 23: Default IP Time-to-Live

This option specifies the default Time-to-Live that the client should use for outgoing datagrams. The TTL is specified as an octet with a value between 1 and 255.

The code for this option is 23, and its length is 1.

```
 Code   Length   TTL
+-----+-----+-----+
|  23 |  1  | ttl |
+-----+-----+-----+
```

A.2.25   Option 24: Path MTU Aging Timeout

This option specifies the timeout (in seconds) to use when aging path maximum transmission unit (MTU) values discovered by the mechanism defined in RFC 1191. The timeout is specified as a 32-bit unsigned integer.

The code for this option is 24, and its length is 4.

```
 Code   Length    Timeout
+-----+-----+-----+-----+-----+-----+
|  24 |  4  |  t1 |  t2 |  t3 |  t4 |
+-----+-----+-----+-----+-----+-----+
```

A.2.26 Option 25: Path MTU Plateau Table

This option specifies a table of MTU sizes to use when performing path MTU discovery as defined in RFC 1191. The table is formatted as a list of 16-bit unsigned integers, ordered from smallest to largest. The minimum MTU value cannot be smaller than 68.

The code for this option is 25, and its minimum length is 2. The length must be a multiple of 2.

```
Code   Length   Size 1       Size 2
+-----+-----+-----+-----+-----+-----+-----+
| 25  |  n  | s1  | s2  | s1  | s2  |[...]|
+-----+-----+-----+-----+-----+-----+-----+
```

A.2.27 Option 26: Interface MTU

This option specifies the MTU to use for this interface. The MTU is specified as a 16-bit unsigned integer. The minimum legal value for the MTU is 68.

The code for this option is 26, and its length is 2.

```
Code   Length   MTU
+-----+-----+-----+-----+
| 26  |  2  | m1  | m2  |
+-----+-----+-----+-----+
```

A.2.28 Option 27: All Subnets Are Local

This option specifies whether or not the client may assume that all subnets of the IP network to which the client is connected use the same MTU as the subnet of that network to which the client is directly connected. A value of 1 indicates that all subnets share the same MTU. A value of 0 means that the client should assume that some subnets of the directly connected network may have smaller MTUs.

The code for this option is 27, and its length is 1.

```
Code   Length Value
+-----+-----+-----+
| 27  |  1  |  n  |
+-----+-----+-----+
```

A.2.29 Option 28: Broadcast Address

This option specifies the broadcast address in use on the client's subnet. The code for this option is 28, and its length is 4.

```
Code   Length      Broadcast Address
+-----+-----+-----+-----+-----+-----+
| 28  |  4  | b1  | b2  | b3  | b4  |
+-----+-----+-----+-----+-----+-----+
```

A.2.30 Option 29: Perform Mask Discovery

This option specifies whether or not the client should perform subnet mask discovery using ICMP. A value of 0 indicates that the client should not perform mask discovery. A value of 1 means that the client should perform mask discovery.

The code for this option is 29, and its length is 1.

```
Code   Length Value
+-----+-----+-----+
| 29  |  1  |  n  |
+-----+-----+-----+
```

A.2.31 Option 30: Mask Supplier

This option specifies whether or not the client should respond to subnet mask requests using ICMP. A value of 0 indicates that the client should not respond. A value of 1 means that the client should respond.

The code for this option is 30, and its length is 1.

```
Code   Length Value
+-----+-----+-----+
| 30  |  1  |  n  |
+-----+-----+-----+
```

A.2.32 Option 31: Perform Router Discovery

This option specifies whether or not the client should solicit routers using the router discovery mechanism defined in RFC 1256. A value of 0 indicates that the client should not perform router discovery. A value of 1 means that the client should perform router discovery.

The code for this option is 31, and its length is 1.

```
Code   Length Value
+-----+-----+-----+
|  31 |  1  |  n  |
+-----+-----+-----+
```

A.2.33 Option 32: Router Solicitation Address

This option specifies the address to which the client should transmit router solicitation requests. The code for this option is 32, and its length is 4.

```
Code   Length     Address
+-----+-----+-----+-----+-----+-----+
|  32 |  4  |  a1 |  a2 |  a3 |  a4 |
+-----+-----+-----+-----+-----+-----+
```

A.2.34 Option 33: Static Route

This option specifies a list of static routes that the client should install in its routing cache. If multiple routes to the same destination are specified, they are listed in descending order of priority. The routes consist of a list of IP address pairs. The first address is the destination address, and the second address is the router for the destination. The default route (0.0.0.0) is an illegal destination for a static route.

The code for this option is 33, and the minimum length for this option is 8. The length must be a multiple of 8.

```
Code   Length   Destination 1            Router 1
+-----+-----+-----+-----+-----+-----+-----+-----+-----+-----+
|  33 |  n  |  d1 |  d2 |  d3 |  d4 |  r1 |  r2 |  r3 |  r4 |
+-----+-----+-----+-----+-----+-----+-----+-----+-----+-----+
  Destination 2              Router 2
+-----+-----+-----+-----+-----+-----+-----+-----+-----+
|  d1 |  d2 |  d3 |  d4 |  r1 |  r2 |  r3 |  r4 | [...]
+-----+-----+-----+-----+-----+-----+-----+-----+-----+
```

A.2.35 Option 34: Trailer Encapsulation

This option specifies whether or not the client should negotiate the use of trailers (RFC 893) when using the ARP protocol. A value of 0 indicates

DHCP Options (RFC 2132)

that the client should not attempt to use trailers. A value of 1 means that the client should attempt to use trailers.

The code for this option is 34, and its length is 1.

```
Code   Length Value
+-----+-----+-----+
|  34 |  1  |  n  |
+-----+-----+-----+
```

A.2.36   Option 35: ARP Cache Timeout

This option specifies the timeout, in seconds, for ARP cache entries. The time is specified as a 32-bit unsigned integer.

The code for this option is 35, and its length is 4.

```
Code   Length      Time
+-----+-----+-----+-----+-----+-----+
|  35 |  4  | t1  | t2  | t3  | t4  |
+-----+-----+-----+-----+-----+-----+
```

A.2.37   Option 36: Ethernet Encapsulation

This option specifies whether or not the client should use Ethernet Version 2 (RFC 894) or IEEE 802.3 (RFC 1042) encapsulation if the interface is Ethernet. A value of 0 indicates that the client should use RFC 894 encapsulation. A value of 1 means that the client should use RFC 1042 encapsulation.

The code for this option is 36, and its length is 1.

```
Code   Length Value
+-----+-----+-----+
|  36 |  1  |  n  |
+-----+-----+-----+
```

A.2.38   Option 37: TCP Default Time-to-Live

This option specifies the default Time-to-Live that the client should use when sending TCP segments. The value is represented as an 8-bit unsigned integer. The minimum value is 1.

The code for this option is 37, and its length is 1.

```
Code  Length  TTL
+-----+-----+-----+
|  37 |  1  |  n  |
+-----+-----+-----+
```

A.2.39 Option 38: TCP Keep-Alive Interval

This option specifies the interval, in seconds, that the client should wait before sending a keep-alive message on a TCP connection. The time is specified as a 32-bit unsigned integer. A value of zero indicates that the client should not generate keep-alive messages on connections unless specifically requested by an application.

The code for this option is 38, and its length is 4.

```
Code  Length   Time
+-----+-----+-----+-----+-----+-----+
|  38 |  4  | t1  | t2  | t3  | t4  |
+-----+-----+-----+-----+-----+-----+
```

A.2.40 Option 39: TCP Keep-Alive Garbage

This option specifies whether or not the client should send TCP keep-alive messages with an octet of garbage for compatibility with older implementations. A value of 0 indicates that a garbage octet should not be sent. A value of 1 indicates that a garbage octet should be sent.

The code for this option is 39, and its length is 1.

```
Code  Length  Value
+-----+-----+-----+
|  39 |  1  |  n  |
+-----+-----+-----+
```

A.2.41 Option 40: Network Information Service Domain

This option specifies the name of the client's Network Information Service (NIS) domain. The domain is formatted as a string consisting of characters from the NVT ASCII character set.

The code for this option is 40, and its minimum length is 1.

```
Code  Length   NIS Domain Name
+-----+-----+-----+-----+-----+-----+
|  40 |  n  | n1  | n2  | n3  | n4  | [...]
+-----+-----+-----+-----+-----+-----+
```

DHCP Options (RFC 2132)

A.2.42   Option 41: NIS Server

This option specifies a list of IP addresses indicating NIS servers available to the client. Servers should be listed in order of preference.

The code for this option is 41, and its minimum length is 4. The length must be a multiple of 4.

```
 Code  Length     Address 1                   Address 2
+-----+-----+-----+-----+-----+-----+-----+-----+-----+
| 41  |  n  | a1  | a2  | a3  | a4  | a1  | a2  | [...]
+-----+-----+-----+-----+-----+-----+-----+-----+-----+
```

A.2.43   Option 42: Network Time Protocol Server

This option specifies a list of IP addresses indicating Network Time Protocol (NTP) servers available to the client. Servers should be listed in order of preference.

The code for this option is 42, and its minimum length is 4. The length must be a multiple of 4.

```
Code Length      Address 1                   Address 2
+----+-----+-----+-----+-----+-----+-----+-----+-----+
| 42 |  n  | a1  | a2  | a3  | a4  | a1  | a2  | [...]
+----+-----+-----+-----+-----+-----+-----+-----+-----+
```

A.2.44   Option 43: Vendor-Specific Information

This option is used by clients and servers to exchange vendor-specific information. The information is an opaque object of n octets, presumably interpreted by vendor-specific code on the clients and servers. The definition of this information is vendor-specific.

The vendor is indicated in the Vendor Class Identifier option. Servers not equipped to interpret the vendor-specific information sent by a client must ignore it, although it may be reported. Clients that do not receive desired vendor-specific information should make an attempt to operate without it, although they may do so, and announce they are doing so, with degraded functionality.

If a vendor potentially encodes more than one item of information in this option, then the vendor should encode the option using "encapsulated vendor-specific options." The Encapsulated Vendor-Specific

Options field should be encoded as a sequence of code/length/value fields of identical syntax to the DHCP Options field with the following exceptions:

- There should not be a "magic cookie" field in the Encapsulated Vendor-Specific Extensions field.
- Codes other than 0 or 255 may be redefined by the vendor within the Encapsulated Vendor-Specific Extensions field, but should conform to the tag/length/value syntax.
- Code 255 (End option), if present, signifies the end of the encapsulated Vendor Extensions, not the end of the vendor extensions field. If no code 255 is present, then the end of the Enclosing Vendor-Specific information field is taken as the end of the Encapsulated Vendor-Specific Extensions field.

The code for this option is 43, and its minimum length is 1.

```
Code   Length   Vendor-Specific Information
+-----+-----+-----+-----+-----+
| 43  |  n  | i1  | i2  | [...] |
+-----+-----+-----+-----+-----+
```

When encapsulated vendor-specific extensions are used, the information bytes (i1 to in) have the following format:

```
Code   Length   Data Item   Code   Length   Data Item   Code
+-----+-----+-----+-----+-----+-----+-----+-----+-----+-----+
| T1  |  n  | d1  | d2  | ... | T2  |  n  | D1  | D2  | ... | ... |
+-----+-----+-----+-----+-----+-----+-----+-----+-----+-----+
```

A.2.45   Option 44: NetBIOS over TCP/IP Name Server Option

The NetBIOS Name Server (NBNS) option specifies a list of RFC 1001/1002 NBNS name servers, such as Shadow IPserver, listed in order of preference. The code for this option is 44, and the minimum length of the option is 4 octets. The length must always be a multiple of 4.

```
Code   Length   Address 1               Address 2
+-----+-----+-----+-----+-----+-----+-----+-----+-----+-----+-----+
| 44  |  n  | a1  | a2  | a3  | a4  | b1  | b2  | b3  | b4  | [...] |
+-----+-----+-----+-----+-----+-----+-----+-----+-----+-----+-----+
```

DHCP Options (RFC 2132)

A.2.46 Option 45: NetBIOS over TCP/IP Datagram Distribution Server

The NetBIOS Datagram Distribution Server (NBDD) option specifies a list of RFC 1001/1002 NBDD servers listed in order of preference. The code for this option is 45, and the minimum length of the option is 4 octets. The length must always be a multiple of 4.

```
Code   Length   Address 1                    Address 2
+-----+-----+-----+-----+-----+-----+-----+-----+-----+-----+-----+
| 45  |  n  | a1  | a2  | a3  | a4  | b1  | b2  | b3  | b4  |[...]|
+-----+-----+-----+-----+-----+-----+-----+-----+-----+-----+-----+
```

A.2.47 Option 46: NetBIOS over TCP/IP Node Type

The NetBIOS Node Type option allows NetBIOS over TCP/IP clients to be configured as described in RFC 1001/1002. The value is specified as a single octet that identifies the client type as follows:

Value (Hex)	Node Type
01	B-node
02	P-node
04	M-node
08	H-node

The code for this option is 46, and the length of this option is always 1.

```
Code   Length   Node Type
+-----+-----+-----------+
| 46  |  1  | See Above |
+-----+-----+-----------+
```

A.2.48 Option 47: NetBIOS over TCP/IP Scope

This option specifies the NetBIOS over TCP/IP scope parameter for the client as described in RFC 1001/1002. (Certain restrictions on the characters that can be used may apply.)

The code for this option is 47, and the minimum length of this option is 1.

```
 Code   Length     NetBIOS Scope
+-----+-----+-----+-----+-----+-----+-----+
|  47 |  n  |  s1 |  s2 |  s3 |  s4 | ... |
+-----+-----+-----+-----+-----+-----+-----+
```

A.2.49   Option 48: X Window System Font Server Option

This option specifies a list of X Window System font servers available to the client. Servers should be listed in order of preference.

The code for this option is 48, and the minimum length of this option is 4 octets. The length must be a multiple of 4.

```
 Code   Length     Address 1                Address 2
+-----+-----+-----+-----+-----+-----+-----+-----+-----+
|  48 |  n  |  a1 |  a2 |  a3 |  a4 |  a1 |  a2 | ... |
+-----+-----+-----+-----+-----+-----+-----+-----+-----+
```

A.2.50   Option 49: X Window System Display Manager

This option specifies a list of IP addresses of systems that are running the X Window System Display Manager and are available to the client. Addresses should be listed in order of preference.

The code for this option is 49, and the minimum length of this option is 4. The length must be a multiple of 4.

```
 Code   Length     Address 1                Address 2
+-----+-----+-----+-----+-----+-----+-----+-----+-----+
|  49 |  n  |  a1 |  a2 |  a3 |  a4 |  a1 |  a2 | ... |
+-----+-----+-----+-----+-----+-----+-----+-----+-----+
```

A.2.51   Option 64: NIS+ Domain

This option specifies the name of the client's NIS+ domain. The domain is formatted as a string consisting of characters from the NVT ASCII character set.

DHCP Options (RFC 2132)

The code for this option is 64, and its minimum length is 1.

```
Code   Length       NIS+ Domain Name
+-----+-----+-----+-----+-----+-----+-----+
|  64 |  n  | n1  | n2  | n3  | n4  |[...]|
+-----+-----+-----+-----+-----+-----+-----+
```

A.2.52   Option 65: S+ Server

This option specifies a list of IP addresses indicating NIS+ servers available to the client. Servers should be listed in order of preference.

The code for this option is 65, and its minimum length is 4. The length must be a multiple of 4.

```
Code   Length     Address 1                Address 2
+-----+-----+-----+-----+-----+-----+-----+-----+-----+
|  65 |  n  | a1  | a2  | a3  | a4  | a1  | a2  |[...]|
+-----+-----+-----+-----+-----+-----+-----+-----+-----+
```

A.2.53   Option 68: Mobile IP Home Agent

This option specifies a list of IP addresses indicating Mobile IP home agents available to the client. Agents should be listed in order of preference.

The code for this option is 68. Its minimum length is 0, indicating no home agents are available. The length must be a multiple of 4. The usual length will be 4 octets, containing a single home agent's address.

```
Code   Length    Address 1
+-----+-----+-----+-----+-----+-----+-----+
|  68 |  n  | a1  | a2  | a3  | a4  |[...]|
+-----+-----+-----+-----+-----+-----+-----+
```

A.2.54   Option 69: Simple Mail Transport Protocol (SMTP) Server

This option specifies a list of SMTP servers available to the client. Servers should be listed in order of preference.

The code for the SMTP server option is 69, and the minimum length for this option is 4 octets. The length must always be a multiple of 4.

```
Code   Length    Address 1              Address 2
+-----+-----+-----+-----+-----+-----+-----+-----+-----+
| 69  |  n  | a1  | a2  | a3  | a4  | a1  | a2  |[...]|
+-----+-----+-----+-----+-----+-----+-----+-----+-----+
```

A.2.55 Option 70: Post Office Protocol (POP3) Server

This option specifies a list of POP3 mail servers available to the client. Servers should be listed in order of preference.

The code for the POP3 server option is 70, and the minimum length for this option is 4 octets. The length must always be a multiple of 4.

```
Code   Length    Address 1              Address 2
+-----+-----+-----+-----+-----+-----+-----+-----+-----+
| 70  |  n  | a1  | a2  | a3  | a4  | a1  | a2  |[...]|
+-----+-----+-----+-----+-----+-----+-----+-----+-----+
```

A.2.56 Option 71: Network News Transport Protocol (NNTP) Server

This option specifies a list of NNTP servers available to the client. Servers should be listed in order of preference.

The code for the NNTP Server option is 71, and the minimum length for this option is 4 octets. The length must always be a multiple of 4.

```
Code   Length    Address 1              Address 2
+-----+-----+-----+-----+-----+-----+-----+-----+-----+
| 71  |  n  | a1  | a2  | a3  | a4  | a1  | a2  |[...]|
+-----+-----+-----+-----+-----+-----+-----+-----+-----+
```

A.2.57 Option 72: Default World Wide Web (WWW) Server

This option specifies a list of WWW servers available to the client. Servers should be listed in order of preference.

The code for the WWW Server option is 72, and the minimum length for this option is 4 octets. The length must always be a multiple of 4.

```
Code   Length    Address 1              Address 2
+-----+-----+-----+-----+-----+-----+-----+-----+-----+
| 72  |  n  | a1  | a2  | a3  | a4  | a1  | a2  |[...]|
+-----+-----+-----+-----+-----+-----+-----+-----+-----+
```

DHCP Options (RFC 2132)

A.2.58 Option 73: Default Finger Server

This option specifies a list of Finger servers available to the client. Servers should be listed in order of preference.

The code for the Finger Server option is 73, and the minimum length for this option is 4 octets. The length must always be a multiple of 4.

```
Code   Length     Address 1               Address 2
+-----+-----+-----+-----+-----+-----+-----+-----+-----+
| 73  |  n  | a1  | a2  | a3  | a4  | a1  | a2  |[...]|
+-----+-----+-----+-----+-----+-----+-----+-----+-----+
```

A.2.59 Option 74: Default Internet Relay Chat (IRC) Server

This option specifies a list of IRC servers available to the client. Servers should be listed in order of preference.

The code for the IRC server option is 74, and the minimum length for this option is 4 octets. The length must always be a multiple of 4.

```
Code   Length     Address 1               Address 2
+-----+-----+-----+-----+-----+-----+-----+-----+-----+
| 74  |  n  | a1  | a2  | a3  | a4  | a1  | a2  |[...]|
+-----+-----+-----+-----+-----+-----+-----+-----+-----+
```

A.2.60 Option 75: StreetTalk Server

This option specifies a list of StreetTalk servers available to the client. Servers should be listed in order of preference.

The code for the StreetTalk server option is 75, and the minimum length for this option is 4 octets. The length must always be a multiple of 4.

```
Code   Length     Address 1               Address 2
+-----+-----+-----+-----+-----+-----+-----+-----+-----+
| 75  |  n  | a1  | a2  | a3  | a4  | a1  | a2  |[...]|
+-----+-----+-----+-----+-----+-----+-----+-----+-----+
```

A.2.61 Option 76: StreetTalk Directory Assistance (STDA) Server

This option specifies a list of StreetTalk Directory Assistance servers available to the client. Servers should be listed in order of preference.

Appendix A

The code for the StreetTalk Directory Assistance Server option is 76, and the minimum length for this option is 4 octets. The length must always be a multiple of 4.

```
Code  Length  Address 1               Address 2
+-----+-----+-----+-----+-----+-----+-----+-----+-----+
| 76  |  n  | a1  | a2  | a3  | a4  | a1  | a2  |[...]|
+-----+-----+-----+-----+-----+-----+-----+-----+-----+
```

A.3 DHCP-Only Options

This section introduces all DHCP-only options that can be defined at the DHCP server and delivered to requesting DHCP clients. Be aware that although most DHCP servers can deliver all options illustrated here to requesting DHCP clients, there are platform-specific dependencies that determine whether or not requesting DHCP clients can actually make use of all delivered information.

A.3.1 Option 50: Requested IP Address

This option is used in a client request (DHCPDISCOVER) to allow the client to request that a particular IP address be assigned. The code for this option is 50, and its length is 4.

```
Code   Length    Address
+-----+-----+-----+-----+-----+-----+
| 50  |  4  | a1  | a2  | a3  | a4  |
+-----+-----+-----+-----+-----+-----+
```

A.3.2 Option 51: IP Address Lease Time

This option is used in a client request (DHCPDISCOVER or DHCPREQUEST) to allow the client to request a lease time for the IP address. In a server reply (DHCPOFFER), a DHCP server uses this option to specify the lease time it is willing to offer. The time is expressed in seconds and is specified as a 32-bit unsigned integer.

The code for this option is 51, and its length is 4.

```
Code   Length    Lease Time
+-----+-----+-----+-----+-----+-----+
| 51  |  4  | t1  | t2  | t3  | t4  |
+-----+-----+-----+-----+-----+-----+
```

A.3.3 Option 52: Option Overload

This option is used to indicate that the DHCP Sname or File fields are being overloaded by using them to carry DHCP options. A DHCP server inserts this option if the returned parameters will exceed the usual space allotted for options. If this option is present, the client interprets the specified additional fields after it finishes interpretation of the standard option fields.

The code for this option is 52, and its length is 1. Legal values for this option are:

```
Value          Meaning

  1        The File field is used to hold options
  2        The Sname field is used to hold options
  3        Both fields are used to hold options

Code   Length Value
+-----+-----+-----+
|  52 |  1  |  n  |
+-----+-----+-----+
```

A.3.4 Option 53: DHCP Message Type

This option is used to convey the type of the DHCP message. The code for this option is 53, and its length is 1. Legal values for this option are as follows:

```
Value      Message Type

  1        DHCPDISCOVER
  2        DHCPOFFER
  3        DHCPREQUEST
  4        DHCPDECLINE
  5        DHCPACK
  6        DHCPNAK
  7        DHCPRELEASE
  8        DHCPINFORM

Code   Length  Type
+-----+-----+-----+
|  53 |  1  |  n  |
+-----+-----+-----+
```

A.3.5 Option 54: Server Identifier

This option is used in DHCPOFFER and DHCPREQUEST messages and may optionally be included in the DHCPACK and DHCPNAK messages.

DHCP servers include this option in the DHCPOFFER in order to allow the client to distinguish between lease offers. DHCP clients use the contents of the Server Identifier field as the destination address for any DHCP messages unicast to the DHCP server. DHCP clients also indicate which of several lease offers is being accepted by including this option in a DHCPREQUEST message. The identifier is the IP address of the selected server.

The code for this option is 54, and its length is 4.

```
Code   Length      Address
+-----+-----+-----+-----+-----+-----+
| 54  |  4  | a1  | a2  | a3  | a4  |
+-----+-----+-----+-----+-----+-----+
```

A.3.6 Option 55: Parameter Request List

This option is used by a DHCP client to request values for specified configuration parameters. The list of requested parameters is specified as n octets, where each octet is a valid DHCP option code as defined in this appendix. The client may list the options in order of preference. The DHCP server is not required to return the options in the requested order but must try to insert the requested options in the order requested by the client.

The code for this option is 55, and its minimum length is 1.

```
Code   Length    Option Codes
+-----+-----+-----+-----+-----+
| 55  |  n  | c1  | c2  |[...]|
+-----+-----+-----+-----+-----+
```

A.3.7 Option 56: Message

This option is used by a DHCP server to provide an error message to a DHCP client in a DHCPNAK message in the event of a failure. A client may use this option in a DHCPDECLINE message to indicate why the client declined the offered parameters. The message consists of n octets of NVT ASCII text, which the client may display on an available output device.

The code for this option is 56, and its minimum length is 1.

DHCP Options (RFC 2132)

```
 Code  Length   Text
+-----+-----+-----+-----+-----+
| 56  |  n  | c1  | c2  |[...]|
+-----+-----+-----+-----+-----+
```

A.3.8 Option 57: Maximum DHCP Message Size

This option specifies the maximum length of a DHCP message that a system is willing to accept. The length is specified as an unsigned 16-bit integer. A client may use the Maximum DHCP Message Size option in DHCPDISCOVER or DHCPREQUEST messages but should not use the option in DHCPDECLINE messages.

The code for this option is 57, and its length is 2. The minimum legal value is 576 octets.

```
 Code  Length     Length
+-----+-----+-----+-----+
| 57  |  2  | 11  | 12  |
+-----+-----+-----+-----+
```

A.3.9 Option 58: Renewal (T1) Time Value

This option specifies the time interval from address assignment until the client transitions to the RENEWING state. The value is in seconds and is specified as a 32-bit unsigned integer.

The code for this option is 58, and its length is 4.

```
 Code  Length      T1 Interval
+-----+-----+-----+-----+-----+-----+
| 58  |  4  | t1  | t2  | t3  | t4  |
+-----+-----+-----+-----+-----+-----+
```

A.3.10 Option 59: Rebinding (T2) Time Value

This option specifies the time interval from address assignment until the client transitions to the REBINDING state. The value is in seconds and is specified as a 32-bit unsigned integer.

The code for this option is 59, and its length is 4.

```
Code   Length      T2 Interval
+-----+-----+-----+-----+-----+-----+
|  59 |  4  |  t1 |  t2 |  t3 |  t4 |
+-----+-----+-----+-----+-----+-----+
```

A.3.11   Option 60: Vendor Class Identifier

This option is used by DHCP clients to optionally identify the vendor type and configuration of a DHCP client. The information is a string of n octets, interpreted by servers. Vendors may choose to define specific vendor class identifiers to convey particular configuration or other identification information about a client. For example, the identifier may include the client's hardware configuration. Servers not equipped to interpret the class-specific information sent by a client must ignore it, although it may be reported. Servers that respond should only use option 43 to return the vendor-specific information to the client.

The code for this option is 60, and its minimum length is 1.

```
Code   Length     Vendor Class Identifier
+-----+-----+-----+-----+-----+
|  60 |  n  |  i1 |  i2 | [...]
+-----+-----+-----+-----+-----+
```

A.3.12   Option 61: Client Identifier

This option is used by DHCP clients to specify their own unique identifiers. DHCP servers use this value to index their database of address bindings. This value is expected to be unique for all clients in an administrative domain. Identifiers should be treated as opaque objects by DHCP servers. The client identifier may consist of type/value pairs similar to Htype/Chaddr fields. For instance, it may consist of a hardware type and hardware address. In this case, the Type field should be a defined ARP hardware type. A hardware type of 0 should be used when the Value field contains an identifier other than a hardware address (for instance, a fully qualified domain name). For correct identification of clients, each client's identifier must be unique among the identifiers used on the subnet to which the client is attached. Vendors and system administrators are responsible for choosing identifiers that meet this requirement for uniqueness.

The code for this option is 61, and its minimum length is 2.

DHCP Options (RFC 2132)

```
Code   Length      Type Client Identifier
+-----+-----+-----+-----+-----+-----+
|  61 |  n  |  t1 |  i1 |  i2 | [...]
+-----+-----+-----+-----+-----+-----+
```

A.3.13 Option 66: TFTP Server Name

This option is used to identify a TFTP server when the Sname field in the DHCP header has been used for DHCP options. The code for this option is 66, and its minimum length is 1.

```
Code   Length      TFTP server
+-----+-----+-----+-----+-----+-----+
|  66 |  n  |  c1 |  c2 |  c3 | [...]
+-----+-----+-----+-----+-----+-----+
```

A.3.14 Option 67: Boot File Name

This option is used to identify a boot file when the File field in the DHCP header has been used for DHCP options. The code for this option is 67, and its minimum length is 1.

```
Code   Length      Boot File Name
+-----+-----+-----+-----+-----+-----+
|  67 |  n  |  c1 |  c2 |  c3 | [...]
+-----+-----+-----+-----+-----+-----+
```

A.4 Unofficial DHCP Options

Several additional options, while not yet part of the official RFC 2132 standard, have achieved some degree of popularity and are in common use. If you are interested in the latest inventory of unofficially assigned DHCP options, the list is available on the Internet at *ftp://ftp.isi.edu/in-notes/iana/assignments*.

Option	Description
62	NetWare/IP Domain Name
63	NetWare/IP Suboptions
77	User Class

Option	Description
78	Directory Agent Information
79	Service Location Agent Scope
80	Naming Authority
81	Client Fully Qualified Domain Name
82	Agent Circuit ID
83	Agent Remote ID
84	Agent Subnet Mask
85	Novell Directory Services Servers
86	Novell Directory Services Tree Name
87	Novell Directory Services Context
88	IEEE 1003.1 POSIX Timezone
89	Fully Qualified Domain Name
90	Authentication
91	Banyan Vines TCP/IP Server
92	Server Selection
93	Client System Architecture
94	Client Network Device Interface
95	Lightweight Directory Access Protocol (LDAP)
96	IPv6 Transitions
97	UUID/GUID-based Client Identifier
100	Printer Name
101	Multicast Scope
102	Start Time
103	Multicast Time-to-Live
104	Multicast Block Size
105	Client Port
106	Cookie
107	Multicast Scope List
108	Swap Path
109	Autonomous System Number (ASN)
110	IPX Compatibility
111	Served IP Range

DHCP Options (RFC 2132)

Option	Description
112	NetInfo Parent Server Address
113	NetInfo Parent Server Tag
114	Universal Resource Locator (URL)
115	DHCP Failover Protocol
126	Extension
127	Extension

By convention, a few vendors, such as IBM, may use additional DHCP options in the 200 to 208 range. You may wish to use these same option numbers for the same purposes, even on non-IBM platforms.

200	Default LPR Printer
201	Default Gopher Server
202	Default WWW Home Page
203	Default WWW Proxy Gateway
204	Default WWW News Server
205	Default SOCKS Server
206	NFS Mount Points
207	Default X Font Servers
208	X Display Manager Servers

A.5 Options Supported by Popular Operating Systems

This section provides information about strengths and weaknesses some DHCP servers and DHCP clients encounter.

A.5.1 Servers

UNIX, Shadow IPserver, and Windows NT Server can serve any and all DHCP options to clients. However, it appears that it is not possible to alter option 1 in at least some releases of Windows NT Server in order to assign a subnet mask to a client that is not identical to the server's own subnet mask.

UNIX tends to provide the most flexibility in defining address pools.

A.5.2 Clients

Most flavors of UNIX support all DHCP options, and DHCP option handlers are provided for most of the standard DHCP options. Others can be interpreted and acted upon by the client using custom option handlers. Windows 95 and Windows NT support a more limited set of options, notably 1, 3, 6, 44, 46, and 47. Third-party products may be required to intercept and handle less commonly used DHCP options.

INDEX

A

A records, 61
Active mode (RIP), 120
Addermask utility, 358–359
Address Lifetime Expectations (ALE), 280
Address Resolution Protocol (ARP), 14, 180
Address(es), 3–6
  care-of, 171, 172, 174, 187
  dynamic, 11
  home, 171, 172
  in IPv6, 292–298
    anycast addresses, 297–298
    Global Unicast address, 294–296
    multicast addresses, 296–297
    unicast addresses, 293–296
  network, 3
  static, 11
  subnets of, 7
Adjacent routers, 131
Adjacent routers (OSPF), 141–143
Admission control (Integrated Services model), 244
Agent advertisement messages, 173–174
Agent discovery, 171–172
Agents:
  foreign, 172, 186–187
  home, 171, 172, 186–190
  mobility, 172
AIX, 212
ALE (Address Lifetime Expectations), 280
Alias names, 13
All bits 0, 5
All bits 1, 5
All Subnets Are Local (Option 27), 402
Anycast addresses, 297–298

APIs (application programming interfaces), 41
Application layer, 228–234
Application programming interfaces (APIs), 41
Area border routers, 128
Area ID (OSPF), 134
Areas (OSPF), 127–128
ARP (*see* Address Resolution Protocol)
ARP Cache Timeout (Option 35), 405
arp command, 221, 224
ARPANET, 51
AS boundary routers, 128
AS external link advertisements, 136
ASs (*see* Autonomous systems)
Audit Manager (QIP Enterprise 5.0), 367
Authentication header, 291–292
Authoritative name servers, 58
Automated subnet masks, 35
Automatic tunneling, 322–326
Autonomous systems (ASs), 108, 109

B

Backbone, OSPF, 128
Backup designated routers, 132
Bandwidth efficiency, 238–240
Bay Networks, 372
B-bit (Mobile IP registration), 176
Berkeley Internet Name Domain (BIND), 65–68
Best-effort, 242, 255
BGP (*see* Border Gateway Protocol)
BGP-4 (*see* Border Gateway Protocol)
BIND (*see* Berkeley Internet Name Domain)
Boot File Name (Option 67), 419

Boot File Size (Option 13), 398
BootP (*see* Bootstrap Protocol)
`BOOTP Address from Pool` **parameter** (BootP), 350
`BOOTP Packet Size` **parameter** (BootP), 349
Bootstrap Protocol (BootP), 11
  and JOIN, 346–350
    Dynamic BootP, 347–348
    Finite BootP, 348
    traditional BootP, 347
  options
    All Subnets Are Local (Option 27), 402
    ARP Cache Timeout (Option 35), 405
    Boot File Size (Option 13), 398
    Broadcast Address (Option 28), 403
    Cookie Server (Option 8), 396–397
    Default Finger Server (Option 73), 413
    Default IP Time-to-Live (Option 23), 401
    Default IRC Server (Option 74), 413
    Default WWW Server (Option 72), 412
    Domain Name (Option 15), 398–399
    Domain Name Server (Option 6), 396
    End (Option 255), 394
    Ethernet Encapsulation (Option 36), 405
    Extensions Path (Option 18), 399
    Host Name (Option 12), 398
    Impress Server (Option 10), 397
    Interface MTU (Option 26), 402
    IP Forwarding Enable/Disable (Option 19), 400
    Log Server (Option 7), 396
    LPR Server (Option 9), 397
    Mask Supplier (Option 30), 403
    Maximum Datagram Reassembly Size (Option 22), 401
    Merit Dump File (Option 14), 398
    Mobile IP Home Agent (Option 68), 411
    Name Server (Option 5), 395–396
    NetBIOS over TCP/IP Datagram Distribution Server (Option 45), 409
    NetBIOS over TCP/IP Name Server Option (Option 44), 408

Bootstrap Protocol (BootP), options (*Cont.*):
    NetBIOS over TCP/IP Node Type (Option 46), 409
    NetBIOS over TCP/IP Scope (Option 47), 409–410
    Network Information Service Domain (Option 40), 406
    Network Information Service Server (Option 41), 407
    Network Time Protocol Server (Option 42), 407
    NIS+ Domain (Option 64), 410–411
    NIS+ Server (Option 65), 411
    NNTP Server (Option 71), 412
    Non-Local Source Routing Enable/Disable (Option 20), 400
    Pad (Option 0), 394
    Path MTU Aging Timeout (Option 24), 401
    Path MTU Plateau Table (Option 25), 402
    Perform Mask Discovery (Option 29), 403
    Perform Router Discovery (Option 31), 403–404
    Policy Filter (Option 21), 400–401
    POP3 Server (Option 70), 412
    Resource Location Server (Option 11), 397
    Root Path (Option 17), 399
    Router (Option 3), 395
    Router Solicitation Address (Option 32), 404
    SMTP Server (Option 69), 411–412
    Static Route (Option 33), 404
    StreetTalk Directory Assistance Server (Option 76), 413–414
    StreetTalk Server (Option 75), 413
    Subnet Mask (Option 1), 394
    Swap Server (Option 16), 399
    TCP Default Time-to-Live (Option 37), 405–406

Index

Bootstrap Protocol (BootP), options (*Cont.*):
    TCP Keep-Alive Garbage (Option 39), 406
    TCP Keep-Alive Interval (Option 38), 406
    Time Offset (Option 2), 395
    Time Server (Option 4), 395
    Trailer Encapsulation (Option 34), 404–405
    Vendor-Specific Information (Option 43), 407–408
    X Window System Display Manager (Option 49), 410
    X Window System Font Server Option (Option 48), 410
  as predecessor of DHCP, 18–19
  relay agents in, 72
Border Gateway Protocol (BGP-4), 152–166
  maintaining connections with, 160–162
  and NLRI, 162, 163
  notification messages in, 165–166
  opening/confirming connections with, 159–160
  path attributes in, 162–164
  path selection in, 156–157
  reachability information, sending of, 161–162
  and routing information exchange, 158–159
  routing policy recommendations for, 157–158
  terminology, 153–156
  withdrawn routes in, 164–165
Bottom-up approach (to troubleshooting), 224–234
Boundary nodes (Differentiated Services), 268–270
Boundless networking, 181
Broadcast Address (Option 28), 403
Broadcast datagrams, 178
Broadcast networks, 132

Bucket capacity, 247
Business travelers, use of Mobile IP by, 185–186

C

Caching-only name servers, 58
Care-of address(es), 171, 172
  co-located, 174, 187
  foreign agent, 187
CDDM (*see* Cisco DNS/DHCP Manager)
Cellular technologies, 182
Centralized database (NetBIOS), 90
CERT (Computer Emergency Response Team), 193
Check BOOTP Client Net **parameter** (BootP), 349
Child name servers, 58–59
CIDR (*see* Classless Inter-Domain Routing)
Cisco, 170, 181
Cisco DHCP/BootP server:
  and multiple logical networks, 344–345
  updating DNS via, 341–344
Cisco DNS/DHCP Manager (CDDM), 334–341
  applications of, 334–335
  DNM server in, 338–341
  features/benefits of, 335–336
  hardware platforms for, 337
  service management with, 345–346
Cisco IOS, 188–190
Class A addresses, 3–4
Class B addresses, 4
Class C addresses, 4
Class D addresses, 5
Class E addresses, 5
Class ID, 33
Classifiers, 268
Classless Inter-Domain Routing (CIDR), 152, 280
Client failures, 211–212
Client ID, 32–33
Client Identifier (Option 61), 418–419

CNAME records, 62
Co-located care-of addresses, 174, 187
.com, 51
Computer Emergency Response Team (CERT), 193
Configured tunneling, 326–328
Connections, severed, 209
Controlled Load Service, 248–249
Cookie Server (Option 8), 396–397
Correspondent node, 172
Counting to infinity, 113–115

D

Daemons, routing, 108–109
Data link layer, 224–225
Datagrams, 2
　broadcast, 178
　NetBIOS, 90–92
D-bit (Mobile IP registration), 176
DDNS (see Dynamic DNS)
Default Finger Server (Option 73), 413
Default IP Time-to-Live (Option 23), 401
Default IRC Server (Option 74), 413
Default WWW Server (Option 72), 412
Delivery vehicles, use of Mobile IP in, 185
Designated routers, 132
Designated routers (OSPF), 138–141
DHCP (see Dynamic Host Configuration Protocol)
DHCP Message Type (Option 53), 415
DHCPACK message, 25, 26
DHCPREQUEST message, 24
Differentiated Services model, 243, 263–277
　architecture of, 264–273
　boundary nodes in, 268–270
　domains in, 267, 271–273
　interior components of, 270–271
　Internet drafts on, 277
　with IPSec, 276–277
　with LDAP, 275–276
　per-hop behavior in, 264–267

Differentiated Services model (*Cont.*):
　with RSVP, 273–275
　Service Level Agreement in, 263–264
Direct routing (delivery), 10
Directed graph, 134
Distance vector reouting, 111–116
Distributed database (NetBIOS), 87–89
DNM (see Domain Name Manager)
DNS (see Domain Name System)
Domain:
　Differential Services, 267, 271–273
Domain Name Manager (DNM), 338–341
　browser, DNM, 340–341
　clients, DNM, 339–340
　users, DNM, 341
Domain Name (Option 15), 398–399
Domain Name Server (Option 6), 396
Domain Name System (DNS), 12, 50–53
　BIND, treatment of database entries in, 65–68
　in IPv6, 314–318
　Meta DNS, 385–387
　QIP Enterprise 5.0, 361–362
　resolvers in, 62–65
　static DNS, 13
　See also Cisco DNS/DHCP Manager; Dynamic DNS; Name servers
Domain names, 12
Domains:
　top-level, 51–52
　zones of authority vs., 54–56
Droppers, packet, 268–269
Dynamic addresses, 11
Dynamic BootP, 347–348
Dynamic DNS (DDNS), 13, 69, 169
　dynamic addressing with, 78
　security with, 194–201
Dynamic Host Configuration Protocol (DHCP), 11, 17–48, 169
　BootP as predecessor of, 18–19
　client identification in, 30–36
　　Class ID, 33
　　Client ID, 32–33
　　MAC address, 31–32

Index

Dynamic Host Configuration Protocol (DHCP), client identification in (*Cont.*):
    multiple qualifiers, use of, 36
    relay agents, qualification from, 34–35
    vendor extensions, qualification from, 33–34
  components, network, 19, 20
  functioning of, 21–30
    changes, implementation of, 27–28
    configuration information, acquisition of, 21–26
    lease renewals, 26, 27
    with multiple pools per subnet, 30
    with multiple subnets per pool, 29–30
    new subnets, moves to, 26–27
    and relay agents, 28–29
  host clients with, 19
  in IPv6, 47–48, 318–319
  leases in, 26, 27, 202–204, 216–218
  messages in, 319
  Meta DHCP, 383–385
  options, 393–422
    All Subnets Are Local (Option 27), 402
    ARP Cache Timeout (Option 35), 405
    Boot File Name (Option 67), 419
    Boot File Size (Option 13), 398
    Broadcast Address (Option 28), 403
    Client Identifier (Option 61), 418–419
    Cookie Server (Option 8), 396–397
    Default Finger Server (Option 73), 413
    Default IP Time-to-Live (Option 23), 401
    Default IRC Server (Option 74), 413
    Default WWW Server (Option 72), 412
    DHCP Message Type (Option 53), 415
    Domain Name (Option 15), 398–399
    Domain Name Server (Option 6), 396
    End (Option 255), 394
    Ethernet Encapsulation (Option 36), 405
    Extensions Path (Option 18), 399
    Host Name (Option 12), 398
    Impress Server (Option 10), 397
    Interface MTU (Option 26), 402

Dynamic Host Configuration Protocol (DHCP), options (*Cont.*):
    IP Address Lease Time (Option 51), 414
    IP Forwarding Enable/Disable (Option 19), 400
    Log Server (Option 7), 396
    LPR Server (Option 9), 397
    Mask Supplier (Option 30), 403
    Maximum Datagram Reassembly Size (Option 22), 401
    Maximum DHCP Message Size (Option 57), 417
    Merit Dump File (Option 14), 398
    Message (Option 56), 416–417
    Mobile IP Home Agent (Option 68), 411
    Name Server (Option 5), 395–396
    NetBIOS over TCP/IP Datagram Distribution Server (Option 45), 409
    NetBIOS over TCP/IP Name Server Option (Option 44), 408
    NetBIOS over TCP/IP Node Type (Option 46), 409
    NetBIOS over TCP/IP Scope (Option 47), 409–410
    Network Information Service Domain (Option 40), 406
    Network Information Service Server (Option 41), 407
    Network Time Protocol Server (Option 42), 407
    NIS+ Domain (Option 64), 410–411
    NIS+ Server (Option 65), 411
    NNTP Server (Option 71), 412
    Non-Local Source Routing Enable/Disable (Option 20), 400
    Option Overload (Option 52), 415
    Pad (Option 0), 394
    Parameter Request List (Option 55), 416
    Path MTU Aging Timeout (Option 24), 401
    Path MTU Plateau Table (Option 25), 402

Dynamic Host Configuration Protocol (DHCP), options (*Cont.*):
  Perform Mask Discovery (Option 29), 403
  Perform Router Discovery (Option 31), 403–404
  Policy Filter (Option 21), 400–401
  POP3 Server (Option 70), 412
  popular operating systems, options supported by, 421–422
  Rebuilding Time Value (Option 59), 417–418
  Renewal Time Value (Option 58), 417
  Requested IP Address (Option 50), 414
  Resource Location Server (Option 11), 397
  Root Path (Option 17), 399
  Router (Option 3), 395
  Router Solicitation Address (Option 32), 404
  Server Identifier (Option 54), 415–416
  SMTP Server (Option 69), 411–412
  Static Route (Option 33), 404
  StreetTalk Directory Assistance Server (Option 76), 413–414
  StreetTalk Server (Option 75), 413
  Subnet Mask (Option 1), 394
  Swap Server (Option 16), 399
  TCP Default Time-to-Live (Option 37), 405–406
  TCP Keep-Alive Garbage (Option 39), 406
  TCP Keep-Alive Interval (Option 38), 406
  TFTP Server Name (Option 66), 419
  Time Offset (Option 2), 395
  Time Server (Option 4), 395
  Trailer Encapsulation (Option 34), 404–405
  unofficial options, 419–421
  Vendor Class Identifier (Option 60), 418
  Vendor-Specific Information (Option 43), 407–408

Dynamic Host Configuration Protocol (DHCP), options (*Cont.*):
  X Window System Display Manager (Option 49), 410
  X Window System Font Server Option (Option 48), 410
  QIP Enterprise 5.0, 361–362
  relay agents with, 21, 28–29
  "rogue" servers, 203
  security with, 194–203
  server administration in, 36–41
    access controls, 39
    database initialization, 37–38
    installation, 37
    remote servers, 40–41
    runtime database manipulation, 38–39
  server availability in, 41–47
    redundant backup servers, 42–47
    reliability, 41–42
  server problems with, 210
  servers with, 21, 72
  See also Cisco DNS/DHCP Manager
Dynamic IP, 68–78
  components of, 71–72
  features of, 68–71
  functioning of, 72–74
  host mobility, enabling, 76–77
  network availability, configuring for, 74–76
  and security, 77–78
Dynamic name servers, 56
Dynamic naming (JOIN), 352
Dynamic Presecured zone (DDNS), 196–197
Dynamic Secured zone (DDNS), 196

E

.edu, 51
EGP (Exterior Gateway Protocol), 152
EGPs (exterior gateway protocols), 150
Egress node, 268
Encapsulating Security Payload (ESP), 292

Index

Encapsulation:
   generic routing (GRE), 188.
   IP-in-IP, 188
End (Option 255), 394
Error messages (BGP), 165–166
ESP (Encapsulating Security Payload), 292
Ethernet Encapsulation (Option 36), 405
`Expand BOOTP Packet` parameter (BootP), 349
Extension headers, 285–287
Extensions Path (Option 18), 399
Exterior Gateway Protocol (EGP), 152
Exterior gateway protocols (EGPs), 150
Exterior routing protocols, 150–151

F

Facility loss, 209–210
Failure events, 208–212
   client failures, 211–212
   DHCP server problems, 210
   facility loss, 209–210
   name server problems, 210–211
   router outages, 210
   server failures, 210–211
   severed connections, 209
FAs (*see* Foreign agents)
Finite BootP, 348
Firewall name servers, 60
Firewalls, 14–15, 203–204
Fixed-Filter style, 257
Fixed-length subnet masking, 356–358
Flat switched networks, 34–35
Flooding, 117–118, 143
Flow labels, 298–299
Fluid model, 250
Foreign agent care-of addresses, 187
Foreign agents (FAs), 172, 186–189
Forwarder name servers, 60
Fragment header, 291
Full resolver, 63–64
Fully qualified name, 12

G

Gated daemon, 109
Gated Version 3, 124
Gateway address, 10
Gateway protocols, 109
G-bit (Mobile IP registration), 176
Generic routing encapsulation (GRE), 170, 188
Global Unicast address, 294–296
`.gov`, 52
Gratuitous ARP, 180
GRE (*see* Generic routing encapsulation)
Guaranteed Service, 249–250

H

HAs (*see* Home agents)
Header (OSPF), 136
Hello protocol (OSPF), 138
HINFO records, 62
Home address, 171, 172
Home agents (HAs), 171, 172, 186–190
Home network, 172
Hop-by-hop header, 287–289
Host address, 3
Host clients (DHCP networks), 19
`host` command, 222, 228
Host Name (Option 12), 398
Hot Standby Router Protocol (HSRP), 189
Hot-standby approach, 45–46
HSRP (Hot Standby Router Protocol), 189

I

ICMP (*see* Internet Control Message Protocol)
ICMP Router Discovery Protocol (IRPD), 186–187
ICMPv6 (*see* Internet Control Message Protocol version 6)
IDs (Internet Drafts), 16

IETF (*see* Internet Engineering Task Force)
IGMP (Internet Group Management Protocol), 14
IGPs (*see* Interior gateway protocols)
Impress Server (Option 10), 397
Indirect routing, 10
Ingress node, 268
Integrated Services model, 242–263
   classes of service in, 246–250
      Controlled Load Service, 248–249
      Guaranteed Service, 249–250
   future of, 261–263
   router components in, 243–245
      admission control, 244
      packet classifier, 244
      packet scheduler, 243–244
   RSVP, 245–246, 250–261
Interface MTU (Option 26), 402
Interfaces (OSPF), 133
Interior gateway protocols (IGPs), 118–150
   Open Shortest Path First (OSPF), 126–150
      adjacencies, establishment of, 141–143
      designated router, election, 138–141
      header, 136
      Hello protocol, 138
      link-state propagation, 143–146
      packets in, 136–138
      routing table, calculation of, 146–150
      terminology of, 137–136
   RIPng for IPv6, 124–126
   Routing Information Protocol (RIP), 118–124
      and OSPF, 119
      packet types in, 120
      version 2 of, 122–124
Internet, 51, 80
Internet Control Message Protocol (ICMP), 14, 106–107, 188

Internet Control Message Protocol version 6 (ICMPv6), 299–314
   Multicast Listener Discovery, 311–314
   neighbor discovery in, 300–310
      and address resolution, 301–303
      and neighbor unreachability detection, 308, 310
      and redirection, 306–309
      router/prefix discovery, 303–306
      stateless autoconfiguration, 310–311
Internet Domain Survey, 279
Internet Drafts (IDs), 16
Internet Engineering Task Force (IETF), 16, 46, 78, 79, 170, 280
Internet Group Management Protocol (IGMP), 14
Internet Protocol (IP), 3
   addressing in, 3–6, 11
   routing with, 10–11
   subnets, IP, 6–9
Internet Protocol next generation (IPng), 281
Internet Protocol version 6 (IPv6), 14, 47–48, 279–331
   addressing in, 292–298
      anycast addresses, 297–298
      Global Unicast address, 294–296
      multicast addresses, 296–297
      unicast addresses, 293–296
   DHCP in, 318–319
   DNS in, 314–318
   drive toward, 330–331
   features of, 281
   flow in, 298–299
   headers in, 281–292
      authentication header, 291–292
      destination options header, 292
      Encapsulating Security Payload, 292
      extension headers, 285–287
      fragment header, 291
      hop-by-hop header, 287–289
      routing header, 289–291

Index

Internet Protocol version 6 (IPv6), (Cont.):
  and ICMPv6, 299–314
    Multicast Listener Discovery, 311–314
    neighbor discovery, 300–310
    stateless autoconfiguration, 310–311
  migration from IPv4 to, 320–330
    and dual IP stack implementation, 321–322
    and header translation, 329
    and tunneling, 322–328
  mobility support in, 320
  priority in, 298
Internet root servers, 52
Intra-area routers, 128
Intranets, 14
Invocation information, 246
IOS, 184–185
IP (see Internet Protocol)
IP Address Lease Time (Option 51), 414
IP Forwarding Enable/Disable (Option 19), 400
IP gateway, 105
IP queue, 237–238
IP-in-IP encapsulation, 188
IPng (Internet Protocol next generation), 281
IPSec protocol, 276–277
iptrace command, 220–221
IPv6 (see Internet Protocol version 6)
IRPD (see ICMP Router Discovery Protocol)
ISDN, 14

J

JOIN:
  BootP services with, 346–350
    Dynamic BootP, 347–348
    Finite BootP, 348
    traditional BootP, 347
  dynamic naming with, 352
  location of IP addresses by, 350

JOIN (Cont.):
  naming with
    client naming, 352–356
    dynamic naming, 352
  resolution of client configuration by, 351
  selection of new IP addresses by, 350

K

KEY records, 62

L

LANs (see Local area networks)
LDAP (see Lightweight Directory Access Protocol)
Leases, 26, 27, 202–204, 216–218
  and choice of lease time, 216–218
  functioning of, 216
  multiple, 218
LEO (low-earth orbit) satellites, 182
Lightly loaded conditions, 248
Lightweight Directory Access Protocol (LDAP), 275–276, 361
Link-state advertisements, 135–136
Link-state database, 134
Link-state packets (LSPs), 117–118
Link-state propagation (OSPF), 143–146
Link-state routing, 116–118
LMDS (Local Microwave Distribution Service), 182
Local area networks (LANs), 15, 174
Local Microwave Distribution Service (LMDS), 182
Log Server (Option 7), 396
Loopback addresses, 5
Low-earth orbit (LEO) satellites, 182
LPR Server (Option 9), 397
LSPs (see Link-state packets)
Lucent Qip Enterprise (see QIP Enterprise 5.0)

Index

Maximum Datagram Reassembly Size (Option 22), 401
Maximum DHCP Message Size (Option 57), 417
Maximum packet size (Tspec), 247–248
Maximum transmission units (MTUs), 14, 173, 188, 285
M-bit (Mobile IP registration), 176
Merit Dump File (Option 14), 398
Message (Option 56), 416–417
Meta IP, 379–392
   benefits of, 380–381
   DHCP, Meta, 383–385
   DNS, Meta, 385–387
   Enterprise, Meta IP, 390–391
   features of, 381–383
   multiplatform support with, 389–390
   security with, 383
   Standard, Meta IP, 390
   system requirements, 392
   user-to-address mapping with, 387–389
Minimum policed unit (Tspec), 247
MLD (see Multicast Listener Discovery)
MMDS (Multipoint Microwave Distribution Service), 182
Mobile IP, 169–191
   applications of, 185–186
      business travelers, 185–186
      delivery vehicles, 185
      wired/wireless VPNs, 186
   and ARP, 180
   broadcast datagrams, forwarding of, 178–179
   care-of addresses in, 187–188
   Cisco IOS enhancements to, 188–190
   features of, 170–171, 183–184
   location discovery with, 186–187
   move detection with, 179–180

Mobile IP (Cont.):
   operation of, 173–174
   registration process, 174–178
   registration requests, 188
   and routers, 181–185
   and security, 180, 190–191
   terminology, 171–173
   tunneling in, 178
Mobile IP Home Agent (Option 68), 411
Mobile node, 172
Mobility agents, 172
Mobility binding, 172
Mobility security association, 172–173
Move detection, 179–180
MTUs (see Maximum transmission units)
Multi-access networks, 132
Multicast addresses, 296–297
Multicast Listener Discovery (MLD), 311–314
Multiple leases, 218
Multipoint Microwave Distribution Service (MMDS), 182
MX records, 61

N

Name challenge, 100–101
Name database (NetBIOS), 86–87
Name refresh, 99–100
Name Server (Option 5), 395–396
Name servers, 11–13, 50, 56–62
   authoritative, 58
   caching-only, 58
   child, 58–59
   dynamic, 56
   firewall, 60
   forwarder, 60
   historical background, 82
   master, 58
   parent, 58–59
   primary, 56
   problems with, 210–211
   and record types, 60–62

Index

Name servers (*Cont.*):
  root, 59
  secondary, 57
  static, 56
Name(s):
  alias, 13
  domain, 12
  fully qualified, 12
NBDD (*see* NetBIOS Datagram Distributor)
NBNS (*see* NetBIOS Name Server)
Neighbor discovery (in ICMPv6):
  and address resolution, 301–303
  and neighbor unreachability detection, 308, 310
  and redirection, 306–309
  router/prefix discovery, 303–306
Neighbor routers, 130
Neighbor unreachability detection (NUD), 308, 310
NetBEUI (NetBIOS over IEEE 802.2), 15
NetBIOS (*see* Network Basic Input-Output System)
NetBIOS Datagram Distributor (NBDD), 91, 92
NetBIOS Name Server (NBNS), 15, 79
  function of, 83
  implementations, 101–104
    Microsoft WINS, 101–103
    Shadow IPserver, 103–104
  RFCs, 82
NetBIOS over IEEE 802.2 (NetBEUI), 15
NetBIOS over TCP/IP Datagram Distribution Server (Option 45), 409
NetBIOS over TCP/IP Name Server Option (Option 44), 408
NetBIOS over TCP/IP Node Type (Option 46), 409
NetBIOS over TCP/IP Scope (Option 47), 409–410
NetID, 372–379
  architecture of, 377–379
  benefits of, 372–374
  features of, 374–377

NetID (*Cont.*):
  system requirements, 379
`netstat` command, 221–222, 226–228
Network address, 3
Network Basic Input-Output System (NetBIOS), 79
  API for, 83–84
  databases, 86–90
    centralized database, 90
    distributed database, 87–89
    name database, 86–87
  datagrams, 90–92
  design criteria for, 92–101
    capacity, 95
    database validation, 99–101
    datagram distribution, 97
    dedicated server, 94–95
    distributed algorithms, 97–98
    extensibility, 98
    flat response time, 95
    load balancing, 96
    performance, 93–94
    reliability, 95–96
    remote management, 99
    scalability, 96–97
    standard hardware platform, 94
    static names, 98–99
    transaction capture, 98
  design of, 84
  functionality of, 83
  and naming, 84–86
  protocol-independent services of, 84
Network Information Service Domain (Option 40), 406
Network Information Service Server (Option 41), 407
Network layer, 225–227
Network layer reachability information (NLRI), 162, 163
Network link advertisements, 136
Network operating systems (NOSs), 81
Network protocols, 2–3
Network Time Protocol Server (Option 42), 407

Networks (OSPF), 132
NIS+ Domain (Option 64), 410–411
NIS+ Server (Option 65), 411
NLRI (network layer reachability information), 162, 163
NNTP Server (Option 71), 412
Nodes, 173
Non-broadcast networks, 132
Non-Local Source Routing Enable/Disable (Option 20), 400
NOSs (network operating systems), 81
NS records, 61
`nslookup` command, 222–223, 229–233
NUD (*see* Neighbor unreachability detection)

O

Open Shortest Path First (OSPF), 126–150
  adjacencies, establishment of, 141–143
  designated router, election, 138–141
  header, 136
  Hello protocol, 138
  link-state propagation, 143–146
  packets in, 136–138
  routing table, calculation of, 146–150
  terminology of, 137–136
Option Overload (Option 52), 415
OSI model, 224
OSPF (*see* Open Shortest Path First)

P

Packet classifier (Integrated Services model), 244
Packet scheduler (Integrated Services model), 243–244
Pad (Option 0), 394
Parameter Request List (Option 55), 416
Parent name servers, 58–59
Path MTU Aging Timeout (Option 24), 401
Path MTU Plateau Table (Option 25), 402

PathTear messages, 255
PCSs (personal communication systems), 182
PDAs (*see* Personal Digital Assistants)
Perform Mask Discovery (Option 29), 403
Perform Router Discovery (Option 31), 403–404
Performance, 215–240
  and bandwidth efficiency, 238–240
  and lease time, 216–218
  monitoring/debugging tools for improving, 218–223
    `arp` command, 221
    `host` command, 222
    `iptrace` command, 220–221
    `netstat` command, 221–222
    `nslookup` command, 222–223
    `ping` command, 219
    `traceroute` command, 219–220
  network tuning, 234–238
    parameters, 235–238
    steps for, 234–235
  See also Troubleshooting
Per-hop behavior (PHB), 264–271
Personal communication systems (PCSs), 182
Personal Digital Assistants (PDAs), 169, 181
PHB (*see* Per-hop behavior)
Physical layer, 224
`Ping BOOTP Clients` parameter (BootP), 350
`ping` command, 219, 225–226
Point-to-multipoint networks, 132
Point-to-point networks, 132
Poison reverse, 115–116
Policy Filter (Option 21), 400–401
POP3 Server (Option 70), 412
Popular operating systems, options supported by, 421–422
PPP, 14
Presentation layer, 228
Primary name servers, 56
Private addresses, 5–6

Index

Probe mechanisms, 88–89
Protocols, network, 2–3
`Provisional TTL` parameter (BootP), 349
Provisioning Manager (QIP Enterprise 5.0), 366–367
Proxy ARP, 180
Proxy firewalls, 14
ProxyArec function, 198–202
PTR records, 62

Q

QIP Enterprise 5.0, 360–372
  across-platform integration with, 365–366
  centralization of network configuration/planning with, 362
  customizable user fields/views with, 366
  database replication with, 365
  directory services, 364–365
  features of, 360–361, 363
  flexibility with, 361, 365
  logical address grouping in, 366
  modules included in, 366–367
  multiple user interfaces with, 366
  multivendor DNS/DHCP services, configuration/management of, 365
  profiling capabilities, 361, 363–364
  servers
    DHCP server, 362
    DNS server, 361–362
  subnet management with, 365
  system requirements, 368–372
Quality of service (QoS), 241–278
  definition of, 242
  Differentiated Services model, 263–277
    architecture of, 264–273
    boundary nodes in, 268–270
    domains in, 267, 271–273
    interior components of, 270–271
    Internet drafts on, 277
    with IPSec, 276–277
    with LDAP, 275–276

Quality of service (QoS), Differentiated Services model, (*Cont.*):
    per-hop behavior in, 264–267
    with RSVP, 273–275
    Service Level Agreement in, 263–264
  Integrated Services model, 243–263
    classes of service in, 246–250
    future of, 261–263
    router components in, 243–245
    RSVP, 245–246, 250–261

R

RADIUS (Remote Authentication Dial-In User Service), 382
RARP (Reverse ARP), 14
Rebuilding Time Value (Option 59), 417–418
Registration Manager (QIP Enterprise 5.0), 366
Registration (with Mobile IP), 173–178
Relay agents:
  BootP, 72
  in DHCP networks, 21, 28–29
Reliability, 207–213
  with AIX, 212
  designing networks for, 208
  and failure events, 208–212
    client failures, 211–212
    DHCP server problems, 210
    facility loss, 209–210
    name server problems, 210–211
    router outages, 210
    server failures, 210–211
    severed connections, 209
  with Shadow IPserver, 213
Renewal Time Value (Option 58), 417
Requested IP Address (Option 50), 414
Requests for Comments (RFCs), 16
Resolvers, 62–65
Resource Location Server (Option 11), 397
Resource Protocol (*see* Resource Reservation Protocol)

Resource records (RR), 60–61
Resource Reservation Protocol (RSVP), 239, 245–246, 250–261
  with Differentiated Services, 273–275
  establishment of reservation with, 251
  features of, 250–251
  and future of Integrated Services, 261–263
  message format, 257–261
  operation of, 251–256
  styles, reservation, 256–257
    Fixed-Filter style, 257
    Shared-Explicit style, 257
    Wild-Card-Filter style, 256
ResvTear messages, 255
Reverse ARP (RARP), 14
RFCs (Requests for Comments), 16
RIP (see Routing Information Protocol)
Roll call mechanisms, 89
Root name servers, 59
Root Path (Option 17), 399
Routed daemon, 108
Router, 105
Router address, 10
Router ID (OSPF), 135
Router link advertisements, 136
Router (Option 3), 395
Router outages, 210
Router priority (OSPF), 135
Router Solicitation Address (Option 32), 404
Routers with partial routing information, 106–107
Routing, 10–11, 105–109
  algorithms, routing, 109–118
  distance vector, 111–116
  exterior (see Border Gateway Protocol; Exterior gateway protocols)
  interior (see Interior gateway protocols)
  link-state, 116–118
  Mobile IP, 181–185
  static, 110–111
Routing header, 289–291

Routing Information Protocol (RIP), 118–124
  and OSPF, 119
  packet types in, 120
  version 2 of, 122–124
Routing protocols, 105–106 (See also Routing Information Protocol)
Routing table (OSPF), 134
Routing tables, 10–11
RP records, 61
RR (*see* Resource records)
RSA public key authentication, 194–197
Rspec (Service Request Specification), 248
RSVP (*see* Resource Reservation Protocol)

S

S-bit (Mobile IP registration), 176
Secondary name servers, 57
Security, 193–206
  domain, presecured, 198
  and firewalls, 204–205
  and lease allocations, 202–204
  Meta IP, 383
  with Mobile IP, 180, 190–191
  and ProxyArec function, 198–202
  and RSA public key authentication, 194–197
  TFTP, 205
Security parameter index (SPI), 173
Server failures, 210–211
Server Identifier (Option 54), 415–416
Servers, 21, 72
Service Level Agreements (SLAs), 263–264
Service Request Specification (Rspec), 248
Services Manager (QIP Enterprise 5.0), 367
Session layer, 228
Severed connections, 209
Shadow IPserver, 103–104, 213
Shapers, packet, 268–269
Shared-Explicit style, 257
Shortest-path tree, 134
Shortest-path-first (SPF), 118

Index

SLAs (*see* Service Level Agreements)
SLIP, 14
SMTP Server (Option 69), 411–412
SNA (Systems Network Architecture), 15
SNMP, 382
SOA records, 61
Sockets interface, 13
SOCKS firewalls, 14
SPF (shortest-path-first), 118
SPI (security parameter index), 173
Split horizon, 115
Split horizon with poison reverse, 115–116
Stateless autoconfiguration, 310–311
Static addresses, 11
Static DNS, 13
Static name servers, 56
Static Route (Option 33), 404
Static routing, 110–111
StreetTalk Directory Assistance Server (Option 76), 413–414
StreetTalk Server (Option 75), 413
Stub area, 130
Stub resolver, 64–65
Subdomains, 51
Subnet base address, 8
Subnet Mask (Option 1), 394
Subnet masks, 7–8 (*See also* Variable-length subnet masks)
Subnet(s), 6–9
   moves to new, 26–27
   multiple, 29–30
   servers, splitting between, 44–45
Summary link advertisements, 136
Supernets, 9
Swap Server (Option 16), 399
System address, 3
Systems Network Architecture (SNA), 15

T

TCP Default Time-to-Live (Option 37), 405–406
TCP Keep-Alive Garbage (Option 39), 406
TCP Keep-Alive Interval (Option 38), 406
TCP/IP (*see* Transmission Control Protocol/Internet Protocol)
Telnet, 40
TFTP (*see* Trivial FTP)
TFTP Server Name (Option 66), 419
Time Offset (Option 2), 395
Time Server (Option 4), 395
TLV format (*see* Type-Length-Value format)
Token rate, 247
Topological database, 134
`traceroute` command, 219–220
Traffic conditioners, 268, 269
Traffic control (Integrated Services model), 243
Trailer Encapsulation (Option 34), 404–405
Transit area, 130
Transmission Control Protocol/Internet Protocol (TCP/IP), 1–16, 280
   applications using, 13
   for enterprise, 80–82
   and IP addresses, 3–6
   and IP routing, 10–11
   and IP subnets, 6–9
   and name servers, 11–13
   as network protocol, 2
Transport layer, 227–228
Triggered updates, 116
Trivial FTP (TFTP), 18, 206
Troubleshooting, 223–234
   bottom-up approach to, 224–234
   prerequisites for, 223–224
Tspec, 247–248
Tuning, network, 234–238
   parameters, 235–238
   steps for, 234–235
Tunneling, 170, 178, 322–328
   automatic, 322–326
   configured, 326–328
Tunnels, 173
TXT records, 61
Type-Length-Value (TLV) format, 287
Type-of-service (TOS) metrics, 133–134

U

UAM (*see* User-to-Address Mapping)
UDP (*see* User Datagram Protocol)
Unicast addresses, 293–296
Uninterruptible power supply (UPS), 209–210
Unofficial options, 419–421
UPS (*see* Uninterruptible power supply)
User Datagram Protocol (UDP), 2–3, 90, 120, 175
User-to-Address Mapping (UAM), 388–389

V

Variable-length subnet masks (VLSM), 356–360
    Addermask utility, 358–359
    fixed-length vs., 356–358
V-bit (Mobile IP registration), 176
Vendor Class Identifier (Option 60), 418
Vendor-Specific Information (Option 43), 407–408
Virtual link (OSPF), 129
Virtual networks, 173
Virtual private networks (VPNs), 15, 204
    mobile, 182
    wireless, 186
Visited networks, 173
Visitor list, 173
VLSM (*see* Variable-length subnet masks)
VPNs (*see* Virtual private networks)

W

Web browsers, 40
Wild-Card-Filter style, 256
Windows Internet Naming Service (WINS), 101–103
Winsock, 13
Wireless services, 181–182
Withdrawn routes (BGP), 164–165

X

X Window System Display Manager (Option 49), 410
X Window System Font Server Option (Option 48), 410

Z

Zone transfers, 57
Zones of authority, domains vs., 54–56

ABOUT THE AUTHOR

Paul. T. Ammann is an independent consultant specializing in installing and configuring Novell, Windows NT, and UNIX servers, configuring and troubleshooting Cisco routers, diagnosing server and client hardware problems, solving network infrastructure (LAN/WAN) problems, and analyzing network performance.